# Engineering Lakehouses with Open Table Formats

Build scalable and efficient lakehouses with
Apache Iceberg, Apache Hudi, and Delta Lake

**Dipankar Mazumdar**

**Vinoth Govindarajan**

# Engineering Lakehouses with Open Table Formats

**Portfolio Director:** Sunith Shetty
**Relationship Lead:** Puneet Kaur
**Project Manager:** Aniket Shetty
**Content Engineer:** Siddhant Jain
**Technical Editor:** Shweta Amale
**Copy Editor:** Safis Editing
**Indexer:** Hemangini Bari
**Proofreader:** Siddhant Jain
**Production Designer:** Alishon Falcon
**Growth Lead:** Varun Nair

First published: December 2025

Production reference: 2070126

Published by Packt Publishing Ltd.

Grosvenor House

11 St Paul's Square

Birmingham

B3 1RB, UK.

ISBN 978-1-83620-723-8

www.packtpub.com

# Foreword

My own professional journey in data systems closely mirrors the evolution described in this book. I began my career at Cloudera, working on Apache Hive at a time when the data lake was still taking shape. Back then, the challenge was straightforward but daunting: how do you make sense of massive volumes of data stored cheaply on distributed file systems? Hive brought SQL to Hadoop and unlocked analytical access at scale, but it also exposed fundamental limitations. Table abstractions were thin, metadata was fragile, and reliability was often something engineers worked around rather than relied upon. The data lake gave us scale and flexibility, but not yet trust.

In 2016, I moved to Uber and witnessed firsthand the birth of Apache Hudi. Uber's data problems were not theoretical; they were operational, real-time, and constantly evolving. Incremental ingestion, updates, deletes, and low-latency analytics were no longer edge cases but core requirements. Hudi emerged from those needs, introducing transactional semantics and incremental processing to data lakes that had previously been append-only. For the first time, I saw a serious attempt to reconcile streaming and batch workloads on the same storage layer. It was an early signal that the industry was moving beyond data lakes as dumping grounds toward something more structured and reliable.

That shift became even clearer during my time at Apple, where I saw Apache Iceberg gain broad adoption across large-scale analytical platforms. Iceberg's design, including its clean separation of metadata, engine-agnostic philosophy, and focus on correctness, felt like a maturation of ideas that had been forming for years. Concepts such as schema evolution, snapshot isolation, and time travel were no longer bolt-ons but foundational capabilities. More importantly, Iceberg demonstrated that openness and rigor were not opposing goals. It showed that systems could be both deeply engineered and broadly interoperable.

Today, at OpenAI, we run Delta Lake in production every day. At this scale, reliability is not an abstract concern; it directly impacts research velocity, cost efficiency, and trust in results. Delta's transaction log, strong guarantees, and ecosystem integration make it a critical component of our data platform. Looking back across these experiences, what stands out is not that one format "won," but that the industry converged on a shared set of principles. These include ACID guarantees on open storage, separation of compute and data, and a commitment to interoperability.

The lakehouse is not a buzzword or a product category. It is the result of years of hard-earned lessons from operating data systems at scale. Apache Iceberg, Apache Hudi, and Delta Lake each reflect different trade-offs shaped by the environments in which they were created. Understanding those trade-offs requires more than high-level comparisons; it demands an appreciation of internals, metadata design, and failure modes. This book succeeds because it treats these systems for what they are: sophisticated distributed systems that require careful engineering.

What I particularly value is the book's resistance to oversimplification. Rather than promoting a single "correct" architecture, it equips readers to reason about trade-offs and make informed decisions in their own environments. Its deep coverage of table format internals, catalogs and metadata management, and multi-engine interoperability reflects the real concerns faced by modern data platform teams. Examples spanning batch, streaming, and machine learning workloads ground these ideas in practical, day-to-day engineering scenarios.

For engineers building or modernizing data platforms, this book offers something rare: a coherent view of where the ecosystem has been, where it stands today, and why certain design patterns have endured. It recognizes that while tools continue to evolve, the core challenges of correctness, scalability, and operational simplicity remain. Open table formats are not a silver bullet, but they represent a meaningful and principled step forward.

Having watched this space evolve from early Hive tables to today's production-grade lakehouses, I see this book as both a reflection on that journey and a guide to what comes next. Whether you are selecting a table format, designing a catalog strategy, or operating a multi-engine lakehouse at scale, you will find insights grounded in experience and informed by real engineering constraints.

This is a book I wish I had earlier in my career, and one I expect many engineers will return to as their systems and responsibilities continue to grow.

*Chao Sun*

*Member of Technical Staff, OpenAI*

# Contributors

## About the authors

**Dipankar Mazumdar** is currently the Director of Developer Advocacy at Cloudera, where he leads global developer initiatives focused on lakehouse architectures and generative AI. Previously, he held developer advocacy roles at Dremio, Onehouse, and Qlik, contributing to open source projects such as Apache Iceberg, Apache Hudi, and XTable, among others. For most of his career, Dipankar has worked at the intersection of data engineering and AI. He has also contributed to O'Reilly's *Apache Iceberg: The Definitive Guide* and has spoken at numerous conferences, including Databricks Data + AI, Netflix Engineering, ApacheCon, Scale By the Bay, and Data Day Texas, among others.

*This book would not have been possible without the support of many people. I would like to thank Packt and the editorial team for the opportunity and guidance throughout the writing process, and Satish and Neelesh for their careful reviews and feedback. Above all, I am grateful to my wife, Madhusmita, for her unwavering love and support, and to my parents for the values they instilled, which continue to shape who I am.*

**Vinoth Govindarajan** is a seasoned data expert and Member of Technical Staff at OpenAI, working on large-scale data and applied AI systems. He offers a unique perspective on modern table formats through his work on Apache Hudi at Uber, Apache Iceberg at Apple, and Delta Lake at OpenAI. Previously, he was a Staff Software Engineer at both Apple and Uber, where he built data platforms, incremental ETL frameworks, and real-time pipelines. Vinoth contributes to open-source projects such as Apache Hudi and dbt-spark and has spoken at events like dbt Coalesce and Hudi community meetups. He holds a bachelor's degree in Information Technology from Madras Institute of Technology, Anna University, and has authored multiple research papers in IEEE journals.

*I am deeply grateful to my wife, Aarthi, for her unwavering support, patience, and encouragement throughout this journey. To my two boys, Vinay and Dev, thank you for giving up many playtimes so I could focus on writing, your understanding and support mean more to me than words can express. I am grateful to my parents for their unwavering support and the values that continue to guide me.*

# About the reviewer

**Satish Kotha** has had the privilege of building and scaling state-of-the-art lake house architectures at major tech companies such as Uber and Apple. These lake houses have helped drive data-driven decision-making at massive scale, enabling faster analytics, more robust machine learning workflows, and seamless integration of diverse data sources. He is a committer on Apache Hudi, where he has significantly shaped the project's evolution, notably shepherding the clustering feature to enhance data layout optimization. In his earlier work at Twitter, he led the development of several foundational 0–1 storage systems, including MetricsDB and BlobStore, both of which have become critical components of Twitter's storage infrastructure.

**Neelesh Srinivas** Salian has built and operated large-scale data platforms and lakehouse architectures across data-intensive organizations, including Datavant, Stitch Fix, dbt Labs, Salesforce, and Cloudera. His work spans distributed storage and metadata systems, large-scale Spark and streaming platforms, and production deployments of modern table formats such as Apache Iceberg. He has led cross-team data platform initiatives in both production and regulated environments, with a focus on correctness, scalability, and long-term maintainability.

# Table of Contents

# Chapter 7: Interoperability in Lakehouses 227

# Chapter 8: Performance Optimization and Tuning in a Lakehouse 247

## Chapter 11: Real-World Applications and Learnings 325

# Preface

The rise of the data lakehouse architecture has redefined how organizations manage, process, and analyze data. As open standards continue to mature, modern data engineering increasingly depends on a new class of technologies known as open table formats, such as Apache Iceberg, Apache Hudi, and Delta Lake, to bring transactional consistency, performance, and flexibility to data lakes.

*Engineering Lakehouses with Open Table Formats* is designed to help data engineers and architects understand, evaluate, and implement these formats in real-world environments. This book walks through the entire lakehouse journey, from understanding table format internals and transactional capabilities to building production-ready lakehouses using software such as Apache Spark, Flink, Kafka, Debezium, MLflow, and Python frameworks. It emphasizes a hands-on, engineering-focused approach with examples, architectural diagrams, and code recipes throughout.

## Who this book is for

This book is intended for data and software engineers, architects, and platform engineers who are building or modernizing data platforms on cloud or on-premises environments. A foundational understanding of distributed systems, data architectures (such as warehouses and data lakes), SQL, and Python will help you get the most out of this book. Familiarity with tools such as Apache Spark or Flink is beneficial but not mandatory. Each concept is explained in a step-by-step, practical manner.

## What this book covers

*Chapter 1, Open Data Lakehouse: A New Architectural Paradigm*, introduces the evolution of data architectures and explains how the lakehouse unifies the flexibility of data lakes with the reliability of data warehouses.

*Chapter 2, Transactional Capabilities of the Lakehouse*, explores how ACID transactions, concurrency control, and table management services ensure reliability in large-scale data processing and how these are implemented by each format.

*Chapter 3, Apache Iceberg Deep Dive*, covers Iceberg's architecture, metadata layers, manifest lists, catalog integration, and unique features such as hidden partitioning, branching, and advanced statistics. It also goes into the practical examples of running various operations.

*Chapter 4, Apache Hudi Deep Dive*, explains Hudi's core design principles, including timeline management, file group layout, indexing, and incremental data processing. It also shows practical examples to run transactions at scale.

*Chapter 5, Delta Lake Deep Dive*, details Delta's transaction log, schema enforcement, and data versioning, and shows (with code) how to use Delta for real-time analytics and machine learning workloads.

*Chapter 6, Catalog and Metadata Management*, examines how catalogs orchestrate data discovery, schema evolution, and version control across engines and environments.

*Chapter 7, Interoperability in Lakehouses,* discusses the importance of cross-format compatibility, showcasing Apache XTable and Delta UniForm as bridges enabling multi-format interoperability.

*Chapter 8, Performance Optimization and Tuning in a Lakehouse,* focuses on various techniques such as partitioning, clustering, compaction, and indexing to improve query efficiency, cost efficiency, and reduce latency.

*Chapter 9, Data Governance and Security in Lakehouses*, highlights strategies for implementing fine-grained access controls, auditing, and regulatory compliance.

*Chapter 10, Evaluating and Selecting Open Table Formats*, helps you evaluate when to use Iceberg, Hudi, or Delta based on workload type (batch, streaming, or incremental) and provides a decision framework for engineers and architects to select specific formats.

*Chapter 11, Real-World Applications and Learnings,* brings everything together with practical implementations of analytical, **change data capture** (**CDC**), and machine learning workloads, integrating open table formats with orchestration and BI tools.

## To get the most out of this book

You'll benefit most from this book if you have experience working with existing data systems such as **online transaction processing** (**OLTP**), **online analytical processing** (**OLAP**), data warehouses, or data lakes. You should also have basic experience with Python and SQL to follow the code examples. Prior knowledge of distributed systems or big data tools will be helpful.

To follow along with the examples, you can run the notebooks locally or in a cloud environment such as AWS.

Before starting, ensure that you have the following:

- Python 3.9 or later
- Spark 3.x
- Java 8 or later

# Download the example code files

The code examples and sample datasets used in this book are available on GitHub at `https://github.com/PacktPublishing/Engineering-Lakehouses-with-Open-Table-Formats`.

Additional repositories and resources related to Apache Iceberg, Apache Hudi, and Delta Lake are also linked within the chapters for reference.

# Conventions used

There are a number of text conventions used throughout this book.

`CodeInText`: Indicates code words in text, database table names, folder names, filenames, file extensions, pathnames, dummy URLs, user input, and Twitter handles. For example: "In Delta Lake, compaction is done using the `OPTIMIZE` command."

A block of code is set as follows:

```
SparkActions.get().rewriteDataFiles(table)
    .filter(Expressions.equal("date", "2020-08-18"))
    .option("target-file-size-bytes", Long.toString(500 * 1024 * 1024))
    //500 MB
    .execute();
```

**Bold**: Indicates a new term, an important word, or words that you see on the screen. For instance, new terms appear in the text like this. For example: "Only **copy-on-write (CoW)** or **read-optimized (RO)** views of tables are supported. Log files from Hudi and deletion vectors (for merge-on-read tables) from Delta and Iceberg are not captured."

Any command-line input or output is written as follows:

```
java -jar xtable-utilities/target/xtable-utilities_2.12-0.2.0-SNAPSHOT-
bundled.jar --datasetConfig my_config.yaml
```

Warnings or important notes appear like this.

Tips and tricks appear like this.

# Get in touch

Feedback from readers is always welcome.

**General feedback**: If you have comments or questions regarding any part of this book, please contact customercare@packt.com and mention the title in your message.

**Errata**: If you find any errors, please report them at https://www.packtpub.com/submit-errata.

**Piracy**: If you come across illegal copies, please notify copyright@packt.com.

If you're interested in authoring or contributing to a Packt title, visit http://authors.packt.com.

# Share your thoughts

Once you've read *Engineering Lakehouses with Open Table Formats*, we'd love to hear your thoughts! Scan the QR code below to go straight to the Amazon review page for this book and share your feedback.

https://packt.link/r/1836207239

Your review is important to us and the tech community and will help us make sure we're delivering excellent quality content.

# Free Benefits with Your Book

This book comes with free benefits to support your learning. Activate them now for instant access (see the "*How to Unlock*" section for instructions).

Here's a quick overview of what you can instantly unlock with your purchase:

**PDF and ePub Copies**

**Next-Gen Web-Based Reader**

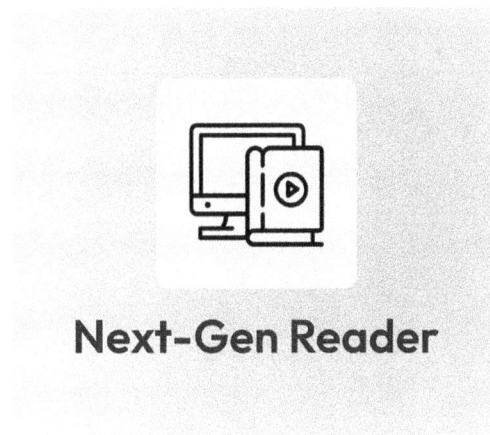

### Free PDF and ePub versions

### Next-Gen Reader

Access a DRM-free PDF copy of this book to read anywhere, on any device.

Use a DRM-free ePub version with your favorite e-reader.

**Multi-device progress sync:** Pick up where you left off, on any device.

**Highlighting and notetaking:** Capture ideas and turn reading into lasting knowledge.

**Bookmarking:** Save and revisit key sections whenever you need them.

**Dark mode:** Reduce eye strain by switching to dark or sepia themes.

## How to Unlock

**UNLOCK NOW**

Scan the QR code (or go to packtpub.com/unlock). Search for this book by name, confirm the edition, and then follow the steps on the page.

*Note: Keep your invoice handy. Purchases made directly from Packt don't require one.*

# 1

# Open Data Lakehouse: A New Architectural Paradigm

Processing large volumes of structured and unstructured data is essential for generating insights and making informed decisions. Over the past few decades, the growing need for both real-time transactional processing and large-scale analytical capabilities has influenced the design of data management systems. Initially, organizations relied on two distinct systems: **online transaction processing (OLTP)** for high-throughput transactional workloads, and **online analytical processing (OLAP)** for historical trend analysis and complex querying.

However, as data volumes grew beyond the capacity of traditional **data warehouses**, particularly due to the rise of semi-structured and unstructured data, a new architectural model emerged: the **data lake**. Built on low-cost cloud or distributed storage, data lakes decoupled compute from storage and allowed organizations to ingest and store raw data of all types at scale. While this architecture addressed scalability and schema flexibility, it lacked the transactional guarantees and governance features necessary for reliable analytics.

These limitations eventually led to the rise of the **lakehouse** architecture, a unification of the best features of both data warehouses and data lakes. Lakehouses offer the scalability and openness of data lakes with the data reliability and query performance traditionally associated with data warehouses.

In this chapter, we will cover the following topics:

- The evolution of data systems
- Emergence of data lakes as centralized storage for diverse data
- An introduction to the data lakehouse and its architecture
- Key attributes that define an open data lakehouse

By the end of this chapter, you'll have a clear understanding of how data management has evolved from OLTP and OLAP systems to the lakehouse architecture. You will also have gained insight into the core components and key attributes that make an open data lakehouse a powerful solution for modern data needs.

---

### Free Benefits with Your Book

Your purchase includes a free PDF copy of this book along with other exclusive benefits. Check the *Free Benefits with Your Book* section in the Preface to unlock them instantly and maximize your learning experience.

---

# The evolution of data systems

OLTP and OLAP systems have long been regarded as foundational for enterprise data management. OLTP systems handle real-time transactions, while OLAP systems focus on long-term data analysis, creating a clear separation between operational and analytical workloads. However, this division brought challenges, including the need for constant **extract, transform, load** (ETL) processes to transfer data between the two systems, which resulted in latency and inconsistencies between operational and analytical data.

In the following subsections, we will dive deeper into the roles and limitations of OLTP and OLAP systems, setting the stage for understanding how modern data architectures such as data lakes and lakehouses address these issues.

## OLTP: The transactional backbone

OLTP systems were designed to handle day-to-day transactional data, excelling at high-speed insert, update, and delete operations optimized for real-time storage and retrieval. They typically manage workloads such as sales transactions, inventory updates, and financial operations. Well-known examples include relational databases such as MySQL, PostgreSQL, and Oracle, which are optimized for rapid insertion and updates in real-time transactional scenarios such as retail purchases, banking transactions, and e-commerce.

The technical components of OLTP include the following:

- Query engine
- Transaction manager
- Storage engine
- Indexing subsystem
- System catalog (metadata store)
- **Write-ahead log** (**WAL**) or redo logs
- Buffer pool/cache layer

OLTP systems can efficiently handle transactional workloads, offering high concurrency, low latency, compliance with **atomicity**, **consistency**, **isolation**, and **durability** (**ACID**) transactions, and normalized data structures. However, they have certain limitations: they are not optimized for analytics or reporting; handling large datasets can be costly and less efficient; and unstructured data is poorly supported.

Because of these limitations, OLTP systems are typically complemented by OLAP systems, which are designed for large-scale data analysis.

## OLAP: Analyzing historical data

OLAP systems were designed for analyzing and reporting on large datasets, primarily for business intelligence workloads such as data warehousing and reporting. Systems such as Amazon Redshift and Google BigQuery have emerged as key OLAP solutions, optimized for large-scale analytics. These systems excel at processing vast amounts of historical data, enabling complex queries and multidimensional analysis, such as time- or region-based sales aggregations. Common OLAP platforms such as Teradata and Snowflake facilitate in-depth analysis of structured data, focusing on data aggregation and multidimensional querying typically stored in data warehouses.

Technical components of OLAP systems are as follows:

- System catalog
- OLAP compute
- Storage engine
- Table format
- File format (column-oriented)
- Storage

OLAP systems are characterized by high query performance, denormalized data structures, and the use of OLAP cubes along with dimensional modeling. Despite these advantages, OLAP systems have certain limitations, including high initial costs, complex ETL processes, and challenges in handling semi-structured or unstructured data.

These shortcomings became more apparent as data volumes grew and data sources became more diverse. A new way had to be devised that could manage the loads of raw data coming from different sources, hence the emergence of the data lake.

## Data lakes: The centralized data storage for a new era

Data lakes are centralized storage facilities for raw data in native formats. Thus, they are designed to handle large volumes from sources such as social media, IoT devices, and sensors, and often run on top of distributed filesystems such as **Hadoop Distributed File System** (**HDFS**) or cloud-based object storage such as Amazon S3.

With big data solutions starting to see demand, enterprises needed a system to capture, process, and analyze unstructured and semi-structured data coming from sources such as logs, sensors, and social media. Over time, data lakes became systems that stored raw data in its native format with less stringent schema enforcement.

Data lakes leverage distributed storage systems designed to scale with volume. This flexibility in scaling lets organizations store many types of data formats in a single location, potentially unlocking advanced analytics, machine learning, and AI capabilities not afforded by the rigidity of traditional OLAP systems.

The key characteristics of data lakes are as follows:

- **Scalability**: Ability to handle large volumes
- **Flexibility**: Ability to store data in its native format
- **Cost-effectiveness**: Implementation on commodity hardware and low-cost storage reduces overall cost of ownership

There are some limitations as well:

- **Lack of governance and metadata**: Data lakes, when unmanaged or improperly governed, often turn into **data swamps**, where data is unorganized, difficult to find, and unreliable for analysis. Without sufficient metadata and data cataloging, it becomes hard to understand the data's structure, quality, or lineage.

- **Performance challenges**: Analyzing data in a data lake can be slow and inefficient without query engines such as Apache Spark, Presto, or Dremio. Without these engines, queries rely on manual code, making operations such as filtering, aggregating, and joining large datasets time-consuming. While formats such as Parquet offer metadata for optimizations, scanning numerous files is still resource-intensive, especially in cloud object stores where higher latency can make metadata reads slower than the queries themselves. This lack of built-in optimization in data lakes results in slower performance for complex and real-time analytics.

- **ACID transactions**: Traditional data lakes built directly on object storage do not natively support ACID transactions, which are essential for ensuring data integrity in systems that process concurrent operations. This limitation makes it difficult to guarantee that data remains consistent during complex workflows, such as multiple simultaneous updates or real-time data processing.

These limitations have driven the evolution of the lakehouse architecture. The challenges of data lakes, combined with their potential, have created a need for a system that blends the flexibility of data lakes with the structure and reliability of traditional data warehouses.

# The emergence of the lakehouse architecture

The lakehouse architecture combines the advantages of data lakes and data warehouses. It introduces a unified platform for both transactional and analytical workloads, addressing the need for scalable, flexible, and high-performance data processing.

Apache Iceberg, Apache Hudi, and Delta Lake (three main open source projects driving the evolution of lakehouse architecture, together with their respective communities) have contributed innumerable feature additions, such as data governance, ACID transactions, and query optimization to data lakes, thereby enabling the lakehouse to prove itself a real solution for the unification of data infrastructure for any organization.

## An introduction to data lakehouses

The data lakehouse architecture has transformed how organizations manage, store, and analyze data at scale. Its rising popularity stems from the need for systems that combine the low-cost, flexible storage of data lakes with the reliability and performance of data warehouses, delivering a unified, open platform for both batch and streaming workloads.

Traditional architectures such as data warehouses (OLAP systems) excel at structured analytics and offer strong consistency guarantees, while data lakes support diverse, semi-structured, and unstructured data types and offer cost-effective storage at scale. However, each comes with trade-offs: data lakes lack transactional reliability, and warehouses are often closed, rigid, and expensive to scale. The lakehouse architecture bridges this gap, combining the best of both worlds.

A modern lakehouse is built on three foundational pillars:

- **Openness**: Storing data in open formats (such as Parquet) and using open table formats (such as Iceberg, Hudi, or Delta Lake) ensures flexibility and interoperability, and helps avoid vendor lock-in
- **Reliability**: ACID transactions, schema enforcement, and governance features make lakehouses reliable for production-grade workloads
- **Scalability and flexibility**: Lakehouses scale storage and compute independently and serve diverse use cases, from machine learning pipelines to real-time dashboards, without the constraints of monolithic systems

What makes the lakehouse architecture particularly powerful is its use of open table formats such as Apache Iceberg, Apache Hudi, and Delta Lake. These formats bring advanced capabilities such as schema evolution, time travel, and ACID compliance to large-scale datasets, while also enabling multi-engine support, allowing you to query the same table with Spark, Trino, Flink, or Presto based on the task at hand.

This separation of storage and compute, coupled with open formats, helps democratize data access, reduce infrastructure costs, and enhance long-term data portability. It also supports critical interoperability as data increasingly spans multiple clouds, databases, and operational systems.

While the lakehouse approach represents a new architectural pattern, the building blocks are not entirely new. The innovation lies in how these components are assembled, using modular, open source technologies to enable enterprises to build solutions tailored to their needs. This is a departure from traditional monolithic data warehouses, which typically lock data into proprietary storage and require using a specific compute engine for all workloads. Open table formats put data ownership back in the hands of organizations, offering them the freedom to evolve their architecture over time.

# Inside the lakehouse architecture

In this section, we'll break down the key components of a lakehouse architecture and understand how they interface with each other to provide an open foundation for the lakehouse architecture. To begin, let's first take a look at the lakehouse architecture breakdown:

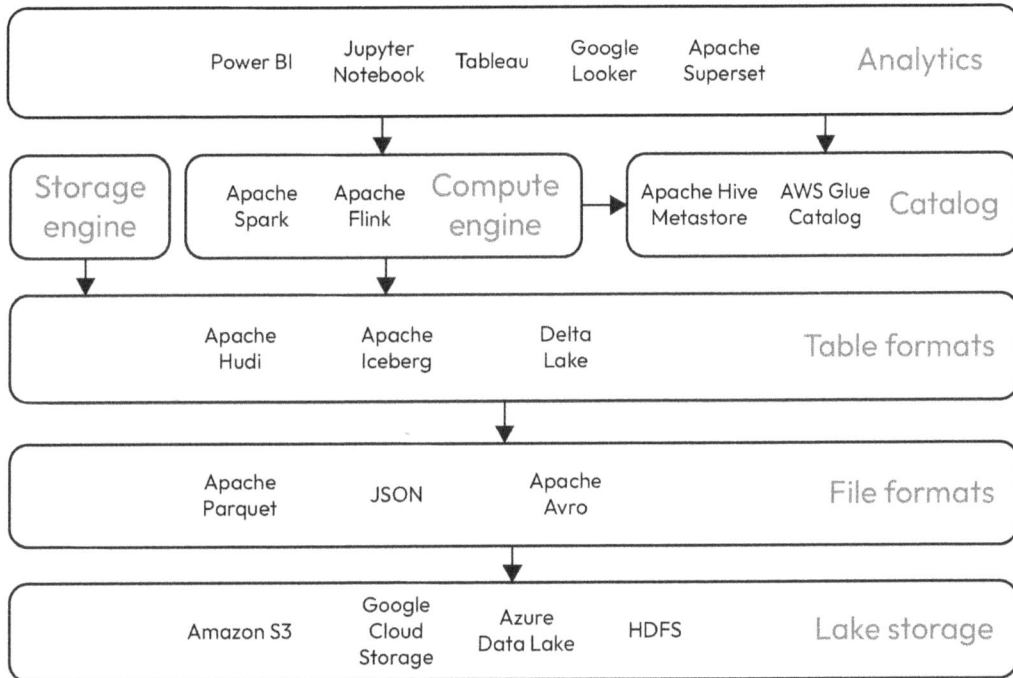

*Figure 1.1 – An architectural breakdown of the lakehouse architecture*

We will discuss the components of the lakehouse architecture in the following sections. The idea is to establish a standard definition for each of these technical components and go over the functionalities and their role in the lakehouse architecture.

## Lake storage

The very first component of a lakehouse architecture is the **storage layer**. It serves as the destination where files from various operational systems are housed after the ingestion process. These systems serve as a repository where all data (whether structured, semi-structured, or unstructured) is stored and organized. For example, consider an on-premises filesystem, such as HDFS, which has been a pioneer in data lake storage infrastructure. In HDFS, large datasets are broken down into blocks and stored across a distributed filesystem on DataNodes. These blocks (stored as separate files) are written to specific paths within the filesystem of each DataNode, which manages the actual data storage. For example, when a block is stored, the DataNode assigns it to a path, like this: `/data/current/{block-id}`. Here's a high-level architecture of a Hadoop-based filesystem:

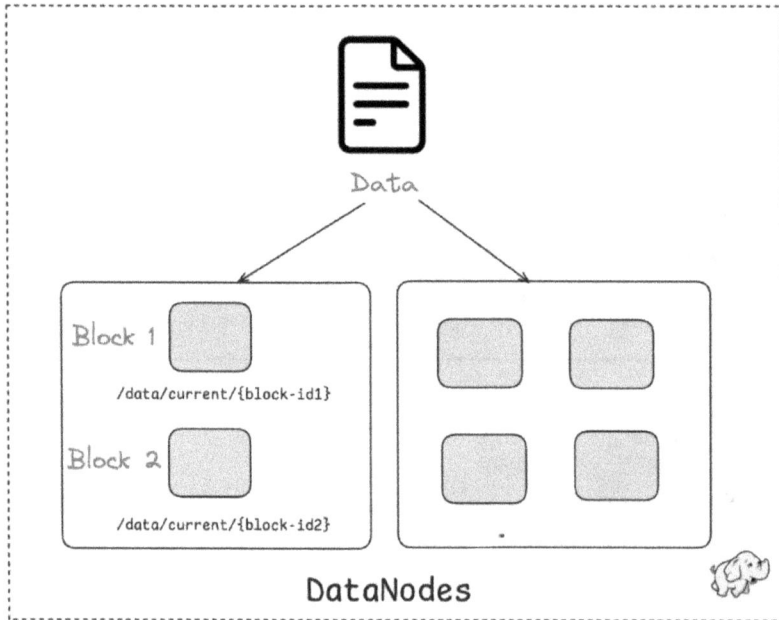

*Figure 1.2 – HDFS architecture showing data organization in the filesystem*

Cloud-based storage such as Amazon S3, Google Cloud Storage, and Azure Blob Storage have seen a huge demand as the preferred choice of storage for the lakehouse architecture, especially because of their ability to scale infinitely and their low-cost options. These systems also have their own way of handling the raw bytes of data under the hood. For example, in Amazon S3, each object is stored within a bucket, which acts like a container for data. Each object is assigned a key, which serves as the path to locate the object. Unlike traditional storage systems that might require complex provisioning to handle growing data volumes, object stores scale elastically to accommodate the needs of the lakehouse. Additionally, cloud storage systems provide high durability and availability, often with built-in mechanisms to replicate data across regions for disaster recovery.

## File formats

**File formats,** part of the storage formats in a lakehouse architecture, hold the actual raw data and define how it is physically stored on the underlying storage system (such as distributed filesystems like HDFS or object stores like Amazon S3), that is, how the raw bytes of data are serialized, compressed, and structured for efficient retrieval and storage. They dictate not only how data is stored but also how it can be queried and compressed. The choice of file format can significantly impact performance, storage efficiency, and the capabilities for processing data. File formats are broadly categorized into *row-based* and *columnar* formats:

- **Row-based formats**: Row-based formats are good for write-heavy workloads because they store data sequentially, row by row, which makes it easier and faster to append new data. This is especially useful in scenarios where entire rows of data need to be written frequently or where updates to the dataset are common, such as in transactional workloads. For example, in row-based formats such as Avro, the data is stored in a serialized binary format, which makes it compact and efficient to write, while still maintaining a self-describing schema for easier interpretation during reads.

- **Columnar formats**: Columnar formats, on the other hand, are optimized for analytical workloads. They store data sequentially by column, which reduces the amount of I/O required to retrieve specific columns in a query. Columnar formats also provide rich metadata, which helps prune irrelevant data, thereby improving query performance. For example, in Parquet (a popular columnar file format), the footer consists of minimum and maximum values of each column, which can be used by query engines to minimize the amount of data scanned.

The following diagram provides insights into the architecture of the Apache Parquet file format and how data and metadata are organized:

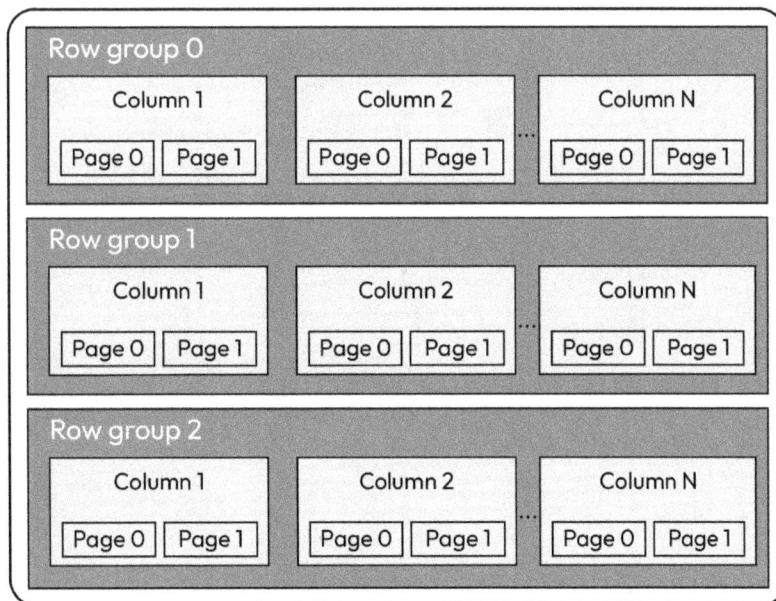

*Figure 1.3 – Apache Parquet file format*

File formats should support diverse data types, including complex types such as arrays, maps, and nested structures. This is important for analytics workloads today, where relational data often coexists with more complex, semi-structured data types. Formats such as Parquet and ORC shine in these aspects, offering robust support for nested and hierarchical data.

## Table formats

Table format is one of the components that play a key role in the data lakehouse architecture. Conceptually, a table format isn't entirely new; it is similar to what databases have traditionally referred to as **storage formats**. Their origins can be traced back to the early development of relational databases, inspired by Edgar Codd's relational model, which was implemented in early systems such as Oracle.

Table formats abstract the complexities of handling the underlying physical file structure and provide a schema for file formats such as Parquet, while keeping track of the metadata of the files, similar to databases. This abstraction enables users to query and work with data via logical representations (tables), without needing to manage or understand the complexities of the underlying file structures, such as individual files, directories, or partitions. The following diagram shows how the table format provides the abstraction and schema on top of file formats:

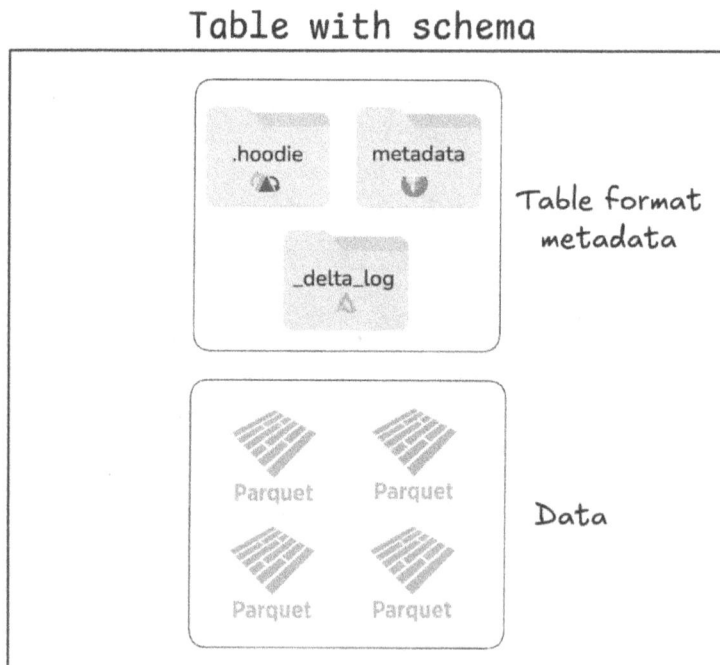

*Figure 1.4 – Table format with schema on top of file format*

Table formats provide a set of reader and writer APIs for query engines such as Spark or Flink to read, write, and update data. Apache Hudi, Apache Iceberg, and Delta Lake are the three widely adopted table formats today in enterprise workloads. All three formats act as a metadata layer on top of the cloud object stores, managing the underlying file format, such as Parquet. Structurally, how the metadata is organized in these three formats is slightly different, with different design goals, but the overall idea is the same. These formats will be explored in more depth in subsequent chapters, where we'll dive into their individual capabilities and how they enable seamless interaction with various compute engines with hands-on examples.

So, what exactly makes up the table format metadata? Here are some of the key components:

- **Data and delete file paths**: Information on the locations of data files and any delete files within the storage system is tracked. These paths point to the file that holds the actual data and mark files for deletion in the case of deletes. This way, the table format keeps information on the relevant state (snapshot/timeline) of a table and which files have been removed or modified.

- **Schema information**: The schema defines the structure of the data, including details such as column names, data types (for example, integers and strings), primary keys, and so on. By maintaining up-to-date schema information, the table format ensures that queries know how to interpret the data and can enforce rules around data integrity and validation.

- **Partition information**: Partitions help optimize data storage and query performance by dividing data into segments based on specific column values (such as dates or customer regions). Partition-related information, such as specific values or ranges that define each partition, is tracked by the table format. This allows query engines to efficiently locate and scan only the necessary partitions, significantly improving query performance.

- **Transaction logs**: Transaction logs track all changes made to the table data over time, including inserts, updates, deletes, and schema modifications. This log provides the necessary information to run transactions in an ACID-compliant way. It also enables powerful features such as time travel, which allows users to query historical versions of the table or rollback to previous versions. We will learn more about these capabilities in the following chapters.

- **Statistics**: Statistical information includes details such as the row count, null counts, and the minimum and maximum values for each column. These statistics are collected from the underlying data files (such as Parquet) and are crucial for query optimization. By utilizing these detailed stats, query engines can perform operations such as filtering, predicate pushdown, and partition pruning more efficiently.

Table format metadata brings together file paths, schema, partitions, transactions, and statistics to keep data consistent, queryable, and optimized for performance. It's the layer that makes modern data lakehouses both reliable and efficient.

## Storage engine

The **storage engine** plays a key role in the lakehouse architecture, serving as the critical layer responsible for how data is stored, retrieved, and maintained on object storage systems such as Amazon S3 or Google Cloud Storage, as well as on-premises storage solutions. Just as in traditional database systems, the storage engine manages the underlying structure of data, ensuring that it is properly organized and efficiently accessible by query engines. It sits on top of raw storage and the table and file formats, providing the necessary guarantees for data consistency, durability, and accessibility, even as the system scales to handle massive amounts of data. The following figure presents how the storage engine interacts with the storage layer, including the file and table format:

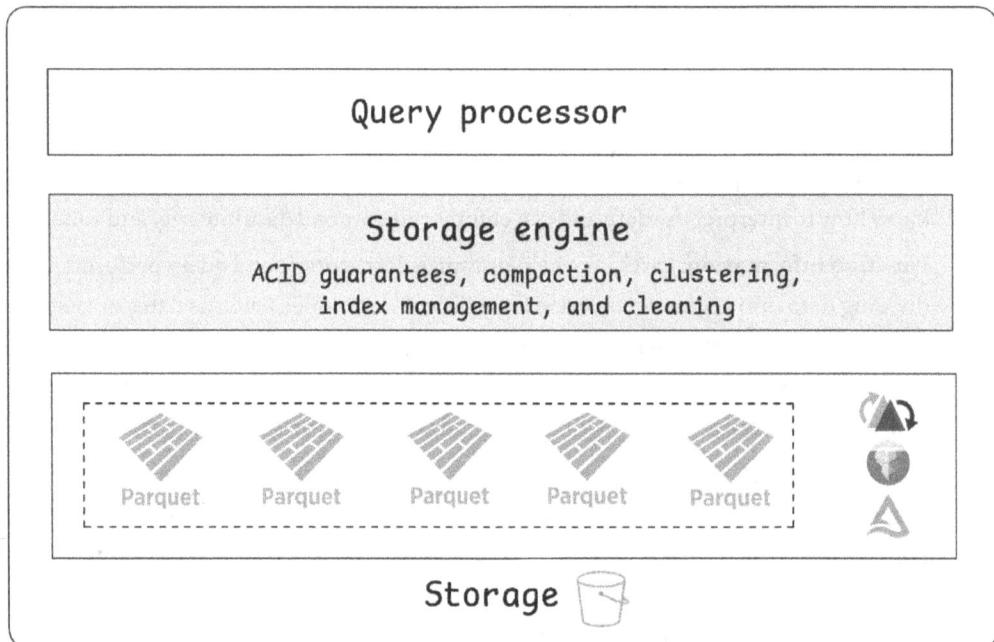

*Figure 1.5 – Storage engine and its interaction with file and table formats*

The storage engine has two fundamental responsibilities: *table management services* and *transactional integrity*. These functions ensure that both the physical organization of the data and its logical correctness are upheld, even under high concurrency. Table management services such as clustering, compaction, cleaning, and indexing are important for optimizing the system's performance and scalability, ensuring that data is organized efficiently for fast access, minimal storage overhead, and smooth read/write operations.

On the transactional side, the storage engine enforces ACID properties to maintain data integrity. Like any database system, these properties are essential in a lakehouse, as they guarantee that every transaction is completed fully or not at all (atomicity), data remains accurate and consistent (consistency), operations are isolated from one another (isolation), and changes are durable, even in the event of a failure (durability). This guarantee becomes especially critical in concurrent write or read scenarios, so multiple users or processes can interact with the data simultaneously without conflicts or data corruption.

To provide a high degree of concurrency, the storage engine employs robust concurrency control and locking mechanisms. These mechanisms allow multiple engines to read from and write to the same dataset simultaneously while avoiding issues such as race conditions, deadlocks, or inconsistent reads. This level of control is non-trivial in environments where high throughput and low latency are required. The storage engine, in combination with table formats (that is, Apache Hudi, Iceberg, and Delta Lake), optimally organizes the data for better query performance. Together, they ensure that data is managed efficiently, consistently, and reliably, even at the scale of petabytes or more. We will explore these capabilities in more detail in *Chapter 2, Transactional Capabilities of the Lakehouse*.

## Compute engine

While the table format component in a lakehouse architecture provides the necessary APIs to read and write data, the **compute engines** are responsible for processing data and running queries, ensuring that the operations are performed efficiently across large-scale datasets. It makes the lakehouse a robust and scalable platform capable of handling a wide range of workloads, from batch processing and real-time analytics to ad hoc querying and machine learning. The compute engine interacts with the underlying table formats (Apache Iceberg, Hudi, or Delta Lake) and utilizes metadata and primitives provided by these formats to optimize query execution and data processing.

An important aspect of a lakehouse architecture is its ability to support multiple compute engines, each tailored to specific types of workloads. For example, Apache Spark is a highly used engine for large-scale batch processing and machine learning, providing robust parallel processing capabilities across distributed environments. Meanwhile, engines such as Apache Flink are designed for real-time streaming analytics. For low-latency, ad hoc SQL queries, Presto and Trino offer the flexibility to run complex, interactive queries with high performance across large datasets.

By supporting multiple compute engines to work on the same table format, the lakehouse architecture provides customers with the flexibility to bring in different engines for specific use cases. The open nature of these table formats enables easy integration on the compute engine side, unlike a traditional data warehouse, where data is only accessible by a single native query engine. This adaptability is crucial, as workloads today can vary significantly, from high-throughput batch jobs to low-latency real-time queries.

Compute engines in a lakehouse architecture perform query optimization by using the metadata provided by the table formats (for example, file statistics, partitioning details, and min/max values) to reduce the amount of data that needs to be scanned. For instance, **predicate pushdown** is a technique where the compute engine filters data at the storage level before scanning, thus reducing unnecessary reads. Additionally, a vectorized way of execution speeds up analytical queries by processing multiple rows of data simultaneously, minimizing CPU overhead. We will learn more about the query optimization techniques in *Chapter 8, Performance Optimization and Tuning in a Lakehouse*.

## Catalog

The **catalog** is a centralized repository for all metadata related to the tables stored within the system. It provides the foundation for data discovery and management, enabling users to search for and access datasets efficiently across large-scale environments. The catalog's main objective is to ensure that the metadata associated with underlying table formats (for example, Apache Hudi, Iceberg, and Delta Lake) is stored and maintained in a central location, often referred to as a **metastore**. This repository keeps track of table definitions, including the schema (column names, data types, and nested structures) and versions of the data, and provides a set of governance policies to make sure that the data stored is secure. By storing this information centrally, the catalog provides a unified view and makes it possible for compute engines (for example, Apache Spark, Flink, and Presto) to interact with the same dataset consistently, ensuring data integrity and performance across different types of workloads. We can see how the catalog component sits between the compute engines and table formats to bring in the necessary security controls and capabilities, such as data discovery and management:

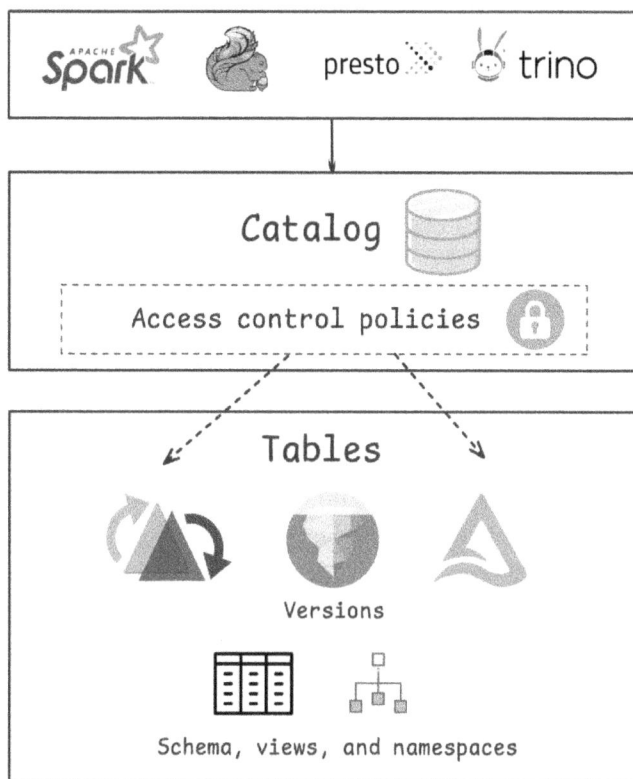

*Figure 1.6 – Catalog component in a lakehouse*

In a more generic sense, the catalog provides a logical separation of the metastore, allowing users to organize metadata into databases or schemas. Each such structure holds not just tables but also views, namespaces, and other objects that are part of the lakehouse. This structure makes it easier to manage metadata, especially in large organizations with many datasets. A key feature of the catalog is its role in data governance and security. It provides the mechanism for defining access controls on tables, databases, and schemas, ensuring that only authorized users can access or modify data. This is important for organizations that need to comply with regulations (such as GDPR or HIPAA) and enforce audit trails for all actions taken on the data. By logging all access and changes, the catalog provides a high level of transparency and traceability, thereby bringing in the required governance otherwise absent in systems such as data lakes. In subsequent chapters, we will explore the different catalog implementations and see how Apache Iceberg, Apache Hudi, and Delta Lake utilize catalogs within a lakehouse architecture.

Now that we have explored the architectural breakdown of a lakehouse, it's important to understand the key attributes that define its open nature.

# Attributes of an open data lakehouse

In this section, we will explore the defining attributes that give the open data lakehouse architecture its edge for today's analytical workloads. These attributes form the foundation of how an open data lakehouse architecture delivers openness, reliability, and cost-efficiency, enabling the running of multiple analytical workloads on the same architecture. As we explore each attribute, you'll see how they come together to optimize data management, reduce costs, and ensure seamless integration across various workloads and compute engines.

## Open data architecture

One of the most important characteristics of a lakehouse architecture is its emphasis on **open data architecture**. In today's context, *openness* refers to open standards and utilizing open storage formats. This is facilitated by the metadata layer (table formats such as Apache Iceberg, Apache Hudi, and Delta Lake) in combination with the data layer (open file formats such as Apache Parquet) that provide common specifications for various compute engines to interact with the data. Here are some important aspects of an open data architecture:

- **Vendor-neutrality**: Open data architecture ensures that data is not locked into any one vendor's proprietary system. This avoids the risk of **vendor lock-in**, where organizations become dependent on a single technology provider for data storage and processing. With open table formats in a lakehouse architecture, organizations have the flexibility to decide where and how to store data and have control over it.

- **Standardized APIs**: Open data architecture is characterized by the use of standard APIs. These APIs adhere to one agreed specification and allow various compute engines to interact with data consistently. Open table formats such as Iceberg, Hudi, and Delta Lake provide a standardized set of APIs to be utilized by various compute engines (for example, Apache Spark, Presto, Trino, and Flink) to read and write data into the storage.

- **Future-proof systems**: An open data lakehouse enables a future-proof architecture. Analytical workloads in an organization will change with time, depending on the maturity level of the organization. For instance, an organization today may have only business intelligence workloads running, but in the future, they may plan to utilize advanced analytics (such as machine learning). In such cases, bringing in a different compute engine or other tools becomes easier with an open data architecture. By adopting open standards, organizations ensure that they can integrate with new technologies as they emerge without being tied to the limitations of any specific platform.

An open data lakehouse architecture contrasts with traditional data warehouses, which require data to be brought to the compute engine, rather than bringing compute to the data. With this new approach, organizations can manage, process, and analyze data more flexibly while ensuring future-proofing and vendor neutrality.

## Unification of batch and streaming

Lakehouse architecture aims to unify batch and streaming workloads, simplifying the complexities that traditional systems face when maintaining separate infrastructures for each. In the previous data architectures, batch processing and real-time streaming operated on distinct platforms, each with its own storage, compute resources, and pipelines. This separation increases operational overhead and introduces challenges in data synchronization, consistency, and efficiently managing resources. A lakehouse architecture is designed for both batch and streaming workloads to be handled on a single platform with a shared storage layer comprising the open table and file formats, eliminating the need for separate systems. This unification streamlines data pipelines by reducing the number of steps involved in data movement and processing, allowing organizations to build more efficient workflows that can handle both historical datasets and real-time data simultaneously.

By using the same data infrastructure for both types of workloads, lakehouses reduce operational costs, particularly by taking advantage of the cost-efficiency of cloud object stores. Writing data to a unified data store (table format) ensures that it is immediately accessible to catalogs, enabling downstream analytical applications to use the most suitable compute engine for each task. For example, Apache Flink, a popular stream processing engine, can be used in combination with Apache Hudi to handle real-time data ingestion. Flink processes streaming data from a source such as Kafka, writing it to Hudi tables in a cloud storage layer such as Amazon S3. Hudi's table format ensures that the ingested streaming data is immediately available for queries using engines such as Trino or Presto, providing transactional guarantees and schema evolution capabilities. On the same platform, Apache Spark-based distributed batch workloads can process raw data and ingest it into Hudi tables, which can then serve as a feature store for machine learning model batch inference.

## Cost efficiency

A key advantage of adopting a lakehouse architecture is the ability to reduce both operational and monetary costs by using low-cost cloud object stores as the storage and multiple data optimization techniques provided by the open table and file formats. Unlike traditional data warehouses, where users need to provision expensive disk space ahead of time, cloud object stores such as Amazon S3 operate on a pay-as-you-go model that lets users pay based on the data stored currently. Through features such as compaction, clustering, compression, and cleanup, open table formats enable organizations to manage large-scale data systems without the typically high operational costs associated with traditional data architectures.

Here are some of the important capabilities offered by open table formats that can help keep both storage and query performance costs in check:

- **Compaction**: Compaction reduces the number of small files by consolidating them into larger, optimized files. This improves query performance and lowers storage costs by reducing file overheads.

- **Clustering**: Clustering groups similar records together to reduce the amount of data scanned, leading to faster queries and lower compute costs.

- **Compression algorithms**: Compression algorithms such as GZip, Snappy, and ZSTD reduce the size of stored data. Using these techniques on file formats such as Parquet helps cut storage costs while maintaining performance by optimizing data retrieval.

- **Data cleanup**: Data cleanup removes files that are no longer referenced or needed by the table format. This process helps reduce storage costs.

- **Open data accessibility**: Open table formats such as Hudi, Iceberg, and Delta Lake allow data to be accessed by multiple compute engines without duplication. This reduces storage needs and eliminates the cost of synchronizing data across platforms.

Organizations have seen significant cost savings by implementing open table formats such as Apache Hudi and Apache Iceberg in their data architecture. *Hudl*, for example, optimized its AWS Glue pipeline with Apache Hudi, resulting in a 90% reduction in pipeline runtime and significant cost savings by focusing on incremental changes instead of processing entire datasets. Similarly, *Insider Engineering* adopted Apache Iceberg and was able to reduce its Amazon S3 storage costs by 90% through optimized file management, compression, and handling of metadata.

## Improvements in query performance

One of the most striking advantages of the lakehouse architecture is significantly better query performance, enabled by a variety of fundamental optimizations. Traditional data lakes have received complaints about slow query performance over rather large, and often unstructured, datasets. The lakehouse architecture addresses these shortcomings by offering a set of features that help improve performance:

- **Partitioning and indexing**: Data can be partitioned based on relevant keys, such as date, region, or customer ID, so that queries only scan a subset of the dataset. This drastically reduces I/O and improves performance, especially for time-series or filtered queries.

In addition to partitioning, indexing further accelerates data access by creating auxiliary data structures, such as Bloom filters, column statistics, or sorted key indexes, that guide the query engine to the most relevant files or data blocks. Instead of scanning every file, the engine consults these indexes to efficiently narrow down the search space, significantly reducing query latency for high-cardinality or point lookup operations.

- **Data caching and query acceleration**: Multilevel caching mechanisms, inclusive of in-memory caching of hot data, are employed to achieve this. This considerably reduces the response time to queries. In addition to caching, query acceleration engines such as Apache Spark or Presto are part of the query acceleration that some lakehouse solutions provide, optimizing query execution plans and parallelizing query tasks across distributed nodes.

- **File format optimizations:** Modern optimized file formats include Parquet and ORC, which are columnar formats, and Avro, which is a row-based format. Parquet and ORC enable faster reads and writes by supporting features such as predicate pushdown, columnar storage, and compression, all of which reduce the amount of data scanned during query execution. While Avro doesn't offer columnar storage, it excels in efficient row-wise data handling and schema evolution, making it valuable for certain use cases. Together, these formats enhance storage efficiency and query performance.

These attributes enable the lakehouse to give interactive, near-real-time query performance for complex analytic queries over large datasets; this enables organizations to drive more rapid and effective insights compared to traditional data lakes.

## Reliable transactions

One of the major limitations of data lakes has been the lack of support for ACID transactions. The lakehouse architecture addresses this by introducing robust transactional capabilities that ensure data integrity and consistency, even in highly concurrent environments. This is achieved through several key mechanisms that guarantee reliable data processing:

- **ACID compliance**: Community-driven developments of table formats such as Apache Iceberg, Apache Hudi, and Delta Lake have ensured the data lake's compliance with ACID transactional guarantees. Consistent reads and writes can be ensured (that is, updates, deletes, and inserts of data are atomic in nature). This is a very important property to avoid data corruption and ensure that queries always return correct and consistent results.

- **Concurrency control**: Advanced concurrency controls, such as optimistic concurrency control, are implemented in lakehouses over the operations against their data. That guarantees that there are no conflicts between various users who read and write to the data, and in case of conflicts, it gracefully handles the system, usually through versioning control or rollbacks.

- **Schema evolution and enforcement**: Traditional data lakes struggle with schema evolution, whereas in a lakehouse, changes can be made to the schema without breaking data integrity. This is critical for modern data workflows, where schemas evolve over time and data is continuously ingested from multiple sources.

With support for ACID transactions, lakehouses integrate the flexibility of a data lake with the typical guarantees around data integrity from traditional data warehouses and thereby provide a stable foundation for both operational and analytical workloads.

## Interoperability across diverse compute engines

A defining strength of the lakehouse architecture is its ability to interoperate seamlessly with multiple, diverse compute engines. Unlike traditional data lakes and warehouses, which often tie users to a single query engine, lakehouses decouple compute from storage, enabling various engines to operate on the same data in place. This architectural flexibility empowers organizations to align the right tool with the right workload, enhancing performance and reducing complexity.

Modern organizations run a wide range of workloads (ETL pipelines, ad hoc analytics, real-time processing, and machine learning inference), often within the same environment. A single engine is rarely optimal for all these use cases. Lakehouses, built on open table formats such as Apache Iceberg, Delta Lake, and Hudi, and open file formats such as Parquet and ORC, allow compute engines to interact with a shared, consistent storage layer without data duplication.

This is how compute engines differ in their strengths:

- Apache Spark is ideal for large-scale batch processing and ML training workloads, benefiting from its rich ecosystem and mature APIs
- Presto/Trino excels at ad-hoc and interactive querying, offering low-latency SQL over large datasets without requiring data movement
- Apache Flink is designed for event-driven, real-time streaming jobs, offering precise event-time semantics and stateful stream processing
- Dremio and Starburst offer high-performance analytics with cost-based optimization and pushdown capabilities for BI-style workloads

By supporting interoperability at the metadata level, lakehouses allow all these engines to access the same data schema and version history, ensuring **a single source of truth** while eliminating siloed data copies.

The benefits of engine-specific interoperability are as follows:

- **Workload specialization**: Different teams (e.g., data science, analytics, and ops) can use the engine best suited to their job without altering the dataset.

- **Cost optimization**: Compute resources can be provisioned independently per engine, reducing overhead and avoiding overprovisioning.

- **Simplified operations**: No need for complex data pipelines to transfer data between systems. Updates made by one engine are immediately visible to others.

In practice, this enables high-throughput ingestion using Flink, heavy transformation with Spark, and instant querying with Trino, all operating on the same Delta or Iceberg table in S3.

This engine-agnostic approach to data access is central to the lakehouse's flexibility, enabling diverse teams to work in parallel on a consistent dataset while meeting the performance and cost requirements unique to each workload.

# Summary

In this chapter, we explored the evolution of data architectures, from OLTP and OLAP systems to data lakes, providing a foundation for understanding the data lakehouse paradigm. This historical context helps explain how the challenges of older systems led to the development of more flexible and scalable solutions, even as foundational components remained the same. You also gained a deep understanding of the core components and principles of open data lakehouse architecture, including storage, file formats, table formats, storage engines, catalogs, and query engines. These building blocks will help you design scalable and flexible systems capable of handling both batch and streaming workloads efficiently. Additionally, you learned about some of the key attributes of the lakehouse architecture, such as open data architecture, modularity, flexibility, and cost-efficiency.

In the next chapter, you will dive deep into the transactional layer of the lakehouse to understand how critical technical components, such as table format and storage engine, play a central role in enabling reliable, concurrent transactions.

# Questions

1. What are the main differences between OLTP and OLAP systems in terms of their primary focus and technical components?

2. Explain the role and characteristics of data lakes in modern data architectures. What limitations do they have that led to the development of the lakehouse architecture?

3.  What are the key attributes of a lakehouse architecture that make it distinct from traditional data lakes and warehouses?

4.  How do table formats such as Apache Iceberg, Apache Hudi, and Delta Lake enhance the functionality of a lakehouse architecture?

5.  What are the benefits of using an open data architecture in a lakehouse setup? Provide examples.

6.  Why is the unification of batch and streaming workloads an important feature of the lakehouse architecture? How is this achieved?

7.  Describe the importance of file formats (row-based and columnar) in a lakehouse. How do they impact query performance and storage efficiency?

8.  What role does the storage engine play in a lakehouse architecture, and how does it ensure data integrity and scalability?

9.  Explain the concept of multi-compute engine support in a lakehouse. Why is this feature critical for modern data workloads?

10. List three key optimizations in lakehouse architectures that improve query performance.

## Answers

1.  OLTP systems focus on real-time transactional processing, optimized for rapid data insertion, updates, and deletions with ACID compliance. OLAP systems target large-scale data analysis with high query performance, often using column-oriented file formats and denormalized schemas.

2.  Data lakes provide centralized storage for raw data in its native format, enabling scalability and cost-effectiveness. However, they face challenges such as a lack of governance, slow query performance, and no native ACID support, which the lakehouse architecture addresses by combining the flexibility of data lakes with the reliability of data warehouses.

3.  Key attributes of a lakehouse architecture include open data architecture, unification of batch and streaming workloads, cost efficiency, reliable transactions, and multi-compute engine support.

4.  Table formats such as Apache Iceberg, Apache Hudi, and Delta Lake provide schema evolution, time travel, and ACID compliance, enabling better data management and interoperability across compute engines.

5. Open data architecture ensures vendor-neutrality, uses standardized APIs, and enables future-proofing by supporting multiple compute engines and avoiding vendor lock-in. For example, data stored in Parquet format can be accessed by engines such as Spark, Presto, and Flink.

6. The unification of batch and streaming workloads reduces operational complexity by enabling both types of processing on the same storage layer. Tools such as Apache Flink for streaming and Apache Spark for batch processing work seamlessly with table formats such as Hudi.

7. File formats such as Parquet and ORC enhance query performance through features such as columnar storage and compression. Row-based formats such as Avro are better for write-heavy workloads and schema evolution.

8. The storage engine organizes and maintains data on object storage, ensuring transactional integrity through ACID properties and handling high concurrency. It also optimizes data layout for efficient querying.

9. Multi-compute engine support allows different engines (for example, Spark for batch, Flink for streaming, and Presto for interactive queries) to operate on the same dataset, ensuring flexibility and cost optimization.

10. Key optimizations include partitioning and indexing to minimize scanned data, data caching for faster access, and file format improvements such as predicate pushdown and compression for efficient query execution.

# 2

# Transactional Capabilities of the Lakehouse

Building on our exploration of the evolution from traditional OLTP and OLAP systems to the lakehouse architecture, we will now look at one of the key features that sets lakehouses apart: their **transactional capabilities**. For years, data management has struggled to balance consistency, reliability, and high concurrency when working with massive datasets. Traditional data lakes excelled in flexibility and scalability but often fell short in providing robust transactional features. While data warehouses introduced limited transactional support for ingestion and ETL processes, they were not designed for fine-grained, concurrent transactional operations. Lakehouses bridge this gap by integrating transactional properties, enabling real-time data operations and large-scale analytics, and we'll explore the inner workings of transactions, ACID properties, and conflict resolution methods that maintain data integrity.

In this chapter, we will cover the following topics:

- Understanding transactions and ACID properties
- Discovering conflict resolution mechanisms
- Understanding the storage engine

By the end of this chapter, you'll have gained a comprehensive understanding of the transactional layer's architecture, how it operates in a lakehouse, and its integration with open table formats and the storage engine to support reliable data operations.

# Understanding transactions and ACID properties

**Transactions** are fundamental units of work in any database system. They represent a series of operations that are executed as a single, indivisible unit. The concept of a transaction ensures that either all the operations within it are executed successfully, or none at all, preserving the integrity of the system. In a transactional context, we focus on the **atomicity**, **consistency**, **isolation**, and **durability** (**ACID**) properties, which govern the behavior of these operations.

ACID properties serve as the backbone of robust data management systems. They are crucial in ensuring that transactional operations are reliable and consistent, even in the presence of multiple concurrent operations or system failures. Without ACID guarantees, data systems could become unreliable, leading to data corruption, inconsistencies, and operational inefficiencies.

## Deep dive into ACID properties

To understand the foundation of transactional systems, let's break down the four core ACID properties that ensure data consistency and reliability:

- **Atomicity**: Atomicity ensures that a transaction is "all or nothing." If any part of a transaction fails, the entire transaction is rolled back, ensuring that partial updates do not leave the system in an inconsistent state. This is especially important in distributed systems where partial updates can lead to a variety of issues, including data loss and corruption.

- **Consistency**: Consistency ensures that a transaction brings the database from one valid state to another. In other words, after the transaction is completed, the data should still satisfy all the integrity constraints (such as foreign keys, unique constraints, and so on). For example, if a table requires a column to have unique values, no transaction should violate this rule.

- **Isolation**: Isolation guarantees that the intermediate states of a transaction are invisible to other transactions. Even though multiple transactions might be running concurrently, they are isolated from each other. Different isolation levels (such as read committed and serializable) can be used based on the system's requirements and the balance between performance and consistency.

- **Durability**: Durability ensures that once a transaction is committed, it is permanently stored in the system, even in the event of a crash or failure. Durability is typically achieved through techniques such as logging and **write-ahead logs** (**WALs**) in storage engines to ensure that all changes are safely written to persistent storage.

## ACID properties in traditional databases

In traditional databases such as MySQL, PostgreSQL, and Oracle, the ACID properties have been well established. These systems use a tightly coupled architecture where both the compute and storage components are integrated, ensuring that transactions can be processed efficiently.

However, the introduction of distributed and cloud-native architectures has brought new challenges. In such environments, ensuring ACID properties across distributed systems requires specialized techniques such as **2-phase commit** (**2PC**) or optimistic concurrency control to handle distributed transactions while maintaining consistency across nodes.

## ACID properties in lakehouse architectures

The lakehouse architecture addresses some of the inherent limitations of traditional data lakes by introducing ACID-compliant transactional capabilities. In data lakes, operations such as updates and deletes were difficult to handle without complex workarounds. However, with open table formats such as Apache Hudi, Apache Iceberg, and Delta Lake, these challenges are addressed, bringing ACID properties to the forefront in a distributed file-based architecture. We will dive deep into each table format's transactional capabilities later in this chapter.

In a lakehouse, the storage engine manages transactions, ensuring that any operation, whether it's a write, update, or delete, is executed in a manner that conforms to ACID guarantees. This ensures that users can trust the consistency and durability of the data, even in large-scale, multi-petabyte environments where high concurrency and distributed operations are common.

Now that we've explored ACID properties in traditional databases and lakehouse architectures, let's dive deeper into the conflict resolution mechanisms in the next section.

# Discovering conflict resolution mechanisms

In any multi-user or concurrent environment, conflicts can arise when multiple transactions attempt to update or modify the same data simultaneously. Conflict resolution is crucial for maintaining data integrity, particularly in systems where high levels of concurrency are expected, like those in distributed databases or lakehouse environments.

Traditional database systems employ various mechanisms to manage conflicts, ensuring that simultaneous operations do not lead to data corruption or inconsistencies. Two key concepts in this space are locking mechanisms (for example, pessimistic and optimistic locking) and concurrency control methods (for example, two-phase locking or timestamp ordering).

# Types of conflict resolutions

To ensure data consistency and integrity, transactional systems employ various concurrency control mechanisms. Three primary strategies address potential conflicts:

- **Pessimistic concurrency control**: Locks data to prevent conflicts
- **Optimistic concurrency control**: Assumes that conflicts are rare and resolves them when they occur
- **Multi-version concurrency control**: Uses multiple versions of data to resolve conflicts

Let's discuss them in detail.

# Pessimistic concurrency control

In **pessimistic concurrency control (PCC)**, the system assumes that conflicts are likely to occur. Therefore, it locks the data before a transaction starts, preventing other transactions from accessing it until the lock is released, as shown:

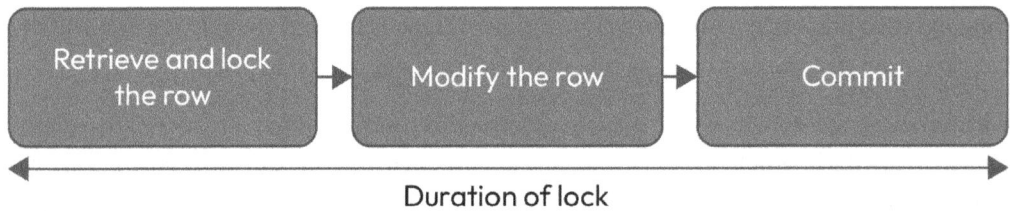

*Figure 2.1 – Pessimistic strategy*

This method is effective in preventing conflicts but can lead to performance bottlenecks, particularly in high-traffic systems where multiple users are accessing the same data concurrently.

# Optimistic concurrency control

**Optimistic concurrency control (OCC)** operates on the assumption that conflicts are rare. Instead of locking data preemptively, the system allows multiple transactions to proceed concurrently and checks for conflicts only at the time of the transaction's commit. If a conflict is detected, such as two transactions trying to modify the same data simultaneously, the system takes corrective action, such as aborting or retrying the conflicting transaction.

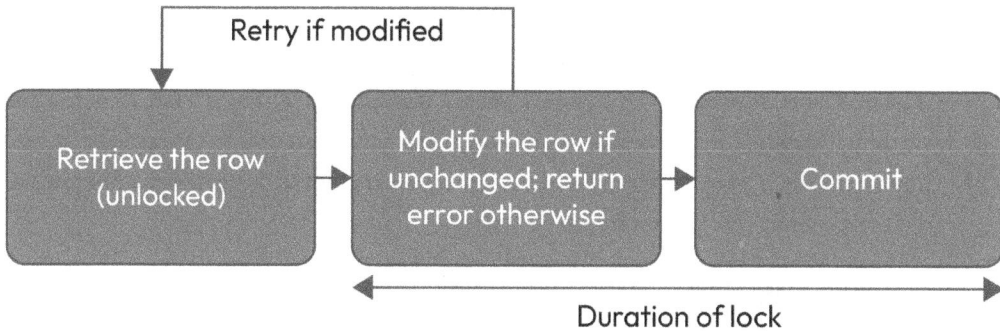

*Figure 2.2 – Optimistic strategy*

OCC is particularly useful in environments where read operations are more frequent than writes, as it enables higher performance and reduced contention among transactions.

## Multi-version concurrency control

**Multi-version concurrency control (MVCC)** offers a more nuanced solution by allowing multiple versions of data to exist simultaneously. Rather than locking data or assuming that conflicts are rare, MVCC creates a new version of the data each time it is modified. When a transaction reads the data, it retrieves the most recent committed version that was available at the time the transaction began.

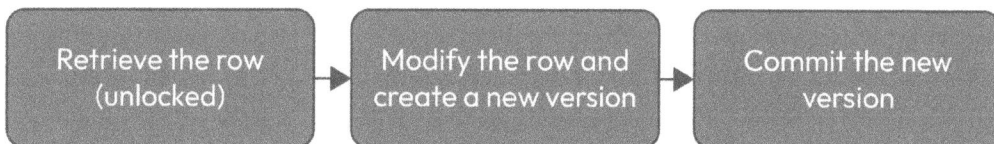

*Figure 2.3 – Multi-version strategy*

This ensures that readers are never blocked by writers, and writers can update data without waiting for readers to finish. MVCC allows for high levels of concurrency while minimizing contention and ensuring consistency:

- **How it works**: When a user reads data, they see a snapshot of the database at a particular point in time, ensuring consistency without the need to lock resources. If multiple versions of the same record exist, each transaction sees the version that was valid at the start of the transaction. Writers create new versions of data rather than overwriting the existing version, which allows for better handling of concurrent operations.

- **Conflict resolution:** In MVCC, all transactions are allowed to complete, with each creating a new version of the data. Readers see a consistent snapshot of the database as of the start of their transaction, while subsequent reads or queries can use the latest committed version. If multiple versions of the same record exist, the system resolves conflicts at read time, typically by exposing the latest version in the metadata or by merging updates as per the system's conflict resolution strategy.

## Locking granularity

Locking granularity refers to the level of data specificity when applying locks. Choosing the right granularity is crucial, as it affects concurrency, performance, and conflict resolution. Here are three common locking granularities:

- **Row-level locking:** Specific rows are locked, allowing more granular control but also increasing the risk of deadlocks
- **Table-level locking:** The entire table is locked, reducing concurrency but simplifying conflict prevention
- **Partition-level locking:** A specific partition of data is locked, often used in distributed databases to allow other partitions to be accessed concurrently

## Conflict resolution in distributed systems

Distributed systems introduce added complexity, as conflicts must be managed across different nodes that might hold different versions of the data. Techniques such as consensus protocols (Paxos and Raft) and MVCC are employed to ensure that conflicts are resolved efficiently and that the data remains consistent across all nodes. In some cases, systems also leverage **conflict-free replicated data types** (CRDTs), which enable concurrent updates to be merged automatically, ensuring eventual consistency without requiring complex coordination.

In distributed systems, MVCC ensures that transactions operate on a consistent snapshot of the data, with any modifications written as a new version. This approach allows multiple transactions to coexist without blocking each other, enabling higher concurrency and efficient resource utilization. While MVCC provides snapshot isolation and version management, replication of these versions across nodes is handled separately by the underlying storage system or coordination service (for example, HDFS, S3, or consensus protocols such as Raft).

# Conflict resolution in lakehouse architectures

In lakehouse architectures, conflict resolution is a key challenge due to the decoupling of compute and storage, which allows multiple engines to operate on the same data. To address this, two concurrency control mechanisms are most widely used: OCC and MVCC.

With OCC, lakehouses allow transactions to proceed concurrently without locking data preemptively. At the time of committing the transaction, the system checks whether a conflict occurred. If a conflict is detected, the system can roll back or retry the conflicting transaction. This method aligns well with the open storage layer in lakehouses, where multiple compute engines may simultaneously access the data.

Lakehouses implement MVCC to manage concurrent reads and writes without introducing locks. When data is modified, a new version of the data is created, allowing readers to continue accessing the previous version. This ensures that readers are never blocked by ongoing write operations, and writers can proceed without waiting for readers.

Apache Iceberg and Delta Lake both implement MVCC to provide snapshot isolation and support concurrent reads and writes. Apache Hudi provides a similar guarantee through its commit timeline and supports snapshot isolation in **Copy-on-Write** mode, while **Merge-on-Read** enables near-real-time incremental views.

By leveraging OCC and MVCC, lakehouse architectures maintain the integrity and consistency of data even in environments with high levels of concurrency. This ensures that users can operate on data without running into conflicts, enabling smooth collaboration and efficient processing of large-scale datasets.

An essential aspect of conflict resolution in lakehouse architecture is version control. Lakehouses maintain versions of data as part of their transactional system, allowing users to view the state of the data at any given point in time. This feature is not only useful for conflict resolution but also for auditing and rollback purposes, allowing users to revert to previous versions of the data if necessary.

This version control ensures that no data is lost and any conflicts can be traced and resolved, ensuring the integrity of the system over time. This is particularly valuable for enterprises with compliance requirements that demand data lineage and historical tracking.

In the next section, we'll explore how these concepts apply to the lakehouse architecture, specifically the storage engine component. We'll delve into table management services and transactional integrity, discussing how lakehouse storage engines provide ACID properties, concurrency control, and more.

# Understanding the storage engine

In *Chapter 1, Open Data Lakehouse: A New Architectural Paradigm*, we introduced the storage engine as the critical component responsible for managing how data is stored, retrieved, and maintained in a data lakehouse architecture. In this chapter, we will deepen that understanding by exploring how the storage engine integrates with the open table format to provide transactional capabilities. However, before we dive into the specific capabilities of a storage engine, let's first examine the various sub-components that make up the storage engine within a traditional database system. This will help clarify why the storage engine is so essential in an open lakehouse architecture.

## Components of a traditional database storage engine

Storage engines enable transactional capabilities in a lakehouse, so it's helpful to first look at what makes up a traditional database storage engine. Understanding its sub-components highlights why this layer is essential for efficient data management. The following diagram illustrates the architecture of a database system, with the storage engine highlighted at the bottom:

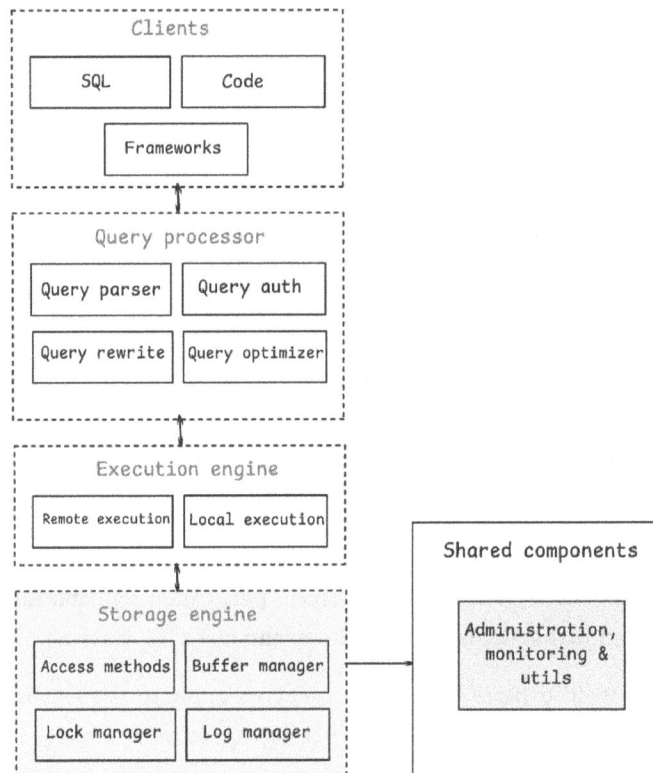

*Figure 2.4 – Architecture of a traditional database management system*

In traditional **database management systems (DBMSs)**, the storage engine is the core layer responsible for managing how data is physically stored, retrieved, and maintained. It handles the low-level operations of the database, such as reading and writing data to storage, managing transactions, and enforcing concurrency. As shown in *Figure 2.4*, the storage engine includes components such as the lock manager, access methods, buffer manager, and recovery manager. Each of these components plays a vital role in ensuring the efficiency, accuracy, and durability of database operations. The lakehouse architecture draws inspiration from traditional database systems by incorporating a storage engine to provide transactional capabilities across massive datasets stored in systems such as Amazon S3, Google Cloud Storage, and Azure Blob Storage.

Let's take a look at the four sub-components of a storage engine and understand their need in today's lakehouse architecture:

- **Lock manager**: The *lock manager* is a critical component in database systems, ensuring that multiple operations can access shared resources without interfering with one another. In a lakehouse architecture, this role becomes crucial due to the distributed nature of data and since different compute engines, such as Spark, Flink, or Presto, operate on the same dataset simultaneously for running diverse sets of workloads. Therefore, a lock manager is needed to prevent conflicts and maintain data correctness under concurrent operations. By bringing effective concurrency control mechanisms to coordinate multiple readers and writers, the lock manager upholds data integrity, ensuring that workloads run smoothly without conflicts or data corruption.

- **Access methods**: In traditional database systems, the *access methods* component determines how data is accessed and retrieved, often relying on storage structures such as B-trees, hashing, or **log-structured-merge-trees (LSM-trees)** for efficient data retrieval. Similarly, in a lakehouse architecture, there is a need to effectively organize data and metadata so that compute engines can access data in storage efficiently. Lakehouse table formats employ a directory-based access method for efficient data retrieval from distributed cloud object stores. For example, the Apache Hudi table format organizes data into file groups and file slices (discussed in *Chapter 4, Apache Hudi Deep Dive*) within its timeline – a type of event log. Indexes operate on top of this structure to help compute engines quickly locate the right file groups for faster reads and writes. Apache Iceberg uses a tree-based structure to organize metadata files (manifests), which enables efficient pruning of irrelevant data files. Similarly, Delta Lake employs a directory-based access method, combined with its transaction log, to track all transactions and help prune data files.

- **Buffer manager**: The *buffer manager* in a database system is essential for improving system performance by caching frequently accessed data, reducing the need to repeatedly access slower storage. In lakehouse architectures, where cloud object stores serve as the storage layer, there is a fundamental trade-off between faster data ingestion and optimal query performance. Writing smaller files or logging deltas can speed up ingestion, but for optimal query performance, it is critical to minimize the number of files accessed and pre-materialize data merges. This is where a buffer manager becomes essential in a lakehouse context. It addresses the issue by caching frequently accessed or modified data, allowing query engines to avoid repeated access to slower lake storage. For example, in Apache Hudi, there are proposals to tightly integrate a columnar caching service that can sit between the lake storage and query engines, using the Hudi timeline to ensure cache consistency across transactions and mutations. This approach will not only improve read performance by serving data directly from the cache but also amortize the cost of merge operations by compacting data in memory.

- **Recovery manager**: The *recovery manager* is responsible for ensuring data durability and consistency, especially in the event of system failures. In a lakehouse architecture, the recovery manager takes on the role of maintaining data reliability across distributed storage systems. This involves mechanisms that allow the system to recover data to a consistent state, even after unexpected disruptions. Open table formats such as Apache Hudi, Apache Iceberg, and Delta Lake use metadata snapshots and WALs to guarantee durability and facilitate recovery. For example, Iceberg uses immutable snapshots to enable data rollback and point-in-time recovery, while Hudi uses a timeline of commits to maintain consistent versions of the dataset and to revert for any unexpected scenarios. Delta Lake employs transaction logs that track all changes, enabling the system to revert to a stable state if needed. These capabilities ensure that lakehouses are resilient and can maintain data integrity, even at a massive scale.

While these four interconnected sub-components form the foundation for executing ACID-based transactions in a traditional database system, the storage engine's role extends beyond just ensuring transactional integrity. Another key responsibility of the storage engine is to continuously optimize the data layout within the storage layer. In traditional databases, the storage engine works closely with the **administration**, **monitoring**, and **utilities** components (as illustrated in *Figure 2.4*) to manage the organization and structure of files, ensuring efficient data access and performance. This concept carries over to modern lakehouse architecture, where the storage engine is not only responsible for maintaining transactional consistency but also for delivering a comprehensive suite of table management services. These services include cleaning, compaction, clustering, archival, and indexing, operations that are essential for ensuring that the storage layout remains optimized for different compute engines to efficiently query the data. By organizing the underlying files and metadata, the storage engine enables query engines to leverage advanced optimization techniques, such as predicate pushdown, data skipping, and pruning, ultimately improving query performance across various workloads.

With this understanding, we can dive deeper into the two fundamental responsibilities of the lakehouse storage engine: transactional capabilities and table management services.

# How a lakehouse handles transactions

One of the defining attributes of the lakehouse architecture is its ability to provide transactional guarantees when running various **Data Definition Language** (**DDL**) and **Data Manipulation Language** (**DML**) operations, something that distinguishes it from traditional data lakes, which often lack such capabilities. These transactional features align the lakehouse architecture with the reliability and consistency typically associated with data warehouses (OLAP databases), while still retaining the flexibility of data lakes. In this section, we will explore how transactional integrity is achieved in the three table formats through ACID guarantees and concurrency control mechanisms, which allow multiple users and applications to safely interact with the same dataset without compromising data integrity.

## ACID guarantees

ACID properties are essential for ensuring that data operations are reliable, consistent, and isolated from each other. In lakehouses, the need for these guarantees arises from the complexities of handling concurrent reads and writes, managing multiple compute engines, and supporting large-scale applications accessing the same data. Each of the table formats, such as Apache Hudi, Apache Iceberg, and Delta Lake, implements ACID properties slightly differently, given the distinct structure of the formats. Let's understand how the design decisions of each table format ensure ACID properties in a lakehouse.

## Apache Hudi ACID

Hudi achieves ACID guarantees via its timeline – a WAL that keeps track of all the transactions occurring in the table. *Atomic* writes in Hudi are achieved by publishing commits atomically to a timeline, where each commit is stamped with an instant time. This instant time denotes the point at which the action is deemed to have occurred, ensuring that changes are either fully committed or rolled back, preventing partial updates. This guarantees that readers never see partially written data, maintaining atomicity.

*Consistency* in Hudi is primarily ensured through its timeline mechanism, which acts as a structured log of all actions (insert, update, and delete) represented as a sequence of "instants." Only committed instants (those that complete the requested → inflight → completed cycle) are visible to readers and writers, ensuring the consistent ordering of events and preventing partial or incomplete writes from affecting the dataset. In concurrent scenarios, each transaction is assigned a unique, increasing timestamp, guaranteeing that operations are applied in the correct order and avoiding conflicts between overlapping modifications.

In addition to this, Hudi enforces primary key uniqueness as a data integrity rule. Each record is assigned a primary key, which helps map data to specific partitions and file groups, allowing efficient updates and ensuring duplicate records are not introduced into the dataset.

Apache Hudi uses a combination of MVCC and OCC to ensure *isolation* between different types of processes. Hudi distinguishes between writer processes (which handle data modifications such as upserts and deletes), table services (which perform tasks such as compaction and cleaning), and readers (which execute queries). These processes operate on consistent snapshots of the dataset, thanks to MVCC, ensuring that readers always access the last successfully committed data, even when writes are ongoing. MVCC enables non-blocking, lock-free concurrency control between writers and table services, and between different table services, allowing for smooth parallel execution. At the same time, Hudi uses OCC to manage concurrency between writers, ensuring that conflicting operations are detected and handled without compromising data integrity. This dual approach provides snapshot isolation across all processes, maintaining isolation while efficiently supporting concurrent operations.

Hudi provides *durability* via its WAL (timeline) that comprises Apache Avro serialized files containing individual actions (such as commit, compaction, or rollback), ensuring that all changes made to the dataset are permanent and recoverable, even in the event of system failures. Any changes made during a transaction are first written to the WAL, which acts as a temporary log of changes before they are applied to the actual dataset. This mechanism ensures that, in case of a crash or failure, the system can recover from the WAL and complete any pending operations or roll back uncommitted changes, preventing data loss. Additionally, both metadata and data files in Hudi are stored in systems such as cloud object stores or HDFS, which enables the formats to take advantage of their durable nature.

## Apache Iceberg ACID

Apache Iceberg guarantees ACID properties by organizing data into a persistent tree structure of metadata and data files, with the entire table state represented by the root of this tree. Each commit to the dataset, such as an insert, update, or delete, creates a new tree with a new root metadata file. The key design element for *atomicity* is Iceberg's use of an atomic **compare-and-swap (CAS)** operation for committing these new metadata files to the catalog.

The catalog stores the location of the current metadata file, which holds the complete state of all active snapshots of the table. When a writer performs a change, it generates a new metadata file and attempts to commit the update by swapping the current metadata location with the new one. This CAS operation ensures that either the entire change is applied successfully or none at all, preventing any partial updates. In the case of concurrent writes, if two writers attempt to commit changes based on the same original metadata file, only the first writer's commit will succeed. The second writer's commit will be rejected, ensuring that no conflicting or incomplete changes are written. Technically, any kind of database or data store can be used as a catalog in Apache Iceberg. The only requirement is that the database should have a locking mechanism to ensure there are no conflicts. The atomic swap mechanism is fundamental to maintaining the integrity of the table and forms the backbone of Iceberg's transactional model.

Iceberg's metadata tree structure and commit process are designed to ensure *consistency* guarantees. At the core of Iceberg's consistency model is the guarantee that every commit must replace an expected table state with a new, valid state. Each writer proposes changes based on the current table state, but if another writer has modified the table in the meantime, the original writer's commit will fail. In such cases, the failed writer must retry the operation with the new table state, preventing the system from introducing any inconsistencies due to concurrent writes. This mechanism enforces a linear history of changes, where each commit builds on the most recent table version (snapshot), avoiding scenarios where the table could be left in a partially updated state. Iceberg ensures that as much of the previous work as possible is reused in the retry attempt. This efficient handling of retries reduces the overhead associated with repeated write operations and ensures that concurrent writers can work independently without causing inconsistencies. Readers only access fully committed data, as changes are atomically applied, maintaining a consistent view of the table without partial updates.

Apache Iceberg supports both *snapshot isolation* and *serializable isolation* to ensure that readers and concurrent writers remain isolated from each other. Iceberg uses OCC, where writers operate on the assumption that the table's current version will not change during their transaction. A writer prepares its updates and attempts to commit them by swapping the metadata file pointer from the current version to a new one. If another writer commits a change before this operation completes, the first writer's update is rejected, and it must retry based on the new table state. This mechanism guarantees that uncommitted changes from multiple writers never overlap or conflict, ensuring *isolation* between concurrent operations. Readers also benefit from isolation, as they access a consistent snapshot of the table, unaffected by ongoing writes, until they refresh the table to see newly committed changes. The atomic swap of metadata (in the catalog) ensures that all operations are isolated and fully applied, preventing partial updates from being exposed to readers or other writers.

Apache Iceberg ensures *durability* by committing both data and metadata updates to fault-tolerant storage systems, such as HDFS, Amazon S3, or Google Cloud Storage. This is reinforced by Iceberg's tree-structured table format, where each committed snapshot represents a consistent, durable state of the table. Once a transaction is committed, both metadata and underlying data files are safely persisted to distributed storage. The commit process is atomic: the new metadata version is updated only after all changes are fully written and conflict-free. This guarantees that partially committed or failed transactions are excluded from valid snapshots, leaving the table in its last consistent state and preventing any risk of data corruption. Since Iceberg's metadata is stored alongside data files in cloud object storage, tables benefit from the durability guarantees of the underlying storage. In the event of a system crash or failure, Iceberg can recover to the latest stable state by referencing the most recent snapshot.

## Delta Lake ACID

Delta Lake ensures *atomicity* by committing all changes, whether adding new data or marking old files for removal, as a single, indivisible transaction. This is achieved through Delta Lake's delta log, a WAL that tracks every operation on the table, ensuring that changes are logged in an all-or-nothing manner. Each write operation generates new data files (typically in Parquet format) and appends a corresponding commit entry to the delta log, recording both the files added and the files logically removed. More importantly, a commit is only considered successful when the entire operation, including all file updates, is fully recorded in the log. If the commit fails at any point, due to a system failure, conflict, or other issue, none of the new files will be visible to the system, guaranteeing that the transaction either fully completes or has no impact at all. The atomic commit process ensures that the table remains in a consistent state, avoiding scenarios where partial writes could lead to data inconsistencies.

*Consistency* in Delta Lake is achieved by ensuring that every transaction adheres to the rules and constraints defined for the dataset. This is enforced through Delta Lake's transaction log, which serves as the system's source of truth for all changes. Every write operation, whether it involves adding new data, updating existing records, or removing files, is validated against the current state of the table, ensuring that schema constraints are maintained and that no conflicting or invalid changes are applied. The delta log keeps a detailed record of each transaction, allowing Delta Lake to enforce data integrity checks, such as ensuring that schema changes are compatible and that records remain unique where required.

Because Delta Lake follows an append-only model, data files are never modified in place. Instead, new data files are created, and older files are logically marked for removal through entries in the delta log. The system uses this log to assemble a consistent, up-to-date snapshot of the dataset for both readers and writers. This design prevents inconsistencies by ensuring that every version of the table is constructed from valid, committed transactions. If a transaction violates a constraint (such as a schema mismatch or an attempt to modify data that has been concurrently updated by another writer), the transaction is aborted and must be retried. This guarantees that no invalid data is committed to the table, preserving the consistency of the dataset.

Delta Lake provides snapshot *isolation* for reads and serializable isolation for writes, ensuring that transactions operate on a consistent view of the data. For reads, snapshot isolation guarantees that readers always see a stable version of the dataset, unaffected by ongoing writes, as they are based on previously committed snapshots of the data. Readers only view the changes once they are fully committed, which prevents any "dirty reads" of uncommitted data.

For writes, Delta Lake uses OCC to enforce serializable isolation. Writers operate on potentially different snapshots of the data, assuming that no other transactions have modified the snapshot they are working on. However, before committing changes, Delta Lake verifies whether the snapshot is still valid. If another writer has committed changes to the same portion of the dataset, the transaction fails, and the writer must retry with the updated snapshot. This prevents conflicting updates from being committed.

The core mechanism that enables this separation of read and write operations is MVCC, which allows Delta Lake to track multiple versions of the dataset over time, ensuring that readers can work on consistent snapshots while writers operate on isolated versions of the data. If a conflict arises between multiple writers, only one can successfully commit, preserving isolation and ensuring that no overlapping changes are applied to the dataset.

Similar to Apache Hudi and Apache Iceberg, Delta Lake guarantees *durability* by storing all transactions in fault-tolerant, persistent storage systems such as Amazon S3, Azure Blob Storage, or HDFS. Once a transaction is successfully committed to the delta log, both the data files and the metadata changes are durably stored, ensuring that they are protected even in the event of a system failure. Delta Lake's use of cloud object storage means that every write is replicated across multiple locations, providing resilience and strong consistency. Delta Lake can recover from any failed state by relying on the last successful transaction recorded in the delta log, making sure that no committed data is ever lost.

## Table management services

In a typical database system, table management services are part of the **administration, monitoring, and utilities** component. The storage engine interfaces with these services to keep the underlying data files optimized, enabling query engines to interact efficiently with the data. This not only ensures that transactions are ACID-compliant but also that the data is accessible in a way that allows for faster reads and writes, better query performance, and optimal storage use. In an open lakehouse architecture, services such as compaction, clustering, indexing, and cleaning focus on organizing and maintaining data in a way that benefits both write-side transactions and read-side analytical queries.

Let's understand how these services can be utilized in all three table formats.

### Compaction/file sizing

**Compaction** refers to the process of merging smaller files into larger, more efficient files. This is critical in lakehouse environments where frequent updates or inserts can lead to the creation of many small files, known as the "small file problem," which can degrade query performance and inflate storage costs. File sizing through compaction optimizes the storage layout by ensuring that file sizes remain optimal for query engines to read efficiently. All three table formats allow compacting the underlying data files using the **bin-packing algorithm**.

Apache Hudi is designed to avoid the creation of small files by dynamically adjusting file sizes during the ingestion process, using several configuration parameters such as *Max File Size, Small File Size*, and *Insert Split Size*. Hudi manages file sizes in two main ways: auto-sizing during writes and clustering after writes. During ingestion, Hudi ensures that data files are written to meet the defined *Max File Size* (for example, 120 MB). If small files, those below the *Small File Size* threshold, are created, Hudi merges them during compaction cycles to maintain optimal file sizes. This automatic merging not only improves query performance but also reduces storage overhead. Hudi helps keep file sizes balanced without requiring manual intervention.

In addition to auto-sizing during writes and clustering after writes, Hudi also manages file merging for its **Merge-on-Read (MoR)** table type (discussed further in *Chapter 4, Apache Hudi Deep Dive*). In a MoR table, each file group contains a base file (columnar) and one or more log files (row-based). During writes, inserts are stored in the base file while updates are appended to log files, avoiding synchronous merges and reducing write amplification, which improves write latency. During the compaction process, the log file updates are merged into the base file to create a new version of the base file. This ensures that users can read the latest snapshot of the table, helping to meet data freshness SLAs. Hudi offers flexibility by allowing users to control both the frequency and strategy of compaction, providing greater management over file sizing and data performance.

Compaction in Iceberg is a maintenance operation that is achieved using the `rewriteDataFiles` action, which can run in parallel on Spark. This action allows users to specify a target file size, ensuring that small files are merged into larger files, typically over 100 MB in size. For example, a user can set the target file size to 500 MB to ensure that data is written optimally, reducing both the number of files and the associated file open costs:

```
SparkActions.get().rewriteDataFiles(table)
    .filter(Expressions.equal("date", "2020-08-18"))
    .option("target-file-size-bytes", Long.toString(500 * 1024 * 1024)) //
500 MB
    .execute();
```

Additionally, Iceberg supports merging delete files with data files, which is particularly needed for MoR tables that generate delete files. This merging process reduces the number of separate files that query engines need to scan, further enhancing performance.

In Delta Lake, compaction is done using the `OPTIMIZE` command. The bin-packing algorithm used by `OPTIMIZE` aims to create files that are more efficient for read queries, focusing on ensuring optimal file sizes rather than the number of tuples per file. This results in fewer but larger files that are easier and faster to read. For example, users can execute the following command to compact all files in a table:

```
from delta.tables import DeltaTable
deltaTable = DeltaTable.forPath(spark, pathToTable)
deltaTable.optimize().executeCompaction()
```

For cases where only a subset of the data needs to be compacted, users can add a partition predicate to target specific partitions, enhancing flexibility:

```
deltaTable.optimize().where("date='2021-11-18'").executeCompaction()
```

The compaction process in Delta is idempotent, meaning that running it multiple times on the same dataset will not result in further changes once the compaction has been completed. Delta Lake 3.1.0 also introduces auto compaction, which automates the process of compacting small files immediately after a write operation. Auto compaction is triggered synchronously on the cluster that performs the write, combining small files within the table partitions that meet the file count threshold. Auto compaction settings can be controlled at both the session and table levels.

By reducing the number of small files, compaction improves both storage efficiency and query performance. Auto compaction abilities in Apache Hudi and Delta Lake allow for a more proactive maintenance of the tables, especially in write-heavy environments. We will learn more about how to execute compaction in the three table formats in *Chapter 8, Performance Optimization and Tuning in a Lakehouse*.

## Clustering

**Clustering** refers to the process of organizing data in a way that groups similar records together, typically based on certain columns. This enables faster data retrieval by allowing query engines to scan fewer files or data blocks, improving the speed of analytical queries that filter based on the clustered columns. The core idea behind clustering is to rearrange data files based on query predicates rather than arrival time.

As data is ingested, it is co-located by arrival time (for example, the same ingestion job). However, most queries are likely to filter based on event time or other business-specific attributes (for example, city ID and order status). The clustering service reorganizes these files so that frequently queried data is grouped together, allowing for data skipping and significantly improving the efficiency of scans. For example, in *Figure 2.5*, data ingested in three separate commits (not sorted by `City_ID`) is later sorted and clustered so that files are rewritten based on a `City_ID` range, allowing queries to target specific ranges more efficiently. Clustering techniques typically involve two main strategies: simple sorting and multi-dimensional clustering (including Z-ordering and Hilbert curves). In all three table formats (Apache Hudi, Apache Iceberg, and Delta Lake), clustering is designed to organize data optimally in the storage.

## UnSorted files

| Commit 1 | Commit 2 | Commit 3 |
|---|---|---|
| File 1<br>City_ID range<br>(1-90) | File 2<br>City_ID range<br>(1-100) | File 3<br>City_ID range<br>(20-90) |

Sort
(cluster)

File 4
City_ID range
(1-50)

File 5
City_ID range
(51-100)

## Sorted files

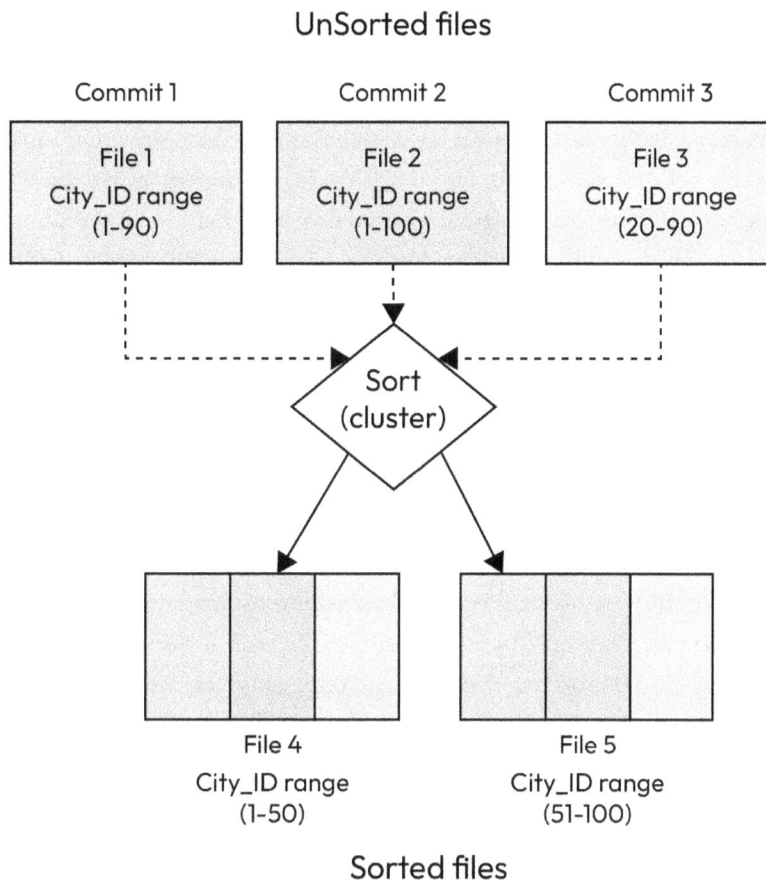

*Figure 2.5 – Clustering based on the City_ID field*

Hudi introduces a clustering service that is tightly coupled with Hudi's storage engine. It reorganizes data for more efficient access based on frequently used query patterns, while still supporting fast data ingestion. The clustering process is asynchronous, which allows new data writes to continue without interruption while clustering is performed in the background. Hudi's MVCC ensures snapshot isolation, so both the clustering process and new data writes can occur concurrently without interference, preserving transactional integrity for readers and writers.

Hudi's clustering workflow consists of two primary steps:

1. **Scheduling clustering**: A clustering plan is generated using a pluggable strategy to identify the optimal way to reorganize files based on query performance.

2. **Executing clustering**: The plan is executed by rewriting data into newly optimized files, replacing the older, less efficient ones, while minimizing query overhead.

Clustering also enhances the scalability of Hudi in handling high-ingestion workloads while maintaining optimized file layouts for fast reads. Beyond simple sorting, Hudi supports advanced techniques such as space-filling curves (for example, Z-ordering and Hilbert curves) to further optimize storage layout. Space-filling curves enable Hudi to efficiently order rows based on a multi-column sort key, preserving the ordering of individual columns within the sort. For instance, a query engine can use Z-ordering to group related data together in a way that minimizes the amount of data scanned. Unlike traditional linear sorting, space-filling curves allow the query engine to reduce the search space significantly when filtering by any subset of the multi-column key, resulting in orders of magnitude speed-up in query performance.

Clustering in Apache Iceberg is handled slightly differently compared to Apache Hudi, but the overall idea is the same. While Hudi integrates clustering as part of its storage engine, Iceberg offers clustering as an API that can be utilized by query engines such as Apache Spark or Apache Flink. Iceberg uses the `rewrite_data_files` API to optimize the layout of data files by sorting them either linearly or hierarchically. This method helps ensure that frequently queried data is organized more efficiently, reducing the need to scan unnecessary data. For example, by using a query engine such as Spark, users can trigger compaction and clustering of data files, ensuring that related data points are stored together in larger, contiguous blocks. Iceberg also allows sorting multiple dimensions using Z-ordering. Z-ordering enables the system to sort data across multiple columns simultaneously, ensuring that related data, across various dimensions, is stored close together. This can be especially beneficial for queries that filter on multiple columns.

In Delta Lake, clustering is achieved via the `executeZOrderBy` API, which allows users to sort data across one or more columns, commonly used in query predicates. For example, running the `OPTIMIZE table ZORDER BY (eventType)` command will reorganize the data to improve query efficiency for predicates filtering on `eventType`.

Z-ordering is especially effective for high-cardinality columns but is not idempotent, meaning it creates a new clustering pattern each time it's executed. This approach balances tuples across files for more efficient access, although the resulting file sizes might vary based on the data itself. In Delta Lake 3.1.0 and above, a new feature called **liquid clustering** was introduced, providing enhanced flexibility in managing data layout. Unlike traditional clustering approaches, liquid clustering allows users to dynamically redefine clustering columns without needing to rewrite existing data. This makes it easier to adapt the data layout as analytical needs evolve over time, ensuring that the system remains optimized for changing query patterns.

With clustering in these table formats, data skipping becomes highly efficient, as queries can avoid scanning unnecessary files, resulting in faster execution and lower compute costs. In *Chapter 8, Performance Optimization and Tuning in a Lakehouse* we will explore the various clustering strategies and see how they can be executed using query engines such as Apache Spark.

## Indexing

**Indexes** are data structures typically used in database systems to accelerate query performance by allowing quick lookups of data. They provide a mechanism to locate specific records without scanning the entire dataset, significantly speeding up read operations. Of the three table formats (Apache Hudi, Iceberg, and Delta Lake), Apache Hudi is the only one that provides explicit support for indexes to enhance both data retrieval and write operations (such as updates and deletes).

Hudi introduces a pluggable indexing subsystem, built on top of its metadata table (discussed in *Chapter 4, Apache Hudi Deep Dive*), which stores auxiliary data about the table essential for organizing and optimizing access to records. Unlike traditional indexing approaches that might lock the system during index creation, Hudi's indexing system operates asynchronously, allowing write operations to continue while indexes are built and maintained in the background. This asynchronous metadata indexing service is an integral part of the storage engine and ensures that write latency is not impacted even during index updates, making it ideal for large-scale tables where indexing might otherwise take hours.

The asynchronous nature of Hudi's indexing brings two key benefits:

- **Improved write latency**: Indexing occurs in parallel with data ingestion, enabling high-throughput writes without delays
- **Failure isolation**: Since indexing runs independently, any failures in the indexing process do not impact ongoing writes, ensuring operational stability

Hudi currently supports several types of indexes, including a `files` index, a `column_stats` index, a `bloom_filter` index, and a `record-level` index. As data continues to grow in volume and complexity, Hudi's pluggable indexing subsystem allows adding more types of indexes to further improve I/O efficiency and query performance. One of the challenges faced by traditional indexing approaches is the requirement to stop all writers when building a new index. In contrast, Hudi's asynchronous indexing allows for dynamic addition and removal of indexes while concurrent writers continue to function, providing a database-like ease of use. This design brings the reliability and performance typical of database systems into the lakehouse paradigm, ensuring that indexing can scale seamlessly as data grows.

## Cleaning

**Cleaning** refers to the removal of obsolete or unreferenced files from the storage layer to free up space and improve performance. As data evolves over time, old versions, snapshots, or deleted records can accumulate, leading to unnecessary storage overhead. The cleaning services provided by Hudi, Iceberg, and Delta Lake ensure that only active data remains, maintaining both storage efficiency and performance.

Apache Hudi offers a cleaner service (as part of its storage engine) that plays a crucial role in managing space reclamation by removing old file slices while maintaining snapshot isolation through its MVCC system. This allows Hudi to balance the retention of data history for time travel and rollbacks while keeping storage costs in check. By default, Hudi automatically triggers cleaning after every commit to remove older, unreferenced files. This behavior can be configured based on user needs, for example, by adjusting the number of commits after which cleaning is invoked using the `hoodie.clean.max.commits` property.

Apache Iceberg provides several APIs for cleaning unused files, such as the `expireSnapshots` operation, which removes old snapshots and the data files they reference. Iceberg uses snapshots for time travel and rollback, but regularly expiring them prevents storage bloat and keeps table metadata small. Iceberg manages metadata cleanup by removing outdated JSON metadata files after each commit, configurable with the `write.metadata.delete-after-commit.enabled` property. Another capability as part of maintenance is the ability to delete orphan files (i.e., unreferenced files left behind by job failures) using the `deleteOrphanFiles` action, ensuring that even files missed by snapshot expiration are cleaned up. It is important to note that these services are not automatic and must be executed as part of a regular, reactive maintenance strategy.

In Delta Lake, the VACUUM command is used to remove files no longer referenced by the Delta table, with a default retention period of 7 days (configurable). Similar to Iceberg's APIs, VACUUM is not automatically triggered, and users must manually invoke it. The VACUUM process only deletes data files, while log files are deleted asynchronously after checkpoint operations. The retention period for log files is 30 days by default, but this can be adjusted with the `delta.logRetentionDuration` property.

By offering these cleaning mechanisms, each system ensures that storage costs are controlled, old or unused data is removed efficiently, and performance remains optimized for large-scale workloads. We will explore more about the cleaning services in *Chapter 8, Performance Optimization and Tuning in a Lakehouse.*

To recap, the storage engine offers two core functionalities in a lakehouse architecture:

- **Transactional integrity**: Guarantees ACID compliance and high concurrency, essential for maintaining data integrity under massive workloads
- **Table management services**: Ensures the efficient organization and access of data through operations such as clustering, compaction, indexing, and cleanup

By incorporating robust cleaning mechanisms, lakehouse storage engines not only manage the data lifecycle effectively but also optimize performance and maintain cost efficiency, ensuring that modern data workloads run smoothly and reliably.

# Summary

This chapter explored the foundational transactional features of the lakehouse architecture, emphasizing their role in enabling robust, reliable, and scalable data management. Beginning with a detailed examination of ACID properties, it highlighted their importance in maintaining data integrity in distributed environments.

The discussion progressed to conflict resolution mechanisms, including pessimistic, optimistic, and multi-version concurrency control types, each of which helps manage concurrent transactions in diverse scenarios. The storage engine's role in maintaining ACID compliance and facilitating efficient data access was analyzed, focusing on components such as lock managers, access methods, and recovery mechanisms.

Finally, the chapter also introduced table management services, such as compaction, clustering, indexing, and cleaning, demonstrating how they optimize query performance and maintain storage efficiency. By integrating these transactional capabilities, lakehouses overcome the limitations of traditional data lakes while ensuring high concurrency and operational resilience.

Building on this understanding of transactional capabilities, the next chapter will delve into Apache Iceberg, a leading open table format powering lakehouse architectures. The chapter will cover Iceberg's architecture, exploring key components such as data files, manifest files, and metadata management. It will highlight Iceberg's critical and unique capabilities, including schema evolution and time travel. The chapter will also provide hands-on guidance for building an Iceberg lakehouse using Spark and Flink, equipping you with practical skills for implementing this powerful technology.

# Questions

1.  What are the four ACID properties, and why are they crucial for transactional systems?

2.  Explain the differences between pessimistic concurrency control and optimistic concurrency control.

3.  What is **multi-version concurrency control (MVCC)**, and how does it manage conflicts?

4.  Describe the role of the lock manager in the storage engine of a lakehouse architecture.

5.  How do access methods in a storage engine facilitate efficient data retrieval?

6.  What is the significance of compaction in table management services?

7.  Explain how clustering improves query performance in lakehouse architectures.

8.  What challenges do traditional data lakes face in ensuring ACID compliance? How do lakehouses address these challenges?

9.  How does the recovery manager ensure data durability and consistency in case of system failures?

10. List two cleaning mechanisms used in Apache Hudi, Apache Iceberg, or Delta Lake, and describe their purpose.

# Answers

1.  The four ACID properties are atomicity, consistency, isolation, and durability. They ensure reliable data management by maintaining data integrity, preventing partial updates, and ensuring that changes are permanent.

2.  Pessimistic concurrency control locks data to prevent conflicts, while optimistic concurrency control assumes that conflicts are rare and resolves them during commit.

3.  MVCC allows multiple versions of data to coexist, enabling high concurrency by ensuring that readers access consistent snapshots while writers create new versions.

4.  The lock manager prevents race conditions and maintains data correctness by coordinating concurrent access in distributed systems.

5.  Access methods organize data and metadata for efficient retrieval, leveraging indexing and directory-based structures such as file groups and slices.

6.  Compaction merges smaller files into larger ones to reduce query overhead, improving performance and storage efficiency.

7.  Clustering reorganizes data based on frequently queried columns, reducing the need to scan unnecessary files and speeding up query execution.

8.  Traditional data lakes lack built-in ACID compliance, making updates and deletes challenging. Lakehouses address this with transactional layers and open table formats such as Hudi, Iceberg, and Delta Lake.

9.  The recovery manager uses techniques such as write-ahead logs and metadata snapshots to restore consistent states after failures.

10. Apache Hudi's *cleaner* service removes old file slices while maintaining snapshot isolation, and Iceberg's *expire snapshots* operation removes unreferenced snapshots to free up storage space.

## Get This Book's PDF Version and Exclusive Extras

UNLOCK NOW

Scan the QR code (or go to packtpub.com/unlock). Search for this book by name, confirm the edition, and then follow the steps on the page.

*Note: Keep your invoice handy. Purchases made directly from Packt don't require an invoice.*

# 3

# Apache Iceberg Deep Dive

Apache Iceberg is a high-performance, open table format that excels in providing reliability, scalability, and flexibility for large-scale data lakehouse architectures. Its architecture is built around several key components such as data files, manifest files, manifest lists, metadata files, and catalogs, that work together to provide advanced functionality such as ACID transactions, time travel, and schema evolution.

In this chapter, we will explore the internals of each of these components, understanding how they contribute to Iceberg's functionality. We will then apply this knowledge through hands-on examples, configuring and running Iceberg with various compute engines, including Apache Spark, Apache Flink, PyIceberg, DuckDB, and Daft.

In this chapter, we will cover the following topics:

- Apache Iceberg architecture
- Apache Iceberg features
- Hands-on with Apache Iceberg and Apache Spark
- Hands-on with Apache Iceberg and Apache Flink

## Apache Iceberg architecture

Apache Iceberg uses a tree-based structure to organize metadata files. This tree consists of three main components: the catalog, a set of metadata files and data files. We will use the following diagram to understand the components that make up the architecture and how it facilitates different capabilities via the table format.

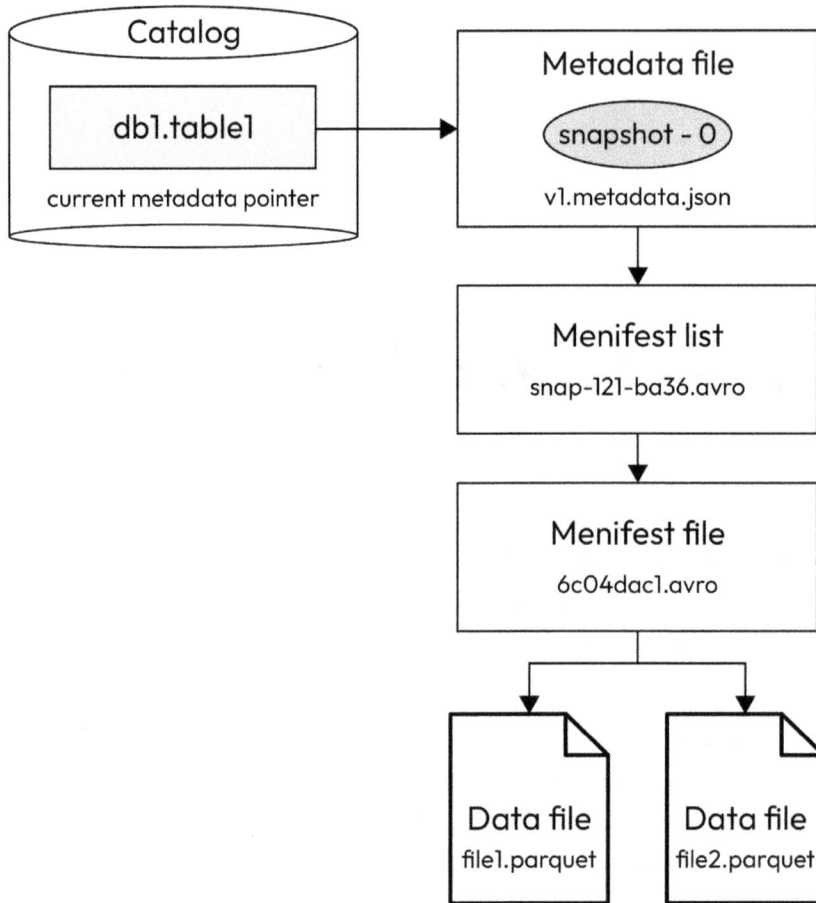

*Figure 3.1 – Apache Iceberg's architecture with various components*

## Catalog

Similar to traditional database systems, a catalog in a lakehouse architecture is essential for storing information about tables. It serves as the single source of truth for managing and accessing various tables within an organization. However, in Apache Iceberg's architecture, the role of the catalog extends beyond being a central repository for tables. It is a key piece for ensuring atomicity and consistency guarantees for transactions and provides a consistent interface for creating, querying, and modifying tables. The catalog in Iceberg stores the location of the *current metadata file* (discussed in the *Metadata* section) for each table, which is essential for coordinating access and ensuring data consistency across different users and compute engines.

Iceberg supports various catalog implementations, such as Hadoop, Hive, AWS Glue, REST, and custom catalogs. Each implementation is responsible for tracking the current version of a table by pointing to its latest metadata file. This reference to the metadata file enables the catalog to serve as an atomic commit log for each table, supporting transactional guarantees in scenarios with multiple concurrent writers.

Technically, any type of database or data store service, such as DynamoDB or PostgreSQL, can be used as a catalog for Iceberg tables. However, the most important requirement is that they have a form of *locking* mechanism to support atomic swaps. The catalog must be capable of coordinating these atomic swaps reliably, as this is fundamental to enabling Iceberg's transactional integrity. Without a catalog, Iceberg tables cannot function correctly, as the system would lack a central authority to manage metadata versioning and concurrency.

If we look at this from a technical sense, Iceberg provides a catalog interface: https://github.com/apache/iceberg/blob/main/api/src/main/java/org/apache/iceberg/catalog/Catalog.java. Different systems can implement the catalog interface to handle reading from and writing to a catalog, including functions such as creating, loading, and dropping tables. For example, here is a default method, createTable, to create tables within the Catalog interface:

```
default Table createTable(
      TableIdentifier identifier,
      Schema schema,
      PartitionSpec spec,
      Map<String, String> properties) {
    return createTable(identifier, schema, spec, null, properties);
  }
```

This method takes four parameters: the table identifier (namespace/name), the schema of the table, the partition specification, and a map of key-value pairs. This way, it provides a simplified way to create a table with the essential attributes.

Other methods such as newCreateTableTransaction and newReplaceTableTransaction allow creating or replacing tables within a transaction, which helps ensure *atomicity*:

```
default Transaction newCreateTableTransaction(
      TableIdentifier identifier,
      Schema schema,
      PartitionSpec spec,
```

```
    String location,
    Map<String, String> properties) {


  return buildTable(identifier, schema)
      .withPartitionSpec(spec)
      .withLocation(location)
      .withProperties(properties)
      .createTransaction();
}
```

These methods help prevent conflicts in concurrent environments by ensuring the table is only created or replaced if no other operation is in progress.

## What happens during writes?

During an insert or update process, the compute engine first consults the catalog to gather info on the current state of the table (i.e., reads the latest version of the metadata file based on the *location* in the catalog). After the new records are inserted or updated in the Iceberg table, the query engine performs an *atomic swap* of the metadata location in the catalog (i.e., it updates the pointer to the new metadata file, but only after verifying that there are no conflicting changes). In *Chapter 2, Transactional Capabilities of the Lakehouse*, we learned how this atomic swap mechanism is vital for ensuring serializable isolation during concurrent write operations. Writers rely on this mechanism to check the current version of the table's metadata file before committing changes. If another writer has modified the metadata in the interim, the catalog will reject the new write, and the writer must retry the operation based on the latest version of the metadata file. This optimistic concurrency control mechanism is crucial for preventing conflicts and maintaining a consistent, linear history of changes to the table.

## What happens during reads?

On the read side, when you run a simple read query, such as `SELECT * from Employee WHERE salary>10000`, the compute engine first queries the catalog and asks for the location of the current metadata pointer. Based on this current location, the engine reads the corresponding records from the data files. Since the catalog is always updated with the *latest version* of the metadata file, users always see the table's latest state data, enabling Iceberg to provide consistency guarantees.

# Catalog considerations for production

By acting as a single source of truth, the catalog ensures that readers and writers are always operating on a consistent view of the data. While Iceberg allows the flexibility to use different types of catalogs, there should be certain considerations when using a catalog in production environments. Here are some recommended practices:

- **One catalog for one Iceberg table**: A specific Iceberg table should be managed by a single catalog only to maintain consistency across data versions and prevent conflicts. Using multiple catalogs may cause query engines to access stale table snapshots, which can introduce consistency challenges. In scenarios where the use of multiple catalogs is unavoidable, a practical solution is to designate one catalog exclusively for write operations, while reserving others strictly for read access.

- **Avoiding file system-based catalogs**: When testing out Apache Iceberg, you may start with a file system-based catalog, such as the Hadoop catalog backed by HDFS, as it requires minimal setup and adheres to file system table specifications. However, file system-based catalogs such as Hadoop are generally unsuitable for production environments. They lack a reliable locking mechanism, which is essential for handling concurrent reads and writes safely. This can lead to issues with atomic operations, such as renaming and dropping tables. Without a lock manager, the Hadoop catalog cannot guarantee atomic behavior, increasing the risk of data inconsistencies.

- **Catalog migration pitfalls**: Iceberg provides a `register_table` method (`https://iceberg. apache.org/docs/1.5.1/spark-procedures/#register_table`) to migrate an existing table to another catalog. However, this approach has several challenges. Registering tables one by one can be time-consuming and inefficient, especially for large numbers of tables. Additionally, this method does not automatically remove table entries from the source catalog. This can lead to missed updates, potential data loss, and table corruption because each catalog may operate independently without awareness of changes made by the other. To streamline migrations and avoid these pitfalls, the `Iceberg-catalog-migrator` tool (`https://github.com/projectnessie/iceberg-catalog-migrator`), part of Project Nessie (`https://projectnessie.org`), a type of custom Iceberg catalog implementation, offers a CLI for bulk catalog migrations, making the process faster and more reliable.

The method of tracking the current metadata file varies by catalog type. For example, in a Hadoop (file-system-based) catalog, the compute engine keeps track of metadata file versions as positive integers (e.g., 1, 2, ...) within a `version-hint.text` file. This file is stored in the same `/metadata` directory as the other metadata files in the data lake storage. We'll dive into these aspects in some more detail with practical examples in our hands-on section.

# Metadata

The metadata layer in Apache Iceberg is composed of three key components: the metadata file, the manifest list, and the manifest file. Together, these components serve as the *core* of the Iceberg tree structure (architecture) and provide a foundation for transactional capabilities. The three components record essential table information, including snapshots (historical versions of the table), partition and schema definitions, and column-level statistics. These components not only enable advanced features such as schema and partition evolution, time-travel, and version rollbacks but also play a crucial role in optimizing query performance. In this section, we'll explore each component in detail and understand their role in the Iceberg architecture.

## Metadata file

The metadata file is the starting point for any operation (read or write) in an Iceberg table. When a new table is created, the compute engine generates the first metadata file in JSON format (`v1.metadata.json`), along with the initial snapshot. This file is populated with critical details such as the table's schema, partition information, and a unique table identifier, is known as `table-uuid`. This unique identifier ensures metadata consistency across operations and serves as a persistent reference for the table in distributed environments.

For subsequent write operations, such as inserts, updates, or upserts, the engine references the current metadata file (`v1.metadata.json`) to retrieve the schema and partition specifications, ensuring new records conform to the table's structure. After new data is written, the engine creates a new snapshot, and a new version of the metadata file (`v2.metadata.json`), and updates the reference to the latest *manifest list* (discussed in the *Manifest list* section). Finally, the engine updates the catalog to point to the location of the latest metadata file version (v2), ensuring that all read and write operations are consistent with the latest table state. This approach enforces immutability for each table version, ensuring that readers and writers operate with a consistent, well-defined state. By versioning metadata files and maintaining snapshots, Iceberg supports advanced use cases such as *branching* and *tagging* (to be discussed in the *Branching and tagging* section), allowing different table versions to coexist for testing, auditing, or sandboxing purposes.

Following is an example of an excerpt of a metadata file:

```
{
  "format-version" : 2,
  "table-uuid" : "9e290419-4cbd-4d66-94e9-fe41ed0f2b40",
  "location" : "s3a://diplakehouse/iceberg_book/customers",
  "last-sequence-number" : 1,
  "last-updated-ms" : 1730678112032,
  "current-schema-id" : 0,
  "schemas" : [ {
    "type" : "struct",
    "schema-id" : 0,
    "fields" : [ {
      "id" : 1,
      "name" : "customer_id",
      "required" : false,
      "type" : "int"
    }, {
      "id" : 2,
      "name" : "first_name",
      "required" : false,
      "type" : "string"
    },
  "partition-specs" : [ {
      "spec-id" : 0,
      "fields" : [ {
        "name" : "state",
        "transform" : "identity",
        "source-id" : 6,
        "field-id" : 1000
      } ]
    } ],
  "snapshots" : [ {
      "sequence-number" : 1,
      "snapshot-id" : 2711640443788239783,
      "timestamp-ms" : 1730678112032,
      "summary" : {
```

```
        "operation" : "append"
    }
}]
```

The metadata file contains several key attributes that define the table's structure, organization, and history. These attributes are crucial for enabling various Iceberg features, including schema evolution, data pruning, and time travel. Let's take a detailed look at these components.

> You can find the complete metadata file from our example in this book's GitHub repository: https://github.com/PacktPublishing/Engineering-Lakehouses-with-Open-Table-Formats/tree/main/ch03.

- **Table-related metadata:** Iceberg includes essential table-specific metadata within the metadata.json file to maintain consistency and control across operations. For instance, in our example file, "format-version": 2 indicates the version of the Iceberg format in use, ensuring compatibility with supported features, and encountering an unsupported version will lead to an exception to prevent data issues. The "table-uuid": "9e290419-4cbd-4d66-94e9-fe41ed0f2b40" field provides a unique identifier for the table, critical for avoiding conflicts during metadata operations. The "location": "s3a://diplakehouse/iceberg_book/customers" field specifies the root storage path for data and metadata files, establishing a common base directory. Meanwhile, "last-updated-ms": 1730678112032 reflects the last time the metadata was modified, serving as a timestamp for the latest changes. Finally, "last-sequence-number": 1 represents the highest assigned sequence number, crucial for maintaining the correct order of snapshots within the table's timeline.

- **Schema information:** The schema section of the metadata file defines the table's structure, listing column names, data types, nullable constraints, and the schema ID. For example, in the example metadata file, the schema includes fields such as customer_id (an integer), first_name (a string), and email (a string). The schema ID (e.g., "schema-id": 0) is critical for tracking schema changes over time, allowing Iceberg to maintain schema versions. Each version is recorded in the "schemas" field, which enables the system to validate incoming data against the current schema and retrieve historical data with the schema active at the time of writing.

- **Partition specification:** Partitioning is defined in the partition-specs field, which details how data is partitioned for optimized access. In the example file, data is partitioned by the "state" field, with an identity transform (meaning it uses the field value directly). The partition-spec-id (e.g., "spec-id": 0) links to this partition specification and allows for changes in partitioning logic over time, enabling Iceberg to manage both current and historical partitioning schemes effectively. Proper partitioning allows for partition pruning, where unnecessary partitions are excluded from query scans, improving performance.

- **Snapshot information:** Iceberg tables maintain a list of snapshots, each representing a specific version of the table. The `current-snapshot-id` field is the most critical property here as it helps identify the current manifest list (which is required to eventually track the actual data files). The `snapshots` array in the metadata file contains pointers to individual snapshots, each with a snapshot ID, timestamp, and manifest list location. For instance, in the provided file, snapshot ID 2711640443788239783 references a manifest list at `"s3a://diplakehouse/iceberg_book/customers/metadata/snap-2711640443788239783-1-6c04dac1-3311-41c5-ba36-eba1451bd89d.avro"`. This list of snapshots enables advanced operations such as *time travel* and *rollback* by allowing users to access previous versions of the data simply by querying a specific snapshot ID or timestamp.

- **Statistical information:** Iceberg allows storing advanced *table related statistics* (such as sketches) in the Puffin file format (discussed in later sections). Each Puffin file for table statistics is registered in the `statistics` field within the metadata file, with attributes such as `statistics-path` (location of the statistics file), `file-size-in-bytes`, and the optional `blob-metadata`, which contains specific statistical properties. Iceberg also stores partition statistics in its metadata layer using manifest files and Puffin files., which offers detailed information at the partition level, enabling more granular query optimization based on partition-specific metrics (partition data tuple, data record count, etc.).

- **Metadata log:** The metadata-log field keeps a record of all previous metadata files, providing a history of changes that can be used for rollback and auditing. Each entry in the log includes a `timestamp-ms` field and a reference to a prior metadata file version (in the example, `"metadata-file" : "s3a://diplakehouse/iceberg_book/customers/metadata/v1.metadata.json"`), enabling Iceberg to restore tables to previous states if necessary.

## Manifest list

In Apache Iceberg, a manifest list is generated with every new snapshot, capturing an up-to-date view of the table's structure. When a new snapshot is created, Iceberg generates a new manifest list that captures the current state of the table by linking to all relevant *manifest files*, which, in turn, point to the actual data files. This provides a cohesive view of the table's structure at a particular moment and is integral to critical capabilities such as time-travel, point-in-time queries, and version rollbacks. In a way, a manifest list acts as an **index** to track all the *manifest files* that are part of a particular snapshot. When a compute engine plans a table scan, the information from the manifest list, such as the number of files added/deleted and upper and lower value bounds of partitions can be used to prune irrelevant manifest files to speed up processing. Iceberg uses Avro as the file format for manifest lists.

Using the example manifest list file provided here: `https://github.com/PacktPublishing/Engineering-Lakehouses-with-Open-Table-Formats/blob/main/ch03/snap-2711640443788239783-1-6c04dac1-3311-41c5-ba36-eba1451bd89d.avro`, let's take a look into some of its essential attributes and how they contribute to the Iceberg architecture:

- **Manifest path**: The `"manifest_path"` field is the most important field in the manifest list and points to the specific *manifest files* that comprise this snapshot. In the example file, the manifest path is as follows:

  ```
  "manifest_path" : "s3a://diplakehouse/iceberg_book/customers/
  metadata/6c04dac1-3311-41c5-ba36-eba1451bd89d-m0.avro"
  ```

  This leads us to the `6c04dac1-3311-41c5-ba36-eba1451bd89d-m0.avro` manifest file, which is saved as an Avro file in the storage system.

- **Partition spec ID**: The `"partition_spec_id"` field represents the partitioning scheme used in this snapshot. In Iceberg, partitioning schemes can evolve over time. This field allows each snapshot to **reference** the specific partition specification that was active when the manifest was created. In the example, `"partition_spec_id": 0` indicates that this manifest follows the initial partition specification, ensuring compatibility even as the table evolves.

- **Content type**: The `"content"` field, **with** a value of 0 in the example, denotes the type of files managed by this manifest. A content type of 0 refers to data files, while 1 indicates delete files. Delete files in Iceberg store information on the rows deleted.

- **Sequence number and min sequence number**: `"sequence_number": 1` represents the point at which this manifest was added to the table, marking the order of operations within Iceberg's versioning system. This monotonically increasing number ensures a linear history of modifications, which is important for consistency guarantees in concurrent scenarios. Additionally, `"min_sequence_number"` records the earliest sequence number of all data files in this manifest, providing insight into the data's evolution over time and enabling features such as time-travel queries by allowing access to specific historical states of the table.

- **Snapshot ID**: Each **manifest** in the list is associated with a specific snapshot ID, seen in the example file as `"added_snapshot_id": 2711640443788239783`. This snapshot ID links each manifest back to the precise snapshot in which it was introduced, enabling

Iceberg to trace changes across the table's history. This ID is fundamental to Iceberg's time-travel capabilities, as it allows users to access or revert to previous snapshots by specifying the snapshot ID.

- **Counts of added, existing, and deleted files and rows:**
  - `"added_data_files_count"`: 5 indicates that five new data files were added in this snapshot.
  - `"existing_data_files_count"`: 0 shows that no data files from previous snapshots were reused in this one.
  - `"deleted_data_files_count"`: 0 means no files were removed in this snapshot. Similar fields track row counts, with `"added_rows_count"`: 5 showing that five rows were added, while `"existing_rows_count"`: 0 and `"deleted_rows_count"`: 0 show that no rows were carried over or deleted.

These counts offer a quick summary of changes within each snapshot, helping query engines understand the relevant manifests without fully scanning them. By analyzing counts of added, existing, and deleted files and rows, query engines can bypass unnecessary manifests that contain only deleted files or data outside the scope of the query, thus optimizing read operations.

## Manifest file

In Apache Iceberg, a manifest file keeps track of individual data files and delete files within a specific partition or group of partitions, associated with a particular snapshot of the table. The manifests are central to Iceberg's architecture and enable efficient data retrieval and query optimization. Each manifest file contains information about the physical data files (such as Parquet) in the table, with properties such as file path, partition values, record counts, and column-level statistics. By organizing this information in manifest files, Iceberg allows query engines to avoid scanning unnecessary data files, significantly improving query performance. Consider this as another level of pruning that allows compute engines to get an aggregated list of statistics without having to read individual Parquet files' footers, which can be costly at scale.

Each time a write operation is run on an Iceberg table (such as an insertion, deletion, or update), the compute engine creates a new manifest file by gathering info about the data files. These manifest files are then linked together in a manifest list, which forms the structure of a snapshot. Ultimately, these snapshots are tracked in a metadata.json file, which enables consistent read and write operations. This approach enables time-travel capabilities by retaining historical manifest files, allowing users to query or revert to past table states without rewriting the data files.

Let's understand some of the key attributes using the manifest file provided in the GitHub repo at `https://github.com/PacktPublishing/Engineering-Lakehouses-with-Open-Table-Formats/blob/main/ch03/6c04dac1-3311-41c5-ba36-eba1451bd89d-m0.avro`:

- **File operation types:** In Iceberg, each manifest entry specifies the type of operation that affected the data file: whether it was added, deleted, or updated. The `"status"` field indicates this: `"status": 0 // 0 means added, 1 means existing, and 2 means deleted`.

- **Data file path within manifest:** Each `data_file` struct within a manifest file is associated with its exact path in storage. In the provided example, you will see entries like the following:

  ```
  "file_path": "s3a://diplakehouse/iceberg_book/customers/data/
  state=CA/00065-2-428e3581-fc2c-44a3-b2fd-458816a59a40-00001.parquet"
  ```

  This path specifies the exact location of the data file within the partition (state=CA) in the storage system (S3 in this case).

- **Partition information:** The `"partition"` struct within each `data_file` struct in the manifest captures the partition tuple. As seen in our example, { state: "NY" } is a tuple containing info on the partition for this data file. Additionally, the table's partition spec helps with transforming row-level predicates into partition-level predicates, which helps during job planning to only get the relevant data files using the manifest file.

- **Statistics information:** Manifest files in Apache Iceberg include column-level statistics such as minimum (`lower_bounds`) and maximum (`upper_bounds`) values, which are stored for each relevant column. For instance, in our data file, we see entries such as `"lower_bounds": {"key": 1, "value": [1, 0, 0, 0]}` and `"upper_bounds": {"key": 1, "value": [1, 0, 0, 0]}` for the first entry in the table, denoting `customer_id=1`.

These statistics help Iceberg perform selective scanning during query planning. For example, if a query requests data that falls outside the range specified by `lower_bounds` and `upper_bounds`, Iceberg can immediately eliminate those files without reading their full content, significantly enhancing query performance by reducing unnecessary I/O operations. Ultimately, manifest files serve as a second layer of pruning in Iceberg by aggregating statistics, enabling query engines to bypass scanning individual data files, which can be very expensive at scale.

## Data layer

The data layer in Apache Iceberg comprises two types of files: **data files** and **delete files**. Let's quickly understand these two different types of files.

# Data files

Data files store the actual table data (i.e., the bytes are written to a file). The most common format typically used in Iceberg is Apache Parquet, although Apache ORC and Apache Avro are also supported. Parquet is often preferred for analytical workloads due to its columnar storage format, which enables efficient compression and fast read performance. Parquet files come with embedded metadata in the form of a footer, which includes min/max statistics and null counts for each column. Iceberg uses this metadata, aggregating it in manifest files, allowing query engines to perform data skipping and avoid reading unnecessary files based on query predicates. This optimization is important to skip irrelevant data, thereby significantly reducing query latency and resource consumption. These data files are immutable, meaning they remain unchanged once written. Instead of modifying data files directly during updates, the compute engine creates new versions of files.

# Delete files

In addition to data files, Iceberg uses delete files to track row-level deletions without modifying the original data files. This file allows Iceberg to do row-level deletes without having to rewrite the original data files (which is expensive at scale). Delete files store details about rows that should be excluded from query results, allowing Iceberg to manage deletions in an efficient way. There are two types of delete files in Iceberg:

- **Position deletes**: These files mark specific rows in a data file for deletion based on their position (row number), making it effective for tracking row-level changes without modifying the data file itself.
- **Equality deletes**: These files store the values of specific columns in deleted rows, marking all rows that match the given values for deletion. This is useful for scenarios where deletions are based on conditions such as column values rather than exact row positions.

Delete files specifically apply to the **Merge-on-Read (MoR)** table type in Iceberg (discussed later in this chapter). These files play a crucial role by tracking records marked for deletion or update without requiring the rewriting of existing data files. Instead, the delete file specifies which records should be ignored during read operations.

Now that we have a thorough understanding of the architecture of Apache Iceberg, let's explore some of the important capabilities that are facilitated by these architectural components.

# Apache Iceberg features

In this section, we will take a look into some of the key capabilities that Apache Iceberg brings to a Lakehouse architecture.

The section is purposefully divided into two parts: the first will focus on three **critical capabilities**, schema evolution, time travel and rollback, and row-level updates/deletes (using **Copy-on-Write (CoW)** and MoR tables), which are essential for supporting transactional workloads within the lakehouse. The second part will explore some of Iceberg's **unique features** that differentiate it from other table formats, such as Apache Hudi and Delta Lake. The goal is to present Iceberg's distinctive attributes so users can evaluate and apply it effectively within their specific workload needs.

## Critical capabilities

Let's understand some of the must-have capabilities in a lakehouse architecture powered by Apache Iceberg.

### Schema evolution

One of the most powerful capabilities of Apache Iceberg is its robust support for schema evolution. Schema evolution is the ability to change the structure of a table without the need to rewrite the tables. Business requirements change very often and in order to cater to the changing needs, a lakehouse format must support evolving schemas. In traditional systems, schema changes can be cumbersome and might often require the need for rewriting the table. However, in Apache Iceberg, schema updates are metadata changes and hence there is no need for rewrites. Iceberg allows schema modifications via operations such as add, drop, rename, update, and reorder columns.

Schema evolution in Iceberg is managed through its *metadata* files, which maintain a versioned history of schema changes. When a new schema is introduced (such as adding a column), Iceberg creates a new metadata file and updates `current-schema-id` and assigns a new `schema-id` to the modified schema entry in the metadata file. This ensures that the latest schema is recognized while retaining prior schemas in the schemas list for historical reference. Following is an example that shows the changes in the two fields (`current-schema-id` and `schema-id`) in the v1 and v2 metadata files after a new column is added.

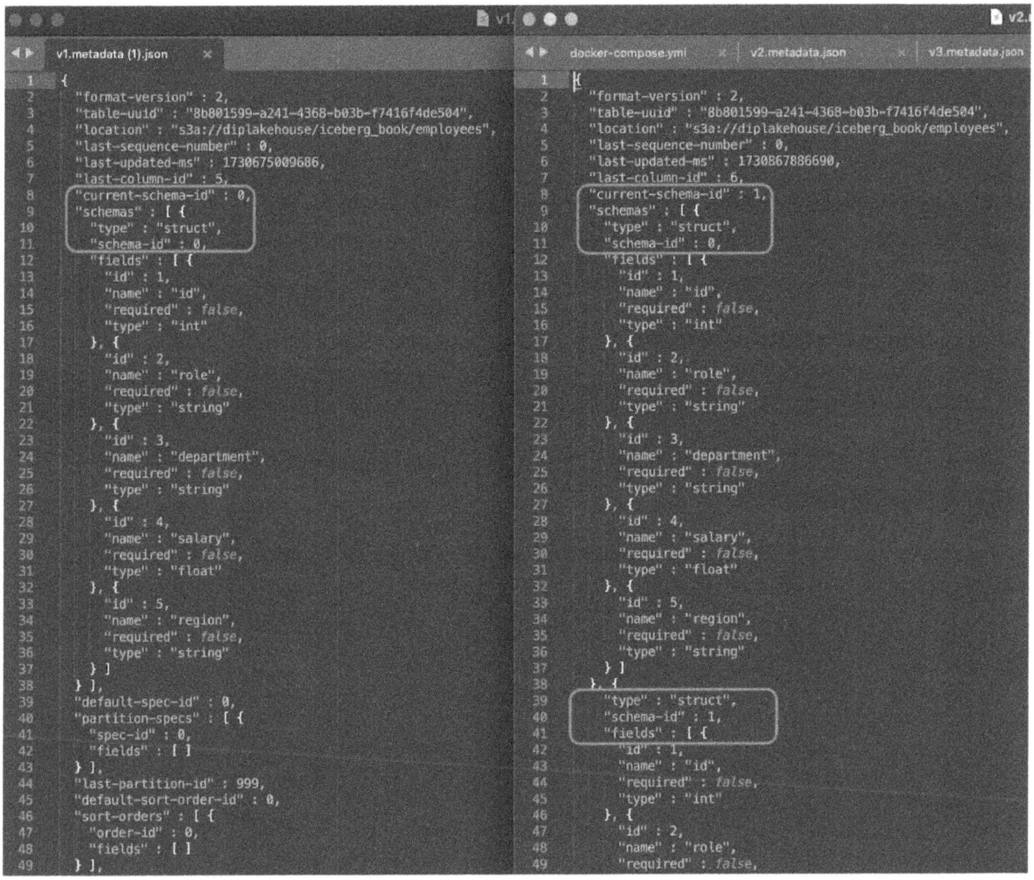

*Figure 3.2 – An example metadata.json file that shows the changes in the two fields (current-schema-id and schema-id) in v1 and v2*

## Time travel and rollback

Time travel is another important capability that allows you to go back to a particular point in time (state) of the table to run analysis. For instance, in financial services, companies must retain and access historical data to comply with strict auditing and regulatory requirements.

Time travel in Iceberg is enabled by *snapshots*, which are organized and tracked within the metadata file. Each snapshot captures a specific state of the table at a particular timestamp, `timestamp-ms`, identified by a unique `snapshot-id`, allowing users to query the dataset as it existed at that specific moment. The snapshots list in the metadata file keeps track of these, along with each snapshot's sequence-number and associated manifest list, creating a log of changes that can be referenced for historical analysis or debugging. The `snapshot-log` field, found in the metadata file is critical here. It records a straightforward history of previous "current snapshots" over time. This log is useful for point-in-time queries, such as in SQL queries with `TIMESTAMP AS OF`, ensuring queries reflect the exact state of the table at a given timestamp.

Let's use the example metadata file (`https://github.com/PacktPublishing/Engineering-Lakehouses-with-Open-Table-Formats/blob/main/ch03/v2.metadata.json`) to illustrate how `snapshot-log` supports time-travel queries. Suppose a user wants to query the state of the table as it existed just before a specific timestamp, say `'2024-11-05T12:00:00Z'`.

Let's say the query engine encounters a SQL query like this:

```
SELECT * FROM my_table TIMESTAMP AS OF '2024-11-05T12:00:00Z';
```

It would refer to `snapshot-log` in the metadata file to locate the latest snapshot that was taken before this timestamp.

In the example metadata file, we can see that `snapshot-log` contains entries in the following structure:

```
"snapshot-log": [
  {
    "timestamp-ms": 1730678112032,
    "snapshot-id": 2711640443788239783
  },
  {
    "timestamp-ms": 1730678110000,
    "snapshot-id": 2711640443788239782
  }
]
```

In this case, the engine will do the following:

1. Convert `'2024-11-05T12:00:00Z'` to a timestamp in milliseconds.
2. Traverse the `snapshot-log` entries to find the highest `timestamp-ms` value that is less than or equal to the specified timestamp. In our example, if the desired timestamp aligns with the first entry in the log, the `snapshot-id` 2711640443788239783 would be selected.

Other than the timestamp ID, Iceberg also enables time travel-based queries with the snapshot ID using the `VERSION AS OF` command in SQL.

# Row-level updates/deletes: Copy-on-Write (CoW) and Merge-on-Read (MoR) tables

Like transactional databases, data lakehouses bring the ability to perform record-level updates and deletes to deal with a range of use cases. Apache Iceberg provides two approaches (or table types) to deal with these kinds of transactions: CoW and MoR. These table types provide flexibility in handling update and delete operations depending on performance and latency needs. Let's understand these two table types in Iceberg and go over the considerations to use them.

- **CoW:** In a CoW table, updates or deletes result in rewriting the affected data files (i.e., which contain those records). This approach is advantageous for read-heavy workloads because it eliminates the need for additional processing during reads. By rewriting files with updated data, CoW ensures that readers can access a clean, merged view of the data without processing any additional files. However, the trade-off is a higher write latency, as the system must rewrite entire files to apply updates or deletes. CoW tables are ideal for scenarios where write performance can be traded off for optimized read performance.

- **MoR:** MoR tables provide a more write-efficient approach by storing updates and deletes in separate files known as *delete files*. Instead of rewriting data files, Iceberg generates delete files that mark certain records as updated or deleted, which are then applied at read time. This approach minimizes the write overhead and is suitable for applications that prioritize low-latency writes over read performance. However, read operations in MoR tables have more operational overhead to merge the base data files with the delete files, which can introduce read latency. MoR tables are ideal for applications with frequent updates or deletions and where write efficiency is crucial.

The choice between CoW and MoR depends on the specific workload requirements. Iceberg's support for both types allows data engineers to select the most appropriate table type based on the workload.

# Unique capabilities

As mentioned previously, this section will focus on the distinct capabilities that make Apache Iceberg a powerful choice in lakehouse architecture. These capabilities stem from Iceberg's unique design and the architectural components covered in *Part 1* of this chapter.

# Hidden partitioning

Partitioning is critical for query optimization and organizing data optimally, but managing and maintaining separate partition columns (as seen with first-generation table formats such as

Hive) can be error-prone and complex for users. Apache Iceberg brings the concept of *hidden partitioning*, which abstracts away the need for users to maintain partition columns explicitly, hence hidden. Instead of manually specifying partition columns, Iceberg automatically derives partition values by transforming base columns. This is made possible by the unique metadata tree structure in Iceberg, and therefore it does not have to rely on a physical directory-based structure for partitioning, unlike Hive.

In Iceberg, hidden partitioning relies on `partition-specs` stored in the `metadata.json` file. When a table is created with a particular partitioning scheme, Iceberg's metadata file records the `spec-id` along with the column details. One important aspect in the column details is the `transform` property, which can either be `identity` (i.e., direct column value) or other available options such as year, month, day, hour, truncate, and so on. For example, if a table uses `date (event_time)` as a transform to partition a table, Iceberg takes the responsibility of doing that transformation and tracking the relationship. Since these transformations are tracked internally, query engines interact with the base columns without needing to be aware of the partition structure.

## Partition evolution

The logical separation from the physical data structure complexity (i.e., data files) allows Iceberg to be independent of the table's physical layout, which also enables a key functionality—*partition evolution*. As datasets evolve, so do the partitioning needs. Iceberg's partition evolution allows partition schemes to be modified without the need for expensive rewrites, a capability that provides extreme flexibility without downtime. Unlike traditional data systems where partitioning is static and any change requires rewriting files, Iceberg stores each partitioning scheme as a new partition spec in the metadata file and assigns a unique `spec-id`. When you evolve a partition spec in Iceberg, the original data remains in its initial layout, while new data adheres to the updated partitioning scheme. For instance, a table initially partitioned by `MONTH(date)` might later switch to `DAY(date)` to allow for more granular queries.

Since Iceberg stores metadata for each partition spec separately, engines can plan queries across different layouts. When a read request is made, the planner identifies the relevant partition spec for each subset of data and applies filters accordingly. This split planning enables access to data across both old and new layouts, without the need for any manual work.

## Branching and tagging

Data architectures often require multi-versioned data environments for testing, experimentation, and auditing purposes. Typically, this involves duplicating datasets (tables), which leads to too many unmanageable versions of data and causes issues such as data drift. Apache Iceberg introduces unique branching and tagging capabilities, enabling users to create isolated branches of a table and tag specific snapshots for easy reference. This is quite similar to how branches and tags work in version control systems such as Git.

## Branching

Branching in Iceberg allows users to create separate "versions" of the table, each with its own sequence of snapshots. A branch, such as dev or staging, operates independently of the main production table, providing a safe environment for testing newly ingested data, applying schema changes, or experimenting with different operations.

Branches are represented in the metadata file by references to the initial snapshot of the branch, creating a lineage that separates the branch's operations from the main table's state. For our example metadata file provided here: https://github.com/PacktPublishing/Engineering-Lakehouses-with-Open-Table-Formats/blob/main/ch03/v3.metadata.json, we see this:

```
"refs" : {
    "main" : {
        "snapshot-id" : 5886256132005027082,
        "type" : "branch"
    }
}
```

This represents a branch within the Iceberg table, specifically the "main" branch, which points to a particular snapshot ID (5886256132005027082). This defines the initial snapshot for that branch, establishing the "starting point" for any subsequent changes that occur within the branch. As changes are made within this branch, new snapshots are added to its sequence. These snapshots are separate from other branches, hence providing isolation from the main table or any other branches.

## Tagging

Tags provide a way to label specific snapshots (snapshot-id) and are immutable. Unlike branches, which can evolve independently, tags are static pointers to a specific snapshot, often used to refer to a specific point in time. For example, a user might tag the snapshot at the end of each quarter as Q1_2024. This allows you to specifically refer to this version of the table for quick access for audits or compliance checks. Similar to branches, tags are recorded in the metadata file alongside snapshots, allowing query engines to retrieve the exact state of the table at any tagged snapshot.

# Advanced statistics with Puffin files

Efficient query planning and execution rely on statistical information. As discussed in the *Manifest files* section, Iceberg aggregates statistical information from individual Parquet files in the manifest files, which provides a more efficient way to skip irrelevant data files. The introduction of *Puffin files* in Iceberg provides a mechanism to store advanced statistics (significantly larger in size) that cannot be directly saved in the manifest files.

Puffin files contain "blobs," which are segments of information about the data, referred to as *sketches*. Sketches, such as apache-datasketches-theta-v1, are produced by **stochastic streaming algorithms**, and provide approximate results for complex calculations (e.g., distinct counts and quantiles) by processing data streams in a single pass. This enables Iceberg to support more efficient query optimization without requiring a full scan of data files.

A significant application of Puffin files is in tracking the approximate **number of distinct values (NDV)** for specific columns. Knowing the NDV is crucial for query engines to plan efficient operations, such as join reordering, especially when a column's distinct values vary greatly. Without Puffin, NDV calculations would require re-scanning the dataset, but with Puffin files, this data is incrementally updated and readily accessible. This persistent sketching approach makes Puffin particularly valuable for large datasets where accurate counts are computationally intensive and where approximate values suffice. Puffin files are optimized for large sketches, which may otherwise occupy substantial space if stored in traditional formats such as Parquet or Avro.

Puffin files are integrated into Iceberg's table statistics and referenced in the *metadata* (metadata.json) file, offering query engines valuable metadata for efficient query planning. They are listed under the "statistics" section, with details such as the snapshot ID, file path, and relevant metadata. For instance, take the example provided:

```
"statistics": [
    {
      "snapshot-id": "5",
      "statistics-path": "s3a://diplakehouse/iceberg_book/customers/
stats/00005.puffin",
      "file-size-in-bytes": 2048,
      "file-footer-size-in-bytes": 64,
      "blob-metadata": [
        {
          "type": "table-stats",
          "snapshot-id": 5,
```

```
          "sequence-number": 150,
          "fields": [1, 2, 3],
          "properties": {
            "statistic-type": "summary"
          }
        }
      ]
    }
  ]
```

These unique capabilities should be carefully considered when building lakehouse architectures based on the Apache Iceberg table format. For example, if your organization requires flexibility to adjust partitioning as data patterns evolve, Iceberg's partition evolution supports seamless updates without rewriting data. If you need to create isolated data environments for testing data or want to enable your analytics team (such as data scientists) to experiment and reproduce specific models, branching and tagging can be invaluable. Together, these capabilities make Iceberg a strong foundation for lakehouse architectures, tailored to meet the demands of dynamic, large-scale data environments.

# Hands-on with Apache Iceberg and Apache Spark

In this section, we will dive into hands-on exercises with Apache Iceberg, using Apache Spark as the compute engine. This part will provide a step-by-step guide to setting up, managing, and utilizing Iceberg tables. By the end of this section, you'll have a practical understanding of Iceberg's unique capabilities, including how to configure catalogs, perform data manipulation through DDL and DML operations, execute read queries with time-travel and schema evolution, and leverage Iceberg's advanced features, such as branching and tagging. We will primarily use Spark's SQL API to run these examples, but will also use the Python (PySpark) API occasionally.

# Installation requirements

Before you get started, make sure you have the following:

- Spark 3.x
- Java
- Downloading required packages (details in the next section)
- Python libraries: `pip install pyspark findspark`

You can find all of these examples in a Docker container in the following repository: `https://github.com/PacktPublishing/Engineering-Lakehouses-with-Open-Table-Formats/tree/main/ch03/ApacheSpark`.

# Write and read operations with Spark and Iceberg

This initial section aims to guide you through the essential configurations needed to start working with Apache Iceberg tables, including the compute engine and catalog setup. Once we have a solid understanding of these configurations, we'll dive into the various read and write operations supported by Iceberg.

## Getting the required packages

To get started with Apache Iceberg and Spark, you'll need to include some essential packages that support Iceberg's functionality, integration with Spark, and access to storage system-specific resources. Here's a breakdown of the key packages required and their roles:

- `org.apache.hadoop:hadoop-aws:3.3.4`: This package enables using an AWS S3 file system (instead of an HDFS directory), allowing Spark to interact with S3 storage for reading and writing data in Iceberg tables.

- `org.apache.iceberg:iceberg-spark-runtime-3.3_2.12:1.4.3`: This is the core Iceberg package for Spark runtime, enabling Iceberg table operations such as reading and writing within Spark environments. The `1.4.3` here denotes the Iceberg version, `3.3` specifies the compatible Spark version, and `2.12` is the Scala version used.

- `software.amazon.awssdk:bundle:2.17.178`: A comprehensive SDK bundle from Amazon required for AWS interactions, including S3 access and other AWS services that may be used with Iceberg tables.

- `software.amazon.awssdk:url-connection-client:2.17.178`: This package provides a URL-based HTTP client for AWS SDK, which supports network communication required for AWS services.

Additionally, Spark SQL extensions are necessary to enable Iceberg-specific SQL syntax within Spark. Configuring `spark.sql.extensions` with `'org.apache.iceberg.spark.extensions.IcebergSparkSessionExtensions'` enables Spark to recognize Iceberg's extended SQL syntax, allowing for specialized commands that support operations such as running stored procedures and perform table modifications, such as adjusting the table's write order, adding partitions, and so on directly within SQL.

# Configuring catalogs

As discussed, catalogs provide consistency guarantees in transactions by enabling compute engines to update the metadata file reference with the latest version after each write operation. Additionally, they provide a unified interface to access all the tables. Setting up a catalog is therefore the *essential* first step when working with Iceberg tables. It is also important to acknowledge that Iceberg provides various APIs to interact with the storage system, but you will need a compute engine to process the data and execute various operations. Hence, our overall configuration will be based on three key components: compute engine, table format, and catalog.

There are various open source and proprietary choices available for using a particular database or data store as a catalog, including Hadoop (file system-based), Hive Metastore (HMS), AWS Glue, Project Nessie, and so on. For this particular section, we will use a simple file-system-based Hadoop catalog.

Catalogs are set up through properties prefixed with `spark.sql.catalog.(catalog_name)`, where `(catalog_name)` represents a specific catalog instance (such as Hadoop or Hive). The most important element in configuring any catalog is its implementation class. This implementation class defines the operational logic and behavior for how Spark will access and manage tables within that catalog. Iceberg provides two built-in catalog implementation classes—`org.apache.iceberg.spark.SparkCatalog` and `org.apache.iceberg.spark.SparkSessionCatalog`—as well as support for *custom catalog* implementations.

Here is a detailed table summarizing the configuration and functionality of the different catalog implementation classes available in Apache Iceberg for Spark.

| Implementation Class | Description |
|---|---|
| `org.apache.iceberg.spark.SparkCatalog` | The general-purpose implementation class for Iceberg catalogs, supporting either a Hadoop or Hive catalog. When type is set to `hive`, it integrates with Hive's Metastore. When set to `hadoop`, it uses a directory-based catalog in Hadoop or any compatible filesystem, storing metadata locally or in distributed storage. |

| | |
|---|---|
| `org.apache.iceberg.spark.`<br>`SparkSessionCatalog` | `SparkSessionCatalog` integrates support for Iceberg tables directly within Spark's built-in catalog. It allows seamless management of both Iceberg and non-Iceberg tables by handling Iceberg tables specifically while delegating non-Iceberg table operations to Spark's native catalog. |
| Custom Catalog Implementation | Allows you to configure a custom catalog implementation beyond the built-in options. Requires a custom class that implements Iceberg's Catalog interface. Use `catalog-impl` to specify the custom catalog class. |

*Table 3.1:  Table summarizing configuration & functionality for different catalog implementations with Apache Spark and Iceberg*

Following are some examples to use these different implementation classes with Iceberg tables using Spark.

## SparkCatalog with Hadoop

```
spark.sql.catalog.hadoop_catalog=org.apache.iceberg.spark.SparkCatalog
spark.sql.catalog.hadoop_catalog.type=hadoop
spark.sql.catalog.hadoop_catalog.warehouse='s3a://diplakehouse/iceberg_
book'
```

These properties will configure a hadoop catalog of the `SparkCatalog` type, named `hadoop_catalog` and use an S3 bucket, `s3a://diplakehouse/iceberg_book`, as the warehouse directory to host all the data and metadata files for a particular table.

## SparkSessionCatalog with Hive

```
spark.sql.catalog.hive_spark_catalog=org.apache.iceberg.spark.
SparkSessionCatalog
spark.sql.catalog.hive_spark_catalog.type=hive
spark.sql.catalog.hive_spark_catalog.uri=thrift://localhost:9083
```

These properties will configure a `hive` catalog of the `SparkSessionCatalog` type, named `hive_spark_catalog`. We inform Spark to use Hive's Metastore at the specified URI (`thrift://metastore-host:port`) for storing and managing Iceberg table metadata.

## Custom catalog (AWS Glue)

```
spark.sql.catalog.glue=org.apache.iceberg.spark.SparkCatalog
spark.sql.catalog.glue.catalog-impl=org.apache.iceberg.aws.glue.
GlueCatalog
spark.sql.catalog.glue.io-impl=org.apache.iceberg.aws.s3.S3FileIO
(spark.sql.catalog.glue.my-additional-catalog-config=my-value)
```

Here, we use an AWS Glue catalog (custom) with the custom class, `org.apache.iceberg.aws.glue.GlueCatalog`, along with an additional config, `spark.sql.catalog.glue.io-impl=org.apache.iceberg.aws.s3.S3FileIO` that changes the default I/O implementation of the catalog to write data to the storage, (i.e., S3).

Now that we know how to configure different types of catalogs in Iceberg and are aware of the required packages, let's bring all of these together and finally configure a Spark, Iceberg, and Hadoop catalog as an example setup for the rest of the sections.

```
import pyspark
from pyspark.sql import SparkSession
import os
conf = (
    pyspark.SparkConf()
        .setAppName('lakehouse_app')
        .set('spark.jars.packages', 'org.apache.hadoop:hadoop-
aws:3.3.4,org.apache.iceberg:iceberg-spark-runtime-
3.3_2.12:1.4.3,software.amazon.awssdk:bundle:2.17.178,software.amazon.
awssdk:url-connection-client:2.17.178')
        .set('spark.sql.extensions', 'org.apache.iceberg.spark.extensions.
IcebergSparkSessionExtensions')
        .set('spark.sql.catalog.hdfs_catalog', 'org.apache.iceberg.spark.
SparkCatalog')
        .set('spark.sql.catalog.hdfs_catalog.type', 'hadoop')
        .set('spark.sql.catalog.hdfs_catalog.warehouse', 's3a://
diplakehouse/iceberg_book/')
        .set('spark.sql.catalog.hdfs_catalog.io-impl', 'org.apache.
iceberg.aws.s3.S3FileIO')
        .set('spark.hadoop.fs.s3a.access.key', 'aws access')
        .set('spark.hadoop.fs.s3a.secret.key', 'aws secret')
)
```

```
spark = SparkSession.builder.config(conf=conf).getOrCreate()
print("Spark Running")
```

If everything downloads successfully, you should see something similar to this in the output.

```
software.amazon.awssdk#url-connection-client;2.17.178 from central in [default]
software.amazon.awssdk#utils;2.17.178 from central in [default]
software.amazon.eventstream#eventstream;1.0.1 from central in [default]
---------------------------------------------------------------------
|         |          |            modules            ||   artifacts   |
|   conf  |  number| search|dwnlded|evicted||  number|dwnlded|
---------------------------------------------------------------------
| default |   13   |   0   |   0   |   0   ||   13   |   0   |
---------------------------------------------------------------------
:: retrieving :: org.apache.spark#spark-submit-parent-5c26ca86-7887-47c4-92b4-3c3f333c172b
    confs: [default]
    0 artifacts copied, 13 already retrieved (0kB/16ms)
24/11/12 05:23:25 WARN NativeCodeLoader: Unable to load native-hadoop library for your platform... using builtin-ja
va classes where applicable
Setting default log level to "WARN".
To adjust logging level use sc.setLogLevel(newLevel). For SparkR, use setLogLevel(newLevel).
Spark Running
```

*Figure 3.3 – Snippet showing Spark, Iceberg, and the Hadoop catalog configured*

Now, we are ready to get started with the write and read operations.

> A Hadoop catalog is usually not recommended for production usage, as discussed in the *Catalog considerations for production* section. However, depending on your data lake storage, this may vary. For example, AWS S3 recently started supporting conditional writes, which could address consistency problems with specific operations: https://aws.amazon.com/about-aws/whats-new/2024/08/amazon-s3-conditional-writes/.

## DDL statements

With the catalog configured, we can now define and create tables using standard SQL **Data Definition Language** (**DDL**) operations.

## CREATE TABLE

Let's start with creating the first Iceberg table:

```
spark.sql("""
    CREATE TABLE hdfs_catalog.default.customers (
        customer_id INT,
        first_name STRING,
        last_name STRING,
        email STRING,
```

```
        charges FLOAT,
        state STRING
    )
    USING iceberg
    PARTITIONED BY (state)
""")
```

This command creates a table in the default namespace of hdfs_catalog with state as the partitioning field. Partitioning on state will allow efficient data pruning by partition, as Iceberg will organize data within each state, optimizing queries that filter by this column.

Alternatively, you can achieve the same using PySpark's DataFrame API. Here's the equivalent code:

```
from pyspark.sql.types import StructType, StructField, StringType,
IntegerType, FloatType
from pyspark.sql.functions import col
schema = StructType([
    StructField("customer_id", IntegerType(), True),
    StructField("first_name", StringType(), True),
    StructField("last_name", StringType(), True),
    StructField("email", StringType(), True),
    StructField("charges", FloatType(), True),
    StructField("state", StringType(), True)
])
df = spark.createDataFrame([], schema)
df.writeTo("hdfs_catalog.default.customers").partitionedBy(col("state")).
create()
```

## CREATE TABLE AS SELECT (CTAS)

CTAS, or CREATE TABLE AS SELECT, allows you to create a new Iceberg table based on the results of a query. This is particularly useful for materializing complex queries directly as tables. This command creates a new high_value_customers table with data from customers where charges exceed 1000:

```
spark.sql("""
CREATE TABLE hdfs_catalog.default.high_value_customers
    USING iceberg
    AS SELECT *
    FROM hdfs_catalog.default.customers
    WHERE charges > 1000
""")
```

In PySpark, we can use the `DataFrame.writeTo()` method to perform a CTAS operation by reading from an existing table and writing to a new one. Here is an example:

```
df_ctas = spark.read.table("hdfs_catalog.customers")
df_ctas.filter(df_ctas.charges > 1000) \
        .select("customer_id", "first_name", "last_name", "state",
"charges") \
        .writeTo("hdfs_catalog.high_value_customers") \
        .partitionedBy("state") \
        .create()
```

## DROP TABLE

Starting from Iceberg version 0.14, the behavior of `DROP TABLE` has changed. By default, `DROP TABLE` only removes the table from the catalog without deleting the underlying data files. To fully delete the table's data, you must use `DROP TABLE PURGE`.

To drop a table without deleting its data files, use the following:

```
spark.sql("DROP TABLE IF EXISTS hdfs_catalog.customers")
```

To drop a table and delete its data files, use the following:

```
spark.sql("DROP TABLE IF EXISTS hdfs_catalog.customers PURGE")
```

This command checks for the existence of the `customers` table and deletes it if present.

## ALTER TABLE

Iceberg offers robust `ALTER TABLE` functionality, providing full support for making various structural and schema changes to tables, such as adding, deleting, or renaming columns, renaming tables, and widen data types, among others. This flexibility is crucial for adapting to evolving data needs without compromising table integrity or requiring complete rewrites. This is called schema evolution, as discussed earlier.

## Adding a column

Adding a column to an Iceberg table allows you to introduce new data fields without impacting the historical schema. In this example, we'll add a phone_number column to the customers table:

```
spark.sql("""
    ALTER TABLE hdfs_catalog.customers
    ADD COLUMN phone_number STRING
""")
```

# Renaming a column

Iceberg allows renaming columns in the table schema. For example, in the following snippet, we change the `charges` column to `total_spent`:

```
spark.sql("""
    ALTER TABLE hdfs_catalog.customers
    RENAME COLUMN charges TO total_spent
""")
```

# Dropping a column

Dropping a column removes it from the table's schema, which can be useful for deprecating old fields that are no longer needed. For instance, if phone_number data is obsolete, we can drop this column:

```
spark.sql("""
    ALTER TABLE hdfs_catalog.customers
    DROP COLUMN phone_number
""")
```

# Adding a partition field

As we learned in the *Getting the required packages* section, configuring `spark.sql.extensions` enables running specialized commands that are not part of standard SQL. Adding or dropping a partition field directly using SQL is one such capability.

The `ADD PARTITION FIELD` command allows you to introduce new partition fields using different transformation functions such as identity, bucket, truncate, and date-based functions. This is a metadata-only operation, meaning existing data files remain unchanged. New data will be stored with the added partition field, while old data remains in its original partition layout. This flexibility is essential for growing tables where partitioning needs evolve over time.

Here, we add a new partition field, `state`, which will organize the physical data files by state:

```
ALTER TABLE hdfs_catalog.customers ADD PARTITION FIELD state;
```

We can also apply a bucket transformation to distribute data evenly across partitions and use it together with an `ALTER TABLE` statement as shown:

```
ALTER TABLE hdfs_catalog.customers ADD PARTITION FIELD bucket(16,
customer_id);
```

This will hash the `customer_id` column into 16 buckets, enabling efficient distribution.

## ALTER TABLE CREATE BRANCH

As we learned *Branching and tagging* section, branches and tags in Iceberg allow you to create named references to specific snapshots of a table. Branches are mutable and can evolve with new snapshots, while tags are immutable pointers to a particular snapshot. Let's see how to create these using Spark SQL.

This command creates a branch called dev-branch at the current state of the customers table:

```
ALTER TABLE hadoop_catalog.customers CREATE BRANCH `dev-branch`;
```

In the following case, the audit branch will retain snapshots for 30 days and keep at least the latest 3 snapshots, plus any snapshots created in the past 2 days at snapshot version 1234:

```
ALTER TABLE hdfs_catalog.customers CREATE BRANCH `audit-branch`
AS OF VERSION 1234
RETAIN 30 DAYS
WITH SNAPSHOT RETENTION 3 SNAPSHOTS 2 DAYS;
```

For tags, this command will create a named reference called EOY-tag on the current snapshot of the customers table:

```
ALTER TABLE hdfs_catalog.customers CREATE TAG `EOY-tag`;
```

Here is another example where we create a tag named historical-tag at snapshot ID 1234, allowing us to retain a specific historical view of the table for analysis purposes:

```
ALTER TABLE hdfs_catalog.customers CREATE TAG `historical-tag`
AS OF VERSION 1234;
```

To drop a branch or tag, we can do the following:

```
ALTER TABLE prod.db.sample DROP BRANCH `dev-branch`
ALTER TABLE prod.db.sample DROP TAG `historical-tag`
```

## DML statements

Apache Iceberg provides full support for common DML operations in Spark, such as INSERT, MERGE INTO, INSERT OVERWRITE, DELETE FROM, and UPDATE. These operations enable efficient data modification in a table while ensuring consistency, even with concurrent reads and writes. Here, we'll cover each of the key DML operations with examples in both SQL and PySpark.

## INSERT INTO

The INSERT INTO command appends new records to an existing Iceberg table:

```
INSERT INTO hdfs_catalog.customers
VALUES (1, 'John', 'Doe', 'john.doe@example.com', 150.75, 'CA');
```

This can also be achieved using PySpark:

```
# Define schema by referencing the existing Iceberg table
schema = spark.table("hdfs_catalog.customers").schema
data = [
    (1, 'John', 'Doe', 'john.doe@example.com', 150.75, 'CA'),
    (2, 'Alice', 'Smith', 'alice.smith@example.com', 200.50, 'NY'),
    (3, 'Bob', 'Brown', 'bob.brown@example.com', 175.25, 'TX'),
    (4, 'Emily', 'Davis', 'emily.davis@example.com', 220.30, 'FL')
]
df_insert = spark.createDataFrame(data, schema)
df_insert.writeTo("hdfs_catalog.customers").append()
```

## MERGE INTO

The MERGE INTO operation, used for upserts, combines records from a source dataset into a target table, updating existing records and inserting new ones based on specified matching criteria. This is particularly useful for handling **slowly changing dimensions (SCDs)** or applying **Change Data Capture (CDC)** updates in real-world scenarios.

```
MERGE INTO hdfs_catalog.customers AS target
USING updates AS source
ON target.customer_id = source.customer_id
WHEN MATCHED THEN
  UPDATE SET *
WHEN NOT MATCHED THEN
  INSERT *
```

This MERGE INTO query updates the customers table by merging data from the updates source. If a customer_id exists in both tables (e.g., customer_id 2), the record in customers is updated to match updates. If there's no match (e.g., customer_id 4), a new record is inserted. This process ensures that customers reflects the latest data without duplicates or outdated entries.

## INSERT OVERWRITE

In Iceberg, INSERT OVERWRITE allows you to replace data in a table or a specified partition with new query results. This operation is atomic, ensuring data consistency during the overwrite process. The scope of the overwrite (i.e., whether it applies to specific partitions or the entire table) depends on the table's partitioning scheme and Spark's partition overwrite mode. There are two partition overwrite modes, static and dynamic:

- **Static overwrite mode**: In static mode, Spark replaces partitions based on the PARTITION clause filter, which must reference existing table columns

- **Dynamic overwrite mode**: In dynamic mode, Spark replaces only the partitions that contain rows produced by the SELECT query, allowing more granular updates

  ```
  -- Static Overwrite Mode: Overwrites only the "CA" partition
  INSERT OVERWRITE hdfs_catalog.default.customers
  PARTITION (state = 'CA')
  SELECT customer_id, first_name, last_name, email, total_spent, state
  FROM staging_updates
  WHERE state = 'CA'
  ```

- In this example, only the partition for state = 'CA' is overwritten with data from staging_updates:

  ```
  -- Dynamic Overwrite Mode: Overwrites all partitions with data in
  the query result
  INSERT OVERWRITE hdfs_catalog.default.customers
  SELECT customer_id, first_name, last_name, email, total_spent, state
  FROM staging_updates
  WHERE state IN ('CA', 'NY')
  ```

In this case, Spark overwrites any partitions with rows in the query result, such as state = 'CA' and state = 'NY', if they exist in the staging_updates table.

Although INSERT OVERWRITE is useful for fully replacing data, MERGE INTO is often preferred because it selectively rewrites only the necessary data files, making it more efficient and intuitive for targeted updates.

## DELETE FROM

The DELETE FROM command in Iceberg allows you to delete records that match a specific condition. Iceberg supports both partition-level and row-level deletions, which enables efficient deletion in large datasets. If the condition matches entire partitions, Iceberg performs a *metadata-only* delete, making the operation faster by simply updating metadata without modifying data files. If the condition matches individual rows, Iceberg will rewrite only the affected *data files* (via the CoW and MoR strategy discussed here). Let's see how to do partition-level and row-level deletions in Iceberg.

- **Row-level delete**

  This example deletes a single customer record where `customer_id` is 1.

  ```
  DELETE FROM hdfs_catalog.customers
  WHERE customer_id = 1;
  ```

- **Partition-level delete**

  This example deletes all records for customers in the state of CA. If Iceberg's partitioning is based on the `state` column, this deletion will be a metadata-only operation.

  ```
  DELETE FROM hdfs_catalog.customers
  WHERE state = 'CA';
  ```

## UPDATE

The `UPDATE` command allows you to modify existing records in an Iceberg table based on a condition. Iceberg handles updates via two strategies—CoW and MoR tables (discussed earlier in the *Row-level updates/deletes: Copy-on-Write (CoW) and Merge-on-Read (MoR) tables section*. By either creating new data files with the modified records or rewriting the updated records in a separate *delete file*. Here is a simple example that updates `charges` for every customer for the CA state.

```
UPDATE hdfs_catalog.customers
SET charges = charges * 1.1
WHERE state = 'CA';
```

## Read queries

To query data from an Iceberg table, you can use standard SQL `SELECT` statements. Iceberg allows Spark to perform snapshot-based reads, allowing for historical querying such as time-travel. Here are some examples:

## Snapshot reads

```
# Read all data from the table
spark.sql("SELECT * FROM hadoop_catalog.customers").show()
```

```
# Read only records from a specific state
spark.sql("SELECT * FROM hadoop_catalog.customers WHERE state = 'CA'").
show()
```

If you were to use the PySpark API, here is how this would look:

```
df = spark.table("hadoop_catalog.customers").filter("state = 'CA'")
df.show()
```

### Time-travel reads

Iceberg's time-travel feature allows querying data at specific points in time using both snapshot ID and timestamp.

This query reads the state of the customers table as it existed on October 26, 2024, at 15:30:00:

```
SELECT * FROM hadoop_catalog.customers TIMESTAMP AS OF '2024-10-26
15:30:00';
```

This query reads the state of the customers table as it was at a specific snapshot, identified by its unique snapshot ID:

```
SELECT * FROM hadoop_catalog.customers VERSION AS OF 12345678901234;
```

## Iceberg procedures

In Iceberg, procedures offer powerful built-in functionalities for managing tables, maintaining snapshots, and optimizing file storage. These procedures are available in Spark when Iceberg SQL extensions are enabled. They can be accessed using the CALL command, with arguments passed either by name (recommended) or by position, but mixing both is not allowed. Each procedure operates within the system namespace of the configured Iceberg catalog. In this section, we will take a look at some of the commonly used procedures and how to use them.

### Expire snapshot

**Purpose**: Each write operation in Iceberg creates a new snapshot. The expire_snapshots procedure removes older snapshots and their unique data files, freeing up storage while ensuring files required by active snapshots are preserved.

Here is an example that removes snapshots older than August 1, 2023, retaining the latest 5 snapshots:

```
CALL hdfs_catalog.system.expire_snapshots(
    table => 'hdfs_catalog.customers',
```

```
  older_than => TIMESTAMP '2023-08-01 00:00:00',
  retain_last => 5
)
```

## Roll back to snapshot

**Purpose**: `rollback_to_snapshot` reverts the table state to a specified snapshot (based on ID), discarding any later changes. This is useful for undoing unintended modifications while preserving prior history. This command rolls back the `customers` table to the specified snapshot, discarding any changes made after it:

```
CALL hdfs_catalog.system.rollback_to_snapshot(
  table => 'hdfs_catalog.customers',
  snapshot_id => 2711640443788239783
)
```

## Remove orphan files

**Purpose**: The `remove_orphan_files` procedure is used to clean up any data files that are no longer tracked by the table's metadata, often due to incomplete operations or updates. This helps in reclaiming storage space and maintaining the integrity of the table's data by removing unreferenced files.

We can run this procedure in a *dry mode* first to check the files that would be removed without actually deleting them:

```
CALL hdfs_catalog.system.remove_orphan_files(
  table => 'hdfs_catalog.customers',
  dry_run => true
)
```

After a dry run, we can call this procedure to remove orphaned files from the specified location in the `customers` table:

```
CALL hdfs_catalog.system.remove_orphan_files(
  table => 'hdfs_catalog.customers',
  location => 's3a://diplakehouse/iceberg_book/customers/data'
)
```

## Rewrite data files

**Purpose:** When tables accumulate many small files, metadata overhead increases, and query performance can suffer due to the cost of opening multiple files. `rewrite_data` handles a variety of optimization tasks, such as *compaction*, which optimizes the table by rewriting small data files into larger ones, enhancing read efficiency. Similarly, you can also execute *linear sorting* and *multi-dimensional clustering* (such as Z-ordering) using this particular procedure. We will cover these techniques in detail in *Chapter 8, Performance Optimization and Tuning in Lakehouse.*

Here is an example that shows how to run compaction to rewrite small files using the `binpack` algorithm and sets the target file size as 512 MB:

```
CALL hdfs_catalog.system.rewrite_data_files(
  table => 'hdfs_catalog.customers',
  strategy => 'binpack',
  target_file_size_bytes => 512 * 1024 * 1024
)
```

## Add files

**Purpose:** `add_files` attempts to directly register untracked files from an external Hive or file-based table into an existing Iceberg table, adding them to Iceberg's metadata. This command does not create a new Iceberg table or verify schema compatibility, so it's ideal when migrating files that are known to match the Iceberg schema. Once registered, these files are treated as part of the Iceberg table and can be managed accordingly.

The following example registers files located at `s3://my-bucket/new_data/` into the existing Iceberg table, `hdfs_catalog.customers`. The files are added to Iceberg's metadata, making them part of the table's data, but they remain in their original location:

```
CALL hdfs_catalog.system.add_files(
  table => 'hdfs_catalog.customers',
  path => 's3://my-bucket/new_data/'
)
```

In this section, we practically explored some of the critical configurations necessary for running various DDL, DML, and advanced commands in Apache Iceberg using Apache Spark. This should provide foundations for building various analytical workload pipelines. We will discuss a few of the workloads in *Chapter 11, Real-World Applications and Learnings.*

# Hands-on with Apache Iceberg and Apache Flink

Apache Flink is an open source distributed compute engine well-suited for stream processing, although it does support batch workloads. It excels in event-time processing, exactly-once semantics, and low-latency, high-throughput processing, all of which are crucial for streaming analytics. Apache Iceberg, as an open table format, offers features such as ACID compliance, schema evolution, hidden partitioning, and time travel. Together, Flink and Iceberg enable a near real-time lakehouse architecture, providing efficient, low-latency access to both streaming and batch data.

In this section, we'll explore practical examples of configuring and running Flink with Apache Iceberg tables. Our goal is to break down key components of this setup, showing how to configure Flink to execute transactions and run DDL, DML, and read queries via Flink SQL. Apache Flink offers three main APIs for data processing: the ProcessFunction, DataStream API, and SQL/Table API. While the DataStream and ProcessFunction APIs provide more flexibility, the SQL/Table API is concise and well-suited for SQL-like operations. For this chapter, we'll focus on the SQL API.

To accomplish our goal, we'll first configure three essential components: the Flink SQL client, a catalog, and the Iceberg table. For ease of following these exercises, we have shared a Docker container with all the required services. Just use `docker-compose` up to start the services.

## Configuration (Flink, Iceberg, storage)

Before integrating Flink with Iceberg, we will need to get a few key libraries and classes that facilitate seamless communication between Flink, Iceberg, and the storage system. Following is a detailed guide to these prerequisites and how they fit into the configuration:

1.  **Apache Flink**: Download the latest compatible version of Flink from the official website: `https://flink.apache.org/downloads/`, and ensure compatibility with the Iceberg version you use. The latest recommended use is Flink 1.19 bundled with Scala 2.12. However, for our exercises we rely on an older, stable version (i.e., 1.16.3).

2.  **Iceberg-Flink runtime JAR**: The `iceberg-flink-runtime` JAR file is a critical one that allows Flink to interact with Iceberg tables. This runtime JAR acts as a bridge, enabling Flink to perform SQL operations on Iceberg-managed tables. Download the latest compatible JAR from Iceberg's Maven repository. We use `iceberg-flink-runtime-1.17-1.3.0` for the examples.

3. **Hadoop common libraries**: For Flink to interact with storage systems such as Amazon S3 or HDFS, you'll need Hadoop common libraries. These libraries include essential classes that facilitate communication with various storage backends and enable file operations. You can download the Hadoop Common libraries here: `https://repo1.maven.org/maven2/org/apache/hadoop/hadoop-common/2.8.3/hadoop-common-2.8.3.jar`.

4. **Hadoop AWS library**: If you plan to use S3 or an S3-compatible API (such as `MinIO`) as the storage for Iceberg tables, the Hadoop AWS library is essential. This library supports S3-specific configurations and includes classes for handling S3 bucket permissions, file management, and data I/O operations.

5. **AWS SDK bundled libraries**: In addition to Hadoop AWS, AWS SDK bundled classes provide support for additional AWS services, such as IAM for authentication, Lambda for serverless operations, and so on. These bundled libraries allow you to do things such as download and upload objects. The AWS SDK can be added from `Maven`.

After downloading these libraries, place them in the `FLINK_HOME/lib` directory, where Flink can automatically load them during startup.

## Setting up Flink SQL

Apache Flink has two main components: *JobManager* and *TaskManager*, which coordinate to execute distributed processing jobs efficiently:

- **JobManager**: The JobManager is the central coordinator for Flink's operations. It manages the scheduling of tasks, oversees resource allocation, and is responsible for critical tasks such as checkpoint coordination, which ensures fault tolerance.

- **TaskManager**: TaskManagers are the workhorses of the Flink cluster. They execute the tasks that have been scheduled by the JobManager. Each TaskManager manages a pool of task slots, where each slot represents a share of the system's resources (such as CPU and memory).

## Flink SQL Client

Flink SQL eliminates the need for Java or Scala code, making it accessible for users familiar with SQL. With the SQL Client, users can interact with a Flink cluster through SQL commands, which are executed on the distributed data engine.

The SQL Client comes bundled with the standard Flink distribution, making it ready to run right out of the box. You can start the SQL Client in embedded mode by running the following command in your terminal:

```
./bin/sql-client.sh
./bin/sql-client.sh embedded (explicit)
```

If everything configures fine, you will be able to see this interface:

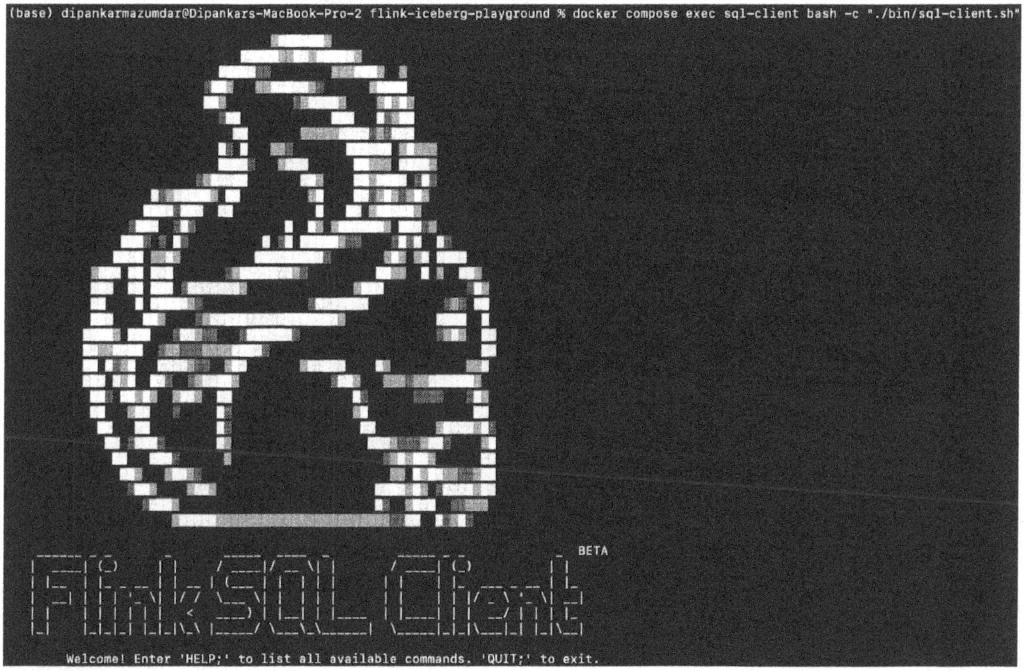

*Figure 3.4 – Snippet showing Flink SQL Client configured and running*

## Catalog configuration

As with any Iceberg setup, configuring a catalog is the first step to interfacing with Iceberg tables using Flink. We learned in the *Catalog* section how the choice of catalog is diverse in the Iceberg world and can be any kind of a database or data store. For our example in the Docker container, we're using DynamoDB as the catalog. Following is an excerpt from our docker-compose.yml file:

```
# Catalog
  dynamodb-local:
    command: "-jar DynamoDBLocal.jar -sharedDb -dbPath ./data"
    image: "amazon/dynamodb-local:latest"
```

```
container_name: dynamodb-local
networks:
  iceberg-dynamodb-flink-net:
ports:
  - "8000:8000"
volumes:
  - "./docker/dynamodb:/home/dynamodblocal/data"
working_dir: /home/dynamodblocal
```

If we want to check the content of the catalog, we can use the AWS CLI to access DynamoDB:

```
aws dynamodb scan --table-name iceberg-catalog --endpoint-url http://
localhost:8000 | jq

{
  "Items": [
    {
      "namespace": {
        "S": "db"
      },
      "identifier": {
        "S": "NAMESPACE"
      },
      "created_at": {
        "N": "1731474231620"
      },
      "updated_at": {
        "N": "1731474231620"
      },
      "v": {
        "S": "1d1e57fe-4914-478e-b1e2-725b47ebaa22"
      }
    },
    {
      "identifier": {
        "S": "db.spotify"
      },
      "updated_at": {
```

```
        "N": "1731474263772"
      },
      "v": {
        "S": "f9d3cd08-4f29-42b4-a47c-b38d69cb0cf5"
      },
      "namespace": {
        "S": "db"
      },
      "created_at": {
        "N": "1731474240918"
      },
      "p.metadata_location": {
        "S": "s3://warehouse/db.db/spotify/metadata/00001-2a5babcd-b060-
4c36-be1b-fa1baa24fbe5.metadata.json"
      },
      "p.previous_metadata_location": {
        "S": "s3://warehouse/db.db/spotify/metadata/00000-612cc05f-5fbf-
4c1f-9676-34704e1613d2.metadata.json"
      },
      "p.table_type": {
        "S": "ICEBERG"
      }
    }
  ],
  "Count": 3,
  "ScannedCount": 3,
  "ConsumedCapacity": null
}
```

This shows the existing Iceberg table, spotify, in the catalog, along with its content within the database, db.

## DDL statements

Let's start by creating some of the DDL statements to interact with Iceberg tables. Flink SQL currently has support for creating tables, altering table properties, and dropping tables.

## CREATE CATALOG

As mentioned, we are using a DynamoDB catalog to manage our Iceberg tables that will be stored in an S3-compatible API (MinIO):

```
CREATE CATALOG dynamo_catalog WITH (
  'type' = 'iceberg',
  'catalog-impl' = 'org.apache.iceberg.aws.dynamodb.DynamoDbCatalog',
  'io-impl' = 'org.apache.iceberg.aws.s3.S3FileIO',
  'client.assume-role.region' = 'us-east-1',
  'warehouse' = 's3://warehouse',
  's3.endpoint' = 'http://storage:9000',
  's3.path-style-access' = 'true',
  'dynamodb.table-name' = 'iceberg-catalog',
  'dynamodb.endpoint' = 'http://dynamodb-local:8000'
);
```

## Key properties

Here are some of the important properties to understand when using Flink with Iceberg:

- type: Specifies that this catalog is of type `iceberg`
- catalog-impl: Defines the catalog implementation as `org.apache.iceberg.aws.dynamodb.DynamoDbCatalog`
- warehouse: All tables under this catalog will reside in this bucket or directory
- s3.endpoint: Specifies the endpoint for an S3-compatible service (i.e., MinIO)
- dynamodb.table-name: Defines the name of the DynamoDB table, `iceberg-catalog`, where Iceberg metadata will be stored
- dynamodb.endpoint: Specifies the endpoint for the DynamoDB instance

You can then list all available catalogs to confirm the creation of dynamo_catalog. Here is the command that lists out all the catalogs:

```
SHOW CATALOGS;
```

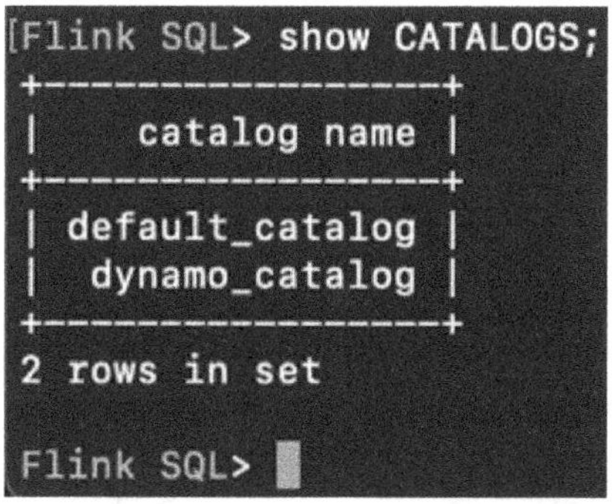

```
[Flink SQL> show CATALOGS;
+------------------+
|   catalog name   |
+------------------+
| default_catalog  |
|  dynamo_catalog  |
+------------------+
2 rows in set

Flink SQL> █
```

*Figure 3.5 – List of catalogs, with the recently created dynamo_catalog*

To use this particular catalog, you can use the following command in Flink SQL:

```
USE CATALOG dynamo_catalog;
```

## CREATE DATABASE

In earlier versions of Iceberg, Flink provided a default database, but as of Iceberg 1.3.1 and later, you can create and manage your own databases within a catalog. To create a new database and set it as the active database, use the following commands:

```
CREATE DATABASE db;
USE db;
```

Here's the list of databases in Flink SQL:

```
[Flink SQL> show databases;
+-----------------+
| database name   |
+-----------------+
|              db |
|         default |
+-----------------+
2 rows in set
```

*Figure 3.6 – List of databases, with the recently created db*

## CREATE TABLE

Let's create a sample Iceberg table, event_logs, to capture real-time logs, such as event type, event source, timestamp, and other relevant details:

```
CREATE TABLE event_logs (
  event_id STRING,
```

```
    event_type STRING,
    event_source STRING,
    event_time TIMESTAMP(3),
    event_details STRING
) PARTITIONED BY (event_time);
```

We can see the newly created table along with the other existing one by using SHOW TABLES;:

```
[Flink SQL> SHOW TABLES;
+--------------+
| table name |
+--------------+
| event_logs |
|    spotify |
+--------------+
2 rows in set
```

*Figure 3.7 – List of tables, with the recently created event_logs table*

## DML statements

Iceberg supports a range of DML statements in Flink SQL, allowing both batch and streaming writes, with commands such as INSERT INTO, INSERT OVERWRITE, and UPSERT. Let's take a look into these practically.

## INSERT INTO

The INSERT INTO command shown here inserts new records to an Iceberg table:

```
-- Insert a single event log directly into the event_logs table
INSERT INTO event_logs VALUES ('event1', 'click', 'app', TIMESTAMP '2023-
10-26 10:15:00', 'User clicked button');
```

Here is the output:

```
[Flink SQL> INSERT INTO `event_logs` VALUES ('event1', 'click', 'app', TIMESTAMP '2023-10-26 10:15:00', 'User clicked button');
[INFO] Submitting SQL update statement to the cluster...
[INFO] SQL update statement has been successfully submitted to the cluster:
Job ID: c9ad1572bd487620041d828729b3cf17
```

*Figure 3.8 – Snippet showing data being written to an Iceberg table using Flink SQL*

This statement submits a job to the active Flink cluster. To access the job information, you can access the Flink UI at http://localhost:8081/ (after running the Docker container). The Job manager log within the UI can be beneficial to debug any failed jobs. Here is a snippet:

insert-into_dynamo_catalog.db.event_logs

| | | | | | | | |
|---|---|---|---|---|---|---|---|
| Job ID | c9ad1572bd487620041d828729b3cf17 | | Job State | FINISHED 2 | | Actions | Job Manager Log |
| Start Time | 2024-11-16 17:28:44 | | End Time | 2024-11-16 17:28:49 | | Duration | 4s |

Overview    Exceptions    TimeLine    Checkpoints    Configuration

Source: Values[8] -> Calc[9]
-> IcebergStreamWriter
**Parallelism: 1**
Backpressured (max): N/A
Busy (max): N/A

FORWARD

IcebergFilesCommitter -> Sin
k: IcebergSink dynamo_catal
og.db.event_logs
**Parallelism: 1**
Backpressured (max): N/A
Busy (max): N/A

| Name | Status | Bytes Received | Records Received | Bytes Sent | Records Sent | Parallelism | Start Time | Tasks |
|---|---|---|---|---|---|---|---|---|
| Source: Values[8] -> Calc[9] -> IcebergStreamWriter | FINISHED | 0 B | 0 | 1.18 KB | 1 | 1 | 2024-11-16 17:28: | 1 |
| IcebergFilesCommitter -> Sink: IcebergSink dynamo_catalog.db... | FINISHED | 1.19 KB | 1 | 0 B | 0 | 1 | 2024-11-16 17:28: | 1 |

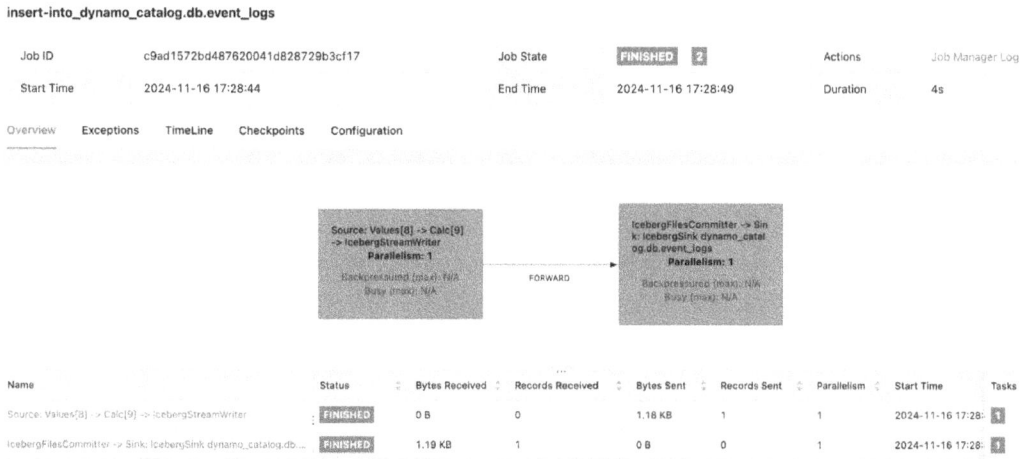

*Figure 3.9 – Flink UI showing the Job Manager with jobs*

# INSERT OVERWRITE

The INSERT OVERWRITE command replaces existing data with new data from a query result. Note that this command is not supported in Flink streaming jobs and can only be used in batch jobs:

```
SET execution.runtime-mode = batch;
INSERT OVERWRITE `event_logs` VALUES('event1', 'click', 'app', TIMESTAMP
'2023-10-26 10:15:00', 'User clicked button');
```

This overwrites the entire event_logs table.

# UPSERT

Iceberg supports UPSERT based on primary keys when using the v2 table format. Flink SQL doesn't offer a dedicated MERGE INTO or UPSERT command, but Iceberg provides two ways to enable upserts:

- **Table-level property**: Enabling write.upsert.enabled as a table property enables UPSERT for all writes to the table, but it requires the table to be created as a v2 ('format-version') table with identifier fields (e.g., PRIMARY KEY (...) NOT ENFORCED in Flink SQL) so Iceberg knows which key to merge on.

  Configuring upsert mode directly on the table allows you to handle updates and inserts automatically with INSERT INTO statements. Iceberg will check the unique identifier (e.g., a primary key) and either update the record if it exists or insert it if it doesn't.

  ```
  CREATE TABLE user_activities (
              `activity_id` STRING UNIQUE,
  ```

```
        `user_id` STRING NOT NULL,
        `activity_type` STRING,
        `activity_time` TIMESTAMP(3),
        `activity_details` STRING,
        PRIMARY KEY(`activity_id`) NOT ENFORCED
) WITH ('format-version'='2', 'write.upsert.enabled'='true');
```

With this configuration, any INSERT INTO statement will perform upserts based on the activity_id. For instance, if an activity_id already exists, Iceberg will update that record instead of creating a duplicate entry.

- **Write options**: Alternatively, you can enable upsert mode during individual writes by passing the upsert-enabled option as a SQL hint. This approach offers more control, as you can decide when to apply upserts without setting it globally on the table.

```
INSERT INTO user_activities /*+ OPTIONS('upsert-enabled'='true') */
VALUES ('activity123', 'user42', 'login', TIMESTAMP '2023-10-26
11:00:00', 'User logged in from mobile');
```

The following screenshot shows how to enable upsert mode by setting the upsert-enabled option as a SQL hint.

```
Flink SQL> INSERT INTO user_activities /*+ OPTIONS('upsert-enabled'='true') */
> VALUES ('activity123', 'user42', 'login', TIMESTAMP '2023-10-26 11:00:00', 'User logged in from mobile');
[>
[INFO] Submitting SQL update statement to the cluster...
[INFO] SQL update statement has been successfully submitted to the cluster:
Job ID: 2ea3c052468f05f0ca8b7af031050472
```

*Figure 3.10 – Snippet showing how to enable upsert mode as a SQL hint*

## Read queries

Apache Iceberg supports both *batch* and *streaming* reads in Flink SQL, allowing you to switch between processing modes easily based on your data requirements. Here is how to do so:

```
SET execution.runtime-mode = streaming;
SET execution.runtime-mode = batch;
```

## Batch reads

In batch mode, you can retrieve the complete dataset as of the latest snapshot:

```
SET execution.runtime-mode = batch;
SELECT * FROM events_logs;
```

Here is the output:

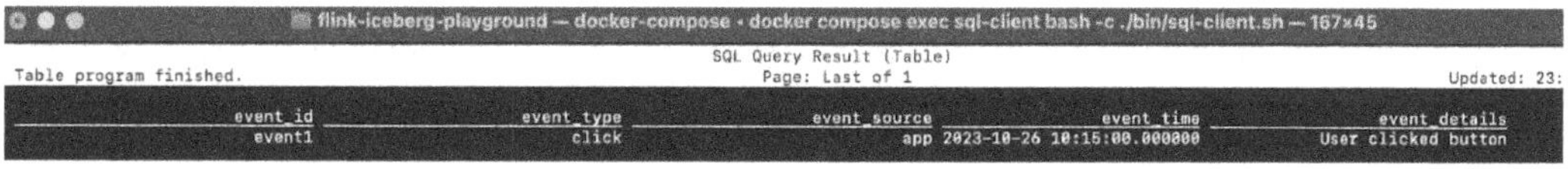

*Figure 3.11 – Snippet showing records read using Batch mode*

# Streaming reads

Iceberg also supports streaming reads in Flink, allowing you to process *incremental* data starting from a specific snapshot ID. This mode is especially valuable for applications that need to react to new data in real time:

```
SET execution.runtime-mode = streaming;
SET table.dynamic-table-options.enabled=true;
SELECT * FROM user_activities /*+ OPTIONS('streaming'='true', 'monitor-
interval'='1s') */;
```

Here is the output:

*Figure 3.12 – Snippet showing records read using Streaming mode*

This query reads all records from the current snapshot in the user_activities table and then continuously monitors for new data in the set interval of 1s, reading incremental changes as they are committed to the table.

This section demonstrated how to set up Flink SQL with Iceberg, configure catalogs, create databases and tables, and perform read/write operations. Integrating Apache Flink with Iceberg allows users to build real-time data pipelines that support low-latency analytics, all within an open lakehouse architecture.

Lakehouse formats are primarily designed for distributed environments, with compute engines such as Spark and prerequisites such as Java, Hadoop, and so on to handle data at scale. However, there's also a growing demand for single-node access to Lakehouse tables for lightweight tasks, such as ad hoc querying and exploratory data analysis. This access is also valuable in data science and machine learning workflows, where fast, direct access to datasets is crucial for quick insights and experimentation. Single-node engines such as *PyIceberg*, *DuckDB*, and *Daft* provide efficient, single-node solutions for working with Iceberg tables without the overhead of JVM-based systems.

# PyIceberg

PyIceberg is a Python-based API that enables users to interact with Iceberg tables directly, without the need for a JVM, offering simplicity and ease of use in Python-centric data workflows.

## Installation

To install the latest release of PyIceberg with optional dependencies, you can use the following:

```
pip install "pyiceberg[s3fs,sql-sqlite]"
```

You can customize the installation by adding optional dependencies based on your catalog and file storage needs. For example, To fetch files from an object store, you'll need at least one of s3fs, adlfs, gcsfs, or pyarrow installed, depending on the storage service you're using.

Other dependencies include pyarrow, numpy, and pandas.

## Connecting to a catalog

Catalog connection is the first step in any Iceberg setup. PyIceberg supports various catalog implementations, including the traditional Hive catalog, AWS Glue, DynamoDB, and Iceberg's REST catalog protocol. For our examples, we'll configure a SqlCatalog implementation, which stores metadata in a local *SQLite* database and data files in the local filesystem.

First, create a directory to store Iceberg data and metadata files:

```
mkdir /tmp/warehouse
```

Then configure the catalog with PyIceberg.

```
from pyiceberg.catalog.sql import SqlCatalog
warehouse_path = "/tmp/warehouse"
catalog = SqlCatalog(
    "default",
    **{
        "uri": f"sqlite:///{warehouse_path}/pyiceberg_catalog.db",
        "warehouse": f"file://{warehouse_path}",
    },
)
```

This configuration allows you to explore PyIceberg's features locally.

If you already have a catalog configured and want to just load the tables, you can do so using the load_table API as shown:

```
from pyiceberg.catalog import load_catalog
catalog_dev = load_catalog(
    "docs",
    {"uri": f"sqlite:///{warehouse_path}/pyiceberg_catalog.db"}
)
cust_table = catalog_dev.load_table("default.customer")
```

## Create table and insert records

Now that we have the catalog configured, we are good to create our first Iceberg table using PyIceberg. Let's do so by loading data from a sample PyArrow DataFrame. In this example, we'll use the Taxi dataset for January 2023 to demonstrate the process.

Let's begin by downloading a sample dataset in Parquet format:

```
curl https://d37ci6vzurychx.cloudfront.net/trip-data/yellow_
tripdata_2023-01.parquet -o /tmp/yellow_tripdata_2023-01.parquet
```

Use PyArrow to load the Parquet data into a DataFrame, which we'll later write to the Iceberg table:

```
import pyarrow.parquet as pq
# Read the Parquet file into a PyArrow Table
df = pq.read_table("/tmp/yellow_tripdata_2023-01.parquet")
```

We will use pyiceberg.schema.Schema and NestedField to create an Iceberg-compatible schema. Let's define each field's data type, ensuring compatibility with Iceberg:

```
from pyiceberg.schema import Schema, NestedField
from pyiceberg.types import LongType, TimestampType, DoubleType,
StringType
iceberg_schema = Schema(
    NestedField(id=1, name="VendorID", field_type=LongType(),
required=False),
    NestedField(id=2, name="tpep_pickup_datetime", field_
type=TimestampType(), required=False),
    NestedField(id=3, name="tpep_dropoff_datetime", field_
type=TimestampType(), required=False),
```

```
    NestedField(id=4, name="passenger_count", field_type=DoubleType(),
required=False),
    NestedField(id=5, name="trip_distance", field_type=DoubleType(),
required=False),
    NestedField(id=6, name="RatecodeID", field_type=DoubleType(),
required=False),
    NestedField(id=7, name="store_and_fwd_flag", field_type=StringType(),
required=False),
    NestedField(id=8, name="PULocationID", field_type=LongType(),
required=False),
    NestedField(id=9, name="DOLocationID", field_type=LongType(),
required=False),
    NestedField(id=10, name="payment_type", field_type=LongType(),
required=False),
    NestedField(id=11, name="fare_amount", field_type=DoubleType(),
required=False),
    NestedField(id=12, name="extra", field_type=DoubleType(),
required=False),
    NestedField(id=13, name="mta_tax", field_type=DoubleType(),
required=False),
    NestedField(id=14, name="tip_amount", field_type=DoubleType(),
required=False),
    NestedField(id=15, name="tolls_amount", field_type=DoubleType(),
required=False),
    NestedField(id=16, name="improvement_surcharge", field_
type=DoubleType(), required=False),
    NestedField(id=17, name="total_amount", field_type=DoubleType(),
required=False),
    NestedField(id=18, name="congestion_surcharge", field_
type=DoubleType(), required=False),
    NestedField(id=19, name="airport_fee", field_type=DoubleType(),
required=False)
)
```

We will then use our `sqlite` catalog to create a namespace and the Iceberg table with the specified schema. The API is `create_table`:

```
catalog.create_namespace("default")
# Create the table in the "default" namespace with the defined schema
table_ice = catalog.create_table(
```

```
        "default.taxi_dataset_ice",
        schema=iceberg_schema
    )
```

Once the Iceberg table is created, we can add data from the PyArrow DataFrame to the Iceberg table:

```
    table_ice.append(df)
```

This loads the data from the Taxi dataset into the `default.taxi_dataset_ice` Iceberg table in the catalog.

## Read queries

To retrieve data from an Iceberg table in PyIceberg, you perform a table scan. A table scan allows you to filter data, select specific columns, limit the number of results, or read data from a specific snapshot. Once you scan the records, you can then read the records directly using other single node compute such as *PyArrow*, *pandas*, *DuckDB*, and so on.

Start by specifying the filters, columns, limit, and snapshot ID (if required) for the scan. In this example, we'll filter records where `trip_distance` is greater than or equal to 10 and select specific columns from the table:

```
from pyiceberg.expressions import GreaterThanOrEqual
scan = ice_table.scan(
    row_filter=GreaterThanOrEqual("trip_distance", 10.0),
    selected_fields=("VendorID", "tpep_pickup_datetime", "tpep_dropoff_
datetime"),
    limit=100,
)
```

### Read in Apache Arrow format

PyIceberg supports reading data directly into Apache Arrow (https://arrow.apache.org/), a columnar format, which is efficient for in-memory processing:

```
# Convert the scan results to an Arrow table
sc_record = scan.to_arrow()
sc_record
```

```
sc_record

pyarrow.Table
VendorID: int64
tpep_pickup_datetime: timestamp[us]
tpep_dropoff_datetime: timestamp[us]
----
VendorID: [[2,2,1,2,2,...,2,2,2,2,2]]
tpep_pickup_datetime: [[2023-01-01 00:27:12.000000,2023-01-01 00:09:29.000000,2023-01-01 00:13:30.000000,2023-01-01
00:41:41.000000,2023-01-01 00:22:39.000000,...,2023-01-01 00:56:24.000000,2023-01-01 00:55:38.000000,2023-01-01 00:
13:36.000000,2023-01-01 00:51:18.000000,2023-01-01 00:27:34.000000]]
tpep_dropoff_datetime: [[2023-01-01 00:49:56.000000,2023-01-01 00:29:23.000000,2023-01-01 00:44:00.000000,2023-01-0
1 01:19:32.000000,2023-01-01 01:30:45.000000,...,2023-01-01 01:26:29.000000,2023-01-01 01:25:34.000000,2023-01-01 0
0:48:23.000000,2023-01-01 01:11:18.000000,2023-01-01 01:05:05.000000]]
```

*Figure 3.13 – Snippet showing Iceberg records read using Apache Arrow*

## Read in pandas format

For Python users who prefer working with pandas, you can easily convert the Iceberg table to a pandas DataFrame:

```
# Convert the scan results to a Pandas DataFrame
sc_record_pandas = scan.to_pandas()
sc_record_pandas
```

```
sc_record_pandas = scan.to_pandas()
sc_record_pandas
```

|     | VendorID | tpep_pickup_datetime | tpep_dropoff_datetime |
|-----|----------|----------------------|------------------------|
| 0   | 2        | 2023-01-01 00:27:12  | 2023-01-01 00:49:56    |
| 1   | 2        | 2023-01-01 00:09:29  | 2023-01-01 00:29:23    |
| 2   | 1        | 2023-01-01 00:13:30  | 2023-01-01 00:44:00    |
| 3   | 2        | 2023-01-01 00:41:41  | 2023-01-01 01:19:32    |
| 4   | 2        | 2023-01-01 00:22:39  | 2023-01-01 01:30:45    |
| ... | ...      | ...                  | ...                    |
| 95  | 2        | 2023-01-01 00:56:24  | 2023-01-01 01:26:29    |
| 96  | 2        | 2023-01-01 00:55:38  | 2023-01-01 01:25:34    |
| 97  | 2        | 2023-01-01 00:13:36  | 2023-01-01 00:48:23    |
| 98  | 2        | 2023-01-01 00:51:18  | 2023-01-01 01:11:18    |
| 99  | 2        | 2023-01-01 00:27:34  | 2023-01-01 01:05:05    |

100 rows × 3 columns

*Figure 3.14 – Snippet showing Iceberg records read using pandas*

We highly recommend exploring the PyIceberg documentation for other operations possible with Iceberg: https://py.iceberg.apache.org/.

# DuckDB

DuckDB is a lightweight, single-node SQL engine that's well-suited for analytical queries. It also has a concept of *extensions* that allows extending DuckDB's functionality and the ability to use additional file formats, new types, and so on. The Iceberg extension in DuckDB (https://duckdb. org/docs/extensions/iceberg.html) allows it to interact directly with Iceberg tables, enabling efficient, SQL-based querying without the need for a distributed computing cluster.

## Installation

DuckDB can be downloaded in different forms depending on the environment it is meant to be used for. For our exercises, we are using a command line (CLI) version of DuckDB (https:// duckdb.org/docs/installation/index?version=stable&environment=cli&platform=maco s&download_method=package_manager). To use DuckDB with Iceberg, you need to install and load the *Iceberg* extension:

```
INSTALL 'iceberg';
LOAD 'iceberg';
```

The extension supports both local and remote object stores, such as S3, when paired with DuckDB's httpfs extension for file system access over HTTP or S3.

## Read queries

Once the Iceberg extension is loaded, you can query Iceberg tables using standard SQL syntax. The iceberg_scan function allows users to read data directly from Iceberg tables by specifying the table path. Here is an example that queries an Iceberg table downloaded locally:

```
select * from iceberg_scan('/Users/dipankarmazumdar/Downloads/customers',
allow_moved_paths = true);
```

| customer_id int32 | first_name varchar | last_name varchar | email varchar | charges float | state varchar |
|---|---|---|---|---|---|
| 3 | Alice | Johnson | alice.j@samplemail.net | 250.0 | TX |
| 1 | John | Doe | john.doe@fakemail.co | 123.45 | CA |
| 5 | Eve | Davis | eve.davis@demoemail.com | 75.5 | WA |
| 2 | Jane | Smith | jane.smith@mockmail.org | 89.99 | NY |
| 4 | Bob | Brown | bob_brown@myemail.biz | 200.0 | FL |

*Figure 3.15 – Snippet showing Iceberg records read using DuckDB*

This fetches all records from the Iceberg table located at the specified path. DuckDB also allows more complex queries, including filtering, aggregations, and joins, making it versatile for analytical use cases.

For example, we can use conditional logic to create custom labels based on the charges amount:

```
SELECT first_name, last_name, charges,
        CASE WHEN charges > 150 THEN 'High spender'
            WHEN charges BETWEEN 100 AND 150 THEN 'Medium spender'
            ELSE 'Low spender' END AS spending_category
    FROM iceberg_scan('/Users/dipankarmazumdar/Downloads/customers', allow_
moved_paths = true);
```

Here is the result:

| first_name<br>varchar | last_name<br>varchar | charges<br>float | spending_category<br>varchar |
|---|---|---|---|
| Alice | Johnson | 250.0 | High spender |
| John | Doe | 123.45 | Medium spender |
| Eve | Davis | 75.5 | Low spender |
| Jane | Smith | 89.99 | Low spender |
| Bob | Brown | 200.0 | High spender |

*Figure 3.16 – Snippet shows complex queries executed on an Iceberg table using DuckDB*

## Read metadata

DuckDB also allows access to Iceberg metadata. For example, you can query the metadata of an Iceberg table to examine its snapshots, schema, or other metadata:

```
select * from iceberg_metadata('/Users/dipankarmazumdar/Downloads/
customers',allow_moved_paths = true);
```

| manifest_path<br>varchar | manifest_sequence_...<br>int64 | manifest_content<br>varchar | status<br>varchar | content<br>varchar | file_path<br>varchar | file_format<br>varchar | record_count<br>int64 |
|---|---|---|---|---|---|---|---|
| s3a://diplakehouse... | 2 | DATA | ADDED | EXISTING | s3a://diplakehouse/iceberg_boo... | PARQUET | 1 |
| s3a://diplakehouse... | 2 | DATA | EXISTING | EXISTING | s3a://diplakehouse/iceberg_boo... | PARQUET | 1 |
| s3a://diplakehouse... | 2 | DATA | EXISTING | EXISTING | s3a://diplakehouse/iceberg_boo... | PARQUET | 1 |
| s3a://diplakehouse... | 2 | DATA | EXISTING | EXISTING | s3a://diplakehouse/iceberg_boo... | PARQUET | 1 |
| s3a://diplakehouse... | 2 | DATA | DELETED | EXISTING | s3a://diplakehouse/iceberg_boo... | PARQUET | 1 |
| s3a://diplakehouse... | 2 | DATA | EXISTING | EXISTING | s3a://diplakehouse/iceberg_boo... | PARQUET | 1 |

*Figure 3.17 – Snippet shows reading metadata of an Iceberg table using DuckDB*

The example shows the manifest path, operation status, and data file path, among other things:

```
SELECT *
    FROM iceberg_snapshots('/Users/dipankarmazumdar/Downloads/customers');
```

| sequence_number<br>uint64 | snapshot_id<br>uint64 | timestamp_ms<br>timestamp | manifest_list<br>varchar |
|---|---|---|---|
| 1 | 2711640443788239783 | 2024-11-03 23:55:1... | s3a://diplakehouse/iceberg_book/customers/metadata/snap-2711640443788239783-1-6c04d... |
| 2 | 5886256132005027082 | 2024-11-05 04:49:5... | s3a://diplakehouse/iceberg_book/customers/metadata/snap-5886256132005027082-1-32c5a... |

*Figure 3.18 – Snippet shows reading Iceberg snapshots using DuckDB*

Here is another one that fetches all the snapshot related details for the Iceberg table.

> DuckDB's Iceberg extension supports both reading and writing Iceberg tables (write support introduced in DuckDB v1.4.0; `UPDATE/DELETE` for Iceberg v2 tables available in v1.4.2).

# Daft

Daft is a unified compute engine that offers both Python and SQL-based APIs to cater to single node workloads locally, but also allows transitioning to run out-of-core on a distributed cluster. Daft integrates natively with Apache Iceberg, which enables high-performance reads and writes on Iceberg tables, taking advantage of Iceberg's advanced features, such as hidden partitioning and file-level statistics to optimize data access.

## Installation

To start using Daft, you'll need to install it via `pip`. Daft also enables tailoring the installation with additional dependencies, based on your use case. Here's how to get started.

To install the core Daft library, simply run the following:

```
pip install daft
```

There are several optional dependencies that enable integration with specific storage systems and compute backends. For example, to interact with AWS services, such as AWS S3, Daft allows you to install using this:

```
pip install -U "daft[aws]"
```

## Read queries

Daft depends on PyIceberg to enable the reading of Iceberg tables. You start by loading the table with PyIceberg and then using Daft to create a DataFrame from it. Once the data is in a Daft DataFrame, you can apply additional filters that benefit from Iceberg's optimizations:

```
from pyiceberg.catalog import load_catalog
import daft
# Load the Iceberg table through PyIceberg
catalog = load_catalog("my_iceberg_catalog")
ice_table = catalog.load_table("default.taxi_dataset_ice")
# Create a Daft DataFrame from the Iceberg table
```

```
df = daft.read_iceberg(ice_table)
# Apply a filter to optimize reads by leveraging Iceberg's partition
pruning
df_filtered = df.where(df["total_amount"] < 20)
df_filtered.show()
```

| VendorID Int64 | tpep_pickup_datetime Timestamp(Microseconds, None | tpep_dropoff_datetime Timestamp(Microseconds, None | passenger_count Float64 | trip_distance Float64 | RatecodeID Float64 | store_and_fwd_flag Utf8 | PULocationID Int64 | DOLo Int64 |
|---|---|---|---|---|---|---|---|---|
| 2 | 2023-01-01 00:32:10 | 2023-01-01 00:40:36 | 1 | 0.97 | 1 | N | 161 | 141 |
| 2 | 2023-01-01 00:55:08 | 2023-01-01 01:01:27 | 1 | 1.1 | 1 | N | 43 | 237 |
| 2 | 2023-01-01 00:10:29 | 2023-01-01 00:21:19 | 1 | 1.43 | 1 | N | 107 | 79 |
| 2 | 2023-01-01 00:39:42 | 2023-01-01 00:50:36 | 1 | 3.01 | 1 | N | 141 | 107 |
| 2 | 2023-01-01 00:53:01 | 2023-01-01 01:01:45 | 1 | 1.8 | 1 | N | 234 | 68 |
| 2 | 2023-01-01 00:13:04 | 2023-01-01 00:22:10 | 1 | 1.52 | 1 | N | 79 | 186 |
| 1 | 2023-01-01 00:03:36 | 2023-01-01 00:09:36 | 3 | 1.2 | 1 | N | 237 | 239 |
| 1 | 2023-01-01 00:51:45 | 2023-01-01 00:58:18 | 1 | 1.4 | 1 | N | 137 | 79 |

(Showing first 8 rows)

*Figure 3.19 – Snippet shows reading Iceberg data using Daft*

Here, Daft reads from the Iceberg `taxi_dataset_ice table` and loads records where `total_amount` is less than 20. This filter is optimized by Iceberg's file-level statistics, so only relevant data is scanned.

## Write data

To write data to an Iceberg table with Daft, you can use Daft's `write_iceberg` method. This allows you to easily append new records to an existing Iceberg table.

```
import daft
from datetime import datetime

new_data = {
    "VendorID": [1, 2],
    "tpep_pickup_datetime": [datetime(2023, 1, 1, 10, 0, 0),
datetime(2023, 1, 2, 11, 0, 0)],
    "tpep_dropoff_datetime": [datetime(2023, 1, 1, 10, 30, 0),
datetime(2023, 1, 2, 11, 20, 0)],
    "passenger_count": [1.0, 2.0],
    "trip_distance": [2.5, 5.0],
    "RatecodeID": [1.0, 2.0],
    "store_and_fwd_flag": ["N", "Y"],
    "PULocationID": [123, 789],
    "DOLocationID": [456, 101],
```

```
        "payment_type": [1, 2],
        "fare_amount": [15.0, 25.0],
        "extra": [0.5, 1.0],
        "mta_tax": [0.5, 0.5],
        "tip_amount": [2.0, 3.5],
        "tolls_amount": [0.0, 5.0],
        "improvement_surcharge": [0.3, 0.3],
        "total_amount": [18.3, 35.3],
        "congestion_surcharge": [0.0, 0.0],
        "airport_fee": [0.0, 1.0]
}
df_new_rec = daft.from_pydict(new_data)
written_df = df_new_rec.write_iceberg(ice_table, mode="append")
written_df.show()
```

**written_df.show()**

| operation Utf8 | rows Int64 | file_size Int64 | file_name Utf8 |
|---|---|---|---|
| ADD | 2 | 7739 | file:///tmp/warehouse/default.db/tax` eeb3-4373-a2d3-339a99c1f104-0.parquet |

(Showing first 1 of 1 rows)

*Figure 3.20 – Snippet shows writing to Iceberg table using Daft*

This adds the two new records to the existing Iceberg table.

# Summary

In this chapter, we explored the architecture of Apache Iceberg, breaking down its essential components that collectively provide the foundation for a resilient and scalable lakehouse solution. By understanding these components and their interplay, we gained insights into how Iceberg supports critical features such as ACID transactions, time travel, and schema evolution. Through practical hands-on examples with various compute engines and catalogs, we demonstrated how to use Iceberg's capabilities to meet the demands of modern data processing. In *Chapter 4, Apache Hudi Deep Dive*, we will explore Apache Hudi, which is another open table format that enables building a lakehouse architecture.

## Get This Book's PDF Version and Exclusive Extras

**UNLOCK NOW**

Scan the QR code (or go to packtpub.com/unlock). Search for this book by name, confirm the edition, and then follow the steps on the page.

*Note: Keep your invoice handy. Purchases made directly from Packt don't require an invoice.*

# 4

# Apache Hudi Deep Dive

Apache Hudi is an open source data lake framework that adds transactional capabilities and data management features to data lakes. This architecture is designed to handle large-scale data ingestion and processing while enabling users to perform updates, deletions, and incremental data processing pulls efficiently. At the heart of Hudi's architecture is its integration with various storage and compute engines, such as Apache Spark, Flink, and Presto. The architecture supports both **Copy-on-Write (CoW)** and **Merge-on-Read (MoR)** table types, which provide flexibility in balancing query performance and write efficiency.

In this chapter, we will cover the following topics:

- Hudi's architecture and metadata layer, including file slices and catalog integration with Hive and AWS Glue
- Core functionalities such as row-level updates, deletes, schema evolution, and real-time ingestion using Hudi Streamer
- Practical exercises with Spark, covering write/read operations, Hive or Glue syncing, and advanced queries such as snapshot, time travel, and **Change Data Capture (CDC)**
- Working with Flink to perform setup, SQL operations, catalog synchronization, and DDL/DML tasks

- Table services that manage compaction, clustering, file sizing, and orphan file cleanup
- Essential configurations for disaster recovery, rollback, and effective table management

By the end of this chapter, you will have gained a thorough understanding of Apache Hudi's architecture, capabilities, and unique features, along with practical examples using Spark and Flink.

## Technical requirements

To try out the examples listed later in this chapter, you need to install these components:

- Spark 3.x
- Java
- Download the required packages:
    - Python libraries
    - `pip install pyspark findspark`

You can find all of the examples in a Docker container in the repository to follow along.

## Architecture

Apache Hudi defines a table format that organizes the data and metadata files within distributed storage engines. Hudi structures data within a directory hierarchy under a designated base path, which serves as the root directory for a Hudi table. The base path includes a reserved directory named `.hoodie`, which holds transaction logs and metadata. Additionally, the `hoodie.properties` file stores table-level configurations that both writers and readers use. Data files are stored within partition paths for partitioned tables, or under the base path for non-partitioned tables.

*Figure 4.1* depicts a typical data layout of a Hudi table under the table's base path in storage.

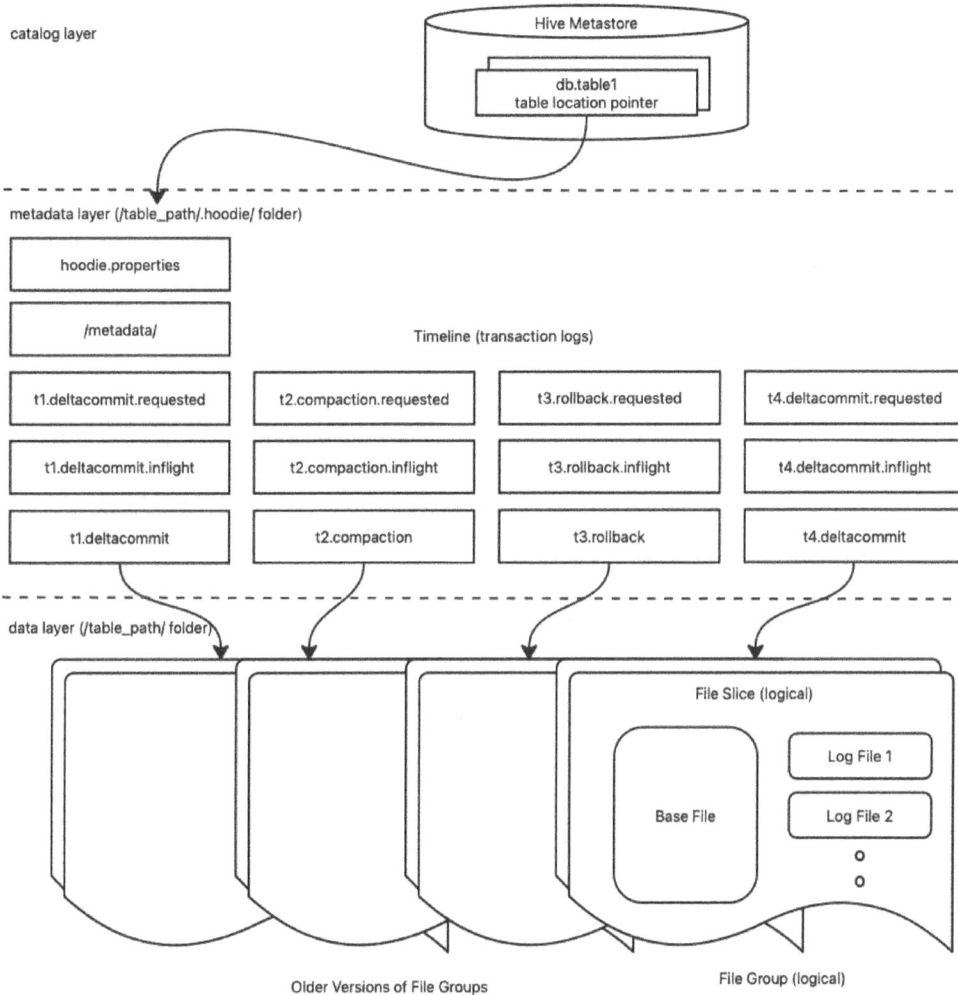

*Figure 4.1 – Hudi file layout architecture*

Hudi's architecture provides a structured and consistent layout for managing both data and metadata. By organizing files under the base path and maintaining a dedicated `.hoodie` directory with transaction logs and configuration properties, Hudi ensures reliable data ingestion, updates, and reads while supporting efficient table management.

## Metadata layer

Hudi relies heavily on metadata to track changes, manage concurrency, and ensure data consistency within the lakehouse. This metadata resides under the `.hoodie` directory within the Hudi table's base path.

## Core metadata files

Hudi maintains several core metadata files that define the structure, configuration, and operational history of a table. These files enable Hudi to efficiently manage data versions, transactions, and timeline events. The key metadata files include the following:

- `hoodie.properties`: This file acts as the central configuration hub for the Hudi table. It stores vital information such as the table name, version, and other critical settings used by both writers and readers interacting with the table.

- **Timeline metadata files**: These files, following a specific naming pattern, record the history of actions performed on the Hudi table. They form the backbone of the Hudi table's "timeline." Here's a breakdown of the naming pattern:

  ```
  <action timestamp>.<action type>[.<action state>]:
  ```

  - `<action timestamp>`: This timestamp indicates the precise moment an action was first scheduled to run. It acts as a unique identifier for that action within the timeline and ensures a monotonically increasing order across different actions.

  - `<action type>`: This element specifies the type of change made by the action. Common action types include the following:

    - `commit`: Represents a new write operation involving inserts, updates, or deletes within the table.

    - `deltacommit`: Similar to `commit` but often used for incremental updates.

    - `compaction`: This action optimizes data organization within the table for improved query performance.

    - `clean`: This action removes obsolete data versions to manage storage space efficiently.

    - `savepoint`: This action creates a snapshot of the table state at a specific point in time, enabling recovery in case of failures.

    - `restore`: This action restores the table state from a previously created savepoint.

  - `<action state>`: This optional element indicates the current stage of the action:

    - `requested`: The action is scheduled to run.

    - `inflight`: The action is currently being executed.

    - `completed` (no suffix): The action has finished successfully.

Following is an example of an excerpt of a committed metadata file:

```
{
  "partitionToWriteStats" : {
    "datestr=2024-10-30" : [ {
      "fileId" : "0596a8fa-0936-43f3-86f2-a98ae10c610e-0",
      "path" : "datestr=2024-10-30/0596a8fa-0936-43f3-86f2-a98ae10c61
0e-0_0-294-368_20241030061457804.parquet",
      "prevCommit" : "20241030060519522",
      "numWrites" : 14,
      "numDeletes" : 0,
      "numUpdateWrites" : 13,
      "numInserts" : 1,
      "totalWriteBytes" : 435648,
      "totalWriteErrors" : 0,
      "tempPath" : null,
      "partitionPath" : "datestr=2024-10-30",
      "totalLogRecords" : 0,
      "totalLogFilesCompacted" : 0,
      "totalLogSizeCompacted" : 0,
      "totalUpdatedRecordsCompacted" : 0,
      "totalLogBlocks" : 0,
      "totalCorruptLogBlock" : 0,
      "totalRollbackBlocks" : 0,
      "fileSizeInBytes" : 435648,
      "minEventTime" : null,
      "maxEventTime" : null
    } ]
  },
  "compacted" : false,
  "extraMetadata" : {
    "schema" : "{\"type\":\"record\",\"name\":\"upsert_partitioned_cow_ta-
ble_record\",\"namespace\":\"hoodie.upsert_partitioned_cow_table\",\"-
fields\":[{\"name\":\"id\",\"type\":[\"null\",\"string\"],\"default\
":null},{\"name\":\"name\",\"type\":[\"null\",\"string\"],\"default-
\":null},{\"name\":\"ts\",\"type\":[\"null\",{\"type\":\"long\",\"logical-
Type\":\"timestamp-micros\"}],\"default\":null},{\"name\":\"datestr\",\"-
type\":[\"null\",{\"type\":\"int\",\"logicalType\":\"date\"}],\"de-
fault\":null}]}"
```

```
    },
    "operationType" : "INSERT",
    "writePartitionPaths" : [ "datestr=2024-10-30" ],
    "fileIdAndRelativePaths" : {
      "0596a8fa-0936-43f3-86f2-a98ae10c610e-0" : "datestr=2024-10-30/0596a-
8fa-0936-43f3-86f2-a98ae10c610e-0_0-294-368_20241030061457804.parquet"
    },
    "totalRecordsDeleted" : 0,
    "totalLogRecordsCompacted" : 0,
    "totalLogFilesCompacted" : 0,
    "totalCompactedRecordsUpdated" : 0,
    "totalLogFilesSize" : 0,
    "totalScanTime" : 0,
    "totalCreateTime" : 0,
    "totalUpsertTime" : 2059,
    "minAndMaxEventTime" : {
      "Optional.empty" : {
        "val" : null,
        "present" : false
      }
    }
  }
}
```

Hudi commit files play a significant role in tracking the details of data writes within a Hudi table. These files contain comprehensive information about partitions, file paths, record counts, and metadata related to the write operations. Analyzing the commit files helps ensure data consistency and allows for operational insights, including write performance and error handling. Next, we will break down the key elements of a Hudi commit file based on the provided example.

**Partition write statistics**

The partitionToWriteStats field outlines write statistics for each partition involved in the commit. In this example, there is one partition (datestr=2024-10-30) with detailed statistics:

- **File ID**: Each file generated during the commit is identified by a unique ID, such as 0596a8fa-0936-43f3-86f2-a98ae10c610e-0.
- **Path**: Specifies the storage location of the written file, e.g., datestr=2024-10-30/0596a8fa-0936-43f3-86f2-a98ae10c610e-0_0-294-368_20241030061457804.parquet.

- **Previous commit**: Points to the previous commit ID (20241030060519522), ensuring the consistency of operations.

- **Write statistics**: Includes counts such as numWrites (14), numDeletes (0), numUpdateWrites (13), and numInserts (1), reflecting the nature of the data written.

- **File size**: The fileSizeInBytes field records the size of the file in bytes (435,648 bytes).

- **Error handling**: Attributes such as totalWriteErrors (0) indicate the number of errors encountered during the write process.

These partition write statistics give a complete snapshot of each partition's activity during a commit, capturing file details, write operations, and error counts to ensure data integrity and traceability.

## Compaction status

The compacted field indicates whether the commit has been compacted. In this case, the value is false, meaning no compaction has taken place yet.

## Schema information

The extraMetadata section contains the schema definition used during the write operation. This JSON-encoded schema outlines the structure of the records:

- **Schema name and namespace**: upsert_partitioned_cow_table_record under hoodie. upsert_partitioned_cow_table

- **Fields**: Specifies the column names (id, name, ts, datestr), their types, and default values

This schema information provides a clear definition of the table structure, ensuring consistent interpretation of records during writes and reads.

## Operation type

The operationType field specifies the type of operation performed during the commit. Here, it is INSERT, indicating that the commit added new data to the table. Other possible types are UPSERT, DELETE, and BULK_INSERT.

## Write partition paths

The writePartitionPaths field lists the partitions affected by this commit. In this example, data was written to the datestr=2024-10-30 partition.

### File ID and path mapping

The `fileIdAndRelativePaths` field maps each fileId to its corresponding relative path. This is similar to the manifest list in other table formats – for instance:

```
"0596a8fa-0936-43f3-86f2-a98ae10c610e-0" : "datestr=2024-10-30/0596a8fa-
0936-43f3-86f2-a98ae10c610e-0_0-294-368_20241030061457804.parquet"
```

This mapping provides a clear association between each file ID and its storage location, enabling efficient tracking and retrieval of data files within the table.

### Performance metrics

Several performance-related fields help evaluate the efficiency of the operation:

- **Total upsert time**: The `totalUpsertTime` recorded is 2,059 milliseconds, indicating the time taken for upsert operations
- **Scan and create time**: Fields such as `totalScanTime` and `totalCreateTime` provide additional details about the operation's execution time, although both are marked as 0 in this instance

These performance metrics offer insight into the efficiency of the operation, highlighting the time taken for upserts and other key execution steps.

### Event time details

The `minAndMaxEventTime` field provides insights into the range of event times captured in the commit. In this case, it is marked as `Optional.empty`, signifying no event times were recorded.

Hudi commit files offer valuable insights into write operations, including data distribution, operation type, performance metrics, and error handling. This detailed metadata enables robust data management, allowing for rollbacks, auditing, and optimization of subsequent operations.

## The importance of metadata

These metadata files, typically stored in JSON or Avro format, hold detailed information about the changes applied or intended to be applied to the table. Maintaining a record of these transactions offers several benefits:

- **Recreating table state**: With the transaction log, it's possible to reconstruct the table's state at any point in its history. This is crucial for recovery purposes or auditing data changes.

- **Snapshot isolation**: By keeping track of historical states, Hudi ensures snapshot isolation. This guarantees that readers always see a consistent view of the data, regardless of concurrent write operations.

- **Reconciling writer conflicts**: Hudi employs concurrency control mechanisms that leverage the metadata to identify and resolve potential conflicts arising from multiple writers modifying the same data concurrently.

The .hoodie directory contains additional metadata files and subdirectories beyond the preceding core elements described.

# Data layer

Hudi employs a two-tiered approach to data storage, categorizing physical data files into base files and log files. This dual-layer design optimizes both read and write operations, ensuring efficient data access and updates.

## Base files: The foundation

Base files serve as the primary storage for records within a Hudi table. They are optimized for read performance, often leveraging columnar file formats such as Apache Parquet. By storing data in a columnar format, Hudi enables efficient querying and filtering on specific columns.

## Log files: The change log

Log files capture incremental changes to the data stored in the corresponding base file. They are designed for efficient write operations and typically use row-based formats such as Apache Avro. As new data is written or existing data is updated or deleted, these changes are appended to the log files.

## File slices and file groups: Organizing data

To further optimize data management, Hudi organizes base files and their associated log files into logical units called file slices and file groups.

- **File slice**: A file slice comprises a single base file and its related log files. Each file slice is tied to a specific timestamp on the timeline, representing a snapshot of the data at that point in time.

- **File group**: Multiple file slices are grouped together into a file group. This grouping helps in efficient data access and management, especially during read operations.

By structuring data in this way, Hudi can do the following:

- **Achieve versioning**: The timeline, coupled with file slices, enables versioning. Each file slice represents a specific version of the data, allowing for time-travel queries and data recovery.

- **Optimize read and write performance**: Base files, optimized for read, provide fast access to historical data, while log files, optimized for write, ensure efficient data ingestion and updates.

- **Handle concurrency and conflict resolution**: Hudi's metadata management and conflict resolution mechanisms, along with the layered data storage, help in handling concurrent writes and ensuring data consistency.

In the subsequent Hudi table services section, we will dive deeper into the specific techniques Hudi employs to manage data, including compaction, cleaning, and other optimization strategies.

Beyond these components, Hudi's internal architecture is designed around key-based record management, indexing strategies, and timeline services. These design principles collectively power Hudi's transactional capabilities, incremental processing, and efficient upserts at scale.

## Design principles of Apache Hudi

Apache Hudi's architecture is built around three core design principles that enable its performance, scalability, and reliability in large-scale data lake environments:

- **Record-level indexing using keys**: Every record in Hudi is identified by a unique *record key*, partition path, and file ID triplet. This enables precise record-level updates and deletions, a capability that sets Hudi apart from other lakehouse table formats such as Iceberg and Delta Lake. Hudi's key-based model allows efficient upserts without rewriting entire partitions.

- **Timeline service and instant-based operations**: Hudi maintains a timeline of all operations (commits, compactions, cleanups) as "instants." This ensures data integrity and consistency across concurrent operations and provides the foundation for incremental pulls and time travel queries.

- **Modular storage and write model:** Hudi lets users choose between read-optimized (CoW) and write-optimized (MoR) layouts at the table level. CoW tables rewrite Parquet base files on updates, while MoR tables append changes to log files that are merged with base files at read or compaction time. Other table formats such as Iceberg and Delta Lake also implement CoW and MoR strategies via delete files or deletion vectors, but Hudi makes these modes first-class with purpose-built table services for compaction, clustering, and cleaning.

Together, these design principles ensure Hudi delivers efficient, consistent, and scalable data management, enabling precise updates, reliable operations, and flexible storage models for large-scale data lakes.

## Hudi's indexing mechanisms

Indexing plays a central role in enabling efficient upserts and deletes in Hudi tables. Each index maps a record key to its file location, allowing Hudi to locate and update records without scanning entire datasets. Hudi supports multiple types of indexing strategies, each optimized for specific workloads:

- **Bloom index (default)**: Uses Bloom filters embedded in Parquet footers to efficiently locate records within files. Ideal for moderately large datasets.

- **Simple index**: A lightweight option that uses file-name–based lookups for small to medium tables.

- **Global bloom index**: Extends the bloom index across partitions for non-partitioned or dynamically partitioned datasets.

- **HFile index**: Uses HBase's HFile format to provide fast, persistent lookups at scale.

- **Bucket index**: Partitions data by hashing record keys, providing predictable file mapping for high-throughput ingestion workloads.

These indexing mechanisms enable Hudi to perform *record-level mutations* efficiently, something that traditional data lakes and even other table formats struggle with at scale.

| Feature | Apache Hudi | Apache Iceberg | Delta Lake |
|---|---|---|---|
| Record/primary keys | Firstclass record keys required; used for indexing, dedup, incremental queries and table services | Optional primary keys/identifier fields for upserts; many tables are keyless | Optional primary keys/identifier fields for upserts; many tables are keyless |
| Index types | Pluggable recordkey indexes: Bloom (`local/global`), Simple (`local/global`), Bucket, `HFile/HBase`, Inmemory, plus metadatatable indexes (`files`, `column stats`, `recordlevel`) | Metadatadriven pruning via manifests (partition + column stats), with optional Puffin sidecar indexes; no general secondary indexes | Metadata and file-stats based data skipping from the transaction log, plus optional Bloom-filter and ZORDER–style data-skipping indexes on some platforms |

| | | Row-level deletes/ updates via equality/ position delete files and file rewrites (no primary-key index); engines combine file-level rewrites with row-level delete metadata | Row-level updates/ deletes via MERGE, UPDATE, DELETE; data is stored CoW-style with deletes/deletion vectors, so engines also combine file rewrites with row- level delete metadata |
|---|---|---|---|
| Update/delete mechanism | Key-based row-level upserts/deletes driven by writer-side indexes; CoW rewrites affected files, MoR writes changes to log files and merges later | | |
| Write models | Explicit CoW/MoR table types | CoW by default; MoR semantics via delete files and read-time mergin | CoW by default; MoR semantics via deletion vectors |

*Table 4.1 – Comparison of key features in Apache Hudi, Apache Iceberg, and Delta Lake*

All three table formats can express row-level updates and deletes. Hudi's differentiator is that **record keys are first-class** and are backed by writer-side indexes, so upserts are directed to the right file groups without scanning the whole table. Iceberg and Delta also support row-level changes, but they typically rely on **delete files or deletion vectors** rather than a primary-key index, so engines implement them by combining file-level rewrites with row-level delete metadata.

Once the Hudi table format and metadata architecture are established, these tables can be registered with external catalogs such as Hive or AWS Glue for discoverability and query federation. The internal .hoodie metadata and timeline are not a replacement for a shared catalog. In production deployments, Hudi tables are typically registered in Hive Metastore, AWS Glue, or another lakehouse catalog so engines can discover them, enforce permissions, and manage governance alongside tables stored in other formats such as Iceberg or Delta Lake, which we will cover in the next section.

## Catalog integration

Apache Hudi integrates with various catalogs, including Apache Hive, AWS Glue, and Google's BigQuery, to manage schema and table metadata efficiently. The catalog layer is vital for simplifying data access by serving as an abstraction layer that organizes and tracks datasets. By utilizing these catalogs, Hudi tables can be seamlessly discovered and incorporated into both read and write workflows. This integration ensures consistent schema enforcement and robust metadata management, which are essential for production-level deployments.

## Hive sync tool

**Hive Metastore (HMS)**, a component of Apache Hive, is an RDBMS-backed service that acts as a catalog for data warehouses and data lakes by storing table metadata, such as partition information, columns, and column types. Apache Hudi supports syncing table metadata with Hive Metastore, enabling the querying of Hudi tables through Hive and interactive query engines such as Apache Spark, Presto, and Trino.

Hudi provides support for HMS sync mode, JDBC mode, and other catalog options.

### HMS sync mode example

To sync a Hudi table using HMS mode, the following configuration is needed:

```
hoodie.datasource.meta.sync.enable=true
hoodie.datasource.hive_sync.mode=hms
hoodie.datasource.hive_sync.metastore.uris=thrift://hive-metastore:9083
```

### JDBC mode example

To sync a Hudi table using JDBC mode, use the following configuration:

```
hoodie.datasource.hive_sync.mode=jdbc
hoodie.datasource.hive_sync.jdbcurl=<jdbc:hive2://hiveserver:10000>
hoodie.datasource.hive_sync.username=<username>
hoodie.datasource.hive_sync.password=<password>
```

These configurations should be specified while creating the table.

# Apache Hudi features

Apache Hudi was designed with the needs of modern data lakes in mind, addressing specific challenges that arise with large-scale data management and streaming data pipelines. Its unique features help organizations manage data more efficiently and make real-time decisions based on the freshest data. Let's understand what these features are:

- **Incremental pulls**: One of Hudi's standout features is its ability to enable incremental data retrieval. With incremental queries, users can access only the data that has changed since the last time a query was run. This greatly reduces the overhead of full data scans, leading to faster and more resource-efficient data processing.

- **Data clustering**: To optimize query performance, Hudi supports data clustering, which organizes data records within files to enhance data locality. Clustering helps minimize query times by arranging records based on access patterns or other criteria, resulting in better storage efficiency and improved data retrieval.

- **Support for both batch and streaming workloads**: Hudi is designed to bridge the gap between batch processing and real-time streaming, supporting use cases that require continuous data ingestion along with traditional batch processing.

- **Transactional data lake operations**: With Hudi, users can perform insert, update, delete, and upsert operations on data within the data lake, mirroring capabilities typically found in databases but at the scale of distributed storage.

These features collectively enable Hudi to provide efficient, real-time, and scalable data management, making it easier to handle large-scale data lakes while supporting both batch and streaming workloads.

## Critical capabilities

Hudi's critical capabilities extend beyond simple data storage to offer advanced data management and querying functionalities. These capabilities provide strong support for scalable, reliable, and low-latency data operations:

- **Schema evolution**: Apache Hudi's flexible schema evolution capabilities allow users to make changes to data structures over time without sacrificing data integrity. This means data engineers can modify table schemas—such as adding or changing columns—without having to rewrite historical data or disrupt existing pipelines.

- **Time travel**: Time travel in Hudi enables users to query historical versions of data, providing the ability to analyze data as it was at specific points in time. This feature is essential for use cases involving auditing, data recovery, and compliance, as it allows teams to review and understand past data states.

- **ACID transactions**: Hudi ensures atomicity, consistency, isolation, and durability in data operations, providing reliable, database-like transactional guarantees within a distributed data lake environment.

These capabilities enable Hudi to efficiently manage large-scale data lakes, providing flexibility, historical insights, and transactional reliability for complex data operations.

# Row-level updates and deletes

Apache Hudi offers support for updating and deleting data at a granular level. This capability is essential for maintaining data consistency and supporting use cases such as GDPR compliance and data correction:

- **CoW**: In CoW tables, data updates result in new versions of entire data files, which simplifies reads since queries directly access the updated data files. Although this approach ensures straightforward query processing, it comes at the expense of slower write performance.

- **MoR**: MoR tables, on the other hand, record updates in delta log files and merge these with base data files during read operations. This strategy provides faster writes and lower latency updates, though it introduces additional complexity at read time as queries must combine base and log data.

These update and delete strategies allow Hudi to maintain data consistency while balancing read and write performance, supporting use cases that require precise, real-time data modifications.

# Schema evolution

Schema evolution is an essential aspect of data management, and Hudi supports schema evolution on write out of the box and experimental support for schema evolution on read.

**Schema evolution on write**: Hudi supports backwards-compatible schema evolution scenarios out of the box, such as adding a nullable field or promoting a field's data type. Furthermore, the evolved schema is queryable across high-performance engines such as Presto and Spark SQL without additional overhead for column ID translations or type reconciliations. The incoming schema will automatically have missing columns added with null values from the table schema. For this, we need to enable the following config: `hoodie.write.set.null.for.missing.columns=true`, otherwise the pipeline will fail.

**Schema evolution on read**: There are often scenarios where it's desirable to have the ability to evolve the schema more flexibly. Here are some examples:

- Columns (including nested columns) can be added, deleted, modified, and moved
- Renaming of columns (including nested columns)
- Add, delete, or perform operations on nested columns of the `Array` type

Hudi has experimental support for allowing backward-incompatible schema evolution scenarios on write while resolving them during read time. To enable this feature, `hoodie.schema.on.read. enable=true` needs to be set on the writer config (Datasource) or table property (SQL).

# Unique capabilities

Hudi distinguishes itself from other data lake solutions through a set of capabilities that are still rare or absent in other open table formats:

- **Database-like indexing subsystem**: Hudi ships with multiple writer-side indexes such as Bloom, Simple, Bucket, HBase/HFile-based, and record-level indexes backed by the metadata table. These indexes map record keys to file groups so upserts and deletes don't require scanning entire partitions, and they can now be built and maintained asynchronously.

- **Efficient MoR design**: Hudi's MoR tables store changes in compact log files alongside Parquet base files, grouped into file slices. Queries merge base + log data only where needed, giving near real-time freshness with lower write amplification than pure CoW, while periodic compaction keeps reads fast. Recent comparisons show meaningful differences in how MoR is implemented across Hudi, Iceberg, and Delta.

- **Built-in table services**: Hudi includes production-ready services for compaction, **clustering, cleaning, rollback, archival, indexing**, and **admin tooling**. These services are part of the project itself and are designed to be idempotent and schedulable alongside ingestion jobs, so you don't have to hand-roll maintenance workflows.

- **Robust concurrency control for the lake**: Hudi combines **MVCC, optimistic concurrency control**, and **external lock providers** (Hive Metastore, Zookeeper, etc.) to support multi-writer workloads and table services running concurrently with ingestion. The concurrency model is tuned for streaming and write-heavy lakehouse workloads rather than just batch analytics.

Together, these capabilities make Hudi feel closer to a **lakehouse database** than a thin table format: the project provides not only a storage layout but also the indexing, concurrency, and maintenance machinery needed to operate primary-key tables at scale.

# Hudi Streamer

The Hudi Streamer utility is a robust, production-grade data ingestion tool tailored for building and managing pipelines for Hudi tables. Integrated within `hudi-utilities-slim-bundle` and `hudi-utilities-bundle`, Hudi Streamer is a Spark-based application offering extensive configurability and seamless integration with diverse data sources, such as **distributed file systems (DFS)** or Kafka. Its unique capabilities include the following:

- **Guaranteed exactly-once ingestion**: Ensures accurate and reliable ingestion of new events from Kafka, incremental imports from tools such as Sqoop, or data pulled via `HiveIncrementalPuller` or `DFS` directories

- **Broad data format support**: Handles incoming data in JSON, Avro, or custom record formats

- **Advanced management features**: Facilitates checkpointing, rollback, and recovery mechanisms to maintain data integrity

- **Schema compatibility**: Utilizes Avro schemas from DFS or the Confluent schema registry for flexible and consistent data schema management

- **Custom transformations**: Allows users to integrate custom transformation logic during ingestion

With its flexible interfaces for configuring source data, defining schemas, scheduling table services, and synchronizing data catalogs, Hudi Streamer empowers teams to efficiently and confidently manage complex data pipelines.

By understanding these concepts, you will gain a thorough understanding of how Apache Hudi balances real-time data processing, efficient storage management, and robust querying capabilities. These features make Hudi an adaptable and powerful solution for modern data lake architectures that require both real-time data ingestion and complex data management.

> To read more about Hudi's differentiators relative to Iceberg and Delta Lake, see the
> *21 Unique Reasons Why Apache Hudi Should Be Your Next Data Lakehouse* blog on the
> Hudi website at https://hudi.apache.org/blog/2025/03/05/hudi-21-unique-differentiators/

# Hands-on with Apache Hudi and Apache Spark

In this section, we will explore practical exercises with Apache Hudi, utilizing Apache Spark as the compute engine. You'll receive a detailed, step-by-step guide on setting up, managing, and working with Hudi tables. By the end, you'll have gained hands-on experience with Hudi's powerful features, such as syncing to various catalogs, performing data manipulations through DDL and DML operations, executing queries with time travel and schema evolution, and using advanced capabilities such as clustering and indexing. While most examples will use Spark's SQL API, we will also incorporate the Python (PySpark) API where applicable.

### Installation requirements

Before proceeding, make sure you have the following prerequisites in place, so the examples run without issues. You can also use the Docker setup in the repository for a preconfigured environment.

- Spark 3.x
- Java
- Downloading required packages (details in the next section)
- Python libraries: `pip install pyspark findspark`

You can find all of these examples in a Docker container in the repository (`https://github.com/PacktPublishing/Engineering-Lakehouses-with-Open-Table-Formats/tree/main/ch04`) to follow along.

# Write and read operations with Spark and Hudi

This introductory section provides a comprehensive guide to the key configurations required for working with `Apache Hudi` tables, including setting up the compute engine and catalog sync. With these foundational setups in place, we'll explore the diverse read and write operations that Hudi supports.

This section offers a concise overview of Apache Hudi's capabilities with Spark. Leveraging Spark Data Source APIs in Python and Spark SQL, we'll explore code snippets demonstrating how to perform inserts, updates, deletes, and queries on a Hudi table.

## Getting the required packages

To get started with Apache Hudi and Spark, you'll need to include key dependencies and configurations that enable Hudi's integration with Spark for reading, writing, and managing Hudi tables. Following is a breakdown of the essential requirements and their roles:

## Supported Spark versions

Hudi supports Spark versions 2.4.3+ and all 3.x releases, with compatibility varying based on the Hudi version:

- **Hudi 0.15.x**: Compatible with Spark 3.5.x (default build), 3.4.x, 3.3.x, 3.2.x, 3.1.x, and 3.0.x
- The default build corresponds to the Spark version used to create `hudi-spark3-bundle`

Hudi provides broad Spark compatibility, allowing users to work with multiple Spark 3.x versions while ensuring that the default build aligns with the Spark version used for the bundle.

## Key configurations for Spark integration

To use Spark SQL with Hudi tables, you must configure Spark with the necessary extensions and bundles. For Spark 3.2 and above, the setup includes the following:

- **Dependency package** (org.apache.hudi:hudi-spark$SPARK_VERSION-bundle_2.12:0.15.0): This package provides runtime support for Spark and Hudi operations, where $SPARK_VERSION is the Spark version (e.g., 3.5, 3.4, 3.3, or 3.2):

```
spark-sql \
--packages org.apache.hudi:hudi-spark$SPARK_VERSION-
bundle_2.12:0.15.0 \
--conf 'spark.serializer=org.apache.spark.serializer.KryoSerializer'
\
--conf 'spark.sql.extensions=org.apache.spark.sql.hudi.
HoodieSparkSessionExtension' \
--conf 'spark.sql.catalog.spark_catalog=org.apache.spark.sql.hudi.
catalog.HoodieCatalog' \
--conf 'spark.kryo.registrator=org.apache.spark.
HoodieSparkKryoRegistrar'
```

- **SQL extensions**: HoodieSparkSessionExtension must be added to spark.sql.extensions to enable Hudi-specific SQL syntax. This allows you to perform operations such as table creation, updates, and schema modifications directly using Spark SQL.

- **Catalog configuration**: Add spark.sql.catalog.spark_catalog=org.apache.spark.sql.hudi.catalog.HoodieCatalog to ensure Hudi tables are managed and queried through the Spark catalog seamlessly.

These configurations allow Spark to interact effectively with Hudi, leveraging its advanced capabilities for incremental data processing, table versioning, and efficient data ingestion.

## Syncing to catalogs

Apache Hudi provides a versatile HiveSyncTool for synchronizing Hudi table metadata with various catalogs, including Hive Metastore, AWS Glue Data Catalog, and even Iceberg REST catalogs. In this section, we will demonstrate how to sync Hudi tables with two widely used production catalogs: Hive Metastore and AWS Glue Data Catalog.

## Syncing Hudi tables with Hive Metastore

Hive Metastore is a metadata service that stores detailed information about tables, including schema, partitions, and column data types. Synchronizing Hudi tables with Hive Metastore enables querying through Hive as well as interactive engines such as `Presto` and `Trino`.

### Prerequisites

Before running the example below, ensure you have a properly configured Hive Metastore, with the `hive-site.xml` file placed under `$SPARK_HOME/conf` so Spark can correctly point to it.

Assume the following:

- HiveServer2 runs on port 10000
- Hive Metastore runs on port 9083

Python example: Syncing a Hudi table to `Hive Metastore`:

```python
from pyspark.sql import SparkSession
from pyspark.sql.types import StructType, StructField, StringType,
LongType, IntegerType
spark = SparkSession.builder \
    .appName("Hudi Hive Sync Example") \
.config("spark.serializer", "org.apache.spark.serializer.KryoSerializer")
\
    .config("spark.sql.extensions", "org.apache.spark.sql.hudi.
HoodieSparkSessionExtension") \
    .config("spark.sql.catalog.spark_catalog", "org.apache.spark.sql.hudi.
catalog.HoodieCatalog") \
    .getOrCreate()

# Table properties
database_name = "my_db"
table_name = "hudi_cow"
base_path = "/user/hive/warehouse/hudi_cow"

# Define schema
schema = StructType([
    StructField("rowId", StringType(), True),
    StructField("partitionId", StringType(), True),
    StructField("preComb", LongType(), True),
```

```
    StructField("name", StringType(), True),
    StructField("versionId", StringType(), True),
    StructField("toBeDeletedStr", StringType(), True),
    StructField("intToLong", IntegerType(), True),
    StructField("longToInt", LongType(), True)
])


# Sample data
data = [
    ("row_1", "2021/01/01", 0, "bob", "v_0", "toBeDel0", 0, 1000000),
    ("row_2", "2021/01/01", 0, "john", "v_0", "toBeDel0", 0, 1000000),
    ("row_3", "2021/01/02", 0, "tom", "v_0", "toBeDel0", 0, 1000000)
]


df = spark.createDataFrame(data, schema=schema)

# Write Hudi table and sync with Hive
df.write.format("hudi") \
    .option("hoodie.datasource.write.precombine.field", "preComb") \
    .option("hoodie.datasource.write.recordkey.field", "rowId") \
    .option("hoodie.datasource.write.partitionpath.field", "partitionId")
\
    .option("hoodie.database.name", database_name) \
    .option("hoodie.table.name", table_name) \
    .option("hoodie.datasource.write.table.type", "COPY_ON_WRITE") \
    .option("hoodie.datasource.write.hive_style_partitioning", "true") \
    .option("hoodie.datasource.meta.sync.enable", "true") \
    .option("hoodie.datasource.hive_sync.mode", "hms") \
    .option("hoodie.datasource.hive_sync.metastore.uris", "thrift://hive-
metastore:9083") \
    .mode("overwrite") \
    .save(base_path)
```

Alternatively, to use JDBC sync mode instead of HMS, replace the sync configurations with the following:

```
.option("hoodie.datasource.hive_sync.mode", "jdbc") \
.option("hoodie.datasource.hive_sync.jdbcurl", "jdbc:hive2://
hiveserver:10000") \
```

```
.option("hoodie.datasource.hive_sync.username", "<username>") \
.option("hoodie.datasource.hive_sync.password", "<password>")
```

With these prerequisites in place and the Hive Metastore correctly configured, you can success-fully write and sync Hudi tables to Hive, ensuring seamless integration and accurate data tracking.

## Syncing Hudi tables with AWS Glue Data Catalog

AWS Glue serves as a fully managed metadata catalog, allowing Hudi tables to sync directly via AwsGlueCatalogSyncTool, which leverages configurations from HiveSyncTool. This integration works seamlessly within AWS EMR or Glue job environments.

### Additional configurations for Glue

Use AwsGlueCatalogSyncTool for metadata syncing:

```
.option("hoodie.meta.sync.client.tool.class", "org.apache.hudi.aws.sync.
AwsGlueCatalogSyncTool")
```

Avoid excessive catalog versions by enabling conditional meta-sync:

```
.option("hoodie.datasource.meta_sync.condition.sync", "true")
```

Optimize sync with parallelism configurations:

```
.option("hoodie.datasource.meta.sync.glue.all_partitions_read_
parallelism", "4") \
.option("hoodie.datasource.meta.sync.glue.changed_partitions_read_
parallelism", "4") \
.option("hoodie.datasource.meta.sync.glue.partition_change_parallelism",
"4")
```

By syncing with Glue, Hudi tables remain updated in AWS environments, supporting a range of analytics workflows.

With these examples, you can configure Hudi to sync table metadata across diverse catalogs, enabling efficient querying and management within both on-premises and cloud environments.

## DDL statements

With the catalog configured, we can now define and create tables using standard SQL **Data Defi-nition Language (DDL)** operations.

## CREATE TABLE

You can create tables using standard CREATE TABLE syntax, which supports partitioning and passing table properties:

```
CREATE TABLE [IF NOT EXISTS] [db_name.]table_name
  [(col_name data_type [COMMENT col_comment], ...)]
  [COMMENT table_comment]
  [PARTITIONED BY (col_name, ...)]
  [ROW FORMAT row_format]
  [STORED AS file_format]
  [LOCATION path]
  [TBLPROPERTIES (property_name=property_value, ...)]
  [AS select_statement];
```

To begin, we'll create a Hudi table. For demonstration purposes, we'll use a partitioned table, but note that Hudi also supports non-partitioned tables:

```
CREATE TABLE hdfs_catalog.default.customers (
        customer_id INT,
        first_name STRING,
        last_name STRING,
        email STRING,
        charges FLOAT,
        state STRING
    )
    USING hudi
    PARTITIONED BY (state)
```

This command creates a table in the default namespace of hdfs_catalog with state as the partitioning field. Partitioning on state, will allow efficient data pruning by partition, as Hudi will organize data within each state, optimizing queries that filter by this column.

Alternatively, you can achieve the same using PySpark's DataFrame API, as you saw in the *Syncing to catalogs* section.

## CREATE TABLE AS SELECT (CTAS)

CTAS, or `CREATE TABLE AS SELECT`, allows you to create a new Hudi table based on the results of a query. This is particularly useful for materializing complex queries directly as tables. This command creates a new `high_value_customers` table with data from customers where charges exceed 1000:

```
CREATE TABLE hdfs_catalog.high_value_customers
    USING hudi
    PARTITIONED BY (state)
AS SELECT
    customer_id, first_name, last_name, state, charges
    FROM hdfs_catalog.customers
    WHERE charges > 1000
```

In PySpark, we can use the `DataFrame.write.format("hudi")` method to perform a CTAS operation by reading from an existing table and writing to a new one.

## DROP TABLE

`DROP TABLE` only removes the table from the catalog without deleting the underlying data files. To fully delete the table's data, you must use `DROP TABLE PURGE`.

Here's how to drop a table without deleting its data files:

```
DROP TABLE IF EXISTS hdfs_catalog.customers
```

Here's how to drop a table and delete its data files:

```
DROP TABLE IF EXISTS hdfs_catalog.customers PURGE
```

These commands check for the existence of the `customers` table and delete it if present.

## ALTER TABLE

Hudi's flexible schema evolution capabilities, enabled by its robust `ALTER TABLE` functionality, support a range of changes, including column modifications, table renames, and data type widening, ensuring seamless data adaptability without sacrificing integrity.

## Adding a column

Adding a column to a Hudi table allows you to introduce new data fields without impacting the historical schema. In this example, we'll add a phone_number column to the customers table:

```
ALTER TABLE hdfs_catalog.customers
ADD COLUMN phone_number STRING
```

Adding a column lets you extend the table schema without affecting existing data, enabling the inclusion of new information in a backward-compatible way.

## Renaming a column

Hudi allows renaming columns in the table schema. For example, in the following snippet, we change the charges column to total_spent:

```
ALTER TABLE hdfs_catalog.customers
RENAME COLUMN charges TO total_spent
```

Renaming a column updates the schema to reflect new naming conventions while preserving the underlying data and its integrity.

### Dropping a column

Dropping a column removes it from the table's schema, which can be useful for deprecating old fields that are no longer needed. For instance, if phone_number data is obsolete, we can drop this column:

```
ALTER TABLE hdfs_catalog.customers
DROP COLUMN phone_number
```

Dropping a column removes obsolete fields from the schema, helping maintain a clean and relevant table structure.

# DML statements

Apache Hudi provides full support for common DML operations in Spark, such as INSERT, MERGE INTO, INSERT OVERWRITE, DELETE FROM, and UPDATE. These operations enable efficient data modification in a table while ensuring consistency, even with concurrent reads and writes. Here, we'll cover each of the key DML operations with examples in Spark SQL.

## INSERT INTO

The INSERT INTO command appends new records to an existing Hudi table:

```
INSERT INTO hdfs_catalog.customers
VALUES (1, 'John', 'Doe', 'john.doe@example.com', 150.75, 'CA');
```

The INSERT INTO command allows you to add new records to a Hudi table while preserving existing data, making it a simple way to expand your dataset.

## MERGE INTO

The MERGE INTO operation, used for upserts, combines records from a source dataset into a target table, updating existing records and inserting new ones based on specified matching criteria. This is particularly useful for handling **slowly changing dimensions (SCDs)** or applying CDC updates in real-world scenarios. This MERGE INTO query updates the customers table by merging data from the updates source:

```
MERGE INTO hdfs_catalog.customers AS target
USING updates AS source
ON target.customer_id = source.customer_id
WHEN MATCHED THEN
  UPDATE SET *
WHEN NOT MATCHED THEN
  INSERT *
```

If a customer_id identifier exists in both tables (e.g., customer_id 2), the record in customers is updated to match updates. If there's no match (e.g., customer_id 4), a new record is inserted. This process ensures that customers reflect the latest data without duplicates or outdated entries.

## INSERT OVERWRITE

In Hudi, INSERT OVERWRITE allows you to replace data in a table or a specified partition with new query results. This operation is atomic, ensuring data consistency during the overwrite process. The scope of the overwrite—whether it applies to specific partitions or the entire table—depends on the table's partitioning scheme and Spark's partition overwrite mode. There are two partition overwrite modes—static and dynamic:

- **Static overwrite mode**: In static mode, Spark replaces partitions based on the PARTITION clause filter, which must reference existing table columns

- **Dynamic overwrite mode:** In dynamic mode, Spark replaces only the partitions that contain rows produced by the SELECT query, allowing more granular updates

```
-- Static Overwrite Mode: Overwrites only the "CA" partition
INSERT OVERWRITE hdfs_catalog.customers
PARTITION (state = 'CA')
SELECT customer_id, first_name, last_name, email, balance
FROM staging_updates
WHERE state = 'CA'
```

In this example, only the partition for state = 'CA' is overwritten with data from staging_updates:

```
-- Dynamic Overwrite Mode: Overwrites all partitions with data in the
query result
INSERT OVERWRITE customers_hudi_demo
SELECT customer_id, first_name, last_name, email, total_spent,
       phone_number, state
FROM staging_updates
GROUP BY customer_id, first_name, last_name, email, total_spent,
       phone_number, state
```

In this case, Spark overwrites any partitions with rows in the query result, such as state = 'CA' and state = 'NY', if they exist in the staging_updates table.

Although INSERT OVERWRITE is useful for fully replacing data, MERGE INTO is often preferred because it selectively rewrites only the necessary data files, making it more efficient and intuitive for targeted updates.

## DELETE FROM

The DELETE FROM command in Hudi allows you to delete records that match a specific condition. Hudi supports both partition-level and row-level deletions, which enables efficient deletion in large datasets. If the condition matches entire partitions, Hudi performs a metadata-only delete, making the operation faster by simply updating metadata without modifying data files. If the condition matches individual rows, Hudi will rewrite only the affected data files (via the CoW and MoR strategy discussed in the *Apache Hudi features* section).

## Row-level delete

This example deletes a single customer record where `customer_id` is 1:

```
DELETE FROM hdfs_catalog.customers
WHERE customer_id = 1;
```

Row-level deletes allow you to remove specific records from a Hudi table while preserving other data, ensuring precise data management.

## Partition-level delete

This example deletes all records for customers in the state of CA. If Hudi's partitioning is based on the `state` column, this deletion will be a metadata-only operation:

```
DELETE FROM hdfs_catalog.customers
WHERE state = 'CA';
```

Partition-level deletes enable efficient removal of entire partitions, often as a metadata-only operation, which helps maintain performance while cleaning up large datasets.

## UPDATE

The `UPDATE` command allows you to modify existing records in a Hudi table based on a condition. Hudi handles updates via two strategies, `CoW` and `MoR` tables by either creating new data files with the modified records or rewriting the updated records in a separate delete file. Here is a simple example that updates the charges for every customer for the CA state.

```
UPDATE hdfs_catalog.customers
SET charges = charges * 1.1
WHERE state = 'CA';
```

The `UPDATE` command lets you modify existing records in a Hudi table based on conditions, ensuring data remains current while maintaining consistency across the dataset.

## Read queries

To query data from a Hudi table, you can use standard `SQL SELECT` statements. Hudi allows Spark to perform snapshot-based reads, allowing for historical querying such as time-travel. Here are some examples.

## Snapshot query

Snapshot queries are the most commonly used query type for Hudi tables. Spark SQL supports snapshot queries on both COPY_ON_WRITE and MERGE_ON_READ tables. You can optimize query performance by configuring session properties, such as enabling data skipping and indexing, as shown:

```
-- Enable data skipping and column statistics
SET hoodie.enable.data.skipping=true;
SET hoodie.metadata.column.stats.enable=true;
SET hoodie.metadata.enable=true;

SELECT * FROM hdfs_catalog.customers
WHERE charges > 1.0 AND charges < 10.0;

-- Enable record-level indexing for point queries
SET hoodie.metadata.record.index.enable=true;

SELECT * FROM hdfs_catalog.customers
WHERE customer_id = 'c8abbe79-8d89-47ea-b4ce-4d224bae5bfa';
```

Snapshot queries provide a straightforward way to read the latest state of a Hudi table, and performance can be enhanced through data skipping, metadata, and indexing configurations.

## Time travel query

Time travel queries allow you to access the state of a table at a specific commit time, which is useful for debugging, auditing, or training machine learning models with data from a specific point in time. Use the AS OF syntax to execute these queries:

```
SELECT * FROM <table_name>
TIMESTAMP AS OF '<timestamp in yyyy-MM-dd HH:mm:ss.SSS or yyyy-MM-dd or
yyyyMMddHHmmssSSS>'
WHERE <filter_conditions>;
```

Time travel queries enable accessing historical table states at specific commit times, supporting auditing, debugging, and analyses based on past data.

## Change Data Capture (CDC) query

CDC queries provide all changes to a Hudi table within a specified time window, including before/after images and the type of change operation. Hudi allows flexible control over supplemental logging levels through the `hoodie.table.cdc.supplemental.logging.mode` configuration, balancing storage, logging, and compute costs.

```
-- Retrieve changes using the `hudi_table_changes` table-valued function
(TVF)
SELECT *
FROM hudi_table_changes(
  <pathToTable | tableName>,
  'cdc',
  <'earliest' | <start_time>>
  [, <end_time>]
);
```

CDC queries provide a detailed view of all changes within a time window, allowing efficient tracking of inserts, updates, and deletes for downstream processing or auditing.

## Incremental query

Incremental queries fetch the latest values for records that have changed after a given commit time. These queries are particularly efficient for incremental data pipelines, as they process only the updated records. Both `COPY_ON_WRITE` and `MERGE_ON_READ` tables support incremental queries.

```
-- Retrieve incremental changes using the `hudi_table_changes` TVF
SELECT *
FROM hudi_table_changes(
  <pathToTable | tableName>,
  'latest_state',
  <'earliest' | <start_time>>
  [, <end_time>]
);
```

Incremental queries efficiently retrieve only the records that have changed since a specified commit, making them ideal for building lightweight, up-to-date data pipelines.

### Incremental versus CDC queries

Incremental queries are more efficient than CDC queries because they focus on fetching the latest state of records, amortizing the cost of compactions across the data lake. For example, if 10 million changes occur to 1 million records in a given window, an incremental query will only process the latest values for those 1 million records. CDC queries, however, process all 10 million changes, making them suitable when you need to analyze every modification in a time window rather than just the latest values.

# Hands-on with Apache Hudi and Apache Flink

Apache Flink is an open source distributed compute engine well-suited for stream processing, although it does support batch workloads. The Flink setup was extensively covered in *Chapter 3*, under the *Configuration (Flink, Iceberg, storage)* section.

## Configuration (Flink, Hudi, storage)

At the time of writing, Hudi 0.15.x supports Flink 1.14.x–1.18.x. Earlier Hudi 0.14.x releases also support Flink 1.13.x. Check the Hudi docs for the latest compatibility matrix.

## Prerequisites

Follow these steps to set up and configure Hudi with Flink in both local and Hadoop-based environments.

1.  Set up Flink as described in *Chapter 3*. For a local setup, do the following:

    a.  Download Hadoop binaries and set the HADOOP_HOME environment variable.

    b.  Export the Hadoop classpath:

    ```
    export HADOOP_CLASSPATH=`$HADOOP_HOME/bin/hadoop classpath`
    ```

2.  Start a Flink standalone cluster in a Hadoop environment:

    ```
    ./bin/start-cluster.sh
    ```

> **Notes for compatibility**
>
> Use Hadoop version 2.9.x or later. Object storage implementations for some filesystems are only available in these versions. The flink-parquet and flink-avro formats are already included in the hudi-flink-bundle JAR.

## Setting up Flink SQL

Hudi provides a pre-packaged bundle JAR for Flink that must be loaded in the Flink SQL Client. You can do either of the following:

- Build the JAR manually from the `hudi-source-dir/packaging/hudi-flink-bundle` directory (refer to Build Flink Bundle JAR instructions)
- Download it directly from the `Apache Maven` repository

Once the bundle JAR is loaded, you can start running Hudi operations directly from the Flink SQL Client.

## Steps to start the SQL CLI

To run `Hudi SQL` commands, you need to set up the `Flink SQL CLI` with the appropriate `Hudi` bundle.

1. Export Flink and Hudi versions:

```
export FLINK_VERSION=1.17
export HUDI_VERSION=0.15.0
```

2. Download the Hudi Flink bundle JAR:

```
wget https://repo1.maven.org/maven2/org/apache/hudi/hudi-
flink${FLINK_VERSION}-bundle/${HUDI_VERSION}/hudi-flink${FLINK_
VERSION}-bundle-${HUDI_VERSION}.jar -P $FLINK_HOME/lib/
```

3. Start the SQL Client:

```
./bin/sql-client.sh embedded -j lib/hudi-flink${FLINK_VERSION}-
bundle-${HUDI_VERSION}.jar shell
```

Once the `SQL CLI` is started with the `Hudi` bundle, you're ready to execute `Hudi SQL` queries and manage your tables.

## Configuration for SQL operations

Set up your tables and base paths correctly so you can run SQL commands smoothly and manage your Hudi workflows without issues:

- **Set up the table and base path in the SQL Client**: Define table names, base paths, and other parameters specific to your Hudi workflow
- **Run SQL commands interactively**: The SQL CLI processes commands line by line, enabling quick experimentation and adjustments

By following this configuration guide, you can seamlessly integrate Hudi with Flink to use both streaming and batch processing capabilities.

## Syncing to a catalog

Similar to in the Spark section, you can use `HiveSyncTool` to sync the datasets to any catalogs. Please refer to the previous *Syncing to catalogs* section for more details.

## DDL statements

Let's start by creating some DDL statements to interact with Hudi tables. Flink SQL currently has support for creating tables, altering table properties, and dropping tables.

## CREATE CATALOG

The catalog facilitates managing SQL tables and allows table definitions to be shared across sessions if the catalog persists with the table metadata. In HMS mode, the catalog also enhances Hive synchronization options:

```
CREATE CATALOG hudi_catalog
WITH (
  'type' = 'hudi',
  'catalog.path' = '${catalog default root path}',
  'hive.conf.dir' = '${directory where hive-site.xml is located}',
  'mode' = 'hms' -- Also supports 'dfs' mode for persisting table DDLs in
the DFS backend
);
```

To use this catalog in Flink SQL, execute the following command:

```
USE CATALOG hudi_catalog;
```

## CREATE DATABASE

To create a new database and set it as the active database, use the following commands:

```
CREATE DATABASE db;
USE db;
```

Creating and using a Hudi catalog allows you to manage tables consistently across sessions while enabling integration with Hive for metadata synchronization.

## CREATE TABLE

You can create tables using standard `FLINK SQL CREATE TABLE` syntax, which supports partitioning and passing Flink options using `WITH`. You can pass all the Hudi configs in the `WITH` clause:

```
CREATE TABLE product_daily_price (
 id BIGINT PRIMARY KEY NOT ENFORCED,
 name STRING,
 price DOUBLE,
 ts BIGINT,
 dt STRING
)
PARTITIONED BY (dt)
WITH (
'connector' = 'hudi',
'path' = 'file:///tmp/hudi_table',
'table.type' = 'MERGE_ON_READ',
'precombine.field' = 'ts',
'hoodie.cleaner.fileversions.retained' = '20',
'hoodie.keep.max.commits' = '20',
'hoodie.datasource.write.hive_style_partitioning' = 'true'
);
```

Using `CREATE TABLE` with Hudi allows you to define table schemas, partitions, and configuration options, enabling both efficient storage and advanced table management within Flink SQL.

## DML statements

Flink SQL provides several **Data Manipulation Language (DML)** actions for interacting with Hudi tables. These operations allow you to insert, update, and delete data from your Hudi tables. Let's explore them one by one.

## INSERT INTO

You can utilize the `INSERT INTO` statement to incorporate data into a Hudi table using Flink SQL. Here is an illustrative example:

```
INSERT INTO product_daily_price
SELECT 1, 'Lakehouse Book', 50, 1732256367, '2024-11-21';
```

The `INSERT INTO` statement lets you append new records to a Hudi table, making it simple to expand your dataset.

# UPSERT

With Flink SQL, you can use the INSERT command to upsert the Hudi table by setting the write operation option. Here is an illustrative example:

```
-- UPSERT
INSERT INTO product_daily_price
/*+ OPTIONS('write.operation' = 'upsert') */
SELECT 1, 'Lakehouse Book', 60, 1732256367, '2024-11-21';

INSERT INTO product_daily_price
/*+ OPTIONS('hoodie.keep.max.commits' = '10') */
SELECT 2, 'Another Book', 40, 1732256367, '2024-11-21';
```

Upserts allow you to insert new records or update existing ones in a single operation, ensuring the table always reflects the latest data.

# UPDATE

With Flink SQL, you can use the UPDATE command to update the Hudi table. Here are a few illustrative examples:

```
UPDATE product_daily_price
SET price = price * 2, ts = 1732258867
WHERE id = 1;
```

The UPDATE query only works with batch execution mode.

The UPDATE command modifies existing records based on a condition, enabling controlled adjustments to your data in batch mode.

# DELETE FROM

With Flink SQL, you can use the DELETE command to delete rows from a Hudi table. Here is an illustrative example:

```
DELETE FROM product_daily_price
WHERE price < 50;
```

DELETE FROM removes specific rows from a Hudi table, helping maintain accurate and relevant datasets.

## Setting writer/reader configs

With Flink SQL, you can additionally set the writer/reader configs along with the query. Here is an illustrative example:

```
INSERT INTO product_daily_price + OPTIONS('hoodie.keep.max.
commits'='true')
```

Configuring writer and reader options alongside queries lets you customize Hudi operations for performance, retention, and consistency according to your workflow needs.

# Hudi table services

Hudi provides a comprehensive set of table services that ensure data consistency, maintain optimal performance, and simplify data management in your data lake. These services address common challenges such as managing the data lifecycle, optimizing query performance, and ensuring data integrity during failures or updates.

## Compaction

Compaction is a key service for managing MoR tables in Hudi, designed to periodically merge updates stored in log files with their corresponding base files to produce optimized columnar formats like Parquet. Unlike CoW tables, where updates are immediately merged during writes, MoR tables prioritize write performance by appending updates to log files asynchronously. This approach reduces write latency and amplification, making MoR tables ideal for high-throughput data ingestion scenarios. By default, Hudi runs compaction asynchronously, allowing ingestion and compaction to proceed in parallel without disrupting write operations. To enable async compaction, users can configure the following:

```
.option("hoodie.compact.inline.max.delta.commits", "10") and
.option("hoodie.datasource.compaction.async.enable", "true").
```

For workloads requiring low-latency ingestion, asynchronous compaction is typically enabled in streaming ingestion models such as Spark Structured Streaming or Flink. This ensures efficient ingestion while maintaining good query performance. Alternatively, users who prioritize immediate read performance or prefer simpler workflows can opt for synchronous inline compactions, where writes and compactions occur in the same job. This mode can be configured by setting hoodie.compact. inline = true for Spark Datasource and Spark SQL writers. Choosing the right compaction strategy depends on the balance between write latency, ingestion performance, and query efficiency.

# Clustering

Clustering in Apache Hudi optimizes data layout in a data lake, balancing ingestion speed with query performance. During ingestion, data is often written into small files or organized by arrival time, which is suboptimal for query engines that perform better with co-located and sorted data. Clustering addresses this by reorganizing files, combining smaller files into larger ones, and sorting data by query predicates. This improves query performance while maintaining ingestion efficiency, building on Hudi's MVCC-based design to ensure snapshot isolation for concurrent readers and writers.

Hudi's clustering service runs asynchronously or synchronously, rewriting data to optimize file layout. The process involves the following:

1. **Scheduling clustering**: Identifying eligible files, grouping, and creating a clustering plan
2. **Executing clustering**: Processing the plan, creating new files, and replacing old ones

Clustering helps maintain an efficient data layout, improving query performance and reducing file fragmentation while preserving Hudi's transactional consistency.

## Clustering types

Similar to compaction, clustering can be performed inline or in async mode.

### Inline clustering

Inline clustering runs synchronously with data ingestion, optimizing data as it's written:

- Synchronous clustering with ingestion
- Enabled by `hoodie.clustering.inline` on the writer

This ensures your data stays optimized in real time, though it may slightly affect write performance.

### Async clustering

Async clustering runs in the background, so ingestion isn't blocked:

- Background clustering without blocking ingestion
- Three deployment modes:
    - Asynchronous execution within the same process
    - Separate process for clustering
    - Scheduling inline and executing async

This approach keeps writes fast while still maintaining optimized data over time.

# Cleaning orphan files

Hudi's cleaning service plays a crucial role in managing storage costs by reclaiming space occupied by older data versions. This ensures snapshot isolation between writers and readers, enabling time travel and rollbacks.

## Importance of cleaning

Cleaning balances storage costs and query performance by doing the following:

- Reclaiming storage space occupied by older data versions
- Managing data history and retention
- Preventing metadata and data storage growth

Regular cleaning ensures efficient storage usage, keeps metadata manageable, and maintains overall query performance.

## Cleaning retention policies

Hudi supports three cleaning policies:

- KEEP_LATEST_COMMITS: Retains the last X commits, ensuring lookback into changes within a specified time frame
- KEEP_LATEST_FILE_VERSIONS: Retains N file versions, useful for maintaining a fixed number of versions
- KEEP_LATEST_BY_HOURS: Retains files based on hours, providing a time-based retention strategy.

Choosing the right retention policy helps balance historical data availability with storage and performance considerations.

## Triggering cleaning

Cleaning can be triggered in two ways:

- **Inline cleaning**: Default mode – cleaning runs after every commit
- **Async cleaning**: Cleaning runs asynchronously with writing, enabled by configuration

Cleaning can be automated or run asynchronously, allowing flexibility in maintaining optimized tables without disrupting ingestion.

# Configuration

Key configurations include the following:

- `hoodie.clean.automatic`: Enables automatic cleaning
- `hoodie.cleaner.commits.retained`: Specifies commits to retain
- `hoodie.clean.async`: Enables async cleaning

Proper configuration of cleaning parameters ensures consistent and effective management of data retention and storage.

# Rollback mechanism

In a data pipeline, failures can occur due to various reasons, such as crashes, bugs, third-party system failures, or job cancellations. A robust system should detect partially failed commits, prevent exposure of incomplete data to queries, and automatically clean up failed writes. Hudi's rollback mechanism handles this cleanup efficiently without requiring manual intervention.

Hudi's timeline ensures that incomplete commits are not read by queries. If a commit is not marked as completed in the timeline, its data is ignored by readers. To manage this, Hudi automatically rolls back failed commits, cleaning up any associated dirty data. The rollback process reverts the commit, removing both the data and its metadata from the timeline. Additionally, Hudi uses rollback operations to restore previous commits when needed.

## Handling failed commits

In any data processing system, commit failures can occur due to crashes, network issues, or concurrent write conflicts. Apache Hudi includes robust mechanisms to automatically detect and recover from such failures, ensuring data integrity and consistency. The rollback process varies slightly depending on whether a **single-writer** or **multi-writer** model is being used:

- **Single-writer**: In a single-writer model, the rollback process is straightforward. Hudi tracks commits through three states—requested, inflight, and completed. If a commit fails midway, Hudi automatically triggers a rollback, cleaning up any associated data and removing the commit from the timeline.
- **Multi-writer**: When multiple writers are involved, the rollback process becomes more complex. Hudi uses heartbeats to determine whether a commit has failed. Each commit emits a heartbeat signal during its execution, and if the heartbeat stops updating (e.g., due to a crash or failure), Hudi deduces the commit as incomplete and triggers a rollback. The

rollback is "lazy" in this case, as Hudi waits for the heartbeat timeout before cleaning up, ensuring that concurrent writers do not mistakenly clean up valid commits. This process is still automatic, requiring no user intervention.

In both cases, the rollback mechanism ensures that failed commits and their associated data are automatically cleaned up, maintaining system integrity and data consistency.

# File sizing

Proper file sizing is crucial for optimizing query performance and pipeline efficiency in data lakes. If files are too small, you may encounter several issues:

- **Slow queries:** Small files require scanning multiple files to retrieve data, causing inefficiencies. Cloud storage systems such as **S3** impose rate limits on requests per second, meaning that more files increase the chances of hitting rate limits and incur additional costs.
- **Slow pipelines:** Excessively small files can result in increased scheduling overhead and memory requirements in frameworks such as Spark, Flink, or Hive.
- **Storage inefficiencies:** A large number of small files can lead to poor compression ratios, increasing storage costs. Additionally, metadata indexing requires more space for tracking small files, making storage management inefficient, especially at large scales (e.g., petabyte- or exabyte-level data).

To address the small file problem, Hudi uses two strategies: **auto-sizing during writes** and **clustering after writes**.

## Auto-sizing during writes

Hudi can automatically size files during ingestion to improve query performance. By default, Hudi targets a Parquet file size of 120 MB (configurable via `hoodie.parquet.max.file.size`). While auto-sizing may slightly increase write latency, it helps ensure more efficient queries once the data is written.

If file sizing is not managed during ingestion and clustering is used afterward, query performance can degrade until clustering is complete. This approach is supported only for append use cases, not for mutable operations.

## File sizing for CoW and MoR tables

For both CoW and MoR tables, file sizing can be managed by setting limits for small files and maximum file sizes. Hudi will attempt to merge small files to meet the specified size limits.

For CoW tables, settings such as hoodie.parquet.small.file.limit (default 100 MB) and hoodie.parquet.max.file.size (default 120 MB) control how small files are handled. For MoR tables, additional configurations such as hoodie.merge.small.file.group.candidates.limit (limits small file groups) and hoodie.logfile.max.size (controls log file size) are also available.

## Clustering after writes

Clustering allows small files to be combined into larger files, improving query performance. It can also reorganize the data layout using techniques such as Z-order or Hilbert curves. Clustering is useful when data ingestion creates small files that need consolidation.

Hudi's clustering service operates asynchronously, so it doesn't block writes. However, if any data is updated while clustering is in progress, the operation will fail.

### Important configuration settings

For CoW tables, important configurations include the following:

- hoodie.parquet.small.file.limit (limits small file size)
- hoodie.parquet.max.file.size (sets target file size)
- hoodie.copyonwrite.record.size.estimate (record size estimate)

For MoR tables, additional settings include the following:

- hoodie.merge.small.file.group.candidates.limit (limits small file groups)
- hoodie.logfile.max.size (log file size limit)

Properly tuning these configuration settings helps optimize file sizing, manage storage efficiently, and maintain performance for both CoW and MoR table types.

### Clustering configuration

Clustering configurations help manage file sizes and improve query efficiency:

- hoodie.clustering.plan.strategy.small.file.limit (sets the size limit for clustering candidates)
- hoodie.clustering.plan.strategy.target.file.max.bytes (sets the target maximum size for output files)

These settings are essential for controlling file sizes and ensuring the storage system is used efficiently.

## Disaster recovery

Disaster recovery is critical for data systems, as data loss or corruption can significantly impact business operations, leading to delays or incorrect decisions. Apache Hudi offers two key operations to help recover data to a previous state: **savepoint** and **restore**.

- **Savepoint**: A savepoint captures the state of the table at a specific commit time. It ensures that the table can be restored to that point later if needed. Hudi guarantees that savepointed data will not be cleaned up by the cleaner. However, savepoints cannot be triggered on commits that have already been cleaned. Essentially, savepoints act like backups, preserving the table's state without duplicating the data.

- **Restore**: The restore operation allows you to revert the table to a savepoint commit. This operation is irreversible, so caution is needed. During the restore process, all data and commit files after the savepoint will be deleted. It is recommended to pause writes to the table while restoring, as they may fail during the process. Additionally, reads might also fail, as snapshot queries could attempt to access files that may be deleted during the restore.

These operations help ensure the ability to recover from critical failures, safeguarding the integrity of the data system.

Each of these services plays a vital role in simplifying data management for modern data lakes, enabling organizations to handle large-scale, incremental, and real-time data processing workloads with ease.

## Summary

This chapter provided an in-depth exploration of Apache Hudi, an open source data lake framework that introduces transactional capabilities to data lakes. We began by understanding Hudi's architecture, including its metadata and data layers, which help ensure efficient storage, schema evolution, and incremental data processing.

We then explored Hudi's core capabilities, such as row-level updates and deletes, time travel, and ACID transactions, making it an ideal solution for managing large-scale datasets in both batch and streaming workloads. Through hands-on exercises, we demonstrated how to perform various data operations using Apache Spark and Flink, including writing, reading, and catalog synchronization with Hive Metastore and AWS Glue.

Additionally, we covered key table services in Hudi, such as compaction, clustering, and data cleaning, which optimize storage efficiency and query performance. The chapter also introduced Hudi's rollback mechanisms, file sizing strategies, and disaster recovery techniques, ensuring robust data management and reliability.

Building on the transactional capabilities of Apache Hudi, the next chapter delves into Delta Lake, another open table format designed for the lakehouse architecture. We will explore Delta Lake's architecture, Delta Log, schema enforcement, and time travel.

In summary, Hudi's unique key-based design and flexible indexing strategies distinguish it as a lakehouse table format purpose-built for record-level operations. These internal mechanisms—combined with Hudi's modular write model and timeline service—form the foundation of its scalability and efficiency in large-scale data lake environments.

## Questions

1. What is Apache Hudi, and how does it enhance data lakes?

2. How does Hudi support both batch and streaming workloads?

3. What are the key differences between CoW and MoR tables in Hudi?

4. How does Hudi's metadata layer contribute to efficient data management?

5. What is the role of the Hive sync tool, and how does it integrate Hudi tables with Hive Metastore?

6. How does Hudi support schema evolution, and what configurations are needed?

7. What are the primary benefits of Hudi's incremental processing capabilities?

8. How does Hudi's compaction process optimize Merge-on-Read tables?

9. What mechanisms does Hudi provide for data recovery and rollback?

10. How does Apache Hudi compare with other open table formats such as Apache Iceberg and Delta Lake?

## Answers

1. Apache Hudi is an open source data lake framework that adds transactional capabilities, enabling upserts, deletes, and incremental processing in data lakes. It ensures efficient data ingestion, consistency, and optimized query performance.

2. **Batch and streaming workloads**: Hudi allows data ingestion in micro-batches while maintaining real-time updates. It supports structured streaming in Spark and Flink, ensuring low-latency data processing.

3. **CoW versus MoR tables**: CoW rewrites entire Parquet files during updates, optimizing read performance but increasing write latency. MoR stores updates in Avro-based log files and merges them with base files during query time, improving write performance but requiring additional read-time processing.

4. **Metadata layer**: Hudi's metadata layer, stored in the `.hoodie` directory, tracks changes, manages concurrency, and maintains historical versions for time travel and rollback operations.

5. **Hive sync tool**: This tool synchronizes Hudi tables with Hive Metastore, enabling seamless querying via Hive, Spark, and Presto. It supports both HMS sync mode and JDBC mode for integration.

6. **Schema evolution**: Hudi allows schema changes such as adding columns, renaming fields, and data type promotions. It ensures backward compatibility with configurations such as `hoodie.write.set.null.for.missing.columns=true`.

7. **Incremental processing**: Hudi supports both incremental and CDC queries that avoid full-table scans by reading only data changed since a given commit. Incremental queries (`latest_state`) return the latest state of each changed record, whereas CDC queries (`cdc`) return the full change history. Both patterns reduce query latency and resource usage and make it easier to build efficient, up-to-date downstream pipelines.

8. **Compaction in MoR tables**: Compaction merges delta log files with base files periodically, improving read performance. It can be scheduled asynchronously using configurations such as `hoodie.compact.inline.max.delta.commits`.

9. **Data recovery and rollback**: Hudi provides `Savepoint` for marking stable states and `Restore` for reverting to previous commits. Failed writes are automatically rolled back to prevent inconsistencies.

10. Hudi versus Iceberg versus Delta Lake:

    - Hudi excels in real-time data ingestion and CDC workloads.
    - Iceberg is optimized for batch queries with advanced snapshot isolation.
    - Delta Lake provides strong ACID guarantees and integrates deeply with Spark.

# 5

# Delta Lake Deep Dive

Delta Lake is another widely used open table format that enables reliable, scalable, and high-performance analytics on top of cloud data lakes. In this chapter, you will explore the foundational architecture of Delta Lake, along with hands-on examples to install and use Delta Lake. The chapter also goes over the mechanics of read and write operations; showcases key features such as time travel, schema evolution, and **Change Data Feed** (**CDF**); and highlights unique subprojects within the Delta ecosystem, such as Delta Sharing.

In this chapter, we will cover the following topics:

- Exploring the Delta Lake architecture
- Understanding the transaction log protocol
- Reviewing Delta Lake features
- Learning the unique capabilities of Delta Lake
- Hands-on with Delta Lake and Apache Spark
- Hands-on with Delta Lake and Apache Flink

By the end, you will have a comprehensive understanding of how Delta Lake enables an open lakehouse architecture.

## Technical requirements

The following installations are required:

- Apache Spark 3.x
- Java 8+ (compatible with your Spark version)

- Download the required packages (details in the next section)
- The following Python libraries:

```
pip install pyspark findspark
```

Spark requires a compatible Java version to run correctly. The supportability matrix defines which Java releases are officially supported for each Spark version at https://community.cloudera.com/t5/Community-Articles/Spark-and-Java-versions-Supportability-Matrix/ta-p/383669

The code files for this chapter are available on GitHub at https://github.com/PacktPublishing/Engineering-Lakehouses-with-Open-Table-Formats/tree/main/ch05.

# Delta Lake architecture

At its core, Delta Lake is powered by three foundational components: the **transaction log**, **log checkpoints**, and **data files**, all of which work together to adhere to the ACID properties and enable reliable data processing for both batch and streaming workloads:

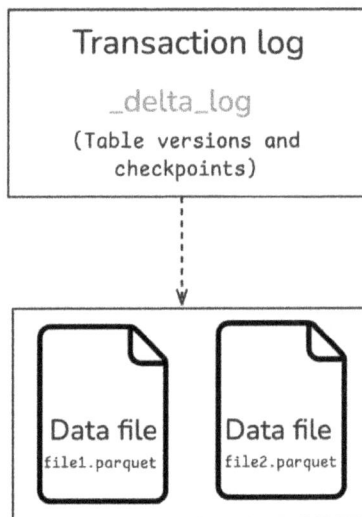

*Figure 5.1 – High-level depiction of Delta Lake's components*

This architecture not only addresses the inherent limitations of traditional data lakes, such as a lack of ACID compliance and data versioning, but also empowers organizations to build analytics solutions that are both performant and cost-effective. In *Chapter 2, Transactional Capabilities of the Lakehouse*, in the *Delta Lake ACID* section, we learned how ACID guarantees are supported by Delta Lake. Let's expand on those understandings and see in detail how the various components of Delta Lake come together to make this work.

# Transaction log

The transaction log is Delta Lake's most critical component, acting as a journal that records every action performed on a table. Unlike traditional data lake storage systems (such as S3), where changes to data are often implicit and untracked, Delta Lake logs every operation in a sequential and immutable manner. Stored as a series of JSON files, the transaction log provides a single source of truth for the table's state, ensuring that every read and write operation adheres to strict ACID guarantees, defined in the `Protocol` subsection of this chapter.

The transaction log is stored in the `_delta_log` subdirectory within the Delta table in a storage system (local filesystems or cloud object stores). Each transaction is represented as a uniquely named JSON file, starting with a zero-padded numerical ID (for example, `00000000000000000000.json`). These files are sequentially ordered, ensuring that the log captures a clear progression of changes to the table over time. The log directory also contains **checkpoint files** in Parquet format, which summarize the state of the table at specific intervals. This combination of JSON files and periodic checkpoints allows Delta Lake to maintain both historical integrity and query efficiency.

Each JSON log file contains a sequence of **attributes** that define how the table evolves with every operation. These attributes include commit info, protocol, metadata, and add/remove actions, all of which collectively describe the table. Let's understand these components now.

Note that the following screenshot is a snippet of the transaction log's content. You can find the complete syntax in this chapter's GitHub repository.

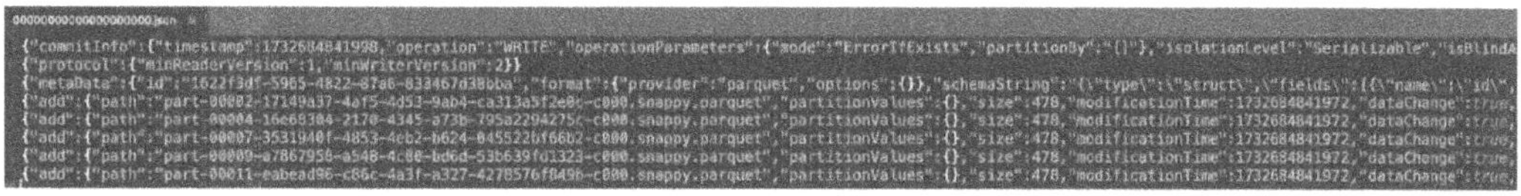

*Figure 5.2 – Content of a transaction log*

## commitInfo

The `commitInfo` entry captures details about the operation that triggered the log entry. In this case, a `WRITE` operation was performed with the following attributes:

- **Isolation level**: `Serializable`, ensuring the highest level of consistency.
- **Metrics**: `numFiles: 6` and `numOutputRows: 5` provide insight into the operation's scale. In our example transaction, we inserted five records, which generated six Parquet files.
- **Engine info**: `Apache-Spark/3.4.1 Delta-Lake/2.4.0` identifies the compute engine and Delta Lake version.

These details make the transaction log an essential tool for auditing and debugging.

## protocol

The protocol entry specifies the minimum reader and writer versions required to interact with the table. minReaderVersion ensures that only clients capable of understanding the table's current state and features can read from it, while minWriterVersion enforces compatibility for write operations, ensuring support for advanced features such as column mapping or CDF. This mechanism enables Delta Lake to evolve by introducing new capabilities without breaking existing workflows. It also safeguards against errors, as older clients that cannot handle the table's features are prevented from accessing or modifying it, ensuring operational stability and consistent data management across all users.

## metaData

The metaData entry in Delta Lake's transaction log provides a blueprint for the table's structure, ensuring that the table's schema, partitioning, and configuration are explicitly defined and consistently enforced. Key attributes include the following:

- **Schema:** The schemaString field defines the table's structure, including column names, data types, and nullability. This allows Delta Lake to enforce schema constraints, enabling features such as schema validation and evolution. For example, in our example log, the table has a single id column of type long that allows null values.

- **Partition columns:** It lists columns used for partitioning the data, enabling query engines to prune irrelevant partitions for faster reads.

- **Storage format:** The format field specifies the file format used to store data files, typically Parquet.

- **Table configuration:** The configuration field allows for custom options that modify the table's behavior.

- **Creation time:** The createdTime attribute captures the timestamp of when the table was created or last modified. This is particularly useful for auditing and tracking the table's life cycle.

The metaData entry ensures reliable table governance, simplifies maintenance, and supports efficient, consistent operations across Delta Lake tables.

## add/remove

Delta Lake uses add and remove attributes within its transaction log to manage the state of a table's data files dynamically. These actions provide the ability to track changes, maintain consistency, and ensure the integrity of the dataset over time.

# add

The add action records information about new data files added to the table. Each add entry specifies information such as the following:

- **File path:** Identifies the physical location of the data file, stored in formats such as Parquet.
- **Statistics:** Includes statistical info of data files, such as the total record count, per-column minimum and maximum values, and null counts. These statistics are crucial for query optimization techniques such as data skipping and predicate pushdown.
- **Modification time:** Captures the timestamp of when the file was added to ensure consistency during concurrent operations.

For example, consider the following snippet:

```
{
"add":{
    "path":"part-00002-17149a37-4af5-4d53-9ab4-ca313a5f2e0c-c000.snappy.
parquet",
    "size":478,
    "modificationTime":1732684841972,
    "dataChange":true,
    "stats":"{\"numRecords\":1,\"minValues\":{\"id\":0},\"maxValues
\":{\"id\":0},\"nullCount\":{\"id\":0}}"
    }
}
```

The add action provides a transparent record of new data files, enabling efficient query planning, consistency checks, and accurate tracking of changes within the Delta Lake table.

## remove

The remove attribute marks files for deletion, signaling that they are no longer part of the active dataset. Key attributes in a remove entry include the following:

- **File path:** Specifies the file to be removed
- **Deletion timestamp:** Records when the removal occurred, enabling time travel and auditing capabilities
- **Data change flag:** Indicates whether the removal represents a logical change in the data
- **Partition values:** Captures the partitioning details of the removed file

For example, consider the following snippet:

```
{"remove":{
  "path":"part-00009-a7867958-a548-4c80-bd6d-53b639fd1323-c000.snappy.
parquet",
  "deletionTimestamp":1732685680656,
  "dataChange":true,
  "extendedFileMetadata":true,
  "partitionValues":{},
  "size":478
}}
```

This entry removes the specified file, retaining its metadata in the transaction log until the file is physically deleted after the retention period (seven days by default). During this retention period, the `deletionTimestamp` attribute ensures that queries using earlier snapshots can still access the file while it remains in storage. This enables features such as time travel or rollback to earlier snapshots where the file is still referenced.

## Log checkpoints

While the transaction log is a powerful mechanism for maintaining a Delta table's state, its size can grow considerably over time, especially for tables subjected to frequent updates or large-scale operations. To address this, Delta Lake employs log checkpoints, a concept designed to balance scalability and performance. A checkpoint consolidates the transaction log's history up to a specific point into a single Parquet file. This Parquet-based snapshot aggregates critical metadata, such as active data files, removed files pending retention, and protocol details, into a format optimized for both storage and retrieval.

Checkpoints serve as an essential tool for query planning and execution. Instead of parsing through every entry in the transaction log, queries can begin from the latest checkpoint and only process the subsequent log entries. For example, in a table with 10,000 log entries, if a checkpoint exists at the 9,000th entry, only the remaining 1,000 entries need to be processed. This approach significantly reduces query latency, ensuring that even large, dynamic tables can deliver consistent and performant results.

Checkpoints are created periodically, with a default frequency of every 10 transactions. This behavior can be tuned using the `delta.checkpointInterval` table property, for example, `ALTER TABLE my_table SET TBLPROPERTIES ('delta.checkpointInterval' = '10');`.

Each checkpoint is uniquely identified as `00000000000000000000.parquet`, indicating that it encompasses all changes up to and including the `00000000000000000000.json` log entry. To further optimize metadata access, Delta Lake maintains a `_last_checkpoint` file, which tracks the latest checkpoint's ID. This ensures that clients can quickly locate the starting point for table state reconstruction without incurring the overhead of scanning the entire `_delta_log` directory.

Beyond performance, checkpoints also enhance the durability and reliability of Delta Lake. By persisting the table state in a compact and efficient format, they act as a fallback mechanism in the event of system failures. This aligns with Delta Lake's commitment to ACID principles, ensuring that the system can recover seamlessly while maintaining data integrity.

## Data files

While the transaction log and checkpoints dictate the logical state of a Delta table, the actual data is physically stored in Apache Parquet files. Parquet, a columnar storage format, is chosen for its efficiency, flexibility, and broad compatibility. Its features, such as columnar organization, compression options, and support for nested data types, make it ideal for handling structured and semi-structured data. Moreover, Delta Lake's reliance on an open and widely supported format such as Parquet ensures interoperability with numerous compute engines.

Each Parquet file represents a specific subset of a table's data, often organized into directories corresponding to partitions. For instance, a table partitioned by date might store all rows for 2024-11-24 in a dedicated directory. This physical arrangement complements Delta Lake's logical organization, as the transaction log explicitly maps each data file to its role (whether added or removed) within the table state. This design ensures that Delta Lake can scale effortlessly, efficiently managing millions of files across massive datasets. When new data is added to a Delta table, Delta Lake creates fresh Parquet files to store this data, each uniquely identified by a **globally unique identifier (GUID)**. The transaction log is then updated to reference these new files, while older files remain intact.

Parquet's footer metadata, such as min/max statistics for each column, facilitates data pruning. This means that during query execution, Delta Lake can skip over files that do not meet the query's criteria, significantly reducing I/O overhead and improving response times.

Now that we have an understanding of the Delta Lake architecture, including the transaction log, checkpoints, and data files, let's explore the transaction log protocol in depth.

## Transaction log protocol

Delta Lake's transaction log protocol is a rigorously designed specification that enforces ACID compliance and ensures consistent transactions for data stored in distributed filesystems or object stores. The protocol bridges the limitations of eventual consistency in object stores (such as S3) by providing strong transactional guarantees required for reliable operations. By using the transaction log with the protocol, Delta Lake provides a unified framework for reads, writes, and concurrent operations, enabling us to build reliable lakehouse architectures.

The transaction log protocol is built around the concept of **serializable transactions**, where every modification to a Delta table results in a new, atomic version of the table. Each version is defined by a contiguous, monotonically increasing integer, and the transaction log serves as the single source of truth, maintaining a complete record of all changes.

One of the other standout features of the transaction protocol is its open design. Clients written in different languages and frameworks, such as Spark, Trino, and Rust, can seamlessly interact with the same Delta table. This is possible because all interactions, whether reading or writing, adhere to the same protocol. For example, a Rust client may write new data, a Spark client may update the table, and a Trino client may query its contents, all without conflict.

## How the transaction log protocol works

Every interaction with a Delta table begins with the transaction log. For users, the log acts as a way to determine which files to process to construct a consistent snapshot of the table. For writers, the protocol defines a clear two-phase process:

1. **Generate changes and stage:** Writers first generate new Parquet files or updated versions of existing ones and stage the changes. These files are not visible to readers or other operations until the commit phase.

2. **Committing transactions:** Once the changes are staged, writers append a new entry to the transaction log. This entry specifies which files to add or remove, along with metadata updates such as schema changes or configuration adjustments. The commit is atomic, ensuring that the table's state transitions seamlessly to its next version.

3. This two-step approach is conceptually similar to the **Two-Phase Commit** (**2PC**) protocol in traditional databases, where a coordinator first prepares all participants and then issues a commit. In Delta Lake, the "staging" phase is analogous to 2PC's prepare step, and the atomic addition of a commit file to the transaction log mirrors 2PC's commit step. The key difference is that Delta Lake's protocol operates on immutable files in cloud/object storage, so rather than coordinating locks across live database nodes, it achieves atomicity through a single, serialized log entry written to _delta_logdirectory.

This transaction log protocol ensures both consistency and isolation, allowing Delta Lake to handle concurrent reads and writes reliably while maintaining a fully versioned history of the table.

# Protocol versions and features

The Delta log protocol initially relied on protocol versions to enforce compatibility for reading and writing tables. Each Delta table specifies the following:

- **Reader version**: The minimum protocol version required to read the table
- **Writer version**: The minimum protocol version required to write to the table

These protocol versions are embedded in the transaction log using the `protocol` entry, as shown:

```
{"protocol": {"minReaderVersion": 1, "minWriterVersion": 2}}
```

In this example transaction log (with default protocol versions), note the following:

- `minReaderVersion: 1` ensures that only clients supporting Reader Protocol Version 1 or higher can read the table.
- `minWriterVersion: 2` requires clients to support Writer Protocol Version 2 or higher to write to the table.

If a client's supported protocol version is lower than the `minReaderVersion` or `minWriterVersion` version number set in the table, the operation will fail immediately.

- **Read attempt with incompatible minReaderVersion**: The query will fail with an error indicating that the client cannot read the table because it uses features not supported by the client's Delta Lake version.
- **Write attempt with incompatible minWriterVersion**: The write will be rejected, preventing partial or corrupt updates. This protects the table from being modified by clients that don't understand the features in use (e.g., generated columns, column mapping, CDF).
- This strict enforcement ensures forward compatibility and prevents data corruption when newer Delta features are introduced.

Each protocol version unlocks specific features, ensuring compatibility between engines and the Delta table. Here are some examples of features tied to specific protocol versions:

- **Reader Protocol Version 1 and Writer Protocol Version 2**: Basic functionality, such as appends and updates
- **Writer Protocol Version 3**: Enables `CHECK` constraints to validate data during writes
- **Writer Protocol Version 4**: Adds support for generated columns and CDF features

- **Writer Protocol Version 5 and Reader Protocol Version 2**: Introduces column mapping for advanced schema evolution capabilities
- In practice, the protocol version acts as a contract between the engine and the table. Maintaining the correct version guarantees both data integrity and long-term interoperability.

Protocol versions provide a clear contract between Delta tables and clients, ensuring data integrity and preventing incompatible operations. By enforcing minimum reader and writer versions, Delta Lake guarantees forward compatibility while enabling safe adoption of new features over time.

## Limitations of protocol versions

Although protocol versions ensured compatibility, they introduced challenges for feature adoption. Since a protocol version bundled multiple features together, clients had to support all features within that version, even if they only needed one. For instance, a Delta table using a newer protocol version might include several new capabilities. However, a client wanting to interact with the table must implement all the features introduced in that protocol version, even if they only need one feature. This coupling slowed down feature adoption, as updating protocol versions required extensive client and table validations.

## Table features

To overcome these limitations, Delta Lake 2.3.0 introduced **table features**, which replace protocol versions as the mechanism to represent table capabilities. Unlike protocol versions, which bundled multiple features together and required clients to support them all, table features enable clients and connectors to selectively implement only the features they need. This decoupling significantly simplifies feature adoption and improves compatibility. For example, if a table uses CDF but not **generated columns**, the table can explicitly enable the CDF feature without requiring support for unrelated features. This approach provides flexibility for both clients and tables, ensuring compatibility without unnecessary overhead.

With Delta Lake 2.3.0+, the migration from protocol versions to table features is transparent for Delta Spark users. There is no need to explicitly upgrade existing tables – the client automatically maps legacy protocol versions to their equivalent features. If you enable a feature that requires a higher protocol version (e.g., CDF or deletion vectors), the client upgrades the table protocol automatically. Once a table reaches reader version 3 and writer version 7, the Delta log starts explicitly listing active features in readerFeatures and writerFeatures. Clients that don't support these features will be blocked from reading or writing the table.

Let's examine how table features work in practice.

When a new table is created without explicitly enabling any features, the transaction log records the minimal reader and writer versions required for basic functionality. Take the following example:

```
spark.sql("""
CREATE TABLE employee_table (
    employee_id INT,
    name STRING,
    department STRING,
    salary FLOAT
)
USING DELTA
LOCATION '/Users/dipankarmazumdar/Downloads/deltawarehouse'
""")
```

This results in the following entry in the transaction log:

```
{"protocol":{"minReaderVersion":1,"minWriterVersion":2}}
```

In this state, the table assumes the lowest possible protocol versions because no advanced features have been enabled.

Now, let's enable CDF for the table:

```
spark.sql("""
ALTER TABLE employee_table
SET TBLPROPERTIES ('delta.enableChangeDataFeed' = true)
""")
```

After this operation, the protocol entry in the transaction log updates to reflect the minimum writer version required to support CDF:

```
{"protocol":{"minReaderVersion":1,"minWriterVersion":4}}
```

By enabling this feature, the table signals that any writer interacting with it must support Writer Protocol Version 4 or higher, which includes support for CDF. This ensures that only compatible clients can write to the table, preventing data corruption or unsupported operations.

We can inspect which features are enabled for a table using the following SQL command:

```
spark.sql("SHOW TBLPROPERTIES employee_table").show()
```

Which results in:

```
spark.sql("SHOW TBLPROPERTIES employee_table").show()

+---------------------+-----+
|                  key|value|
+---------------------+-----+
|delta.enableChang...| true|
|delta.minReaderVe...|    1|
|delta.minWriterVe...|    4|
+---------------------+-----+
```

*Figure 5.3 – Properties of a Delta table*

This system of table features and corresponding protocol versions ensures that Delta Lake tables remain both flexible and compatible, allowing for the selective adoption of new capabilities without sacrificing data integrity for clients interacting with the data.

## Reader and writer features in the transaction log

When a Delta table uses table features, the transaction log explicitly lists the features required for reading and writing under the readerFeatures and writerFeatures fields. These fields ensure that only clients supporting the necessary features can interact with the table.

For example, after enabling **deletion vectors**, the transaction log entry looks like this:

```
{"protocol":{"minReaderVersion":3,"minWriterVersion":7,"readerFea-
tures":["deletionVectors"],"writerFeatures":["deletionVectors","checkCon-
straints","generatedColumns","invariants","changeDataFeed","appendOnly"]}}
```

In this case, readerFeatures specifies that any client reading the table must support the deletionVectors feature and writerFeatures lists all features that a writer must support to modify the table, such as deletionVectors, checkConstraints, and generatedColumns. Additionally, writers must also implement all features listed in readerFeatures because they need to read the table state before committing changes.

## Enforcing ACID properties via the transaction protocol

The transaction log protocol is the backbone that enforces Delta Lake's ACID properties. By meticulously tracking and validating every operation, it ensures that Delta Lake remains consistent and reliable in distributed environments. In Chapter 2, Transactional Capabilities in Lakehouse, we learned about how Delta Lake achieves ACID properties. Let's elaborate on these

# Atomicity — all-or-nothing transactions

As described in the previous section, Delta Lake's transaction log protocol ensures that every write operation, whether adding new data or marking files for removal, follows a clear two-phase process of generating changes and committing transactions. This protocol guarantees that all changes are treated as a single, indivisible unit.

During the commit phase, the protocol ensures that a new transaction log entry is appended **atomically**. This entry consolidates all changes, specifying which files to add, remove, or update, along with metadata adjustments such as schema changes. If a conflict or failure occurs at any stage during the commit, the protocol prevents partial changes from being applied. For instance, a failed INSERT operation will not result in incomplete or orphaned data files being referenced in the log, preserving the consistency of the table.

This all-or-nothing behavior is integral to the transaction log protocol, ensuring that the table's state transitions seamlessly without exposing incomplete or inconsistent data to readers.

# Consistency — validating transactions against rules

Delta Lake enforces consistency by validating each transaction against the current state of the table as recorded in the transaction log. This ensures that all changes adhere to the defined constraints, such as NOT NULL and CHECK. By maintaining a detailed record of table metadata, the transaction log serves as the source of truth, enabling Delta Lake to validate operations before they are committed.

When a schema change is applied, such as adding a new column or modifying an existing field, the transaction log protocol plays a critical role in ensuring compatibility. The transaction log stores the table schema in the metaData entry, under the schemaString attribute. Before committing changes, the protocol compares the new schema with the existing definition to ensure that the update does not violate compatibility rules. For instance, Delta Lake would reject changes that conflict with existing data types or constraints.

In our example transaction log, we can see how Delta Lake tracks the schema:

```
{
  "metaData": {
    "id": "1622f3df-5965-4822-87a6-833467d38bba",
    "format": {"provider": "parquet", "options": {}},
    "schemaString": "{\"type\":\"struct\",\"fields\":[{\"name\":\"id\",\"-
type\":\"long\",\"nullable\":true,\"metadata\":{}}]}",
    "partitionColumns": [],
```

```
        "configuration": {},
        "createdTime": 1732684840504
    }
}
```

In this example, the `schemaString` property defines the table schema, indicating that the `id` column is of type `long` and allows null values. During a write operation, any new records must comply with this schema. If a transaction attempts to write data that violates the schema, such as adding a column of a mismatched data type or setting `NOT NULL` for a nullable column, the protocol will reject the transaction, preventing invalid changes from being committed.

## Isolation – preventing interference in concurrent operations

Delta Lake achieves isolation through a combination of **Optimistic Concurrency Control (OCC)** and **Multi-Version Concurrency Control (MVCC)**, which are governed by the transaction log protocol.

The transaction log protocol ensures that every transaction interacts with a consistent snapshot of the table. By appending changes as new log entries (for example, `000000.json` and `000001.json`), Delta Lake creates a serializable sequence of table versions. These log entries record metadata, schema updates, and file operations, enabling the system to manage concurrent operations without conflicts.

### Optimistic Concurrency Control (OCC)

OCC ensures serializable isolation for writers by validating changes during the commit phase. Writers operate on isolated snapshots, assuming no other transactions have modified the same data files in the table. Before committing, the protocol compares the writer's staged changes against the latest state of the transaction log. If a conflict is detected, such as two writers attempting to modify the same partition, the protocol prevents the second commit and requires a retry with the updated state. This ensures that conflicting updates are never applied simultaneously.

### Multi-Version Concurrency Control (MVCC)

MVCC allows Delta Lake to maintain multiple snapshots of the table simultaneously. The transaction log records these snapshots by incrementing version numbers and storing the corresponding metadata and file changes. You can use the transaction protocol to query a specific version of the table, processing only the files referenced in the transaction log for that version. This ensures that queries remain consistent and are unaffected by ongoing writes or uncommitted changes.

Consider a scenario where a query starts while a writer is committing new data. The query reads from the snapshot represented by the latest committed log entry (for example, `000005.json`), which includes all prior changes but excludes the uncommitted data staged by the writer. Once the writer successfully commits, a new log entry (`000006.json`) is created, representing the updated state of the table. This separation ensures that the query processes a consistent view of the data while the writer operates in isolation.

## Durability – preserving changes across failures

Delta Lake ensures durability by persisting all changes in fault-tolerant storage systems such as Amazon S3, Azure Blob Storage, or HDFS. Once a transaction is committed, its details, including metadata changes and data file additions or deletions, are durably stored in the transaction log. This ensures that no committed data is lost, even in the event of system or network failures.

Removed files are retained as "tombstones" in the transaction log for a configurable retention period (default is seven days). This enables time travel and recovery of accidentally deleted data. When the retention period expires, the VACUUM operation can be used to clean up these files, re-claiming storage while preserving the durability of committed changes.

## Highlights

To summarize, the Delta Lake transaction protocol supports some of the critical features in Delta Lake:

- **Snapshot isolation for reads**: Readers operate on consistent snapshots from the trans-action log, ensuring reliable results during concurrent writes
- **Atomic writes**: All write operations create unified table versions through atomic commits, ensuring data integrity by preventing partial or inconsistent updates
- **Efficient incremental processing**: The protocol enables readers to process only new data via incremental reads, making it ideal for streaming and real-time analytics
- **Durability**: Tombstones and retained transaction logs allow recovery of deleted data and historical states, while VACUUM reclaims storage after the retention period

This demonstrate how Delta Lake's transaction protocol combines consistency, reliability, and efficiency. Together, these features ensure safe concurrent operations, support real-time process-ing, and protect data against loss or corruption.

# How read and write work in Delta Lake

Delta Lake's architecture revolves around the transaction log – the single source of truth for managing table state, governed by the transaction protocol. It ensures consistent, reliable table interactions, even in distributed and eventually consistent environments. In this section, we will explore how read and write queries work in Delta Lake.

## Life cycle of a read query

When a read query is issued on a Delta table, Delta Lake begins by identifying a reliable starting point for reconstructing the table's current state. If a checkpoint exists in the log directory, it provides a compact summary of the table at a specific version, saving time by reducing the number of log records that need to be processed.

Next, Delta Lake evaluates the changes recorded in the log files since the checkpoint. By combining the checkpoint data and newer log entries, the system reconstructs the table's state. This involves isolating all active data files that were added but not removed, ensuring a consistent view of the table. Metadata stored within the transaction log, such as min/max column values and null counts, is used to prune unnecessary files, ensuring that only those relevant to the query are selected for reading.

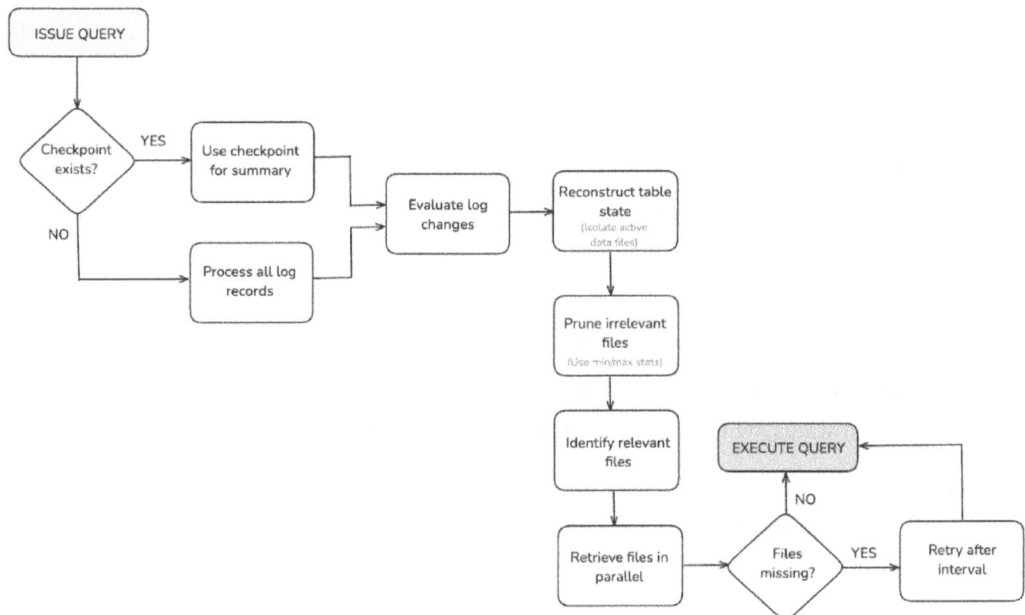

*Figure 5.4 – How a read query works in Delta Lake*

Once the relevant files are identified, Delta Lake retrieves them from the object store in parallel, using the cluster's resources. To account for eventual consistency in object stores, the system gracefully handles missing files by retrying after short intervals, ensuring reliable query execution.

## Life cycle of a write query

Writing data to a Delta table is a carefully coordinated process that builds upon the principles of consistency and atomicity established by the transaction protocol. The process begins by identifying the most recent checkpoint in the transaction log. This checkpoint provides a consolidated snapshot of the table's state at a specific version, reducing the need to process earlier log entries. If no checkpoint exists, the log directory is scanned from the beginning to establish the current state.

After locating the checkpoint, the transaction log is scanned for newer `.json` and `.parquet` files to identify changes made since the checkpoint was created. These log records, combined with the checkpoint, help reconstruct the latest snapshot of the table. If the write operation involves updating or merging data, the relevant data files are read to ensure that the operation is performed on an up-to-date and consistent view of the table.

Once the current state is established, the transaction generates new Parquet files for the data it intends to write. Each file is uniquely named using GUIDs to prevent naming conflicts and maintain traceability. These files are written to the table's directories and staged for inclusion in the table. At this stage, the new files are not visible to readers.

To finalize the write, the system appends a new log entry to the transaction log. This entry records the paths of the newly added files, metadata updates (such as schema changes or table properties), and details about files marked for removal. The atomic nature of this step ensures that either the entire log entry is written, making the changes visible to readers, or no changes are made, leaving the table in its previous state. If the write fails due to a conflict, for instance, when another writer has modified the same portion of the table, the operation retries after refreshing its snapshot of the table.

To further optimize future read performance, Delta Lake periodically generates new checkpoints after a set number of log updates (for example, every 10 updates). These checkpoints consolidate the current table state into a compact format, reducing the overhead of reconstructing the state from multiple log records. Once the checkpoint is written, the `_last_checkpoint` file is updated to reflect it, ensuring that future reads and writes can start from the most recent table state.

Here is the flow:

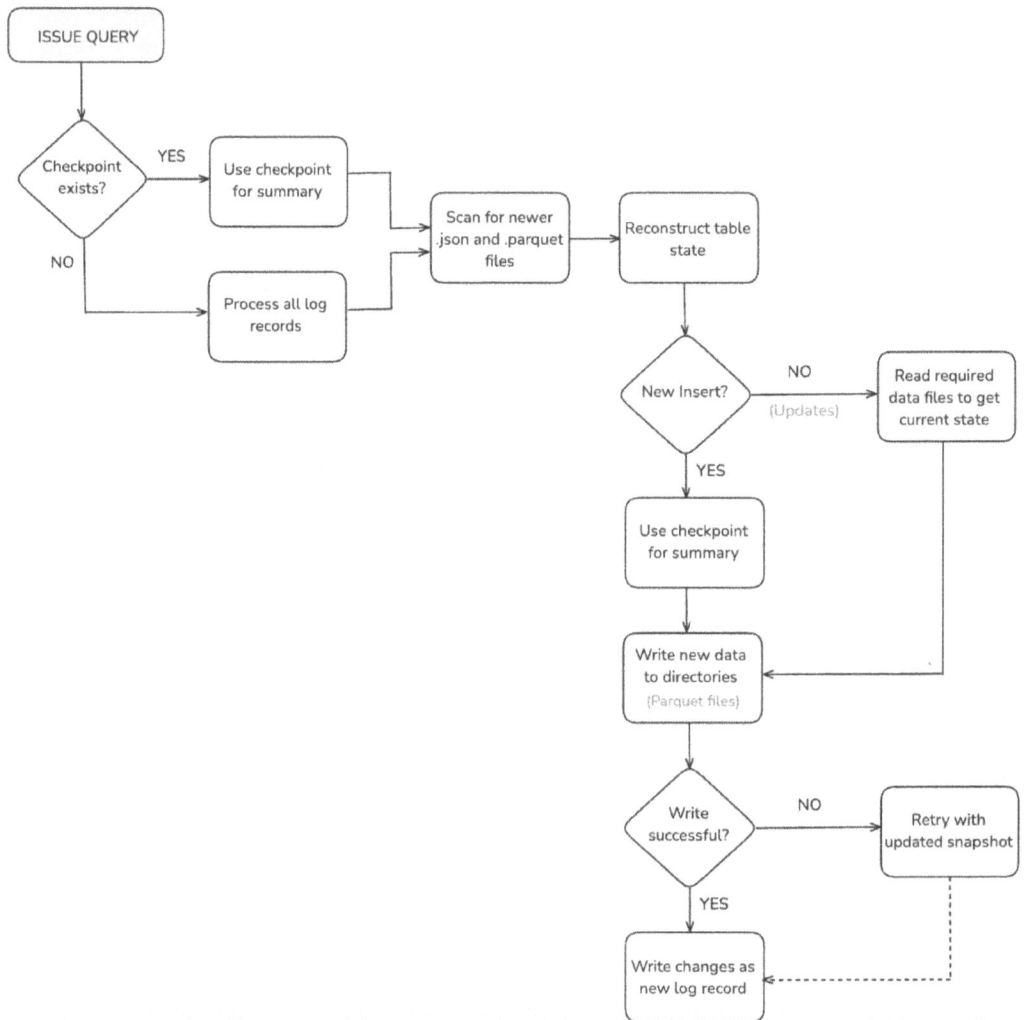

*Figure 5.5 – How a write query works in Delta Lake*

Now, let us go over some of the key capabilities offered by Delta Lake that are critical to run analytical workloads in a data lake.

# Delta Lake features

Delta Lake's transaction log and protocol not only enable ACID compliance but also form the foundation for some of the core features that it brings to a lakehouse architecture. In this section, we will explore some of these important functionalities, such as schema evolution, time travel, and row-level upserts and deletes. These features bring transactional capabilities and enable you to run analytical workloads on top. For each feature, we will also examine the internal workings and understand how the transaction log and protocol underpin their functionality.

# Schema enforcement and evolution

Schema enforcement and evolution are essential pillars of Delta Lake's design, ensuring that data remains consistent and reliable even as table structures change over time. In this section, we will understand how these capabilities enable users to confidently manage evolving datasets while preventing unexpected schema mismatches.

## Schema enforcement

Schema enforcement in Delta Lake ensures that incoming data adheres to predefined table schemas, preventing inconsistencies. When new data is written, Delta Lake validates it against the schema defined in the table's metadata. Any deviation, such as missing required fields or mismatched data types, results in an error. This feature is critical in maintaining data quality and integrity across multiple writes.

In the example log file (00000000000000000000.json), the schema is defined within the metaData entry under the schemaString field:

```
"schemaString": "{\"type\":\"struct\",\"fields\":[{\"name\":\"em-
ployee_id\",\"type\":\"integer\",\"nullable\":true,\"meta-
data\":{}},{\"name\":\"name\",\"type\":\"string\",\"nul-
lable\":true,\"metadata\":{}},{\"name\":\"department\",\"-
type\":\"string\",\"nullable\":true,\"metadata\":{}},{\"name\":\"sala-
ry\",\"type\":\"float\",\"nullable\":true,\"metadata\":{}}]}"
```

This JSON schema specifies that the table consists of four fields (employee_id, name, department, and salary), each with a defined type and nullability. Before writing new data, Delta Lake ensures that the incoming records conform to this schema, rejecting any that do not match these constraints.

## Schema evolution

Schema evolution in Delta Lake is the ability to adapt a table's schema as requirements change over time. It allows users to add new columns or make modifications without disrupting ongoing operations or breaking existing queries. This capability ensures that Delta Lake tables remain flexible and can grow alongside evolving data models, making it easier to incorporate new data sources or adjust to business needs.

For instance, consider a scenario where an organization starts collecting additional information about employee bonuses in a dataset that previously only tracked `employee_id`, `name`, `department`, and `salary`. With schema evolution, a new bonus column can be added to the table, ensuring that historical data remains intact while future records can include this additional field.

When a schema change is applied, Delta Lake records the modification in its transaction log under the `commitInfo` and `metaData` sections. Let's break this down using our example log file, `00000000000000000002.json`. The `commitInfo` section of the log records the operation type as `ADD COLUMNS`, indicating that new columns were added to the table:

```
"operation": "ADD COLUMNS",
"operationParameters": {
  "columns": "[{\"column\":{\"name\":\"bonus\",\"type\":\"float\",\"nul-
lable\":true,\"metadata\":{}}}]"
},
"readVersion": 1,
"isolationLevel": "Serializable",
"isBlindAppend": true,
"txnId": "d4eb1183-4dd0-4594-9d18-96d1b9bd19e6"
```

The `operation` field specifies the type of modification, in this case, the addition of a bonus column of type `float`. The `operationParameters` field provides further details, including the name, data type, and nullability of the new column. The `readVersion` field indicates that this change was applied to version 1 of the table, ensuring compatibility with previous versions. Finally, the `isolationLevel` field guarantees that the schema change adheres to Delta Lake's ACID properties by enforcing serializable isolation, preventing conflicts or inconsistencies during the operation.

## Time travel

Time travel is a powerful feature in Delta Lake that allows users to query the state of a table as it existed at a specific point in time or at a particular version. It allows debugging or rolling back changes by restoring tables to a prior state in case of pipeline errors. For data scientists, it ensures reproducibility by providing consistent historical versions for training machine learning models. Additionally, businesses can perform trend analysis, auditing, and compliance checks by accessing older snapshots without affecting the current table state.

Delta Lake's time travel is built on the foundation of its immutable transaction log and MVCC. Every change to a table, such as data writes, updates, or schema changes, is recorded in a versioned transaction log. These logs, represented as files (`00000000000000000001.json`, `00000000000000000002.json`), capture the sequence of operations applied to the table, as follows:

- `00000000000000000001.json` corresponds to version 1 of the table
- `00000000000000000002.json` corresponds to version 2

Each log file records metadata about the operation, including the `add` and `remove` entries that define the physical data files for that version. By analyzing these entries, Delta Lake reconstructs the state of the table at a given version. In addition to the version number, the transaction log includes a `commitInfo` section. For instance, in `00000000000000000001.json`, the `commitInfo` entry shows the following:

```
"operation": "WRITE",
"readVersion": 0
```

This indicates that version 1 was created based on version 0 through a write operation. By understanding the lineage of versions, Delta Lake ensures accurate reconstruction of table states.

Delta Lake provides intuitive SQL syntax for querying historical versions:

- `VERSION AS OF n`: Queries the state of the table at version n (for example, `VERSION AS OF 1` to query version 1).
- `AS OF timestamp`: Queries the table's state at a specific timestamp. Delta Lake maps the timestamp to the corresponding log version.

Time travel in Delta Lake ensures users can reliably access historical table states for debugging, auditing, or analysis. By leveraging the versioned transaction log, it provides reproducible, consistent views of data without impacting ongoing operations.

## Row-level upserts/deletes — copy-on-write and merge-on-read

Delta Lake supports fine-grained modifications to datasets, such as row-level updates, inserts, and deletes, enabling use cases such as deduplication, GDPR compliance, and real-time data corrections. These operations are powered by **Copy-on-Write (CoW)** and **Merge-on-Read (MoR)** table types. Let's understand these two types.

## Copy-on-Write (CoW)

CoW tables physically rewrite data files whenever updates or deletes are performed. For example, if a row in a Parquet file is updated, a new version of the file is created with the changes, while the old version is marked as logically removed in the transaction log. This ensures that readers only access consistent data versions, but it can result in higher write amplification for frequent updates.

This is how CoW works:

1. File rewriting: When an update or delete operation is performed, the affected Parquet file is entirely rewritten. The updated rows are written to a new file, while rows that remain unchanged are copied as is.

2. **Log entries:** The Delta transaction log records.

3. **Remove entries:** The entries with remove mark the outdated files as logically removed. See the following example:

```
{
   "remove": {
     "path": "part-00000.snappy.parquet",
     "dataChange": true
   }
}
```

These files are excluded from future queries, but they remain accessible for time travel or rollback operations.

4. **Add entries:** The add entries reference the new files containing the updated rows:

```
{
   "add": {
     "path": "part-00001.snappy.parquet",
     "dataChange": true
   }
}
```

The transaction log ensures that either all updates are successfully written (via the add entries) or none at all. If a failure occurs, the old files remain active, guaranteeing consistency.

## Merge-on-Read (MoR)

MoR tables optimize row-level updates and deletes by avoiding full-file rewrites. Instead, they use **deletion vectors** to track rows marked for deletion. For updates, Delta Lake encodes changes as a combination of DELETE and INSERT operations; that is, the old row is marked as deleted, and a new row with updated values is appended. A deletion vector is an optimized bitmap structure that tracks rows within a specific Parquet file that are no longer valid or have been logically "deleted" in a particular version of a Delta table. Instead of physically removing these rows, the deletion vector provides a lightweight mechanism to mark them as deleted, enabling efficient row-level operations without rewriting entire files.

Here's how MoR works:

1. Marking old metadata as invalid: For each file containing rows marked for deletion, a remove entry is added to the transaction log. This entry effectively marks the old metadata for the file as invalid because it no longer references the new deletion vector. Take the following example:

```
{
        "remove": {
            "path": "part-00010.snappy.parquet",
            "deletionTimestamp": 1735678901234,
            "dataChange": true,
            "extendedFileMetadata": true,
            "size": 1203
        }
}
```

2. **Adding updated metadata with the deletion vector**: A new add entry is created in the transaction log to include updated metadata for the affected file, incorporating a reference to the associated deletion vector, as follows:

```
{
        "add": {
            "path": "part-00010.snappy.parquet",
            "deletionVector": {
                    "storageType": "u",
                    "pathOrInlineDv": "H$zK^mPLYT@9!FNxQ#Vr",
                    "offset": 10,
                    "sizeInBytes": 48,
                    "cardinality": 3
            },
            "dataChange": true
```

```
            }
      }
```

Moving on, let's explore some of the unique capabilities that Delta Lake brings to a data lake-house architecture.

# Unique capabilities

In this section, we will go over some of the unique capabilities and components that set Delta Lake apart.

## Change data feed

CDF in Delta Lake is designed to track and surface row-level changes (inserts, updates, or deletes) across versions of a table. It is particularly beneficial for incremental processing workloads, where minimizing the volume of data processed directly translates to reduced latency and cost. By categorizing changes as insert, update_preimage, update_postimage, and delete, Delta Lake provides granular visibility into how data evolves over time. This makes it an ideal solution for scenarios requiring data replication, debugging, or compliance audits. Unlike traditional CDC systems that rely on external tools or databases, Delta Lake achieves this functionality natively through its transaction log.

### How CDF works

CDF's integration with Delta Lake's transaction protocol enables efficient tracking of changes. The transaction log plays a key role by recording both the metadata of operations and references to the change data files generated. During any write operation, such as INSERT, UPDATE, or DELETE, the transaction log records the operation details in the commitInfo field. For example, let's say you execute a DELETE operation. The transaction log records the operation details in the commitInfo field, as shown:

```
{
   "commitInfo": {
      "timestamp": 1733916781786,
      "operation": "DELETE",
      "operationParameters": {
         "predicate": "[\"(employee_id#1162 = 3)\"]"
      },
      "readVersion": 1,
      "isolationLevel": "Serializable",
```

```json
      "isBlindAppend": false,
      "operationMetrics": {
        "numRemovedFiles": "1",
        "numRemovedBytes": "1264",
        "numCopiedRows": "0",
        "numAddedChangeFiles": "1",
        "executionTimeMs": "1014",
        "numDeletedRows": "1"
      },
      "engineInfo": "Apache-Spark/3.4.1 Delta-Lake/2.4.0"
    }
  }
```

Here, the operationMetrics property provides key details, such as the number of rows deleted (numDeletedRows: 1) and the change file generated (numAddedChangeFiles: 1). The log also includes a remove entry to mark the affected file as logically deleted.

```json
  {
    "remove": {
      "path": "part-00002-62810220-8389-4033-ae01-df44b6641419-c000.snappy.
  parquet",
      "deletionTimestamp": 1733916781775,
      "dataChange": true
    }
  }
```

This ensures that future queries against the table exclude the invalidated file. In parallel, a cdc action is recorded in the transaction log, referencing the change data file that contains details about the deleted row.

```json
  {
    "cdc": {
      "path": "_change_data/cdc-00000-c37f4865-27af-4e69-b088-de72314e53fd.
  c000.snappy.parquet",
      "size": 1535,
      "dataChange": false
    }
  }
```

The changed file (cdc-00000-c37f4865-27af-4e69-b088-de72314e53fd.c000.snappy.parquet), located in the table's _change_data directory (seen in the following figure), stores the modified row along with its _change_type field (delete).

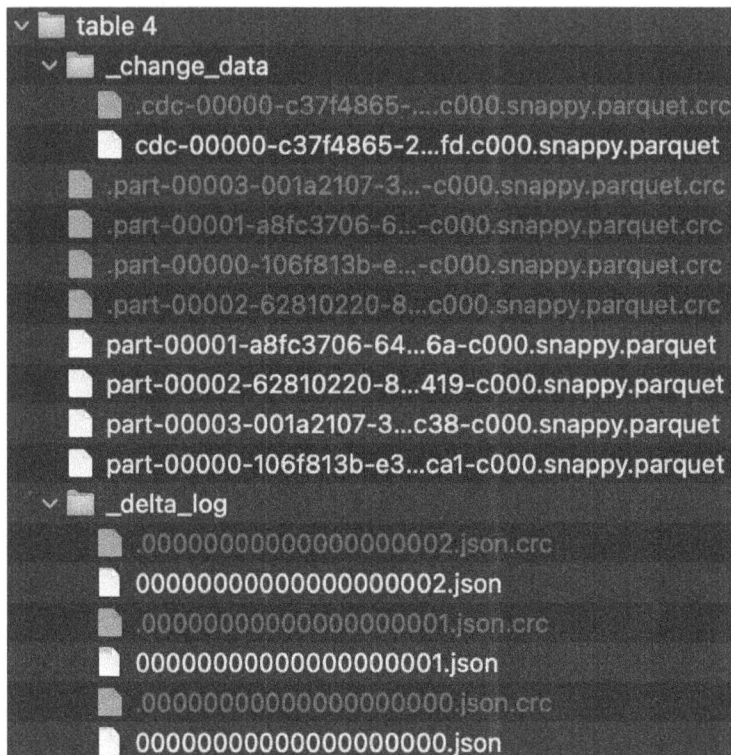

*Figure 5.6 – _change_data directory shows the changed data file*

Here's a snippet of the content of the changed file:

| # employee_id | # name | ᴬᴮ department | ᴬᴮ salary | # _change_type |
|---|---|---|---|---|
| 3 | Charlie | Finance | 65000 | delete |

*Figure 5.7 – Content of the changed file*

This modular approach ensures that changes are isolated and tracked independently of the main data files, enabling precise reconstruction of the affected rows. Additionally, by storing these changes in a compact and structured format, Delta Lake ensures that querying the _change_data files incurs minimal overhead, even as the table size grows.

# Liquid clustering

Efficient data clustering is important for optimizing query performance in large-scale datasets. Traditional clustering methods, such as Z Order in Delta Lake (to be discussed in detail in *Chapter 8, Performance Optimization and Tuning*), have proven effective but come with inherent limitations. For instance, Z Order requires rewriting all data during each optimization operation, regardless of whether new data has been added since the last execution. This results in the following:

- **Excessive write amplification**: Rewriting unchanged data adds unnecessary overhead, particularly in environments with frequent ingestions.

- **Fragility in optimization jobs**: When an optimization job fails, all intermediate progress is lost. Subsequent attempts must restart from scratch, consuming additional time and resources.

- **Manual configuration complexity**: Clustering operations often require users to repeatedly specify clustering columns, increasing the likelihood of errors and inconsistencies.

To address these challenges, Liquid clustering introduces an incremental and intelligent clustering mechanism. By combining advanced metadata with multi-dimensional clustering algorithms such as the **Hilbert curve**, Liquid clustering offers a more efficient solution for large datasets.

## How Liquid clustering works

At the core of Liquid clustering is the concept of incremental clustering powered by ZCubes. A ZCube represents a logical group of files clustered together during a single optimization pass. Each time Liquid clustering is executed, it identifies unoptimized files in the dataset. These files are grouped into a new ZCube and clustered using the Hilbert curve. A unique identifier, ZCUBE_ID, is assigned to each ZCube and stored in the Delta transaction log as part of the file metadata.

By tracking the clustering status of files through their ZCUBE_ID, Delta Lake ensures that already-clustered files remain untouched in future optimization passes. Only files without ZCUBE_ID are rewritten, significantly reducing I/O operations. Optimization tasks are processed in smaller batches, with each batch committing its changes independently. This ensures that intermediate progress is preserved even if a job fails, allowing subsequent runs to resume from the last successful batch. Liquid clustering eliminates the need for users to repeatedly specify clustering columns during every optimization run. The clustering column configuration is stored as part of the table metadata, ensuring consistency and reducing manual errors.

# Generated column

Data engineering workflows often require deriving new columns from existing ones during data ingestion or transformation. Without built-in support for managing such columns, engineers must rely on external preprocessing steps, increasing pipeline complexity and the risk of inconsistencies. Delta Lake's support for generated columns addresses these challenges by embedding derivation logic directly into the table schema.

Consider a real-world scenario – an organization ingests event logs with timestamps stored in a TIMESTAMP column. For optimal querying and partitioning, the data needs to be grouped by a DATE column derived from the timestamp. Without generated columns, this transformation must be handled in the data pipeline, requiring the following:

- Precomputing the DATE column before ingestion, adding complexity and compute costs
- Ensuring the DATE column consistently matches the TIMESTAMP column, which can be error-prone over time

These manual processes are inefficient and can lead to inconsistencies, especially as datasets scale or transformation logic evolves.

Generated columns tackle this problem. They are a special type of column whose values are automatically computed based on a user-defined expression referencing other columns in the table. These columns are always derived during data writes and are governed by strict constraints to ensure consistency.

For example, a table schema with a generated column might look like this:

```
CREATE TABLE events (
    event_id STRING,
    event_timestamp TIMESTAMP,
    event_date DATE GENERATED ALWAYS AS (CAST(event_timestamp AS DATE))
)
```

In this schema, event_date is a generated column computed from event_timestamp. Compute engines only need to provide values for event_timestamp and Delta Lake computes event_date automatically.

## How generated columns work

Generated columns are defined in the table schema using the GENERATED ALWAYS AS keyword, along with an expression that dictates how their values are computed. The expression ensures the generated column's value is always derived in the same way. When data is written to a Delta table, the following occurs:

- If no value is provided for a generated column, Delta Lake computes the value automatically based on the expression.

- If a value is explicitly provided, Delta Lake validates it against the expression, for instance, `event_date <=> CAST(event_timestamp AS DATE) IS TRUE`. If this condition is not satisfied, the write operation fails.

Similar to regular column values, the computed values for generated columns are stored in Parquet files. While this could increase storage costs (depending on the scale), it eliminates the need to recompute values during queries, reducing compute costs and improving query performance.

> Generated columns require a higher writer protocol version to ensure compatibility. This safeguards against older Delta Lake versions interacting with unsupported features.

# Delta Kernel

Delta Kernel provides a modular, engine-agnostic library that encapsulates the core Delta transaction protocol. Similar to how the Linux kernel abstracts hardware complexities and exposes a unified interface to applications, Delta Kernel abstracts low-level Delta operations such as metadata parsing, protocol enforcement, file-level actions, and transaction semantics. By centralizing this logic into a reusable library, Delta Kernel ensures that any compute engine, whether Spark, Flink, Trino, DuckDB, or custom systems, can interact with Delta tables consistently, reliably, and without re-implementing complex protocol details, which we'll cover in the following subsections.

## Core functionality

Delta Kernel serves as the backbone for interacting with Delta Lake tables, providing essential functionality that allows engines to do the following:

- Read and write Delta tables seamlessly

- Handle complex Delta protocol operations, such as ACID transactions, versioning, and schema evolution

- Manage metadata, including log files and data files, without requiring the engine to understand the internal details

Like a Linux kernel handling system calls, Delta Kernel ensures that engines focus on processing data without worrying about underlying Delta Lake mechanisms.

## Abstraction and simplification

One of Delta Kernel's key strengths lies in its ability to abstract the complexities of the Delta protocol. With simplified APIs for operations such as table reads and writes, it hides intricate details such as managing partition columns, deletion vectors, and log files. Engines can rely on Delta Kernel to handle these operations internally, enabling a streamlined development experience. This is comparable to the Linux kernel abstracting complex hardware operations such as file I/O and memory management, making it easier for applications to interact with underlying resources.

## Cross-engine compatibility

Designed to work across a variety of data engines and programming environments, Delta Kernel offers the following:

- A Java kernel for JVM-based engines such as Apache Spark and Trino
- A Rust kernel with bindings for languages such as C, C++, and Python, enabling broader ecosystem adoption

By acting as a universal translator, Delta Kernel ensures that any engine, regardless of its architecture, can interact with Delta tables efficiently.

Delta Kernel is built with distributed processing engines in mind, providing the following:

- Table metadata, such as schema and file lists, which is crucial for job planning in engines such as Spark or Trino
- Opaque file metadata, enabling engines to split data into subsets for worker distribution, similar to how Linux manages scheduling and resource allocation in distributed systems

This design ensures optimal performance and compatibility with large-scale distributed workloads.

## Extensibility and advanced integration

Delta Kernel offers customizable plugin interfaces that enable engines to manage system resources such as memory, CPU, and disk efficiently. Resource-intensive operations, such as Parquet reading and JSON parsing, are encapsulated behind these interfaces, allowing engines to tailor performance optimizations to their specific workloads. This flexibility mirrors the Linux kernel's modular design, where drivers and modules can be tailored to specific hardware or application needs.

A significant advantage of Delta Kernel is its ability to simplify the adoption of new Delta Lake features. Developers can access the latest features by updating the kernel version without modifying their code, ensuring compatibility and quick adoption across the Delta ecosystem. This streamlined upgrade path parallels how the Linux kernel enables consistent innovation by maintaining backward compatibility across hardware platforms.

Delta Kernel provides specialized APIs to handle core functionalities such as reading JSON and Parquet files and evaluating expressions over data. These APIs simplify the integration process for engines, ensuring they can leverage Delta Lake's advanced capabilities without needing to reinvent basic functionality.

## The Delta Kernel advantage

The primary advantage of Delta Kernel is standardization. Historically, each compute engine that wanted to read or write Delta tables had to implement parts of the Delta protocol independently, often resulting in fragmented feature coverage, inconsistent behavior, and slower adoption of new Delta features. Delta Kernel eliminates these discrepancies by providing a single, authoritative implementation of the protocol. This accelerates engine integrations, improves interoperability across the lakehouse ecosystem, and guarantees predictable behavior regardless of the engine used. Additionally, centralizing the protocol logic enables the Delta community to ship new features, such as protocol upgrades, optimized metadata handling, or new file-level actions, once in Delta Kernel, with all downstream engines benefiting immediately.

## Delta Sharing

Delta Sharing is an innovative feature that extends the power of Delta Lake beyond organizational boundaries. This open protocol enables secure, real-time data sharing across platforms, cloud providers, and environments, making Delta Lake a powerful tool for building an interconnected and collaborative data ecosystem.

Some of the key aspects of the delta sharing include the following features:

- Open and cross-platform sharing

  Delta Sharing facilitates the seamless sharing of live data directly from a Delta table without requiring data replication or migration. Its open design allows sharing across cloud providers such as AWS, Azure, and GCP, or even on-premises setups, avoiding vendor lock-in. This capability enables organizations to collaborate efficiently, regardless of the recipient's technology stack or location.

- Real-time access to live data

  One of the standout features of Delta Sharing is its ability to provide recipients with real-time access to the most up-to-date data. Unlike traditional sharing methods that rely on static copies, Delta Sharing ensures that users work with the latest version of the dataset, reducing inconsistencies and enabling better decision-making.

- Scalability and performance

  Delta Sharing is built to handle terabyte-scale datasets by leveraging efficient cloud storage systems such as S3, ADLS, and GCS. This design ensures high performance and reliability even for large-scale sharing operations, making it suitable for enterprise-grade workloads.

- Security and governance

  Security is at the core of Delta Sharing. It allows data providers to implement centralized governance, track access, and maintain compliance with data protection regulations. Providers can audit sharing activities and ensure that recipients only access authorized datasets, preserving data integrity and trust.

- Diverse client support

  Delta Sharing supports a wide range of tools and frameworks, including pandas, Apache Spark, and Rust. This compatibility allows recipients to connect using their preferred platforms, reducing barriers to access and enabling seamless integration into existing workflows.

- The Delta Sharing advantage

  By incorporating Delta Sharing, Delta Lake goes beyond traditional data lake functionalities to enable secure, scalable, and real-time data sharing. It fosters collaboration across organizational boundaries while maintaining rigorous security and governance standards, making it a cornerstone feature for building an open, connected data ecosystem.

Delta Sharing transforms Delta Lake into a platform for secure, real-time, and scalable cross-organizational data collaboration. It ensures users can access live, consistent data while maintaining governance, performance, and broad compatibility across tools and environments.

# Hands-on with Delta Lake and Apache Spark

In this section, we'll dive into practical exercises with Delta Lake, leveraging Apache Spark as the compute engine. We will walk you through setting up, managing, and working with Delta tables. By the end, you'll have hands-on experience with Delta Lake's robust capabilities, including syncing to catalogs, performing data operations with **Data Definition Language** (DDL) and DML, running time travel and schema evolution queries, and utilizing advanced features such as VACUUM and OPTIMIZE for data maintenance. Most examples will use Spark's SQL API, with the Python (PySpark) API incorporated for flexibility where applicable.

# Write and read operations with Spark and Delta

This section aims to guide you through the essential configurations needed to start working with Delta tables, including the compute engine and catalog setup. Once we have a solid understanding of these configurations, we'll dive into the various read and write operations supported by Delta tables.

## Getting the required packages

To begin working with Delta tables and Apache Spark, you'll need to install essential packages that enable Delta table operations, including reading, writing, and managing tables, along with a local installation of Apache Spark.

For the most up-to-date version compatibility, refer to the official Delta Lake documentation at https://delta.io/learn/getting-started/. At the time of writing, Delta Lake version 4.0.x is compatible with Spark 4.0.x. The following example uses Delta 3.2.0 on Spark 3.x for wider compatibility; for the latest supported versions.

To interact with Delta Lake using Spark SQL, Scala, or Python, a local installation of Apache Spark is required. You can choose the appropriate shell based on your preferred language: SQL, PySpark, or Spark shell for SQL, Python, or Scala, respectively.

## Setting up Spark SQL session

Once Apache Spark is installed, you can launch the interactive Spark SQL shell with Delta Lake support by including the necessary Delta packages and configurations. For many Delta Lake operations, you need to set the Spark SQL extension to DeltaSparkSessionExtension:

```
bin/spark-sql --packages io.delta:delta-spark_2.12:3.2.0
--conf "spark.sql.extensions=io.delta.sql.DeltaSparkSessionExtension"
--conf "spark.sql.catalog.spark_catalog=org.apache.spark.sql.delta.
catalog.DeltaCatalog"
```

This setup ensures that your Spark SQL session is fully configured to interact with Delta Lake tables, enabling transactional operations, time travel, and other Delta-specific features.

## Configuring catalogs for Delta Lake

Catalogs in Delta Lake play a vital role in enabling transactional consistency, simplifying table management, and ensuring seamless integration with various compute engines. By using a catalog, compute engines such as Apache Spark can manage and interact with Delta tables efficiently. Configuring a catalog is often the first step in setting up a Delta Lake environment. Delta Lake supports multiple catalog implementations, offering flexibility to integrate with popular metadata stores such as Hive Metastore, AWS Glue, and Databricks Unity Catalog.

In this chapter, we will explore how to configure and interact with catalogs for Delta Lake. We will focus on key components: compute engine, table format, and catalog setup. While Delta Lake can operate without a catalog, using a catalog unlocks advanced capabilities, including schema enforcement, time travel, and optimized query execution.

Delta Lake integrates with catalogs through Spark SQL extensions, using properties prefixed with `spark.sql.catalog.<catalog_name>`. These properties define the catalog instance and its implementation details, allowing seamless interaction with Delta tables. We will explore three common catalog configurations – Hadoop, Hive Metastore, and AWS Glue – along with their use cases and setup steps.

### Hadoop catalog

A Hadoop catalog provides a lightweight, file-based solution for managing Delta tables. Metadata is stored within the directory structure of the filesystem (HDFS, S3, or other compatible systems), making it easy to configure and use.

To configure a Hadoop-based catalog, add the following properties to your Spark session:

```
spark.sql.catalog.hadoop_catalog=org.apache.spark.sql.delta.catalog.
DeltaCatalog
spark.sql.catalog.hadoop_catalog.type=hadoop
spark.sql.catalog.hadoop_catalog.warehouse=s3a://deltalake/warehouse
```

The key components are as follows:

- `hadoop_catalog`: The catalog instance name
- `type`: Set to hadoop to specify a filesystem-based catalog
- `warehouse`: Defines the root path for storing Delta table data and metadata

**Use case:** The Hadoop catalog is suitable for small to medium-scale deployments where simplicity and local storage are priorities. It is also ideal for environments without a dedicated metadata service.

## Hive Metastore catalog

The Hive Metastore catalog enables Delta tables to integrate with Apache Hive's metadata service. This configuration is widely used in production environments where centralized metadata management and compatibility with multiple query engines are required.

To configure a Hive Metastore catalog for Delta Lake, use the following properties:

```
spark.sql.catalog.hive_catalog=org.apache.spark.sql.delta.catalog.
DeltaCatalog
spark.sql.catalog.hive_catalog.type=hive
spark.sql.catalog.hive_catalog.uri=thrift://metastore-host:9083
```

The key components are as follows:

- `hive_catalog`: The catalog instance name
- `type`: Set to `hive` to integrate with Hive Metastore
- `uri`: Specifies the Thrift URI for the Hive Metastore server

**Use case:** The Hive Metastore catalog is ideal for enterprise environments requiring advanced schema management, multi-engine compatibility, and centralized table metadata storage.

## AWS Glue Data Catalog

The AWS Glue Data Catalog is a managed metadata store provided by AWS. It integrates seamlessly with Delta Lake, allowing metadata to be stored in AWS Glue while data resides in Amazon S3. This setup is commonly used in cloud-native deployments.

To configure Delta Lake with AWS Glue, add the following properties:

```
spark.sql.catalog.glue_catalog=org.apache.spark.sql.delta.catalog.
DeltaCatalog
spark.sql.catalog.glue_catalog.type=glue
spark.sql.catalog.glue_catalog.warehouse=s3a://deltalake/warehouse
```

The key components are as follows:

- `glue_catalog`: The catalog instance name
- `type`: Set to `glue` to use AWS Glue as the metadata store
- `warehouse`: Specifies the S3 bucket path for Delta table data

**Use case:** AWS Glue is suitable for large-scale, cloud-native environments that require a fully managed metadata solution. It works well with Amazon EMR and other AWS services.

## DDL statements

With the catalog configured, we can now define and create tables using standard SQL DDL operations.

## CREATE TABLE

Let's start with creating the first Delta table:

```
CREATE TABLE customers_delta_demo (
        customer_id INT,
        first_name STRING,
        last_name STRING,
        email STRING,
        charges FLOAT,
        state STRING
    )
    USING delta
    PARTITIONED BY (state)
```

This command creates a table in the `default` namespace of `hdfs_catalog` with `state` as the partitioning field. Partitioning on `state` will allow efficient data pruning by partition, as the Delta table will organize data within each state, optimizing queries that filter by this column.

Alternatively, you can achieve the same using PySpark's DataFrame API. Go to Python packages, look for the compatible `delta-spark` package version, and install it. Here's the equivalent code:

```
from pyspark.sql import SparkSession
from pyspark.sql.types import StructType, StructField, IntegerType,
StringType, FloatType

# Initialize SparkSession with Delta Lake support
spark = SparkSession.builder \
    .appName("DeltaTableExample") \
    .config("spark.sql.extensions", "io.delta.sql.
DeltaSparkSessionExtension") \
    .config("spark.sql.catalog.spark_catalog", "org.apache.spark.sql.
delta.catalog.DeltaCatalog") \
    .getOrCreate()

# Define schema for the DataFrame
```

```
schema = StructType([
    StructField("customer_id", IntegerType(), True),
    StructField("first_name", StringType(), True),
    StructField("last_name", StringType(), True),
    StructField("email", StringType(), True),
    StructField("charges", FloatType(), True),
    StructField("state", StringType(), True)
])

# Create data for the DataFrame
data = [
    (1, "John", "Doe", "john.doe@example.com", 250.50, "CA"),
    (2, "Jane", "Smith", "jane.smith@example.com", 300.00, "NY"),
    (3, "Alice", "Brown", "alice.brown@example.com", 180.75, "TX")
]

# Create DataFrame
df = spark.createDataFrame(data, schema=schema)

# Write data to Delta table
df.write \
    .format("delta") \
    .mode("overwrite") \
    .partitionBy("state") \
    .save("customers_delta_demo")

print("Delta table created and records inserted.")
```

This demonstrates how to create and populate a Delta table using both SQL and PySpark, laying the foundation for efficient queries, partition pruning, and full Delta Lake functionality.

## CREATE TABLE AS SELECT (CTAS)

In Delta Lake, you can create a new table based on the results of a query using the DataFrame. write.format("delta") method. The following example creates a high_value_customers Delta table with data filtered from the customers table where charges exceed 1000:

```
CREATE TABLE high_value_customers

USING delta
```

```
PARTITIONED BY (state)
AS SELECT
    customer_id, first_name, last_name, state, charges
FROM customers_delta_demo
WHERE charges > 200
```

This approach efficiently creates new Delta tables from query results, enabling filtered or transformed datasets while retaining partitioning and Delta Lake capabilities.

## DROP TABLE

In Delta Lake, DROP TABLE removes the table definition from the catalog. However, the data files remain intact unless explicitly purged.

- **Drop table without deleting data**: To remove the table definition but retain the underlying data files, use the following:

  ```
  DROP TABLE IF EXISTS high_value_customers
  ```

- **Drop table and delete data files**: To delete both the table definition and the underlying data files, use the following:

  ```
  DROP TABLE IF EXISTS high_value_customers PURGE
  ```

Dropping a table provides flexibility to manage metadata and storage independently, allowing either safe removal of the table definition or complete deletion of both the table and its data.

## ALTER TABLE

Delta Lake supports schema evolution and provides the flexibility to modify table schemas using ALTER TABLE commands:

- **Adding a column**: To add a new column (phone_number) to the customers table, use the following:

  ```
  ALTER TABLE customers_delta_demo
  ADD COLUMN phone_number STRING
  ```

- **Renaming a column**: To rename the charges column to total_spent, use the following:

  ```
  ALTER TABLE customers_delta_demo
  RENAME COLUMN charges TO total_spent
  ```

- **Drop column**: To remove the phone_number column from the table schema, use the following:

```
ALTER TABLE customers_delta_demo
DROP COLUMN phone_number
```

These Spark SQL commands demonstrate how to manage Delta Lake tables effectively, including creating new tables, dropping tables, and altering schemas. The SQL interface makes it easy to implement these operations while leveraging Delta Lake's transactional consistency and schema evolution capabilities.

## DML statements

Delta Lake provides full support for common **Data Manipulation Language** (DML) operations, such as INSERT INTO, MERGE INTO, INSERT OVERWRITE, DELETE FROM, and UPDATE. These operations ensure consistency and enable efficient data modification while leveraging Delta Lake's ACID compliance. Let's go through some examples for each operation.

## INSERT INTO

The INSERT INTO command appends new rows to an existing Delta table without altering the existing data. It ensures that the new data integrates seamlessly while maintaining the table's structure and consistency. This is useful for adding incremental data to a table, such as new customer records or updated metrics from a periodic data pipeline.

The INSERT INTO command appends new records to an existing Delta table:

```
INSERT INTO customers_delta_demo
VALUES
(1, 'John', 'Doe', 'john.doe@example.com', 150.75, 'CA'),
(2, 'Alice', 'Smith', 'alice.smith@example.com', 200.50, 'NY'),
(3, 'Bob', 'Brown', 'bob.brown@example.com', 175.25, 'TX'),
(4, 'Emily', 'Davis', 'emily.davis@example.com', 220.30, 'FL');
```

Using INSERT INTO allows continuous growth of a Delta table by safely appending new data while preserving existing records and maintaining transactional integrity.

## MERGE INTO

The MERGE INTO command enables upserts (a combination of updates and inserts) by merging records from a source dataset into a target table based on a specified condition. This operation is ideal for implementing **Slowly Changing Dimensions** (SCDs) and **Change Data Capture** (CDC) workflows, or other scenarios where you need to update existing records while inserting new ones. By ensuring that only necessary changes are made, it avoids duplication and keeps the target table consistent with the latest data.

The `MERGE INTO` command performs upserts, updating existing records and inserting new ones based on the matching criteria:

```
MERGE INTO customers_delta_demo AS target
USING staging_updates AS source
ON target.customer_id = source.customer_id
WHEN MATCHED THEN
  UPDATE SET *
WHEN NOT MATCHED THEN
  INSERT *;
```

This query updates or inserts data from the `updates` table into the `customers` table, ensuring no duplicates or outdated entries.

## DELETE FROM

The `DELETE FROM` command removes rows from a Delta table based on a specified condition. Delta Lake handles deletions efficiently by rewriting only the affected data files while keeping the rest of the table intact. For partitioned tables, Delta Lake can perform partition-level deletions as a metadata-only operation, significantly improving the performance of large-scale deletions. This command is especially useful for cleaning up outdated or invalid data. Delta Lake supports both partition-level and row-level deletions:

- **Row-level delete**: To delete the record with `customer_id = 1`, use this statement:

    ```
    DELETE FROM customers_delta_demo
    WHERE customer_id = 1;
    ```

- **Partition-level delete**: To efficiently remove all records for the `CA` partition based on a condition, if the state column is used as a partition key, use this statement:

    ```
    DELETE FROM customers_delta_demo
    WHERE state = 'CA';
    ```

`DELETE FROM` allows precise removal of data while maintaining overall table integrity, supporting both row-level and partition-level deletions for efficient management of large Delta tables.

# UPDATE

The UPDATE command modifies existing rows in a Delta table based on a condition. Delta Lake uses two strategies – CoW and MoR – to perform updates. These updates can include adjusting column values, recalculating metrics, or fixing errors in existing records. By ensuring that only the necessary data is rewritten, Delta Lake minimizes the overhead associated with updates, making it an efficient choice for transactional workloads:

```
UPDATE customers_delta_demo
SET charges = charges * 1.1
WHERE state = 'CA';
```

This increases the charges for all customers in the CA partition by 10%.

# Read queries

Delta Lake supports different types of read queries that allow users to access both the latest and historical states of a dataset. These capabilities ensure reliable analytics even in the presence of concurrent updates, making it easier to serve diverse workloads ranging from real-time dashboards to compliance-driven audits.

## Snapshot reads

Snapshot reads allow you to query the current state of a Delta table using standard SQL SELECT statements. These queries are commonly used for data analysis, reporting, and integration into downstream systems. Delta Lake's snapshot mechanism ensures consistency and accuracy even during concurrent read and write operations:

```
SELECT * FROM customers_delta_demo;

SELECT * FROM customers_delta_demo
WHERE state = 'CA';
```

Snapshot reads provide a consistent view of the table at a specific point in time, enabling reliable queries and analytics even when concurrent writes are occurring.

## Time travel reads

Delta Lake's time travel feature enables querying data as it existed at a specific point in time, by using either a timestamp or a version number. This functionality is particularly useful for auditing, debugging, or recreating historical states of the data for compliance purposes. Time travel queries provide deep insights into how data has evolved over time, making them a powerful tool for modern data engineering workflows.

Query data as of a specific timestamp:

```
SELECT * FROM customers_delta_demo
TIMESTAMP AS OF '2024-10-26 15:30:00';
```

Query data as of a specific version:

```
SELECT * FROM customers_delta_demo VERSION AS OF 42;
```

These Delta Lake SQL commands provide equivalent functionality to the examples given for Iceberg. Delta's ACID guarantees, time travel support, and efficient DML operations make it an excellent choice for handling transactional workloads in modern data pipelines.

## Delta Lake commands and procedures

Delta Lake provides powerful built-in commands to manage tables, optimize storage, and ensure data consistency. These commands can be executed using Spark SQL or PySpark and are equivalent to procedures in Iceberg. They are designed to handle critical table operations, manage historical snapshots, and optimize file storage, enabling efficient data management in large-scale systems. In this section, we will explore some commonly used Delta Lake commands and their usage.

## VACUUM

VACUUM removes files no longer referenced by the Delta table, such as those created by overwrite operations or older snapshots. This helps reclaim storage space while maintaining data consistency.

By default, Delta retains data files for seven days for time travel. You can modify this retention period to suit your requirements:

```
VACUUM customers_delta_demo RETAIN 168 HOURS;
```

This command removes files older than the retention period of 168 hours (7 days). Use it with caution when reducing the retention period, as it may prevent time-traveling to older snapshots.

## RESTORE

RESTORE reverts a Delta table to a specific version or timestamp. This is useful for recovering from accidental overwrites or unwanted changes while preserving the history for future reference:

- **Restore by version:** This command reverts the table to the specified version, discarding all subsequent changes:

  ```
  RESTORE TABLE customers_delta_demo TO VERSION AS OF 42;
  ```

- **Restore by timestamp**: This command reverts the table to the specified timestamp, discarding all subsequent changes:

```
RESTORE TABLE customers_delta_demo TO TIMESTAMP AS OF '2024-10-01
12:00:00';
```

RESTORE provides a safe way to recover a table to a known good state, ensuring data integrity while preserving the ability to track and analyze historical changes.

## VACUUM (remove orphan files)

- The VACUUM command cleans up untracked files in the storage layer, which may have been left behind by aborted or incomplete operations. This helps maintain table integrity and optimize storage usage.

The DRY RUN option lists files eligible for removal without actually deleting them:

```
VACUUM customers_delta_demo DRY RUN;
```

After verifying, run the command without DRY RUN to permanently delete the orphaned files.

## OPTIMIZE

OPTIMIZE merges small files into larger ones, improving query performance by reducing metadata overhead and minimizing the number of files read during query execution. Delta Lake also supports Z-ordering for multi-dimensional clustering:

- **Bin-packing**: This command compacts small files into larger ones using default optimization strategies:

```
OPTIMIZE customers_delta_demo;
```

- **Z-ordering**: Z-ordering optimizes data layout by co-locating related records, enhancing the performance of queries that filter by the state column:

```
OPTIMIZE customers_delta_demo ZORDER BY (state);
```

OPTIMIZE improves query efficiency by reducing file fragmentation and leveraging Z-ordering to colocate related data, making read operations faster and more resource-efficient.

## CONVERT TO DELTA

`CONVERT TO DELTA` converts an existing Parquet or Hive table to a Delta table while preserving the existing data. This command is useful for adopting Delta Lake's capabilities without recreating the table from scratch, as shown:

```
CONVERT TO DELTA customers_delta_demo;
```

For partitioned tables, specify the partitioning columns:

```
CONVERT TO DELTA customers_delta_demo PARTITIONED BY (state);
```

`CONVERT TO DELTA` enables a seamless transition from traditional tables to Delta Lake, unlocking transactional guarantees, time travel, and optimized query performance without needing to rebuild the table.

These commands provide a comprehensive toolkit for managing Delta tables and optimizing storage, making Delta Lake a powerful choice for large-scale data pipelines. They enable users to reclaim storage, revert changes, clean up unreferenced data, and improve query performance through compact storage layouts. This foundation supports robust, scalable, and efficient analytical workflows, which we will explore further in *Chapter 11, Real-World Applications and Learnings*.

# Hands-on with Delta Lake and Apache Flink

Delta Lake integrates seamlessly with Apache Flink, enabling high-performance, fault-tolerant stream and batch processing on Delta tables. This combination offers robust capabilities such as ACID compliance, schema enforcement, and real-time processing, making it an excellent choice for lakehouse architecture.

In this section, we explore how to configure and perform various Delta Lake operations with Apache Flink using its SQL API.

You can find all of these examples in a Docker container in the repository (`https://github.com/PacktPublishing/Engineering-Lakehouses-with-Open-Table-Formats/tree/main/ch05`) to follow along.

## DDL statements

Delta Lake supports standard SQL DDL operations for managing tables and schemas. With these commands, you can create catalogs, databases, and Delta tables, laying the foundation for a structured and queryable lakehouse.

# CREATE CATALOG

Delta Lake requires a catalog to manage table metadata and provide a unified interface for accessing Delta tables. The Delta catalog can be set up as an in-memory catalog or backed by an external Hive Metastore.

```
CREATE CATALOG delta_catalog WITH (
  'type' = 'delta-catalog',
  'catalog-type' = 'in-memory');
USE CATALOG delta_catalog;
```

This command creates a Delta catalog named `delta_catalog` backed by a Hive Metastore, pointing to a specific Hadoop configuration directory.

# CREATE DATABASE

Delta Lake supports creating namespaces or databases within a catalog, organizing your tables efficiently.

```
CREATE DATABASE customer_data;
USE customer_data;
```

This command creates a database called `customer_data` and sets it as the active namespace.

# CREATE TABLE

Delta tables can be created with partitioning to optimize query performance.

```
CREATE TABLE customers (
    customer_id BIGINT,
    first_name STRING,
    last_name STRING,
    email STRING,
    charges FLOAT,
    state STRING
) PARTITIONED BY (state) WITH (
    'connector' = 'delta',
    'table-path' = 'file:///warehouse/customers'
);
```

This command creates a Delta table customers partitioned by the state column, storing the table data at the specified path.

# DML statements

Delta Lake supports standard SQL DML operations, allowing you to insert, update, delete, and merge data in a transactional and ACID-compliant manner. These operations enable efficient and reliable modifications to your Delta tables.

## INSERT INTO

Delta Lake allows inserting new records into tables efficiently.

```
INSERT INTO customers VALUES (1, 'John', 'Doe', 'john.doe@example.com',
100.0, 'CA');
```

This command appends a record to the customers table.

## Read queries

Delta Lake supports both bounded (batch) and continuous (streaming) reads, allowing you to process data efficiently based on your use case. Let's explore how to implement these reading modes using PySpark.

## Bounded mode (batch reading)

Bounded mode is used for reading a specific snapshot of data from a Delta table.

Here's how to perform a bounded read:

```
# Read the latest version of the Delta table
df = spark.read.format("delta").load("/path/to/delta/table")


# Read a specific version of the Delta table
df = spark.read.format("delta").option("versionAsOf", "10").load("/path/
to/delta/table")


# Read the table as of a specific timestamp
df = spark.read.format("delta").option("timestampAsOf", "2023-01-01
00:00:00").load("/path/to/delta/table")
```

You can also use time travel capabilities to read historical versions of the data:

```
# Read changes since version 5
df = spark.read.format("delta").option("startingVersion", "5").load("/
path/to/delta/table")
```

```
# Read changes since a specific timestamp
df = spark.read.format("delta").option("startingTimestamp", "2023-01-01
00:00:00").load("/path/to/delta/table")
```

This is useful for batch processing or when you need to analyze data up to a certain point in time.

## Continuous mode (streaming)

Continuous mode allows you to read a Delta table as a stream, processing new data as it arrives. This is ideal for real-time analytics and event-driven applications. Here's how to set up a streaming read:

```
# Create a streaming DataFrame
stream_df = spark.readStream.format("delta").load("/path/to/delta/table")

# Process the stream (example: count by customer ID)
query = (stream_df
    .groupBy("customer_id")
    .count()
    .writeStream
    .outputMode("complete")
    .option("checkpointLocation", "/path/to/checkpoint")
    .start("/path/to/output"))

# Wait for the streaming query to terminate
query.awaitTermination()
```

You can also specify a starting point for the stream:

```
# Start streaming from a specific version
stream_df = spark.readStream.format("delta").option("startingVersion",
    "5").load("/path/to/delta/table")

# Start streaming from a specific timestamp
stream_df = spark.readStream.format("delta").option("startingTimestamp",
    "2023-01-01 00:00:00").load("/path/to/delta/table")
```

Continuous mode enables real-time processing of incoming data, allowing Delta tables to power streaming analytics and event-driven workflows while maintaining consistency and fault tolerance.

# Best practices

Delta Lake supports both batch (bounded) and streaming (continuous) processing, each optimized for specific workloads. Understanding the differences in latency, throughput, consistency, and operational patterns is key to building scalable and resilient pipelines. The table below summarizes the best practices for leveraging Delta in each mode.

| Dimension | Bounded (Batch) | Continuous (Streaming) |
|---|---|---|
| What it reads | A snapshot (latest or time-traveled) | New commits appended after a starting point (version/timestamp) |
| Latency | Minutes to seconds per job; optimized for large scans | Seconds to sub-seconds (micro-batch/continuous); optimized for small, incremental reads |
| Throughput | Very high (full-table scans, vectorized Parquet) | High sustained ingest; incremental tailing of the Delta log |
| Consistency | Snapshot isolation: a single, consistent view | Exactly once semantics via checkpoints + commit log; incremental state updates |
| Startup cost | Full plan + file pruning on manifests; can be heavy on very large tables | Fast start (tail transaction log), low-cost incremental planning |
| Typical use | Backfills, periodic analytics, machine learning feature builds, compaction/`OPTIMIZE` windows | Real-time dashboards, event-driven metrics, CDC pipelines |
| Failure recovery | Re-run job; idempotent by version/timestamp | Automatic from `checkpointLocation` + last committed batch ID |
| Performance knobs | Z-order/`OPTIMIZE`, data skipping, partition pruning, vectorization | Trigger interval, state store tuning, watermarking, auto/`OPTIMIZE` + small-file mitigation |

*Table 5.1 – Comparison of best practices for bounded and continuous Delta Lake reads*

The following explains why Delta performs well in both:

- Batch (bounded) leverages snapshot isolation, manifest/file pruning, vectorized Parquet, and layout optimizations (e.g., Z-Order, OPTIMIZE, compaction) to push very high throughput on large historical windows.

- Streaming (continuous) avoids expensive file listing by tailing the Delta transaction log, reading only new commits since startingVersion/startingTimestamp. Combined with checkpointing, this yields low-latency, exactly-once incremental processing.

**Practical guidance:**

- Choose bounded when your goal is complete, reproducible snapshots (backfills, daily/hourly analytics, machine learning training sets) and you can make up for heavy scans with layout optimizations

- Choose continuous when you need freshness (seconds) and incremental metrics; keep latency stable by managing small files (auto-compaction/OPTIMIZE), setting a reasonable trigger interval, and tuning state store and watermarking for streaming aggregations

- Hybrid patterns are common: use streaming to maintain near-real-time derived tables, and run periodic batch jobs to rebalance layout (OPTIMIZE/compaction) and serve heavy backfills

**Rule of thumb**: If your SLA is **freshness**, start streaming. If your SLA is **completeness** and **reproducibility**, run bounded reads with time travel. With Delta as the abstraction, both modes share the same table and lineage, so teams can mix them safely without data copies.

The following is a recap of the best practices:

- Use bounded reads for historical analysis or batch jobs, and continuous reads for real-time pipelines

- Leverage time travel to recover from errors or analyze changes

- Always specify a checkpoint location for streaming queries

- Apply partitioning for large datasets to improve query performance

Following these practices ensures scalable, resilient pipelines, whether you are analyzing snapshots or streaming fresh data.

# Summary

In this chapter, we explored Delta Lake, a robust and open source storage layer designed to power lakehouse architectures with transactional integrity and scalability. You were introduced to Delta Lake's core capabilities, such as ACID transactions, schema evolution, and time travel, which address common challenges in managing large-scale, real-time data workloads. The chapter provided a detailed walk-through of Delta Lake's features, including its mechanisms for managing metadata, implementing incremental updates, and ensuring data consistency through advanced indexing and caching techniques. Hands-on exercises demonstrated how to perform CRUD operations, optimize tables with VACUUM and compaction, and leverage Delta Lake's advanced functionalities such as Z-ordering and CDC.

You have gained a solid understanding of how Delta Lake enhances the functionality of data lakes, transforming them into fully transactional lakehouses. The practical exercises provided a foundation for implementing Delta Lake in real-world scenarios, ensuring performance, reliability, and governance across diverse use cases.

In the next chapter, we will explore the vital role of catalogs in lakehouse architectures. The chapter will delve into different catalog solutions, such as Unity Catalog, AWS Glue, and Iceberg REST, and demonstrate how to synchronize and manage metadata across these systems.

## Questions

1.  What is Delta Lake, and how does it address challenges in traditional data lakes?
2.  Explain the role of ACID transactions in Delta Lake.
3.  What are Delta Lake's capabilities for handling schema evolution?
4.  How does time travel work in Delta Lake, and why is it useful?
5.  What is the purpose of the `VACUUM` command in Delta Lake?
6.  Describe how Delta Lake achieves scalability and performance through Z-ordering.
7.  What are the benefits of Delta Lake's CDC feature?
8.  How does Delta Lake ensure data reliability during concurrent operations?
9.  What is the significance of Delta Lake's `MERGE INTO` operation?
10. Why is Delta Lake considered a key enabler of the lakehouse architecture?

## Answers

1.  Delta Lake is an open source storage layer that brings ACID transactions, schema enforcement, and time travel capabilities to data lakes. It addresses issues such as data inconsistency, lack of governance, and inefficiencies in querying large datasets.
2.  ACID transactions ensure reliable and consistent data updates by maintaining atomicity, consistency, isolation, and durability. They enable concurrent operations without data corruption and guarantee the integrity of write and read operations.
3.  Delta Lake supports schema evolution by allowing changes such as adding or modifying columns without breaking existing queries or compromising data consistency. Schema checks can be enforced to ensure compatibility during data writes.
4.  Time travel allows querying historical data by accessing snapshots of the table at specific points in time, identified by version numbers or timestamps. It is useful for auditing, debugging, and recovering from unintended changes.

5. The VACUUM command removes unused or orphaned files that are no longer referenced by the Delta table, freeing up storage space. By default, Delta retains files for seven days to support time travel.

6. Z-ordering optimizes query performance by physically clustering data based on one or more columns. This minimizes the number of files scanned during queries, improving efficiency, especially for range-based filters.

7. CDC captures and tracks data changes, enabling efficient incremental processing. This is particularly useful for streaming pipelines and updating downstream systems with minimal latency.

8. Delta Lake uses a transaction log to serialize operations, ensuring consistency even during concurrent reads and writes. It also employs optimistic concurrency control to handle conflicts gracefully.

9. The MERGE INTO operation facilitates upserts (updates and inserts) by merging data from a source into a target table based on matching conditions. This is vital for handling SCDs and deduplication.

10. Delta Lake unifies the flexibility of data lakes with the transactional reliability of data warehouses. Its features enable structured and unstructured data processing, real-time analytics, and governance, making it a cornerstone of the lakehouse paradigm.

## Get This Book's PDF Version and Exclusive Extras

UNLOCK NOW

Scan the QR code (or go to packtpub.com/unlock). Search for this book by name, confirm the edition, and then follow the steps on the page.

*Note: Keep your invoice handy. Purchases made directly from Packt don't require an invoice.*

# 6

# Catalog and Metadata Management

In modern data ecosystems, managing data efficiently is critical for deriving insights and making informed decisions. Lakehouse architectures combine the best aspects of data lakes and data warehouses, offering scalability and performance while supporting diverse workloads such as analytics, machine learning, and real-time processing. A key enabler of this architecture is the catalog, a metadata management layer that acts as the backbone of a lakehouse.

In this chapter, we will cover the following topics:

- The importance of catalogs in a lakehouse architecture
- Iceberg REST catalog specification
- Popular catalog options for lakehouses

By the end of this chapter, you will have a comprehensive understanding of how catalogs play a pivotal role in lakehouse architecture, knowledge of key catalog options, and hands-on experience with their integration and configuration for modern data platforms.

## Technical requirements

You can find the code files for this chapter on GitHub at https://github.com/PacktPublishing/ Engineering-Lakehouses-with-Open-Table-Formats/tree/main/ch06.

# The importance of catalogs in a lakehouse architecture

In modern lakehouse architecture, catalogs play a foundational role in managing metadata consistently across multiple compute engines and table formats. They act as a unified interface that tracks table schemas, locations, and versions, enabling reliable operations, efficient query planning, and transactional guarantees. Without a catalog, managing large volumes of structured and semi-structured data across distributed environments becomes error-prone and operationally complex.

In the sections that follow, we explore what catalogs are, why they matter, their essential features, and how they support different open table formats such as Apache Iceberg, Hudi, and Delta Lake.

## Introduction to catalogs

A catalog is essentially a service or database that stores metadata about datasets, tables, and their schemas. In the context of a lakehouse, a catalog provides a unified interface to manage data across multiple engines and formats. Unlike direct object storage access, where metadata management is minimal and decentralized, a catalog centralizes metadata, ensuring that all operations, such as reading, writing, and querying are consistent and efficient.

For example, a catalog keeps track of the following:

- Table schemas (column names, types, and constraints)
- Partitioning and clustering information
- Historical versions and snapshots for time travel queries
- Access control and governance policies

By managing this metadata centrally, catalogs eliminate manual intervention, reduce errors, and enhance the reliability of data operations.

Governance in this context refers to the policies and controls that regulate how data is accessed, shared, and audited. This includes **role-based access control (RBAC)**, column- or row-level security rules, data retention policies, and audit logging to meet compliance requirements (for example, GDPR or HIPAA).

# Why metadata management matters

Metadata serves as the "map" of your data ecosystem. Without effective metadata management, navigating a lakehouse architecture becomes cumbersome and error-prone. Here are the core reasons why metadata management is indispensable:

- **Consistency across engines**: Modern lakehouses support multi-engine compatibility (for example, Apache Spark, Presto, and Flink). A catalog ensures all engines work with the same view of the table metadata, avoiding mismatches and errors.

- **Transaction support**: Catalogs are integral for ensuring **Atomicity, Consistency, Isolation, Durability (ACID)** compliance. They record transactional changes and allow rollback or recovery in case of failures.

- **Optimized query performance**: By maintaining information about partitions and file locations, catalogs enable query engines to prune irrelevant data early, reducing scan times and improving performance.

- **Data discovery and governance**: A catalog serves as a searchable registry for datasets, making it easy to discover and govern data. This is particularly useful in organizations with thousands of datasets.

Consider a scenario where a data engineer adds a new column to a table. Without a catalog, ensuring that all downstream systems recognize this change can be tedious and error-prone. Each consumer, such as Spark jobs, BI dashboards, or ETL pipelines would need to be manually updated to align with the new schema.

With a catalog, schema changes are centrally managed and immediately reflected across all systems interacting with the table. Modern table formats such as Apache Iceberg, Hudi, and Delta Lake embed schema evolution as a first-class feature. Here are some examples:

- **Additive changes** (e.g., adding a new column) are tracked in the catalog's metadata. Downstream consumers can query the table without breaking, and by default, systems either ignore the new column or include it in results, depending on query settings.

- **Column renames and reordering** are supported by maintaining column IDs in the schema metadata, so readers don't misinterpret columns even if their order or names change.

- **Type promotions** (e.g., INT $\rightarrow$ BIGINT) are supported in a controlled way, ensuring compatibility between old and new data.

- **Backward/forward compatibility** is achieved because each snapshot of the table preserves the schema at the time of commit. This allows readers to time-travel to historical data using the schema that was valid at that point.

In practice, this means a BI tool reading from the catalog will always see a consistent schema, while Spark or Flink jobs can continue to process older data versions without breaking. The catalog serves as the **single source of truth** for schema definitions, and table formats ensure that schema evolution happens in a way that maintains both consistency and compatibility across the system.

## Core features of a catalog

Catalogs in a lakehouse architecture provide several critical features that make them indispensable:

- **Schema management:** Catalogs maintain and enforce table schemas, preventing incompatible data from being ingested. This is essential for analytics and machine learning workloads, where schema consistency is critical.

- **Time travel and versioning:** A catalog tracks historical snapshots of tables, enabling time travel queries. Users can retrieve data as it existed at a specific point, aiding in debugging, auditing, and reproducibility.

- **Partitioning and clustering:** These configurations are stored as part of the table's metadata, not in the catalog itself. Table formats such as Iceberg, Delta Lake, and Hudi record partition specs and, in some cases, clustering or sort order in their metadata files. Query engines access this metadata through the catalog to prune partitions, skip files, and optimize scan performance.

- **Access control and governance:** Catalogs provide RBAC to protect sensitive data. They also log actions such as table modifications, helping organizations comply with data privacy regulations such as GDPR.

- **Multi-engine interoperability:** A catalog ensures different engines such as Spark, Flink, and Trino can interact with the same dataset seamlessly, providing a unified experience across tools.

A well-managed catalog keeps your lakehouse reliable and scalable by unifying schema control, governance, and optimization so every engine works from the same trusted source of truth.

## Role of catalogs across table formats

Catalogs are foundational for table formats such as Apache Iceberg, Delta Lake, and Apache Hudi, which are central to lakehouse architectures. Let's explore how catalogs support these formats:

- **Apache Iceberg:** Iceberg leverages catalogs for transactional metadata management, enabling features such as schema evolution, partitioning, and time travel. Iceberg supports various catalog implementations, such as Hive Metastore, AWS Glue, and its own REST catalog.

- **Delta Lake**: Delta Lake uses catalogs to manage its transaction logs and provide governance capabilities. Tools such as Unity Catalog enhance Delta Lake's ability to enforce access controls and manage multi-engine queries.

- **Apache Hudi**: Hudi integrates with catalogs such as Hive Metastore and AWS Glue for schema registration, table discovery, and synchronization. Catalogs enable Hudi to provide snapshot isolation and incremental processing.

In a multi-cloud environment, a single dataset may need to be queried from both AWS Glue and Google BigQuery. A catalog ensures metadata consistency, enabling seamless operations across platforms.

## Challenges without a catalog

Operating a lakehouse without a catalog can lead to several challenges:

- **Inconsistent views**: Metadata inconsistencies can lead to incorrect query results or operational failures

- **Data duplication**: Without a central catalog, managing multiple versions of the same dataset across engines can result in data duplication and increased costs

- **Manual interventions**: Engineers may need to manually manage metadata, increasing the risk of human errors

- **Lack of governance**: Absence of centralized access control and logging makes it difficult to enforce governance and comply with regulations

Catalogs are the backbone of a lakehouse architecture, providing consistency, efficiency, and governance. By enabling transactional metadata management, catalogs ensure that diverse engines and tools can operate seamlessly in a distributed environment. As lakehouse adoption grows, catalogs will continue to play a pivotal role in managing complex data ecosystems, enabling organizations to unlock the full potential of their data.

With this foundation in place, let's now turn our attention to one of the most significant advancements in catalog design: the Iceberg REST catalog specification.

## Iceberg REST catalog specification

The Apache Iceberg REST catalog is a pivotal component introduced in Iceberg version 0.14.0, designed to enhance flexibility and control in metadata management within data lake architectures. By decoupling catalog implementations from client-specific logic, it offers a standardized approach to managing table metadata across diverse environments.

# What is the REST catalog?

Traditionally, Iceberg tables relied on catalog backends such as Hive Metastore, AWS Glue, or JDBC-based catalogs. While these catalogs work, each has its own APIs and client logic, which creates tight coupling between compute engines and the catalog implementation. This leads to fragmentation and makes it harder to standardize features such as schema evolution, transactions, or multi-engine interoperability.

The Iceberg REST catalog represents a significant advancement in managing Iceberg tables across diverse computing environments. At its core, it's a server-side catalog implementation that exposes Iceberg catalog functionality through a standardized REST API. This approach creates a powerful abstraction layer between Iceberg clients and the underlying catalog implementation, offering numerous benefits to data engineers and architects.

One of the key strengths of the REST catalog lies in its standardization. By adhering to the Apache Iceberg REST API specification, it ensures consistency across different implementations. This standardization is particularly valuable in heterogeneous environments where multiple programming languages and compute engines coexist. The REST catalog's flexibility extends to its storage support, seamlessly working with various systems such as HDFS and S3.

Security and governance are paramount concerns in modern data architectures, and the REST catalog addresses both with robust features. It supports OAuth2 authentication and HTTPS to provide secure communication channels for sensitive data operations. In addition, it enables fine-grained access control, audit logging, and policy enforcement at the metadata layer, ensuring not only that data is protected but also that organizations can meet governance and compliance requirements such as GDPR or HIPAA.

The REST catalog finds its niche in several key use cases. In multi-language environments, it serves as a unifying interface, reducing the need for language-specific implementations. For vendors offering Iceberg-based solutions, it simplifies support for various client environments. When enhanced features such as server-side deconfliction or multi-table commits are required, the REST catalog stands out as an ideal choice. It also excels in scenarios demanding secure table sharing across organizational boundaries, and its centralized management of root metadata simplifies version upgrades, a critical aspect of maintaining a healthy data ecosystem.

# Architecture of the REST catalog

The architecture of the Iceberg REST catalog is designed with flexibility, scalability, and interoperability in mind. At its foundation, the REST API layer serves as the primary interface, implementing the API specification and handling crucial aspects such as authentication and authorization. This layer acts as the gatekeeper, ensuring that all interactions with the catalog are secure and compliant with defined protocols.

Behind the API layer, the catalog backend takes center stage in managing metadata storage and retrieval. This component is crucial for maintaining the integrity and organization of table metadata, a cornerstone of Iceberg's powerful capabilities. The storage layer complements this by handling the physical storage of table data and metadata files, interfacing with various storage systems to provide a unified data management experience.

On the client side, the architecture includes a client layer that implements the REST catalog client in various languages. This diversity in client implementations is key to the catalog's broad applicability across different programming environments. Optionally, a metrics store can be integrated to manage and track Iceberg-specific metrics, providing valuable insights into catalog performance and usage patterns.

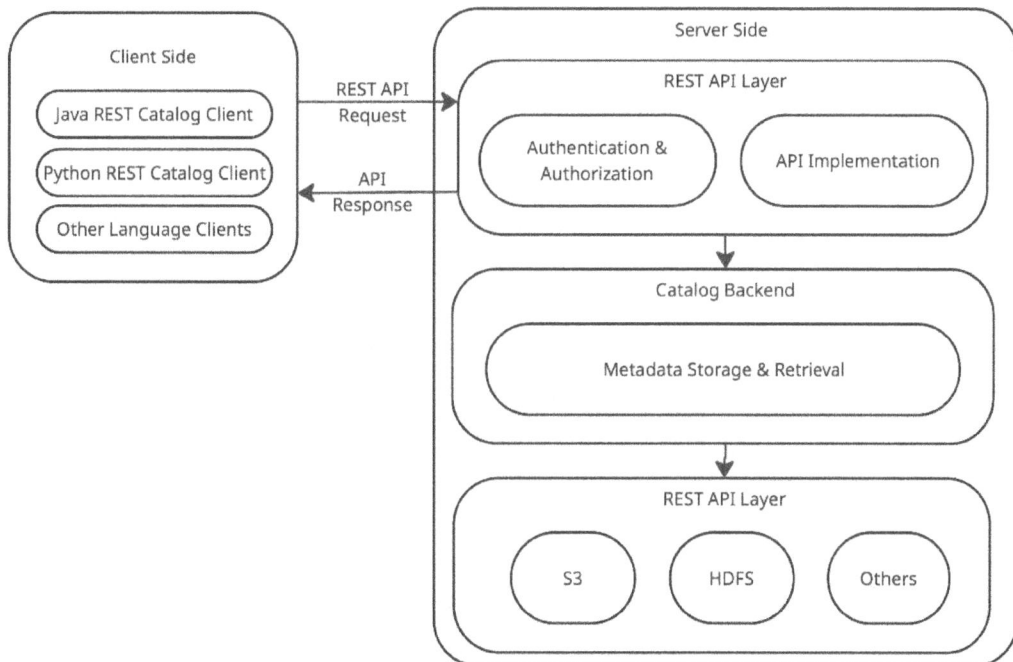

*Figure 6.1 – Iceberg REST catalog architecture*

The interaction flow within this architecture is streamlined for efficiency. When a client sends a REST API request, it first passes through the authentication and authorization checks at the API layer. Once validated, the server processes the request, often involving interactions with the catalog backend. For operations that require access to data or metadata files, the catalog backend communicates with the storage layer. Finally, the server compiles and sends the API response back to the client.

This architectural design brings several key advantages:

- Client-side decoupling
- Standardized API
- Extensibility
- Scalability
- Interoperability

We will dive deep into these advantages in the following sections.

## Benefits of using the REST catalog

The adoption of the Iceberg REST catalog brings a host of benefits that address many of the challenges faced in modern data architectures. One of its most significant advantages is the interoperability it offers. By providing a unified interface across different programming languages and compute engines, it breaks down the silos that often exist in diverse technical environments. This means that whether your team is using Python for data science, Java for engineering, or SQL for analytics, they can all interact with the same Iceberg tables through a single, consistent interface.

Scalability is another crucial benefit of the REST catalog. Its server-side implementation can be scaled independently of clients, allowing for more efficient resource management. As data volumes grow and user access increases, the catalog can be horizontally scaled to handle the increased load without necessitating changes to client applications. This flexibility is particularly valuable in dynamic data environments where demand can fluctuate rapidly.

The decoupling effect of the REST catalog cannot be overstated. Separating client implementations from the underlying catalog logic allows for independent evolution of these components. This means that organizations can upgrade or even completely change their catalog backend without requiring modifications to the various client applications and compute engines accessing the data. Such flexibility is invaluable in long-term data strategy planning.

Enhanced commit mechanisms provided by the REST catalog contribute significantly to data integrity and consistency. The ability to perform server-side deconfliction and retries results in fewer failures, especially in high-concurrency environments. This feature is particularly beneficial in scenarios where multiple processes are writing to the same table simultaneously.

The REST catalog also simplifies metadata upgrades, a critical aspect of maintaining a healthy data ecosystem. With root metadata managed centrally by the catalog service, version upgrades become more controlled and consistent across all tables. This centralized approach reduces the complexity and potential errors associated with distributed metadata management.

Security and governance are enhanced through the REST catalog's support for secure table sharing. It can manage access control and generate temporary credentials, allowing for secure, fine-grained data sharing without exposing underlying storage systems. This capability is particularly valuable when sharing data with external partners or across different organizational units.

Lastly, the standardization brought by the REST catalog ensures consistency across different implementations. This is especially beneficial for organizations operating in multi-cloud environments or those looking to maintain a consistent data interface across various systems and platforms.

# Implementing an Iceberg REST catalog

Implementing the REST catalog involves setting up a server that adheres to the Iceberg REST API specification and configuring clients to communicate with it.

## Server implementation and setup

Setting up the Iceberg REST catalog begins with selecting a server-side implementation that adheres to the Iceberg REST API specification. A popular choice is Apache Gravitino, which offers a robust and open source implementation out of the box. Gravitino is particularly flexible because it supports multiple catalog protocols—including the traditional **Hive Metastore** (**HMS**) API, as well as the newer Iceberg REST API. This dual capability allows organizations to migrate gradually: existing workloads that depend on HMS can continue to function, while new workloads can take advantage of the REST catalog's standardized, decoupled interface.

Once the implementation is selected, the next step is configuring the backend storage where the catalog metadata will reside. This typically involves specifying the backend type (e.g., JDBC), the connection URI, and the data warehouse path. For example, a JDBC-based setup using PostgreSQL and HDFS might include the following configuration parameters:

```
gravitino.iceberg-rest.catalog-backend=jdbc
gravitino.iceberg-rest.uri=jdbc:postgresql://127.0.0.1:5432
gravitino.iceberg-rest.warehouse=hdfs://127.0.0.1:9000/user/hive/
warehouse-jdbc
```

Security is another key consideration in the server setup. Depending on organizational policies, this might include setting up OAuth2 authentication, TLS encryption, or custom authentication modules to control access to catalog operations.

Finally, the REST catalog server must be deployed in an environment that ensures high availability, scalability, and reliability. This typically involves containerization or VM-based deployment with considerations for load balancing, fault tolerance, and monitoring.

Once all configurations are in place, the server can be started following the documentation of the chosen implementation (e.g., Apache Gravitino). At this point, the Iceberg REST catalog becomes accessible to client engines via standardized RESTful endpoints, enabling metadata operations such as table creation, listing, and retrieval in a decoupled and language-agnostic manner.

## Client implementation and configuration

The client-side setup for interacting with an Iceberg REST catalog depends on the compute engine or programming language in use. The goal is to configure the client to communicate with the REST server using standard Iceberg APIs over HTTP.

For **Apache Spark**, this is done through the Spark configuration, where users must define the catalog implementation class and specify the catalog type as rest. Additionally, the URI of the REST catalog server must be provided. An example configuration in spark-defaults.conf or a notebook session might look like this:

```
spark.sql.catalog.rest_catalog = org.apache.iceberg.spark.SparkCatalog
spark.sql.catalog.rest_catalog.type = rest
spark.sql.catalog.rest_catalog.uri = http://localhost:9001/iceberg/
```

For Java clients, configuration involves using the RESTCatalog class provided by Iceberg. Developers create a map of properties that includes the URI of the REST catalog server and any required authentication credentials. The catalog is then initialized using these properties:

```
Map<String, String> properties = new HashMap<>();
properties.put("uri", "http://localhost:9001/iceberg/");
properties.put("credential", "t-1234:secret");

Catalog catalog = new RESTCatalog();
catalog.initialize("rest_catalog", properties);
```

To summarize, the client setup process includes the following:

- **Setting the catalog type:** Configure the client to use the REST interface by setting the catalog type to rest
- **Providing connection details:** Include the catalog server URI and authentication credentials if required

- **Initializing the catalog**: Use the appropriate client library (e.g., Spark or Java API) to initialize and access the REST catalog, enabling metadata operations such as table creation and queries

This setup allows compute engines and custom applications to interact with Iceberg tables via a standardized RESTful interface, ensuring consistency and interoperability in distributed environments.

# Using the REST catalog

Once the setup is complete, using the REST catalog involves operations such as creating tables, loading tables, performing scans, and committing changes. These operations abstract away the complexities of direct file system interactions, providing a clean and consistent interface for metadata and data manipulation.

## Creating a table

Define the schema, partition specification, and properties for your Iceberg table, and use the catalog to create the table in the specified database:

```
Schema schema = new Schema( Types.NestedField.required(1, "id", Types.
LongType.get()), Types.NestedField.required(2, "data", Types.StringType.
get()) );
PartitionSpec spec = PartitionSpec.builderFor(schema) .identity("id")
.build();
catalog.createTable(TableIdentifier.of("my_database", "my_table"), schema,
spec, properties);
```

**Expected output:**

Upon successful creation, the method returns a `Table` instance pointing to the new table. No explicit console output is produced, but internally a metadata file (e.g., `00000.metadata.json`) is created at the catalog's warehouse location.

## Loading a table

Retrieve an existing Iceberg table from the catalog by specifying its database and table name:

```
Table table = catalog.loadTable(TableIdentifier.of("my_database", "my_
table"));
System.out.println("Loaded table schema: " + table.schema()); System.out.
println("Table location: " + table.location());
```

**Expected output:**

```
Loaded table schema: Struct<1: id: required long, 2: data: required
string>
Table location: hdfs://warehouse/my_database/my_table
```

Once the table is loaded, the next step is to inspect its underlying files by planning a scan.

## Performing a scan

Plan a scan on the table to retrieve file scan tasks and iterate through them:

```
TableScan scan = table.newScan();
CloseableIterable<FileScanTask> tasks = scan.planFiles();
for (FileScanTask task : tasks) {
    System.out.println("Processing file: " + task.file().path());
}
```

**Expected output:**

```
Processing file: hdfs://warehouse/my_database/my_table/data/00001.parquet
Processing file: hdfs://warehouse/my_database/my_table/data/00002.parquet
```

After reviewing the table's contents, you can apply updates by starting a transaction and committing your changes.

## Committing changes

Initiate a transaction, append a data file, and commit the transaction:

```
Transaction txn = table.newTransaction();
txn.newAppend()
    .appendFile(dataFile)
    .commit();
txn.commitTransaction();
System.out.println("Transaction committed successfully.");
```

**Expected output:**

```
Transaction committed successfully.
```

This operation results in a new metadata version being written and the appended file being reflected in subsequent scans.

# Best practices for REST catalogs

Implementing and maintaining an Iceberg REST catalog in a production environment requires adherence to a set of best practices to ensure reliability, performance, and security. Security should be a top priority, with strong authentication mechanisms such as OAuth2 or mutual TLS in place. All communications should be encrypted using HTTPS, and a system of fine-grained access control should be implemented at the catalog level. Regular rotation of credentials and comprehensive audit logging are also crucial security measures.

To maximize the benefits of the REST catalog, consider the following best practices:

- **Adhere to specifications**: Ensure that both server and client implementations strictly follow the Iceberg REST OpenAPI specification to maintain compatibility and interoperability

- **Implement robust security measures**: Protect the REST catalog with appropriate authentication and authorization mechanisms to safeguard metadata from unauthorized access

- **Monitor performance**: Regularly assess the performance of the REST catalog server, identifying and addressing potential bottlenecks to maintain optimal responsiveness

- **Plan for scalability**: Design the REST catalog infrastructure to accommodate future growth, including considerations for scaling storage and compute resources as data volumes increase

- **Maintain documentation**: Keep comprehensive documentation of the REST catalog implementation, including configuration settings and operational procedures, to facilitate maintenance and troubleshooting

By implementing these best practices, organizations can ensure that their REST catalog deployments are secure, efficient, and capable of supporting their evolving data management needs.

In summary, the Iceberg REST catalog offers a flexible and standardized approach to metadata management in data lakehouse architectures. By decoupling client applications from catalog implementations, it enhances interoperability, scalability, and maintainability, making it a valuable component for organizations seeking to optimize their data management strategies.

With this understanding of the Iceberg REST catalog, we now broaden our perspective to examine the broader ecosystem of catalog solutions used in lakehouses.

# Popular catalog options for lakehouses

Modern lakehouse architectures depend heavily on metadata catalogs to manage schemas, partitions, and other crucial metadata across diverse data processing engines. These catalogs not only ensure seamless metadata management but also enable data governance, security, and scalability. In this section, we will explore some of the most popular catalog options for lakehouses, focusing on their unique features, integration capabilities, and practical use cases.

> While open source and standards-based catalogs (for example, Hive Metastore, Apache Gravitino, or Iceberg REST) can be adopted across multiple platforms, some catalogs are vendor-specific. Unity Catalog (Databricks), Polaris (Snowflake), and AWS Glue (AWS) offer deep integration and governance features but also introduce varying degrees of vendor lock-in. You should weigh the trade-off between convenience and flexibility when evaluating these options.

## Hive Metastore (HMS) — the established option

**Hive Metastore** (**HMS**) has been the backbone of metadata management in traditional big data ecosystems for years. Originally developed as part of Apache Hive, HMS serves as a relational database-backed service that stores metadata about tables, partitions, and schemas. While it was designed to work with Apache Hive, its widespread adoption has led to compatibility with modern table formats such as Apache Iceberg and Hudi.

Key features of HMS are as follows:

- Centralized metadata repository for managing table schemas and partitions
- Compatibility with table formats such as Iceberg, Hudi, and Delta Lake
- Integration with multiple processing engines, including Apache Spark, Presto, and HiveQL

Before looking at how HMS fits into today's ecosystems, it's useful to understand why it continues to hold its place in many deployments.

### Modern relevance

Although considered legacy, HMS is still widely used in lakehouse architectures for managing metadata, especially in on-premises environments. Its support for schema evolution and table partitioning makes it suitable for modern data lake use cases.

### Hands-on example

To sync an Iceberg table with HMS, you can configure the Iceberg catalog to use HMS as the backend. A configuration example is as follows:

```
CREATE CATALOG hive_catalog
WITH (
```

```
    'type'='hive',
    'uri'='thrift://localhost:9083',
    'warehouse'='hdfs://namenode:8020/warehouse'
);
USE CATALOG hive_catalog;
```

With the HMS setup in place, the next step is to explore how newer systems like Unity Catalog extend these capabilities.

# Unity Catalog – a unified governance solution

Unity Catalog, developed by Databricks, offers a comprehensive governance solution tailored for Delta Lake. It simplifies data governance by providing a single pane of control for managing metadata, access permissions, and audit logs across multiple cloud environments. Unity Catalog ensures that all data in a lakehouse adheres to strict governance and compliance standards.

Its key features are as follows:

- Centralized governance for data and AI workflows
- Built-in support for Delta Lake tables, with schema enforcement and lineage tracking
- Integration with identity providers for RBAC

Overall, Unity Catalog brings consistency, security, and transparency to lakehouse environments, making it a reliable choice for teams that need unified governance across data and AI workloads.

## Governance in action

Unity Catalog supports fine-grained access controls, enabling administrators to define policies at the database, table, and column levels. This ensures compliance with data protection regulations such as GDPR and CCPA.

> Unity Catalog has recently been open-sourced, providing an API specification that can interoperate with multiple compute engines. However, its most advanced features—such as tight Databricks workspace integration, lineage UI, and enterprise governance controls—remain Databricks-specific, meaning full adoption still carries a degree of vendor lock-in.

## Hands-on example

Here is an example configuration for syncing and enabling Unity Catalog with Delta tables:

```
CREATE CATALOG sales_catalog
WITH (
  'type'='unity',
  'databricks.workspace'='https://<workspace-url>',
  'databricks.token'='<personal-access-token>'
);
USE CATALOG sales_catalog;
```

This setup establishes a governed workspace where Delta tables can be managed seamlessly under Unity Catalog's unified controls.

# Polaris — a next-generation metadata service

Polaris, developed by Snowflake, is a modern, cloud-native metadata service designed for lakehouse architectures. It overcomes the limitations of traditional metadata stores by offering advanced features tailored for multi-engine and distributed environments.

Let's go through the key features:

- **Multi-engine support**: Polaris integrates seamlessly with engines such as Apache Spark, Flink, and Trino, enabling unified metadata management across diverse platforms
- **Atomic multi-table transactions**: Ensures data consistency across multiple tables through a centralized transaction manager
- **Versioning and time travel**: Provides advanced capabilities to track changes, roll back to previous states, and perform point-in-time queries
- **Robust security**: Offers fine-grained access controls and encryption for metadata at rest and in transit

> Polaris Catalog was open-sourced in 2024, making it available as a vendor-neutral implementation of the Iceberg REST specification. That said, the enterprise-grade, fully managed Polaris service is operated by Snowflake, so organizations adopting the managed option may still face vendor dependency.

# Hands-on example

The following example demonstrates how to configure Polaris as the metadata service:

```
CREATE CATALOG polaris_catalog
WITH (
  'type'='iceberg',
  'catalog-impl'='com.starburstdata.polaris.catalog.PolarisCatalog',
  'metadata-cache.enabled'='true',
  'warehouse'='s3://lakehouse-data/iceberg'
);
USE CATALOG polaris_catalog;
```

This configuration enables Polaris to serve as the centralized metadata service, allowing Iceberg tables to be efficiently managed and queried within the specified warehouse.

# AWS Glue Catalog — a cloud-native option

AWS Glue Catalog is a serverless, cloud-native metadata catalog service that integrates seamlessly with other AWS services. Designed for scalability, Glue is ideal for managing metadata in distributed and multi-cloud environments. It supports table formats such as Delta Lake, Iceberg, and Hudi, making it versatile for lakehouse architectures.

Here are the key features:

- Fully managed service with automatic schema discovery
- Integration with AWS Athena, EMR, and Redshift
- Support for schema evolution and partition pruning

> AWS Glue Catalog is optimized for AWS services such as Athena, EMR, and Redshift. This makes it highly convenient for AWS users, but also creates dependency on the AWS ecosystem.

# Hands-on example

The following configuration demonstrates how to use AWS Glue as a catalog:

```
CREATE CATALOG glue_catalog
WITH (
  'type'='glue',
  'region'='us-east-1',
```

```
      'warehouse'='s3://delta-lakehouse-data'
);
USE CATALOG glue_catalog;
```

This setup allows AWS Glue to manage metadata centrally, enabling seamless integration and efficient querying of Delta tables stored in the specified S3 warehouse.

# Apache Gravitino — an emerging open source catalog

Apache Gravitino is a cutting-edge, open source metadata lake designed for modern lakehouse architectures. It provides a high-performance, scalable, and multi-tenant solution for managing metadata across distributed systems. Gravitino's flexibility and support for multiple catalog protocols make it a promising choice for organizations looking for a vendor-neutral alternative to traditional metadata solutions.

The key features include the following:

- **Multi-protocol support**: Gravitino integrates with widely used APIs such as HMS and Iceberg REST catalog, enabling smooth interoperability with existing tools
- **Scalability**: Designed to handle large-scale metadata management, Gravitino ensures high performance and fault tolerance in distributed environments
- **Multi-tenancy**: Enables multiple teams or applications to share a single Gravitino instance with complete isolation
- **Extensibility**: Supports custom plugins for authentication, authorization, and metadata processing, ensuring adaptability to diverse requirements

Apache Gravitino offers a modern, flexible alternative for metadata management, combining scalability, multi-tenancy, and extensibility to meet the demands of next-generation lakehouse architectures.

## Hands-on example

Gravitino can be configured as a catalog for Iceberg tables using SQL commands. Here is an example configuration:

```
CREATE CATALOG gravitino_catalog
WITH (
    'type' = 'iceberg',
    'catalog-impl' = 'org.apache.iceberg.gravitino.GravitinoCatalog',
    'uri' = 'https://gravitino-server:8090',
    'catalog-name' = 'my_catalog',
```

```
    'warehouse' = 's3://warehouse-path'
);
USE CATALOG gravitino_catalog;
```

This configuration illustrates how Gravitino can be seamlessly set up as a catalog, enabling Iceberg tables to leverage its scalable and multi-tenant metadata management capabilities.

# Other popular catalogs

In addition to the catalogs we discussed in detail, there are several other notable options in the market. Let's briefly introduce three of them: Project Nessie, Azure Purview, and Google Cloud Data Catalog.

## Project Nessie

Project Nessie is an open source catalog that brings Git-like semantics to data lakes. It introduces concepts such as branching and merging to data management, allowing data teams to experiment with data changes in isolation before merging them into production. This approach can significantly streamline data engineering workflows and enable more agile data practices.

## Azure Purview

Azure Purview is Microsoft's data governance solution for hybrid and multi-cloud environments. It offers features such as automated data discovery, sensitive data classification, and end-to-end data lineage. While not strictly a catalog in the traditional sense, Purview provides many catalog-like features and integrates well with Azure's data services.

## Google Cloud Data Catalog

Google Cloud Data Catalog is a fully managed and scalable metadata management service that integrates with Google Cloud's data analytics services. It offers features such as automatic metadata ingestion from Google Cloud services, a search interface for data discovery, and integration with data governance tools.

Together, these emerging and complementary catalog solutions reflect the diversity of approaches in metadata management, enabling organizations to choose tools best aligned with their architecture, cloud environment, and governance needs.

# Summary

This chapter explored the critical role of catalogs in a lakehouse architecture, detailing their necessity in managing metadata, ensuring consistency across engines, and optimizing performance. We discussed the importance of metadata management, the core features of catalogs, and their integration with table formats such as Apache Iceberg, Delta Lake, and Apache Hudi. The Iceberg REST catalog specification was highlighted as a modern approach to metadata management, emphasizing flexibility, scalability, and interoperability. We also reviewed popular catalog options, such as Hive Metastore, Unity Catalog, Polaris, AWS Glue, and Apache Gravitino, illustrating their unique features and use cases with practical examples.

As data ecosystems grow in complexity, catalogs are pivotal in enabling seamless operations, governance, and multi-engine interoperability, ensuring the lakehouse architecture's potential is fully realized.

Building on the foundation of catalogs, the next chapter delves into the challenges of working with multiple table formats in a lakehouse architecture. It introduces Apache XTable and Delta UniForm as solutions for interoperability and data federation, enabling seamless integration across Apache Iceberg, Hudi, and Delta Lake.

# Questions

1. What is the primary role of catalogs in a lakehouse architecture?
2. How does metadata management enhance query performance in a lakehouse?
3. Name three core features of a catalog.
4. Why is multi-engine interoperability important in lakehouse environments?
5. What is the Iceberg REST catalog, and what problem does it solve?
6. What are the key advantages of using Unity Catalog with Delta Lake?
7. How does Polaris support multi-table transactions?
8. Name three key features of the AWS Glue Catalog.
9. What is unique about Apache Gravitino's multi-tenant support?
10. Compare the use cases of Project Nessie, Azure Purview, and Google Cloud Data Catalog.

# Answers

1. Catalogs act as a centralized metadata management layer, ensuring consistency, governance, and performance across a lakehouse architecture.

2. Metadata management helps optimize query performance by enabling partition pruning and reducing scan times, ensuring efficient data access.

3. Schema management, time travel/versioning, and access control/governance are core features of a catalog.

4. Multi-engine interoperability allows various tools such as Apache Spark, Flink, and Trino to work seamlessly with the same datasets, reducing duplication and inconsistencies.

5. The Iceberg REST catalog standardizes metadata management through a REST API, enabling interoperability across languages and compute engines while simplifying client-server interactions.

6. Unity Catalog provides centralized governance, schema enforcement, and lineage tracking, ensuring compliance and data consistency in Delta Lake environments.

7. Polaris uses a centralized transaction manager to maintain consistency across multiple tables, supporting complex operations in distributed systems.

8. AWS Glue Catalog is serverless, supports schema evolution, and integrates seamlessly with AWS analytics services such as Athena and Redshift.

9. Apache Gravitino supports multiple tenants in a single instance while maintaining isolation, making it suitable for diverse organizational requirements.

10. Project Nessie introduces Git-like version control for data lakes, Azure Purview focuses on automated data discovery and lineage, while Google Cloud Data Catalog integrates with Google Cloud services for metadata management.

# 7

# Interoperability in Lakehouses

The growing adoption of lakehouse architectures has changed the way organizations store, process, and analyze data. Open table formats such as Apache Hudi, Apache Iceberg, and Delta Lake offer flexibility and avoid vendor lock-in by keeping the data tier open and independent, enabling teams to choose best-in-class tools for their specific needs. Yet, as organizations scale out their operations or onboard newer workloads, they encounter challenges that demand interoperability between these formats and systems.

Practitioners care deeply about this because table format lock-in can introduce costly friction—limiting the ability to switch query engines, complicating cross-team collaboration, and increasing operational overhead due to unnecessary data copying or format migration. Whether it's a data engineering team relying on Spark with Apache Hudi, or an analytics team using Trino with Apache Iceberg, the ability to operate across formats without rewriting pipelines or duplicating data is essential for agility, scalability, and cost-efficiency in modern data platforms.

In this chapter, we will learn about the following:

- The key aspects that allow us to understand the need for interoperability among table formats
- The technical solutions, such as Apache XTable and Delta UniForm, that cater to these issues, including their working mechanisms and architectural details
- How to enable interoperability between open table formats without changing existing data pipelines through hands-on exercises

By the end of this chapter, you will be able to confidently apply the concepts and techniques covered, using solutions such as Apache XTable and Delta UniForm to address interoperability challenges while maintaining existing data pipelines efficiently.

# Need for interoperability

The need for interoperability among open lakehouse formats (i.e., Iceberg, Hudi, and Delta Lake) stems from their distinct origins and the unique design trade-offs they embody. Each format originated in different contexts to address specific problems. This means there are distinctive features in each of these formats. The other perspective is that, although these formats started with different use cases, they ultimately have one common goal: serving as the *metadata layer* on top of existing data file formats such as Apache Parquet. So, in a technical sense (as we learned from our previous chapters), although each format has a different metadata design, the content of the metadata is very similar. This has been one of the most important considerations in the design of interoperability solutions that we will explore in our next section.

Now, let's understand the critical needs for interoperability in a bit of detail:

- **Flexibility in table format selection**: Choosing a single table format is often limiting. Each open table format offers unique features tailored for specific use cases. For instance, Apache Iceberg has hidden partitioning; Delta Lake offers a richer set of connectors, while Apache Hudi enables incremental queries. Additionally, the performance of compute engines varies with the choice of format, as some engines are optimized only for a particular format. Organizations must avoid being locked into a single format, as this decision can impact compute decisions when workloads evolve or when newer features in other formats become necessary. Interoperability ensures that switching between formats or supporting multiple formats simultaneously does not become a high-cost, disruptive operation.

- **Collaboration across teams in the same organization**: In large-scale organizations, it is common for different data teams to adopt different table formats based on their specific use cases. For example, a machine learning team may store training datasets in Apache Iceberg to use its branching and tagging capabilities for experimentation purposes, while a streaming team may ingest high-velocity **Change Data Capture** (**CDC**) data in cloud data lakes using Apache Hudi, optimizing for upserts and incremental queries. Without interoperability, collaboration across these teams using different formats would be cumbersome. Interoperability enables teams to run federated queries that combine datasets stored in various open table formats without rewriting or duplicating data.

- **Cost and efficiency**: The most common way to collaborate across different teams in an organization that uses multiple open formats involves migrating a particular set of required data into other formats and making additional data copies. This is also the case for organizations that want to use specific compute engines with specific table formats to take advantage of their performance optimizations. Rewriting or migrating data between formats is both cost-intensive (compute resources) and involves huge engineering efforts with operational downtime. Additionally, maintaining multiple copies of data in different formats results in increased storage costs. Interoperability eliminates the need for these one-off migrations by enabling seamless metadata translation, allowing the same data files to be accessible in multiple formats.

- **Future-proofing the lakehouse architecture**: The pace of innovation in table formats means that the optimal format for a specific workload today may not remain so in the future. Organizations need the ability to adapt to newer formats and integrate emerging tools and technologies. Interoperability ensures that the underlying data remains accessible regardless of the format, creating a future-proof architecture that can evolve with the organization's needs.

In short, interoperability ensures flexibility, collaboration, cost-efficiency, and future-proofing, allowing organizations to leverage multiple open table formats without duplicating data or compromising performance.

# Apache XTable (incubating)

Apache XTable is a metadata translation solution designed to address the interoperability challenges inherent in open lakehouse architectures. Unlike table formats such as Apache Hudi, Apache Iceberg, or Delta Lake, which provide their own metadata structures and APIs, XTable is not a new format. Instead, it functions as a bridge between these formats, enabling seamless translation of metadata while preserving the underlying data files (Parquet) in their original storage layer. This design philosophy ensures that XTable works as an enabler for multi-format compatibility without introducing new storage or computational overhead.

The core idea behind XTable is to facilitate *omnidirectional* interoperability. This means it is not just limited to one-directional conversion but allows you to initiate conversion from any format to another without the need to copy or rewrite data. Hence, data written in one table format can be queried and processed as if it were originally written in another.

Core design principles of Apache XTable include the following:

- **Non-intrusive metadata translation**: XTable operates at the metadata level, leaving the actual data files untouched. This provides the following:

  - **Efficiency**: Metadata translation is lightweight compared to data rewriting
  - **Preservation of data integrity**: Since the data files are not modified, there is no risk of data corruption during translation

- **Minimal overhead:** By focusing solely on metadata (which is much smaller in size), XTable ensures that performance remains unaffected

- **Omnidirectional interoperability:** XTable's ability to translate metadata between any combination of supported formats (Hudi, Iceberg, or Delta) makes it truly omnidirectional:

  - A Hudi table designed for streaming workloads can be queried using Iceberg-compatible engines, which are often optimized for batch processing or interactive querying

  - Similarly, Delta Lake tables can be seamlessly accessed by Hudi-compatible engines, enabling incremental updates

- **Shared characteristics of table formats:** XTable uses the commonalities between open table formats to achieve seamless translation:

  - **Common storage file format:** All three formats (Hudi, Iceberg, and Delta Lake) use Apache Parquet as their primary file format. This ensures that the physical data files are already compatible.

  - **Similar metadata structures:** While the implementation differs, these formats share common metadata elements, including the following:

    - **Schema definitions:** Column names, types, and structures
    - **Partitioning information:** Logical grouping of data for query optimization
    - **Transaction logs:** Commit history, file additions, and deletions

- **Incremental and full synchronization:** XTable supports two synchronization modes:

  - **Full sync:** Translates the entire metadata, typically used for initial setup or when metadata corruption occurs

  - **Incremental sync:** Only processes new or modified commits, ensuring that metadata translation remains efficient for large tables

Apache XTable enables seamless, efficient, and non-intrusive interoperability across Hudi, Iceberg, and Delta Lake by translating metadata without touching the underlying data, preserving integrity, and supporting both full and incremental synchronization for flexible multi-format access.

## Apache XTable architecture

XTable uses a standard model for table representation, achieved through lightweight abstraction layers. This unified model can interpret and translate various elements such as schema, partitioning information, and file metadata, including column-level statistics, row count, and file size. Here is the high-level architecture of Apache XTable:

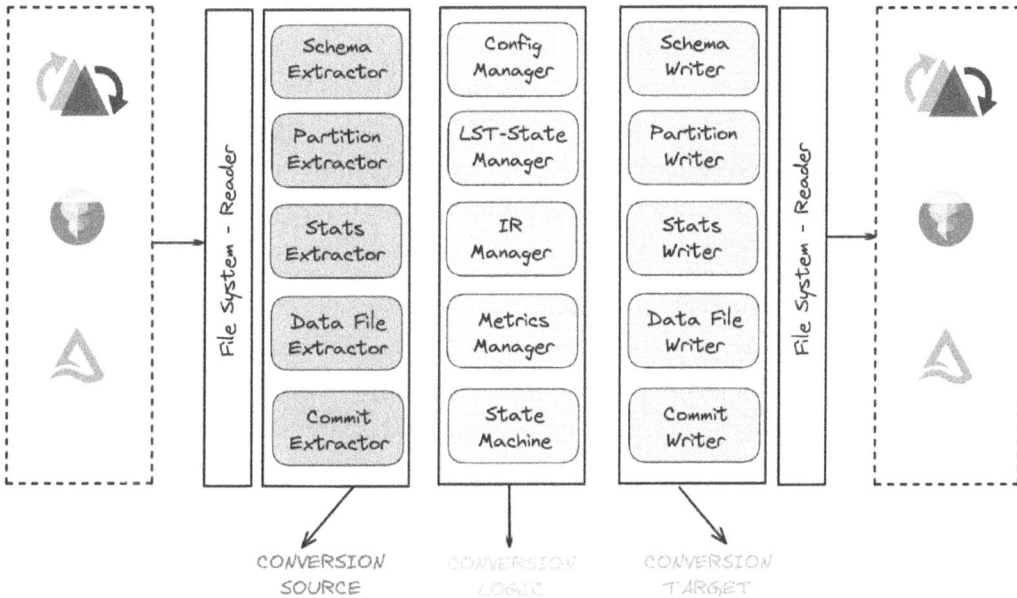

*Figure 7.1 – Apache XTable*

XTable's architecture is built around three core components:

- **Conversion source**: Conversion source is a critical part of XTable's architecture. It serves as format-specific modules responsible for extracting metadata from the source table formats. The modules interact directly with the APIs of their respective table formats to fetch essential metadata and file-level statistics. These readers operate using pluggable filesystems, making XTable compatible with various storage backends such as Amazon S3 for cloud object storage.

  Key responsibilities of conversion source include the following:

  - **Parsing metadata**: Conversion sources extract critical metadata from the source table, including schema definitions, partition layouts, and transaction logs
  - **File-level statistics**: They parse and capture file-level details such as row counts, min/max values, and file sizes to support advanced query optimizations
  - **Pluggable filesystem support**: These readers are designed to operate on multiple storage backends, such as Amazon S3 for cloud object storage

From a technical internals perspective, XTable implements the `ConversionSource` interface for the three different table formats. For example, `IcebergConversionSource.java` is the Iceberg-specific implementation. This class interacts with Iceberg's API to perform schema extraction, partition layout retrieval, snapshot handling, and file-level metadata collection. The process begins with the initialization of the Iceberg table connection. `IcebergConversionSource` uses the `IcebergTableManager` class to retrieve the table object, which acts as the entry point for interacting with Iceberg's metadata. Using the configuration provided, it identifies the table's catalog, namespace, and name, ensuring compatibility with different storage backends such as Amazon S3, Azure Blob Storage, or HDFS.

Once the table is initialized, `IcebergConversionSource` extracts the table's schema, which defines the structure of the data. It fetches this information using Iceberg's `Table.schema()` API. If a specific snapshot is being processed, the schema is retrieved based on the snapshot's schema ID, ensuring that the extracted schema accurately represents the state of the table at the given point in time. The schema includes details such as column names, data types, and nested structures, which are then passed to `IcebergSchemaExtractor`. This class converts the Iceberg schema into XTable's internal schema representation, aligning it with XTable's universal model.

- **Conversion logic:** The conversion logic in Apache XTable acts as the central processing unit for the system. It orchestrates the entire metadata translation process, managing the flow of metadata between the source and target formats while ensuring consistency and compatibility. The conversion logic initializes and coordinates the key components of XTable, including source readers, target writers, and models such as InternalTable (`https://github.com/apache/incubator-xtable/blob/main/xtable-api/src/main/java/org/apache/xtable/model/InternalTable.java`) and InternalSnapshot (`https://github.com/apache/incubator-xtable/blob/main/xtable-api/src/main/java/org/apache/xtable/model/InternalSnapshot.java`), which collectively form the internal representation of the table metadata. This logic is also responsible for ensuring fault-tolerant synchronization workflows, handling both incremental and full syncs as required by the state of the source and target tables.

  At its foundation, the conversion logic enables metadata normalization by using the models defined in the models package (`https://github.com/apache/incubator-xtable/tree/main/xtable-api/src/main/java/org/apache/xtable/model`). These models provide the schema, snapshot, and file-level metadata abstractions necessary to represent any supported table format (e.g., Iceberg, Hudi, or Delta Lake) in XTable's unified internal representation. The conversion logic normalizes the metadata into instances of

InternalTable, InternalSchema, and InternalSnapshot. These classes represent a table's schema, partition structure, and snapshot state in an abstract, format-agnostic way.
For example, the InternalTable class encapsulates fields such as the table name, format,
base path, and latest commit time, while InternalSnapshot captures details about the
current snapshot and its associated data files.

The conversion logic manages the flow of metadata through several stages. First, it validates the extracted metadata to ensure consistency and resolve potential conflicts, such
as mismatched schemas or expired snapshots, using models such as InternalSchema and
InternalSnapshot. Next, it processes the metadata using synchronization workflows,
either performing a full sync (translating all commits) or an incremental sync (processing
only new commits). During an incremental sync, the core logic uses the CommitsBacklog
class to track snapshots or commits that need to be processed:

```
CommitsBacklog<Snapshot> commitsBacklog = sourceReader.
getCommitsBacklog(lastSyncInstant);
```

The getCommitsBacklog method identifies snapshots that occurred after the last sync
and returns them for processing. This ensures that only new metadata is translated, minimizing overhead.

If an incremental sync fails due to missing snapshots, the logic automatically falls back
to a full sync:

```
if (!sourceReader.isIncrementalSyncSafeFrom(lastSyncInstant)) {
    performFullSync();
}
```

Finally, the normalized metadata is passed to the conversion target, which translates it
into the structure and storage requirements of the target format. This involves invoking
the conversion target to generate the appropriate metadata files (e.g., _delta_log for Delta
Lake, and metadata for Iceberg). The DataFilesDiff class helps track file-level changes
(e.g., added and removed files) that need to be reflected in the target format:

```
DataFilesDiff filesDiff = DataFilesDiff.builder()
    .filesAdded(addedFiles)
    .filesRemoved(removedFiles)
    .build();
```

By decoupling format-specific logic from the core functionality, XTable ensures that the
translation process remains modular, scalable, and extensible.

- **Conversion target:** The conversion target is designed to handle the final stage of the metadata translation workflow. These components are responsible for taking XTable's internal representation of metadata, generated during the normalization process, and mapping it to the structure required by the target table format. This process ensures that the translated metadata conforms to the specific APIs, file structures, and conventions of the target format while preserving compatibility and performance.

In essence, the conversion target mirrors the functionality of the conversion source. While the conversion source extracts metadata from the source table format, the conversion target writes the normalized metadata into the required format for the target table. This design symmetry allows XTable to maintain a modular and extensible architecture where new formats can be added seamlessly by implementing format-specific conversion targets.

The ConversionTarget interface defines the contract that all target implementations must fulfill. Each format (Hudi, Iceberg, and Delta) provides its own implementations of this interface. For example, the HudiConversionTarget class is responsible for translating the internal representation into Hudi-specific metadata. Some of the key methods in this interface are as follows:

- syncToTarget(InternalTable internalTable): The central method for metadata translation. It accepts an InternalTable object (i.e., XTable's normalized representation) and writes the metadata into the target format's structure.
- finalizeTarget(): Performs any cleanup or post-processing tasks after the translation is complete, such as closing connections or committing changes.

The HudiConversionTarget class is one such example of the implementation of the ConversionTarget interface for Apache Hudi. HudiConversionTarget begins by validating the target table configuration and setting up the Hudi metadata directory. This ensures that the target environment is ready for metadata translation. The syncToTarget method handles the core translation process. It takes an InternalTable object, extracts the schema, partitions, and commit details, and writes them into Hudi's .hoodie directory:

```
public void syncToTarget(InternalTable internalTable) {
    InternalSchema schema = internalTable.getReadSchema();
    List<InternalPartitionField> partitionFields = internalTable.
getPartitioningFields();
```

```
        Instant latestCommit = internalTable.getLatestCommitTime();

        // Convert internal schema to Hudi schema
        HudiSchema hudiSchema = HudiSchemaConverter.
    fromInternalSchema(schema);

        // Write schema, partitions, and commit details to Hudi metadata
        writeToHudiMetadata(hudiSchema, partitionFields, latestCommit);
    }
    After all metadata has been translated, the finalizeTarget method
    commits the changes to the Hudi catalog and cleans up temporary
    resources.
    public void finalizeTarget() {
        commitMetadataChanges();
    }
```

XTable's architecture provides a robust and modular framework for metadata translation, where source readers extract format-specific metadata, the conversion logic normalizes and synchronizes it, and target writers seamlessly translate it into the desired table format, ensuring efficient, consistent, and extensible interoperability across Hudi, Iceberg, and Delta Lake.

## Inner workings of XTable sync

The synchronization process is the core of Apache XTable, enabling seamless translation of metadata between table formats. It ensures that metadata from a source table format is accurately mapped to the structure of one or more target formats, making the data interpretable as if it were originally written in those formats. XTable achieves this through two distinct synchronization workflows: full sync and incremental sync, each optimized for different scenarios.

Apache Hudi, Iceberg, and Delta Lake share foundational similarities. As you can see in the figure, they use Parquet as the data file format and serve as a metadata layer (each with a unique structure) that provides abstractions for the underlying file formats:

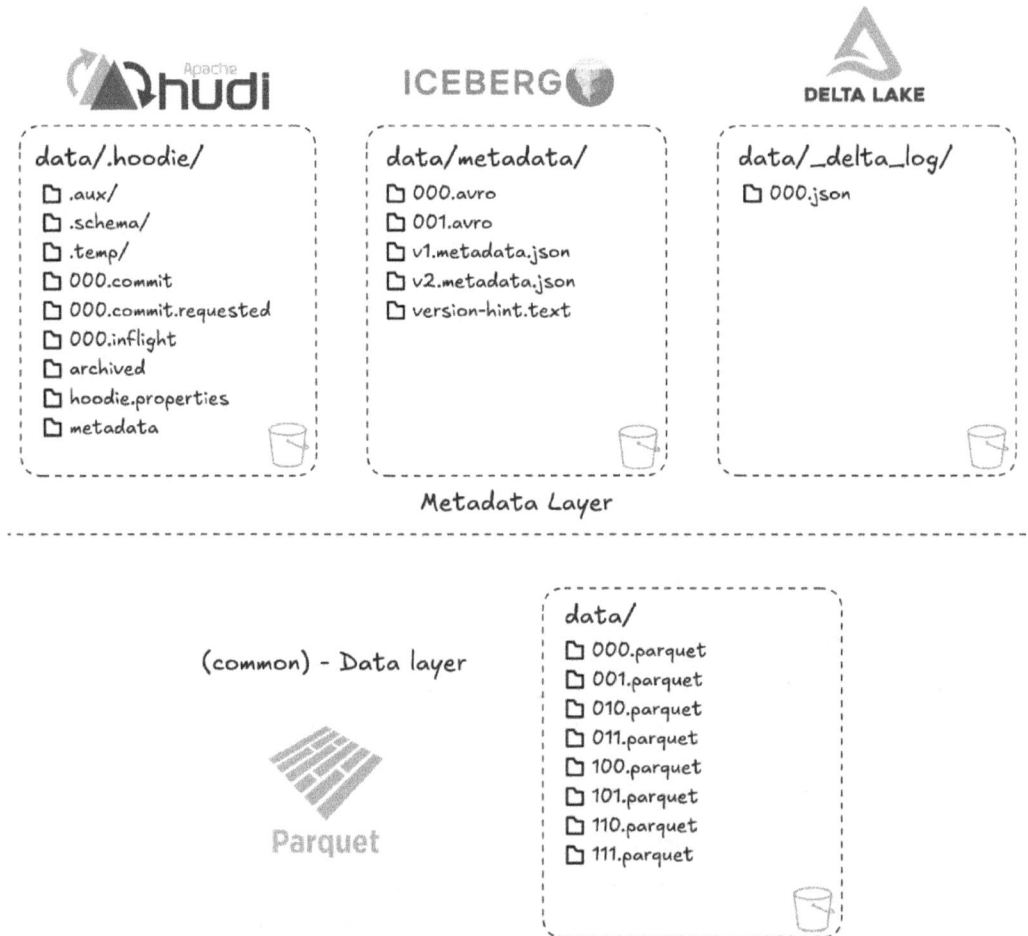

*Figure 7.2 – Apache Hudi, Iceberg, and Delta Lake using Parquet*

XTable uses these commonalities to normalize metadata into its internal representations (InternalTable, InternalSnapshot, etc.) and synchronize this metadata across formats.

As we learned in our previous section, the sync process involves three primary stages:

- **Metadata extraction:** The source table's metadata is read using its respective APIs

- **Metadata normalization:** The extracted metadata is converted into XTable's internal representation for a unified structure

- **Metadata translation:** The normalized metadata is written into the target format's metadata structures (e.g., _delta_log for Delta Lake, metadata for Iceberg, and .hoodie for Hudi)

XTable offers two synchronization modes: full and incremental sync. Let's elaborate on these.

# Full sync

The full sync process translates all metadata commits from the source table into the target format, regardless of whether they have already been synchronized. This method ensures that the entire metadata history is replicated in the target format. During the initial synchronization of a table, a full sync is performed. It is also beneficial when there might be missing or corrupted snapshots, and a complete sync is deemed necessary.

The workflow looks like this:

1. The process begins by retrieving the entire commit history of the source table. This includes all snapshots or commits that define the table's state over time. For example, in Iceberg, the `Table.snapshots()` API is used to fetch the full list of snapshots.

2. Each snapshot is converted into XTable's internal representation using the `InternalSnapshot` and `InternalTable` classes. This ensures that the metadata is stored in a format-agnostic structure that can be translated to any target format.

3. The normalized metadata is then written to the target format's metadata structure and stored in a specific folder structure. So, for Delta Lake, the transaction log is written to `_delta_log`. For Hudi, the properties file, internal metadata table, and other related info are written to the `.hoodie` directory, and for Iceberg, the catalog file reference and manifests are written to the `metadata` directory.

The full sync logic in XTable is implemented in the `ConversionController` class, specifically in the `fullSync` method:

```
public void fullSync() {
    List<Snapshot> allSnapshots = sourceReader.getAllSnapshots();
    for (Snapshot snapshot : allSnapshots) {
        InternalSnapshot internalSnapshot = normalizeSnapshot(snapshot);
        targetWriter.writeMetadata(internalSnapshot);
    }
}
```

This method retrieves all snapshots using the `getAllSnapshots` method, normalizes them into `InternalSnapshot` objects, and writes them to the target format using the `writeMetadata` method.

# Incremental sync

The incremental sync process is designed for efficiency, translating only new commits or snapshots that have not yet been synchronized. This approach reduces the overhead of metadata translation, making it well-suited for large tables with frequent updates. If any issues arise during the incremental sync process, such as missing or expired snapshots, the synchronization process automatically falls back to a full sync to ensure consistency.

Here is the workflow:

1.  The process starts by determining which snapshots or commits have been added since the last synchronization. This is done by comparing the latest commit in the source table with the last commit translated to the target format. For example, in Iceberg, the `Table.currentSnapshot()` API retrieves the latest snapshot.

2.  The identified new snapshots are extracted and converted into XTable's internal metadata representation (`InternalSnapshot`), ensuring compatibility with the target format.

3.  The normalized metadata for the new snapshots is written to the target format's structure, updating it incrementally.

The incremental sync logic is implemented in the `ConversionController` class, specifically in `incrementalSync` method:

```
public void incrementalSync(Instant lastSyncInstant) {
    CommitsBacklog<Snapshot> backlog = sourceReader.
getCommitsBacklog(lastSyncInstant);
    for (Snapshot snapshot : backlog.getCommitsToProcess()) {
        InternalSnapshot internalSnapshot = normalizeSnapshot(snapshot);
        targetWriter.writeMetadata(internalSnapshot);
    }
}
```

Here, the `getCommitsBacklog` method identifies new snapshots that need processing. Each snapshot is normalized and written to the target format.

# How to run translation with Apache XTable and Apache Spark

In this section, we'll walk through the steps to set up Apache XTable and run metadata translation between open table formats such as Apache Hudi, Apache Iceberg, and Delta Lake using Apache Spark as the compute for the table formats. This hands-on guide will demonstrate how to configure XTable, initialize source and target table formats, and perform a translation between them, providing a practical understanding of XTable's capabilities. Our goal would be to use Apache Hudi as the source format and translate it to Apache Iceberg for read-side (analytics).

# Prerequisites

Before you begin, ensure you have the following:

- **Apache Spark environment**: A compute instance capable of running Spark. This can be your local machine, a Docker container, or a distributed service such as Amazon EMR.

- **Apache XTable repository**: Clone the Apache XTable repository and build the xtable-utilities_2.12-0.2.0-SNAPSHOT-bundled.jar file by following the installation instructions provided in the official documentation at https://xtable.apache.org/docs/setup/.

- **Optional**: If you plan to read from or write to distributed storage services such as Amazon S3 or Google Cloud Storage, ensure you have the necessary access configured.

With all prerequisites in place and your environment ready, we can now move on to executing the actual metadata translation using Apache XTable.

# Run translation

Now that we have everything configured, we can go ahead and start with our sync process:

1. Execute the following command from your terminal within the cloned Apache XTable directory to perform the metadata translation:

```
java -jar xtable-utilities/target/xtable-utilities_2.12-0.2.0-
SNAPSHOT-bundled.jar --datasetConfig my_config.yaml
```

If everything runs successfully, you should see the output as presented in the figure:

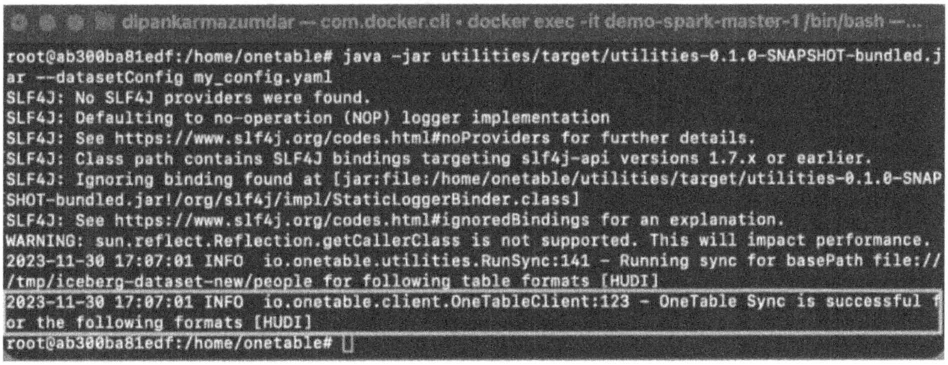

*Figure 7.3 – Translation output*

2.  If you inspect the storage system (such as S3/local) now, you should see the necessary metadata files (e.g., the `metadata` directory in our example for Iceberg) in your specified path. These files enable query engines to interpret the data in the target table format. So, the source Hudi table can now be interpreted as an Iceberg table without users having to worry about the details.

3.  Depending on your source table format, initialize a PySpark shell with the appropriate packages and configurations. Since, in our example, we want to interoperate between Hudi and Iceberg, let's first use Hudi-specific packages with the Spark shell:

```
pyspark \
  --packages org.apache.hudi:hudi-spark3.2-bundle_2.12:0.14.0 \
  --conf "spark.serializer=org.apache.spark.serializer.
KryoSerializer" \
  --conf "spark.sql.catalog.spark_catalog=org.apache.spark.sql.hudi.
catalog.HoodieCatalog" \
  --conf "spark.sql.extensions=org.apache.spark.sql.hudi.
HoodieSparkSessionExtension"
```

> Additional configurations may be required to write to external cloud storage locations such as Amazon S3, Google Cloud Storage, or Azure Data Lake Storage when working with Spark locally. Refer to the respective cloud provider's documentation for more information.

4.  Now, let's write a source table locally using Hudi as our table format. Here is an example:

```
from pyspark.sql.types import *
table_name = "people"
local_base_path = "file:/tmp/hudi-dataset"
records = [
    (1, 'John', 25, 'NYC', '2023-09-28 00:00:00'),
    (2, 'Emily', 30, 'SFO', '2023-09-28 00:00:00'),
    (3, 'Michael', 35, 'ORD', '2023-09-28 00:00:00'),
    (4, 'Andrew', 40, 'NYC', '2023-10-28 00:00:00'),
    (5, 'Bob', 28, 'SEA', '2023-09-23 00:00:00'),
    (6, 'Charlie', 31, 'DFW', '2023-08-29 00:00:00')
]
schema = StructType([
    StructField("id", IntegerType(), True),
```

```
        StructField("name", StringType(), True),
        StructField("age", IntegerType(), True),
        StructField("city", StringType(), True),
        StructField("create_ts", StringType(), True)
    ])
    df = spark.createDataFrame(records, schema)
    hudi_options = {
        'hoodie.table.name': table_name,
        'hoodie.datasource.write.partitionpath.field': 'city',
        'hoodie.datasource.write.hive_style_partitioning': 'true'
    }
    (
        df.write
        .format("hudi")
        .options(**hudi_options)
        .save(f"{local_base_path}/{table_name}")
    )
```

5. Create a configuration file, my_config.yaml, in the cloned Apache XTable directory with the following content:

```
sourceFormat: HUDI
targetFormats:
    - ICEBERG
datasets:
    - tableBasePath: file:///tmp/hudi-dataset/people
      tableName: people
      partitionSpec:
        city: VALUE
```

6. Finally, the translated table (Iceberg) is available to be queried by the preferred compute engine, for example, using Spark SQL. This query should return the data from the source Hudi table, now accessible in the target table format:

```
SELECT * FROM people;
```

By following these steps, you can effectively use Apache XTable to translate metadata between different table formats, facilitating interoperability without the need to copy or move underlying data files.

## XTable limitations

Here are some of the limitations of Apache XTable:

- Only **copy-on-write (CoW)** or **read-optimized (RO)** views of tables are supported. Log files from Hudi and deletion vectors (for merge-on-read tables) from Delta and Iceberg are not captured.

- Hudi requires version 0.14.0 or higher when reading Hudi target tables.

- Field IDs in the Parquet schema may be required when syncing from Hudi or Delta to Iceberg.

- Generated columns in Delta tables are not synced to the target schema.

While Apache XTable provides powerful metadata translation capabilities, these limitations highlight areas where careful planning is needed, especially when working with advanced table features or specific version requirements.

# Delta UniForm

**Universal Format (UniForm)** is an extension to the Delta Lake table format that facilitates interoperability between Delta Lake and other open table formats, such as Apache Iceberg and Apache Hudi. With UniForm, Delta Lake bridges the gap between various table formats by generating metadata that is compatible across formats.

At its core, Delta UniForm is built on the idea of metadata alignment. It ensures that data stored in Delta Lake can be seamlessly queried or operated on using compute engines that natively support only Iceberg or Hudi, without requiring data rewriting or additional transformations. This capability is particularly valuable in multi-team and multi-tool ecosystems, where different teams might use different table formats or compute engines.

Here are some of the key capabilities of UniForm:

- **Interoperability**: Enabling Delta Lake tables to be directly used as Iceberg or Hudi tables without duplicating or migrating data

- **Open ecosystem support**: Compatibility with other compute engines and tools that natively support Iceberg or Hudi

- **Ease of adoption**: Organizations using Delta Lake can enable UniForm on their existing tables or create new tables with UniForm enabled, making it a seamless addition to existing workflows

To understand how UniForm achieves this seamless interoperability, let's dive into its internal mechanisms and see how it manages metadata across multiple table formats.

# Inner workings of UniForm

Similar to Apache XTable, UniForm operates by exploiting the shared foundation of open table formats, which all use Apache Parquet as the underlying data file format. The key differentiation between these formats lies in the metadata layer, which governs how data is managed, queried, and updated. While these metadata layers differ in structure, their core purpose and the type of information they contain are largely aligned. Delta UniForm bridges these subtle differences by providing a unified approach to metadata generation and management.

Under the hood, UniForm automatically generates metadata for multiple table formats (Iceberg and Hudi) alongside the native Delta Lake _delta_log metadata. This means that without duplicating or rewriting data files, UniForm enables a single Delta Lake table to appear as an Iceberg (metadata directory) or Hudi (.hoodie directory) table for compatible compute engines. This metadata alignment is performed dynamically, ensuring live interoperability for all readers.

# Metadata generation in UniForm

The metadata generation process in UniForm is a key enabler of its interoperability capabilities. This process is designed to maintain efficiency, minimize latency, and ensure consistency across all supported formats. Here's how it works.

After a Delta Lake write transaction (e.g., INSERT, UPDATE, or DELETE) completes, UniForm triggers metadata generation for Iceberg and Hudi asynchronously. This process uses the same compute resources that performed the Delta Lake transaction, ensuring tight integration and alignment between Delta Lake and the additional metadata layers.

UniForm also optimizes performance by bundling multiple Delta Lake commits into a single Iceberg or Hudi commit. For example, in a high-frequency transactional workload where Delta commits occur every few seconds or minutes, UniForm consolidates these changes into fewer, larger commits for Iceberg and Hudi, reducing the overhead of frequent metadata updates.

UniForm enforces concurrency control by ensuring that only one metadata generation process per format (Iceberg or Hudi) is active at a time within a single cluster. If a new Delta Lake transaction occurs while metadata generation for Iceberg or Hudi is still in progress, the new transaction will successfully commit to Delta Lake, but it will not trigger additional metadata generation. This mechanism prevents cascading delays and ensures that high-frequency Delta workloads remain efficient.

## How to use UniForm

There are two different ways to use UniForm. Let's understand these two methods from a practical standpoint.

## Create a new Delta Lake table with UniForm

When creating a new table in Delta Lake with UniForm enabled, you can configure it to generate metadata that is compatible with a specific table format, such as Iceberg or Hudi. Here is an example using Spark SQL:

```
CREATE TABLE delta_uniform_table (
  id INT,
  name STRING,
  age INT,
  city STRING
)
USING DELTA
TBLPROPERTIES (
  'delta.enableIcebergCompatV2' = 'true',
  'delta.universalFormat.enabledFormats' = 'iceberg'
)
LOCATION 's3://my-delta-uniform-table/';
```

In this example, the delta.universalFormat.enabledFormats option specifies the target format for interoperability. In this case, Iceberg is chosen.

After successful execution of this table, UniForm will maintain _delta_log for transactional consistency and generate additional Iceberg-compatible metadata in the metadata/ directory.

## Enable UniForm on an existing Delta Lake table

For existing Delta Lake tables, UniForm can be enabled without rewriting the data. This is done by running a table upgrade command:

```
ALTER TABLE existing_delta_table
SET TBLPROPERTIES (
 'delta.minReaderVersion' = '2',
 'delta.minWriterVersion' = '5',

  'delta.enableIcebergCompatV2' = 'true',
```

```
    'delta.universalFormat.enabledFormats' = 'iceberg'
);
```

Similar to the previous method, UniForm will enable metadata for the Iceberg format for the existing_delta_table table.

## UniForm limitations

While UniForm introduces a powerful mechanism for enabling interoperability between Delta Lake, Iceberg, and Hudi, it comes with certain limitations that users must consider before adopting it for production workloads:

- Iceberg and Hudi clients can only read Delta tables with UniForm enabled, and write operations are not supported. External writes could corrupt the Delta table by removing files critical to its transactional consistency.

- Delta tables with deletion vectors enabled are incompatible with UniForm.

- UniForm-enabled Delta tables do not support the VOID data type, which might require schema modifications for certain use cases.

- Delta-specific features such as *Change Data Feed* and *Delta Sharing* are not supported.

While UniForm enables powerful cross-format querying, its limitations around writes, deletion vectors, certain data types, and Delta-specific features mean it is primarily suited for read-only interoperability scenarios.

## Use cases for interoperability

Interoperability unlocks concrete value across diverse workloads where flexibility, performance, or ecosystem fit matter. Here are some real-world use cases where interoperability is key:

- **Incremental ingestion with Hudi, BI with Iceberg**: Apache Hudi excels in ingesting **change data capture (CDC)** streams from transactional sources due to its built-in support for *incremental processing* and its efficient handling of frequent updates and deletes via *indexes*. Once ingested into a Hudi table, the Hudi metadata can be translated into Iceberg using Apache XTable, and the same data can be queried by Iceberg-compatible engines that offer broader ecosystem integrations (e.g., ODBC/JDBC connectors, BI tools, and ML systems).

- **Data sharing across teams using different engines**: A specific team within an organization may write into Delta Lake using Databricks or Spark Structured Streaming, while analysts from other teams, using Apache Iceberg and Iceberg-compatible engines such as Trino, can query the same table. Interoperability enables this without duplicating datasets or maintaining multiple sinks.

- **Migration between ecosystems without rewrite**: Organizations migrating from Databricks (Delta-native) to another stack using Iceberg can use interoperability layers to transition read layers without rewriting terabytes of data or breaking downstream pipelines.

- **Mixed workloads on a single dataset**: A single copy of data may serve both fast ingestion workloads (via Hudi) and batch OLAP workloads (via Iceberg), each format optimized for different latency, concurrency, and query profile needs. Interoperability allows sharing the same data files while interoperating within the metadata layer.

Interoperability enables organizations to maximize flexibility, avoid costly data duplication, and support diverse workloads, all while allowing different teams and tools to seamlessly access and operate on the same underlying data.

## Summary

Interoperability is emerging as a cornerstone of modern lakehouse architecture as organizations adopt multiple open table formats, each optimized for specific use cases. This chapter introduced how solutions such as Delta UniForm and Apache XTable are bridging the gaps between formats by enabling cross-engine reads, schema sync, and format translation.

We explored the architectural trade-offs, real-world use cases (such as CDC ingestion and cross-format ML pipelines), and current limitations, offering a practical lens into the evolving landscape of format interoperability in lakehouse systems.

In the next chapter, we will look at performance optimization techniques and how they help us in data analysis.

# 8

# Performance Optimization and Tuning in a Lakehouse

Performance optimization is critical for managing and analyzing large-scale datasets in modern data systems. As the volume of data continues to grow exponentially and different types of analytical workloads (BI, machine learning, streaming, and so on) emerge, ensuring that systems can provide low-latency queries, efficient storage, and scalability becomes a core challenge. In big data ecosystems, performance bottlenecks typically stem from two critical areas: unoptimized storage and query execution overheads. To address these challenges, data systems have evolved to incorporate techniques that minimize data scanning, optimize resource usage, and improve data organization. In this chapter, we will explore how widely used performance optimization techniques (storage and query engine) from the traditional database world are applied to lakehouse table formats such as Apache Hudi, Apache Iceberg, and Delta Lake, and learn how they are run within these systems.

We will cover the following topics:

- Performance optimization
- Optimization techniques in open table formats
- Query optimization techniques

## Performance optimization

At a fundamental level, storage optimization techniques ensure that data is structured and managed in a way that minimizes redundant operations and improves data locality. Techniques such as partitioning, compaction, and clustering have become integral to addressing the challenges of large-scale storage. Partitioning logically segments data based on specific columns, allowing query engines to target only relevant partitions. Without effective partitioning, systems risk scanning massive amounts of irrelevant data, which increases query latency and resource consumption. Compaction addresses a common issue in the big data world: the small file problem. It combines small data files, typically created during ingestion, to create larger ones, as querying large files is more efficient than processing many small files. This improves I/O performance, reduces the number of files read, and ultimately enhances overall query performance. Clustering, on the other hand, reorganizes data within the storage system to align with query patterns, ensuring that frequently accessed data is stored together to minimize read operations. Finally, as data undergoes continuous writes, updates, and deletions, old file versions and metadata naturally accumulate. Over time, this buildup can result in excessive storage consumption and longer file listing times, both of which degrade query performance. Hence, cleaning is a critical technique to optimize storage.

Another equally important aspect is query engine-side optimization, which utilizes techniques to reduce the amount of data read and processed during query execution. These methods range from data skipping, where query engines use auxiliary information such as row- or column-level statistics provided by storage formats (such as Apache Parquet) to avoid scanning files that do not satisfy query predicates, to using vectorized execution that processes data in batches rather than row by row, using modern processing capabilities for faster computation.

These techniques form the foundation of performance optimization in large-scale data systems. Lakehouse table formats build upon these methods to address challenges unique to distributed, large-scale data environments.

# Optimization techniques in open table formats

This section explores how open table formats such as Apache Iceberg, Apache Hudi, and Delta Lake implement optimization techniques such as partitioning, compaction, clustering, and cleaning. It also explores practical examples of executing these techniques using compute engines such as Apache Spark. This should provide insights into how to tune performance in lakehouse architectures for practical use cases.

## Partition pruning

Partitioning is a fundamental optimization technique that enhances query performance by dividing large datasets into small, manageable segments based on commonly queried columns such as time, region, or category. This logical segmentation significantly reduces the amount of data scanned, improving efficiency in query execution. For example, as shown in the following diagram, in a Logs table with millions of entries, a query for event_date = '2018-12-02' would require scanning all records if the dataset was unpartitioned, whereas partitioning by event_date allows the query engine to retrieve only the relevant partition. This approach minimizes I/O operations, optimizes storage, and ensures that queries scale efficiently as data volume grows.

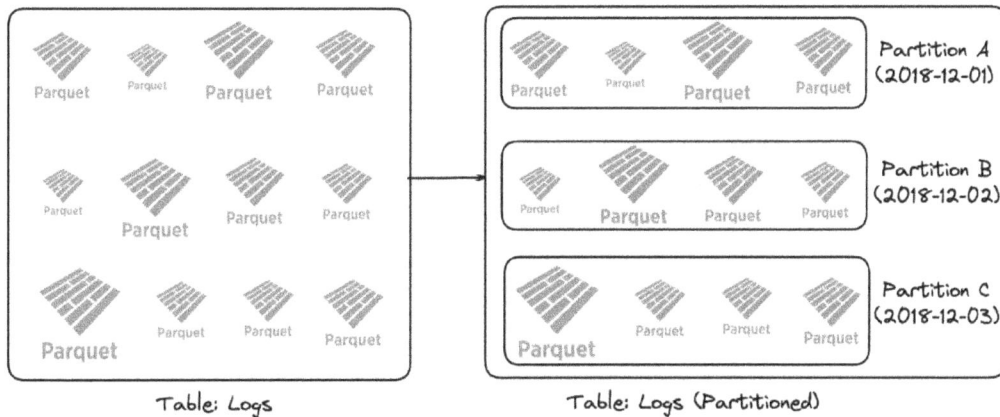

*Figure 8.1 – Parquet table reorganized into date partitions*

## Apache Iceberg

Apache Iceberg simplifies partitioning by eliminating the complexities of traditional table formats such as Apache Hive, which rely on explicit partition columns and directory structures. Instead, Iceberg abstracts partitioning logic, enabling hidden partitioning (discussed in *Chapter 3, Apache Iceberg Deep Dive*), where partition values are automatically derived using transformations (e.g., month(event_time)) and stored in metadata files. This allows users to query the base column (event_time) without explicit partition filters, while Iceberg optimizes queries by pruning unnecessary partitions. Additionally, partition evolution allows modifying partitioning schemes without rewriting existing data, enabling seamless transitions to finer-grained partitions as query needs evolve.

Here is an example that shows how to create a partitioned table:

```
CREATE TABLE logs (
    id BIGINT,
    event_time TIMESTAMP,
    log_message STRING
) USING iceberg
PARTITIONED BY (month(event_time));
```

If we query this table using `event_time`, Iceberg will take care of internally handling the transformation:

```
SELECT * FROM logs WHERE event_time >= '2023-06-01' AND event_
time < '2023-07-01';
```

## Apache Hudi

Partition pruning in Apache Hudi optimizes query performance by ensuring that only relevant partitions are scanned instead of reading the entire dataset. Hudi follows a directory-based partitioning model, where partitioned tables are structured hierarchically under the table's base path. When a query includes filters on partition columns, Hudi reads only the subset of data stored for that specific key.

Hudi also uses its internal metadata table (`https://hudi.apache.org/docs/metadata/`) to quickly identify and prune unnecessary partitions, significantly reducing query latency. Hudi's metadata table is structured as an internal **merge-on-read** (**MoR**) table that hosts different types of table metadata in each partition. This design is similar to traditional databases that maintain internal tables to track metadata. A key requirement for any engine interacting with Hudi tables is the ability to identify all files associated with the table, which typically involves listing table partitions and folders. However, performing such operations at scale, especially in cloud storage environments, can become a significant bottleneck, as directory listing operations may take several seconds or even minutes for large, deeply partitioned tables. Hudi tracks the file listings so they are readily available for readers/writers without listing the folders containing the data files. Ultimately, metadata tables enhance partition pruning by maintaining partition-level info as a file index, which is then utilized to prevent direct storage calls such as `exists`, `listStatus`, and `listFiles` on the cloud storage.

Here is an example of creating a partitioned Hudi table:

```
CREATE TABLE hudi_table (
    ts BIGINT,
    uuid STRING,
    rider STRING,
    driver STRING,
    fare DOUBLE,
    city STRING
) USING HUDI
PARTITIONED BY (city);
```

When filtering on the partition columns (city), Hudi uses partition pruning along with the metadata table to quickly locate relevant partitions, ensuring efficient pruning:

```
SELECT * FROM hudi_table WHERE city = 'SFO';
```

## Delta Lake

Similar to Hudi and Iceberg, Delta Lake offers partition pruning as a key performance optimization method that allows query engines to skip scanning unnecessary data files based on partition filters. When a query contains a filter on a partitioned column, Delta Lake analyzes its transaction log to identify only the relevant files, significantly reducing query execution time. For example, if a table is partitioned by country, and a query includes a filter such as WHERE country = 'Canada', Delta Lake ensures that only the data files stored under country=Canada/ are read, skipping irrelevant partitions.

Delta Lake does not offer explicit partition management commands such as ADD PARTITION or DROP PARTITION. Instead, new partitions are automatically created when data is written, and existing partitions are updated dynamically. Delta Lake's transaction log maintains partition column metadata, allowing query engines to efficiently prune partitions without needing to list files in storage. This metadata-driven approach improves query performance, particularly in cloud environments where file listing operations can be slow and expensive.

The following example demonstrates how to create a Delta table partitioned by country, enabling partition pruning for queries filtering on the country column:

```
data = [
    ("Canada", "2024-02-01", 120),
    ("Germany", "2024-02-02", 250),
    ("Canada", "2024-02-03", 180),
    ("Germany", "2024-02-04", 310)
]
df = spark.createDataFrame(data, ["country", "date", "sales"])
df.write.format("delta").partitionBy("country").save("/path/to/delta-
sales")
```

When executing a query with a partition filter, Delta Lake only reads the relevant partitions:

```
df = spark.read.format("delta").load("/path/to/delta-sales")
df.filter("country = 'Canada'").show()
```

This query will only scan the data stored under country=Canada/, improving efficiency.

For workloads that frequently filter on multiple columns, Delta Lake supports multi-column partitioning. The following example partitions data by both country and date:

```
df.write.format("delta").partitionBy("country", "date").save("/path/to/
delta-sales-multi")
```

When filtering on both partitioned columns, Delta Lake prunes partitions at a finer granularity, further optimizing query performance:

```
df = spark.read.format("delta").load("/path/to/delta-sales-multi")
df.filter("country = 'Germany' AND date = '2024-02-02'").show()
```

## Compaction

As data lakehouse architectures scale, continuous ingestion often leads to the small file problem, where numerous small files accumulate over time. This is also more applicable to streaming workloads, where small chunks of data are written as part of a stream. Each file carries overhead in terms of storage, metadata management, and query execution. When query engines process these dispersed files, they must open and process numerous files, significantly increasing I/O costs and slowing down performance. If we leave them unaddressed, the issue escalates with data growth, resulting in inefficient storage utilization and slower query performance.

**Compaction**, also known as **file sizing**, is a key optimization technique that merges small files into larger, well-sized ones, reducing the file count and improving query efficiency. By ensuring that files meet a system-defined target size, compaction helps minimize metadata overhead, speeds up query execution, and enhances overall system scalability. One of the most widely used approaches for compaction is the **bin packing algorithm**, which intelligently groups small files into near-optimal sizes without exceeding the defined threshold. This structured approach ensures that storage remains efficient while queries perform optimally, making compaction a key method in managing large-scale lakehouse environments.

For example, as shown in the following diagram, smaller files such as 40 MB, 80 MB, and 90 MB can be combined into larger files that align with the system's target size of 120 MB. This reduces the total file count while maximizing file utilization, leading to more efficient queries.

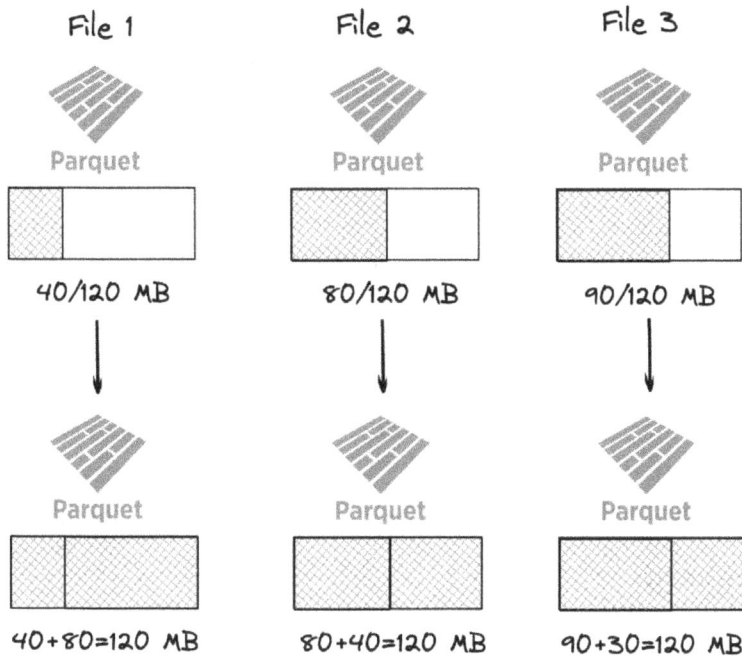

*Figure 8.2 – Smaller files combined into larger files that align with the system's target size of 120 MB*

## Apache Hudi

In Apache Hudi, it is important to distinguish between compaction and small file management. Compaction (https://hudi.apache.org/learn/tech-specs/#compaction) is a table service that merges Avro log files into new Parquet base files for MoR tables. Separately, Hudi manages small Parquet files for both CoW and MoR tables through write-time file sizing and optional clustering. In this section, we use *file sizing* to refer to small file management, and reserve *compaction* for Hudi's MoR log-to-base merge service. As discussed in the *Compaction* section earlier, small files can significantly impact query performance. Hudi addresses this through two file sizing strategies: write-time auto-sizing and post-write clustering mechanism to handle small files after data is written. Let's discuss these two primary file sizing strategies in Hudi:

- **Auto-sizing during writes**: Hudi intelligently manages file sizes at write time by ensuring that incoming data is distributed across existing files before creating new ones. This prevents the creation of small files, which can negatively impact query performance. Using configuration parameters such as hoodie.parquet.max.file.size and hoodie.parquet. small.file.limit in the ingestion job, Hudi automatically limits the size of new data files, typically targeting 120 MB per file by default. For MoR tables, since the goal is to reduce write amplification, Hudi limits the number of base data files (i.e., Parquet) to one. This is controlled via the property hoodie.merge.small.file.group.candidates.limit. By writing optimally sized files from the outset, Hudi reduces the need for post-processing, ensuring that queries benefit from efficient file layouts immediately after ingestion without user intervention.

- **Clustering after writes for file sizing**: Even with auto-sizing, some small files may still be created due to variable data ingestion patterns. To address this, Hudi supports file sizing post ingestion as part of its clustering table service. The configurable parameter in Hudi to select candidates for file sizing is hoodie.clustering.plan.strategy.small.file.limit. We will learn about clustering in the next section, but this service can be triggered manually or scheduled as an automated background process, helping optimize file layout without disrupting ingestion workflows. This post-write optimization further improves query efficiency.

## Apache Iceberg

Apache Iceberg addresses the small file problem by compacting data files to reduce metadata overhead and improve query efficiency. Iceberg can compact data files in parallel using Apache Spark with the rewriteDataFiles action, which combines small files into larger ones. This process utilizes a bin-packing algorithm to produce files that are close to the table's target size, controlled by the table property write.target-file-size-bytes, which defaults to 512 MB.

The bin packing algorithm does the following:

- Takes a target file size
- Has a lookback parameter to control how many bins to look back when packing
- Groups files into bins that are close to but don't exceed the target size

The actual rewrite process (Spark action) works this way:

- Reads the source files into a Spark DataFrame
- Configures the split size based on the target file size
- Writes the data back into new files of the target size

This rewrite process is performed atomically; that is, old files are only removed after new files are successfully written. Various configuration parameters, such as target file size, minimum input files to compact, and maximum file size, can be tuned for this process.

Here is an example using the Spark procedure:

```
CALL catalog_name.system.rewrite_data_files(
  table => 'db.sample',
  strategy => 'binpack',
  options => map(
    'target-file-size-bytes', '536870912',  -- 512MB
    'min-input-files', '5',
    'max-file-group-size-bytes', '107374182400' -- 100GB
  )
);
```

## Delta Lake

Delta Lake provides multiple strategies to handle small files and maintain efficient storage, ensuring that query performance remains optimal as data grows. Delta Lake offers manual compaction, auto compaction, and optimized writes to consolidate inefficiently sized files into larger, more manageable ones. Let's go over these processes:

- **Manual compaction with optimize**: Delta Lake provides the optimize command, which allows you to manually run a compaction operation to merge small files into larger files within each partition. By default, the operation aims for 1 GB file sizes. The compaction process can be triggered manually with the following command:

  ```
  from delta.tables import DeltaTable
  delta_table = DeltaTable.forPath(spark, "path/to/delta-table")
  delta_table.optimize().executeCompaction()
  ```

  This approach is particularly useful for batch-processing workloads, where many small files accumulate over time and need periodic consolidation.

- **Optimized writes:** Instead of waiting for manual compaction, Delta Lake allows users to optimize file sizes during data ingestion by enabling optimized write. This feature performs a data shuffle before writing, ensuring that small writes to the same partition are consolidated into fewer, larger files at the time of ingestion. Optimized writes can be enabled at different levels:

  For a specific write operation:

  ```
  df.write.format("delta").option("optimizeWrite", "True").
  save("path/to/delta")
  ```

For the entire Delta table:

```
ALTER TABLE delta_table SET TBLPROPERTIES ('delta.autoOptimize.
optimizeWrite' = 'true');
```

> Because Optimized Writes introduce an additional shuffle phase to coalesce
> small batches into larger files, they typically take longer to execute compared
> to standard (non-optimized) Delta writes that do not perform this shuffle.

- **Auto compaction**: Delta Lake also provides auto compaction, where small files are automatically merged after each write operation without manual intervention. This is particularly beneficial for workloads such as streaming and incremental data loads where small files are frequently generated. Auto compaction, in such cases, automatically triggers a lightweight optimization step after every write, consolidating files below a certain size threshold into larger, more efficient ones. Unlike manual compaction, which requires explicit execution of the optimize command, auto compaction runs in the background, periodically monitoring table partitions and merging small files only when necessary. You can enable auto compaction at different levels:

  - **Table level:**

    ```
    ALTER TABLE delta_table SET TBLPROPERTIES ('delta.
    autoOptimize.autoCompact' = 'true');
    ```

  - **Entire Spark session:**

    ```
    SET spark.databricks.delta.autoCompact.enabled = true;
    ```

> The OPTIMIZE command and table properties such as delta.autoOptimize.
> optimizeWrite and delta.autoOptimize.autoCompact are available in managed
> platforms like Databricks Runtime and some cloud runtimes that bundle Delta Lake.
> In pure open-source Delta Lake deployments, only the OPTIMIZE operation may be
> available depending on the Delta Lake version and catalog integration; auto-optimize
> features and their configuration flags can vary by platform.

# Balancing the cost of compaction

While compaction improves query performance by reducing the number of small files and optimizing layout, it is itself a resource-intensive operation that rewrites data. In practice, there is a trade-off between the additional write I/O and compute cost of compaction versus the read-time savings it enables.

A practical way to tune this balance is to observe a few key indicators over time:

- **File counts and average file size per partition**: If you see many very small files in frequently queried partitions, or average file sizes well below the target, compaction is likely to help. After a compaction run, you should see fewer files and a more consistent file size distribution.

- **Query planning and scan time**: Use your query engine's metrics (e.g., query profile or execution details) to compare planning time and total scan time before and after compaction. Successful compaction typically reduces the number of files scanned and the overall I/O cost.

- **Compaction job duration and resource usage**: Monitor how long compaction jobs run and their impact on cluster utilization. If compaction frequently overlaps with peak workloads or causes contention, consider running it less often, using smaller target file sizes, or scheduling it during off-peak windows.

In general, compaction and clustering are most effective when applied selectively: focus on hot tables and partitions that are read often and accumulate many small files, and avoid over-compacting rarely queried or archival data. This allows you to capture most of the performance benefits without incurring unnecessary maintenance costs.

# Clustering

Clustering is a storage optimization technique used in open table formats such as Apache Hudi, Apache Iceberg, and Delta Lake to enhance query efficiency by minimizing unnecessary file scans. At its core, clustering reorganizes data based on frequently queried attributes, aligning physical storage with expected query patterns. In the following diagram, you can see how records with different cities (color-coded) are spread across different files (on the left) and how, after clustering, similar cities are part of the same files (on the right).

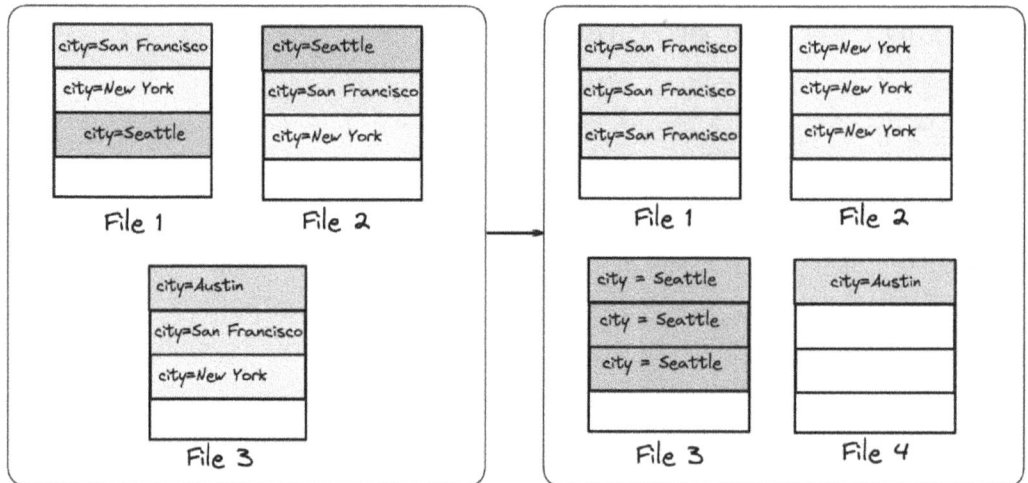

*Figure 8.3 – Records with different cities (color-coded) are spread across different files (on the left). After clustering, similar cities are part of the same files (on the right)*

As discussed earlier in the Compaction section, poorly sized and poorly organized files can increase I/O and slow down queries. Clustering builds on this idea by not only consolidating files but also reordering data within those files along key dimensions to align with query patterns.

There are two primary clustering strategies:

- **Linear sorting (single-dimensional clustering)**: This method orders data based on a single column to improve data locality and reduce scan overhead. Sorting ensures that values within a column (for example, event_date or region) are grouped together in files, making range-based queries significantly faster. However, single-column sorting may not be sufficient for queries involving multiple predicates, where filtering by one column does not sufficiently eliminate unnecessary scans.

- **Multi-dimensional clustering**: To further optimize queries involving multiple filtering conditions, multi-dimensional clustering techniques such as Z-ordering and Hilbert curves are used. These methods preserve spatial locality across multiple columns, meaning that records with similar attributes are stored closer together, significantly reducing query scan overhead.

  - **Z-ordering**: Z-ordering is a widely used multi-dimensional clustering technique that improves query efficiency by preserving locality across *multiple* dimensions. Unlike traditional sorting, which orders data based on a single column, Z-ordering arranges records in a way that groups similar values from multiple columns together. This significantly reduces the number of files scanned when queries involve filters on multiple attributes, making it particularly useful for analytical workloads. For example, in location-based analytics, where queries frequently filter on latitude and longitude, Z-ordering ensures that geographically close records are stored within the same data files. This minimizes the number of files that need to be read. By reducing unnecessary file scans, Z-ordering provides a significant performance boost, particularly for workloads involving range-based filtering across multiple dimensions.

- **Hilbert curves**: Hilbert curves are another space-filling curve-based clustering technique. Like Z-ordering, Hilbert curves map high-dimensional data into a one-dimensional space while preserving data locality, but they offer superior clustering in *high-dimensional* datasets.

   Hilbert curves are particularly beneficial in scientific and geospatial applications, where access patterns involve multiple attributes, such as time, depth, and location. For example, in climate modeling datasets, where queries frequently filter based on temperature, altitude, and geographic coordinates, Hilbert curves maintain better spatial proximity, ensuring that relevant data points are grouped together efficiently.

   However, Hilbert curves are computationally more complex than Z-ordering, requiring additional processing to determine the optimal clustering layout. While they offer better data locality preservation in high-dimensional clustering, the tradeoff lies in the increased computational overhead during writes. Therefore, choosing between Z-ordering and Hilbert curves depends on the specific data distribution, query workload, and performance considerations.

# Apache Hudi

Clustering in Apache Hudi allows users to reorganize data files for efficient query execution without disrupting ongoing ingestion. Unlike traditional approaches that require dedicated maintenance windows, Hudi's clustering service is designed to run *asynchronously* in the background, ensuring continuous ingestion while still optimizing data layout. This flexibility makes Hudi particularly well-suited for real-time and streaming workloads, where data arrives incrementally, often in an unorganized fashion. Hudi supports the three major clustering strategies: linear sorting, Z-ordering, and Hilbert curves.

## Hudi's clustering service

Hudi manages clustering as a table service, structured into two main phases: scheduling and execution. This design ensures that clustering can be orchestrated efficiently while minimizing query latencies and maintaining ACID guarantees.

Let's go over these two phases:

- **Scheduling clustering**: Hudi identifies eligible files that would benefit from clustering, such as small files or fragmented records. Files are grouped together to meet the target file size, ensuring optimal performance while preserving parallelism. The clustering plan is recorded in the Hudi timeline, stored in Avro format, and marked for execution.

- **Executing clustering**: Hudi retrieves the clustering groups from the saved plan and applies the chosen execution strategy (for example, sorting by event time). Data is rewritten into new, well-organized files, improving query efficiency. A REPLACE commit is made, updating Hudi's metadata to reflect the new data layout while preserving previous versions for time travel and rollback.

Hudi primarily provides two deployment models for clustering, allowing users to balance query performance with ingestion throughput:

- **Inline clustering**: Clustering occurs synchronously within the ingestion job. This mode ensures data is clustered immediately after ingestion, but it may delay the ingestion of new data until clustering completes. Here is an example using Spark's DataSourceWriter API:

```
df.write.format("hudi")  \
        .option("hoodie.clustering.inline",  "true")  \
        .option("hoodie.clustering.inline.max.commits",  "4")  \
        .option("hoodie.clustering.plan.strategy.sort.
columns",  "column1,column2")  \
        .mode("append").save("s3a://data-lake")
```

- **Async clustering**: Clustering runs in the background, separate from ingestion, allowing new data to be written without waiting for clustering to complete. Hudi provides three different modes to deploy async clustering.

  - **Async mode (same job)**:

    - **Schedule**: Clustering plans are scheduled after each commit within the ingestion job.

    - **Execute**: Execution of clustering occurs asynchronously in a separate thread spun up within the same ingestion job.

    This mode runs asynchronously within the same job after each commit and allows ingestion to proceed without waiting for clustering to complete, as clustering is handled in parallel.

- **Async mode (standalone job):**

  - **Schedule:** A separate clustering job schedules and plans the clustering operations independently of the ingestion job.

  - **Execute:** The same standalone clustering job executes the clustering plans it schedules.

  By isolating clustering into a separate job, this mode allows users to allocate independent compute resources for clustering. This ensures that ingestion latency remains stable and unaffected by clustering. No clustering configurations need to be set in the ingestion writer for this mode. However, proper lock providers should be configured to ensure concurrency control between ingestion and clustering jobs.

- **Async mode (manual trigger):**

  - **Schedule:** Clustering plans are scheduled inline during the ingestion job.

  - **Execute:** Execution of clustering occurs in a separate process or job, which users trigger manually at their convenience.

  This mode allows users to decouple clustering from ingestion entirely. Ingestion proceeds uninterrupted, and clustering plans are executed independently based on operational needs.

Here is an example of manually triggering and running async clustering using Spark SQL:

```
spark.sql("""
    CALL run_clustering(
        table => 'customer_data',
        op => 'scheduleAndExecutee',
    order_strategy => 'linear',
        options => 'hoodie.clustering.async.max.commits=4,
                    hoodie.clustering.plan.strategy.small.file.
limit=629145600,
                    hoodie.clustering.plan.strategy.sort.columns=Country,
                    hoodie.write.lock.filesystem.path = file://tmp/
hudilock/dip_hudi,
                    hoodie.fs.atomic_creation.support = s3a,
                hoodie.clustering.plan.strategy.target.file.max.
bytes=1073741824'
    )
""").show()
```

# Apache Iceberg

Apache Iceberg enables clustering through the `rewrite_data_files` Spark procedure. Unlike Apache Hudi, Iceberg does not have a dedicated clustering service, meaning clustering operations must be triggered *manually*. Since Iceberg's clustering is a reactive process, users must decide when to run it based on query performance degradation, storage inefficiencies, or planned maintenance windows. This approach prioritizes control and flexibility, but there is no automated mechanism to balance ingestion with optimized data layout. Iceberg supports two clustering strategies, linear sorting and Z-ordering, which define how data is reorganized to minimize file scans and improve query efficiency.

Linear sorting reads the input files, applies the specific sort order, and writes the new sorted files. It allows you to specify sort columns, sort direction (`ASC`/`DESC`), and `NULL` ordering. Here is an example:

```
CALL catalog_name.system.rewrite_data_files(
  table => 'db.table',
  strategy => 'sort',
  sort_order => 'id DESC NULLS LAST, name ASC NULLS FIRST'
);
```

Z-ordering takes multiple columns and interleaves their bits to create a Z-value. It then sorts by this Z-value to cluster related data together, thereby maintaining data locality across multiple dimensions. Here is an example that shows how to run Z-order clustering in Iceberg using the Spark procedure by specifying the clustering strategy and order:

```
CALL catalog_name.system.rewrite_data_files(
  table => 'db.table',
  strategy => 'sort',
  sort_order => 'zorder(c1, c2)'
);
```

Some of the configurable parameters are as follows:

- `max-output-size` = 2147483647 (default): Controls bytes interleaved in Z-order algorithm
- `var-length-contribution` = 8 (default): Bytes considered from variable length columns

The `rewrite_data_files` procedure returns metrics about the rewrite operation, such as the number of files rewritten, the number of new files added, the number of bytes rewritten, and the number of failed files (if partial progress has been enabled).

Since clustering in Iceberg requires explicit execution, organizations typically schedule it during low-traffic periods or as part of maintenance workflows to minimize impact on concurrent queries and ingestion processes.

# Delta Lake

Delta Lake provides clustering capabilities through Z-ORDER and the recently introduced Hilbert curve–based liquid clustering in Delta Lake 3.1.0. Z-ORDER clustering must be triggered manually using the OPTIMIZE command. Liquid clustering, on the other hand, supports eager clustering of newly written data depending on the version and configuration, and can also be invoked via OPTIMIZE. Unlike Apache Iceberg, Delta Lake does not provide a fully automated background clustering service.

In Delta Lake 3.1, liquid clustering is a preview feature gated by the spark.databricks.delta. clusteredTable.enableClusteringTablePreview configuration and has some limitations, with broader Python and Scala API support becoming available in Delta Lake 3.2 and later.

Z-order clustering is the most widely used clustering method in Delta Lake. This is what happens when a Z-order operation is performed:

1. Columns selected for Z-ordering are mapped to range partition IDs – each unique value in the selected columns is assigned an internal ID.

2. These partition IDs are then interleaved at the bit level to generate Z-values, ensuring that related values across different dimensions maintain spatial locality.

3. Data is physically reordered according to these Z-values, grouping similar records within the same data files.

This mechanism reduces the number of files scanned when queries filter on multiple Z-order columns by preserving spatial locality at the storage level. Since queries in Delta Lake leverage the transaction log for partition pruning, Z-ordering further enhances efficiency by ensuring that only the most relevant files are accessed during query execution.

For example, applying Z-order clustering on a sales dataset with customer_id and transaction_ date:

```
OPTIMIZE sales_table ZORDER BY (customer_id, transaction_date);
```

This ensures that records with similar customer_id and transaction_date values are stored close together, reducing unnecessary file scans when filtering on these attributes simultaneously.

Delta Lake 3.1 introduced liquid clustering, an incremental approach to clustering that reduces write amplification while preserving spatial locality better than Z-ordering. Unlike traditional clustering, which rewrites all files each time it's executed, liquid clustering only reclusters unoptimized files in subsequent runs, making the process more efficient.

This technique uses a Hilbert curve, which organizes multi-dimensional data with better spatial locality than Z-ordering, making it particularly useful for queries filtering on multiple correlated attributes. An added benefit of liquid clustering is that it automatically tracks clustering metadata in the transaction log, eliminating the need for users to manually specify clustering columns every time they invoke `optimize`.

This is how liquid clustering works:

- **Uses Hilbert space-filling curves to map multidimensional data**: Unlike Z-ordering, which interleaves bits from partitioned columns, Hilbert curves offer superior spatial locality preservation in higher dimensions

- **Creates ZCubes to group related data**: Delta Lake organizes data into logical clusters, ensuring that records with similar values across multiple dimensions are stored together

- **Supports incremental clustering**: Unlike traditional clustering methods that require a full rewrite of data, liquid clustering only reclusters unoptimized files while keeping already optimized data intact

- **Minimizes write amplification**: Since only unclustered files are rewritten in subsequent operations, liquid clustering significantly reduces storage costs and improves query performance without excessive data movement

## Cleaning

In lakehouse architectures, cleaning plays a crucial role in managing storage efficiency, reducing metadata overhead, and maintaining query performance. As data is continuously written, updated, and deleted, old versions of files accumulate, leading to unnecessary storage consumption and long file listing times. Over time, this can degrade system performance, as query engines must process an increasing number of outdated file references and metadata entries.

Cleaning helps address this issue by removing obsolete file versions, optimizing metadata structures, and reclaiming storage space, ensuring that only relevant, up-to-date data remains accessible. This process is comparable to *vacuuming* in traditional databases, where old tuples and logs are periodically purged to prevent excessive bloat. By efficiently managing data retention, cleaning ensures that queries remain performant, storage costs are controlled, and the system operates with minimal overhead.

# Apache Iceberg

As Iceberg tables grow with continuous updates and new writes, old snapshots, metadata files, and unreferenced data accumulate, leading to storage inefficiency and increased query latency. To counter this, Iceberg provides built-in maintenance Spark procedures and table properties to manage data retention, optimize storage, and improve query performance.

Here are the three different procedures to maintain an Iceberg table in production:

- **Expire snapshots**: Every write operation in Iceberg generates a new snapshot, which is stored by Iceberg to enable time-travel queries and rollback capabilities. However, as snapshots accumulate, they increase metadata storage costs and slow down query planning. The `expire_snapshots` procedure removes outdated snapshots and their associated data files that are no longer referenced by active snapshots. This process helps reclaim storage while maintaining consistency. For instance, to remove snapshots older than one day, we can execute this:

```
CALL  catalog_name.system.expire_snapshots(
    table  =>  'catalog_name.db.table_name',
    older_than  =>  TIMESTAMP  '2024-02-10  00:00:00'
);
```

- **Remove old metadata files**: Iceberg maintains table metadata in JSON files, capturing details of table schema, snapshots, and partitioning. Frequent updates (such as streaming writes) generate new metadata files, and without periodic cleanup, these files can accumulate, affecting query performance. The `write.metadata.delete-after-commit.enabled` property enables automatic metadata cleanup after each table commit. To configure Iceberg to retain a specific number of historical metadata files, use the following code:

```
ALTER  TABLE  catalog_name.db.table_name  SET  TBLPROPERTIES  (
    'write.metadata.previous-versions-max'  =  '10'
);
```

This ensures that only a limited number of metadata files are kept, and older ones are automatically deleted after reaching the specified threshold.

- **Delete orphan files**: Orphan files are data files left behind due to failed write operations, schema changes, or snapshot expiration that doesn't immediately remove all unreferenced files. These files increase storage costs and create inconsistencies in data management.

The remove_orphan_files procedure deletes such untracked files by scanning the storage location and identifying files not referenced in Iceberg's metadata. Here's how you can delete the unreferenced files:

```
CALL  catalog_name.system.remove_orphan_files(
    table  =>  'catalog_name.db.table_name',
    location  =>  's3a://lakehouse/data'
);
```

> Since deleting orphan files can be risky if retention settings are not carefully managed, Iceberg allows setting a retention interval (the default is three days) to prevent the mistaken removal of files still in progress.

## Apache Hudi

Apache Hudi incorporates a built-in cleaning service to efficiently manage storage by removing outdated file versions while maintaining data integrity. Since Hudi operates on **Multi-Version Concurrency Control** (**MVCC**), multiple file versions are retained to support snapshot isolation, which ultimately enables features such as rollback, time travel, and incremental queries. However, retaining too many historical versions can lead to storage inefficiency, making cleaning a crucial part of table maintenance.

Hudi's cleaning process is designed to be automatic and asynchronous, ensuring that old file versions are pruned without disrupting ongoing ingestion or queries. By default, cleaning is triggered immediately after a commit, preventing excessive file accumulation. Users can also configure the cleaning frequency by setting hoodie.clean.max.commits, defining how often cleaning runs (e.g., after every 10 commits instead of after each commit). This allows flexibility in balancing query rollback capabilities and storage efficiency.

Hudi offers multiple cleaning strategies, allowing users to fine-tune how obsolete data files are removed:

- **Version-based cleaning**: Retains only the most recent *N* versions of a file while deleting older ones. This ensures that rollback and time travel operations are supported up to a certain number of historical versions.
- **Commit-based cleaning**: Retains files based on a fixed number of past commits. For example, setting hoodie.cleaner.commits.retained=10 keeps only the last 10 commits' data files and deletes older ones.

- **Time-based cleaning**: Deletes files that exceed a specified age threshold (e.g., files older than 24 hours). This method is useful for use cases where only recent data is relevant, such as streaming workloads with short retention windows.

To configure cleaning in a Hudi table, you can set properties such as the following:

```
-- Retain the latest 5 versions of each file
SET hoodie.cleaner.policy=KEEP_LATEST_FILE_VERSIONS;
SET hoodie.cleaner.fileversions.retained=5;
-- Run cleaning every 10 commits
SET hoodie.clean.max.commits=10;
```

If you want to run the cleaner service asynchronously along with writing, enable the following properties:

```
hoodie.clean.automatic=true
hoodie.clean.async=true
```

The important thing to take away is that Hudi's automatic cleaning ensures storage remains optimized by intelligently removing outdated file versions without disrupting ingestion or queries.

## Delta Lake

Delta Lake manages storage cleanup using the VACUUM command, which removes data files that are no longer referenced by the Delta transaction log. Similar to Iceberg and Hudi, since Delta Lake retains historical versions of data for time travel and rollback, unreferenced files can accumulate over time, increasing storage costs. VACUUM in Delta Lake is a manual operation, giving users control over when to delete obsolete files.

By default, Delta Lake retains deleted files for seven days, ensuring that long-running transactions and streaming queries can still access required data. This retention threshold can be modified based on workload requirements, but reducing it too aggressively can lead to data corruption risks, especially for ongoing queries that depend on past snapshots. Additionally, VACUUM only removes data files (Parquet), while log files (metadata) are managed separately and are automatically purged after 30 days (configurable via delta.logRetentionDuration).

To clean a Delta table while maintaining a safe retention window, run the following command:

```
VACUUM eventsTable;
```

This command runs in FULL mode, scanning the table directory and removing all unreferenced files outside the retention period. For more efficient execution, Delta Lake 3.3 introduced LITE mode, which speeds up the cleanup process by relying on the transaction log instead of scanning the full directory:

```
VACUUM eventsTable LITE;
```

If you need to check which files would be deleted before executing the command, a dry run can be performed:

```
VACUUM eventsTable DRY RUN;
```

Together, LITE mode and DRY RUN make VACUUM far safer and more predictable, letting you preview deletions before committing and clean up faster when you're ready. These options turn table maintenance into a controlled, low-risk operation.

# Practical Tuning Cheat Sheet

The optimal file size and maintenance strategy depend on your workloads and platform, but each table format ships with sensible defaults based on production experience. This section summarizes those defaults, the key configuration knobs, and when you might adjust them.

## Apache Hudi

### Typical target file size

By default, Hudi writes Parquet base files with a target size of roughly 120 MB, controlled by the hoodie.parquet.max.file.size setting (in bytes). Hudi also uses hoodie.parquet.small.file. limit to decide when a file should be considered "small" and eligible for consolidation.

### Key configuration knobs

- hoodie.parquet.max.file.size – target size for Parquet base files
- hoodie.parquet.small.file.limit – threshold below which files are treated as small
- hoodie.clustering.plan.strategy.target.file.max.bytes – target size for files produced by clustering

### When to increase the target file size

Consider raising the target size (for example into the 200–500 MB range) when:

- Queries are I/O-bound and scan many small files.
- Your executors have enough memory and CPU to process larger splits without spilling.
- Compaction and clustering jobs are running comfortably within your maintenance windows.

Larger files reduce the number of file opens and metadata entries, which can help on cloud object stores.

## When to decrease the target file size

Consider lowering the target size or running compaction/clustering less aggressively when:

- Compaction or clustering jobs take too long or compete with other workloads.
- Your cluster has small executors or limited memory, and large splits cause spills.
- You are ingesting data continuously and want lighter, more frequent maintenance cycles.

For streaming-heavy pipelines, it's often better to keep write-time files moderate (around 100–200 MB) and rely on periodic clustering rather than very large files.

# Apache Iceberg

This section looks at how Apache Iceberg manages data file sizing and the configuration options that control it. Understanding these defaults and tuning points helps balance write efficiency, query performance, and metadata overhead as tables grow.

## Typical target file size

Iceberg's default target file size is 512 MB, controlled by the `write.target-file-size-bytes` table property. Compaction operations such as `rewrite_data_files` also accept their own `target-file-size-bytes`, `min-file-size-bytes`, and `max-file-size-bytes` options.

## Key configuration knobs

- `write.target-file-size-bytes` – target size for new data files
- `rewrite_data_files` options – `target-file-size-bytes`, `min-file-size-bytes`, `max-file-size-bytes`

## When to increase the target file size

Keeping the default 512 MB is a good starting point for most batch analytics workloads. You might increase it when:

- You are running large, scan-heavy queries and want to minimize the number of files.
- Your cluster handles large scan tasks well and you are not seeing memory pressure or spills.

Bigger files can reduce planning and metadata overhead, especially on append-only tables.

## When to decrease the target file size

Consider lowering `write.target-file-size-bytes` (for example to 128–256 MB) when:

- You are ingesting data via micro-batches or streaming and don't want to wait long for files to fill.
- You see tasks spilling or long garbage-collection pauses due to very large splits.
- You prefer more granular parallelism for mixed workloads.

Smaller, but not tiny, files often strike a good balance between freshness and efficiency.

# Delta Lake (managed runtimes such as Databricks or Fabric)

The settings and behavior in this subsection describe managed runtimes that include Delta Lake (for example, Databricks or Microsoft Fabric). Open-source Delta Lake installations may expose a subset of these options depending on the catalog and engine.

## Typical target file size

On these platforms, `OPTIMIZE` typically aims for files around 1 GB in size, controlled by settings such as `spark.databricks.delta.optimize.maxFileSize` (in bytes). Some environments also provide auto-optimize features that write smaller files (often around 128–256 MB) during streaming or high-frequency ingestion.

## Key configuration knobs

`spark.databricks.delta.optimize.maxFileSize` or `delta.targetFileSize` – target size for `OPTIMIZE`.

Platform-specific auto-optimize / auto-compaction settings – control how small files are combined automatically

## When to increase the target file size

It is usually safe to keep the 1 GB default for large, read-heavy tables that you compact periodically. You might raise or leave it unchanged when:

- You primarily run large analytical queries that benefit from scanning fewer, larger files.
- `OPTIMIZE` jobs complete within acceptable maintenance windows.

## When to decrease the target file size

Lower the target size (for example to 256–512 MB or even 128 MB) when:

- OPTIMIZE or maintenance jobs are taking too long or putting pressure on cluster resources.
- You have many incremental updates and want compaction to complete faster.
- Your workload is dominated by streaming or near-real-time ingestion, and extreme file sizes would cause long stalls.

Auto-optimize features can often manage file sizes for you in streaming workloads; you can then use occasional OPTIMIZE passes to clean up historical data.

## Putting it together

As a rule of thumb:

- Start with the defaults for each format.
- Monitor the number of files per partition and the time spent in planning and I/O.
- If you see many small files and high metadata overhead, increase the target file size or run compaction/clustering more often.
- If maintenance jobs are slow or disruptive, reduce the target file size and schedule them during off-peak hours.
- For streaming and near-real-time workloads, prefer moderate file sizes with frequent, lightweight maintenance rather than infrequent, heavy rewrites.

This cheat sheet gives you a starting point and a rubric for tuning rather than a single "magic" number, so you can adapt settings to your own cluster size, workload mix, and service-level objectives.

# Query optimization techniques

As data lakehouses continue to grow in scale and complexity, the need for efficient query performance becomes increasingly important. Query optimization techniques play a pivotal role in reducing data I/O, improving scan efficiency, and accelerating data retrieval. In modern data lakehouses, leveraging advanced metadata, indexing strategies, vectorized execution, **cost-based optimization (CBO)**, intelligent caching, and unified materialized views has become essential for achieving high performance. This approach is particularly effective for time-series workloads, where efficient data pruning can lead to orders of magnitude performance improvements.

Some of the examples in this section reference public talks or engineering blog posts from companies such as Netflix, Microsoft, Uber, Pinterest, and Databricks. These are intended to illustrate how these techniques have been applied in practice rather than to prescribe specific performance expectations.

# Leveraging column statistics and metadata for efficient data pruning

Efficient data pruning is fundamental to minimizing I/O during query execution. For example, in a typical enterprise data warehouse scenario, effective pruning can reduce scan sizes significantly for time-based queries, significantly improving query response times.

## Apache Iceberg

Iceberg maintains file-level metrics in manifest entries, allowing query engines to bypass entire files without scanning their footers. For example, if a query filters on `transaction_date > '2025-01-01'`, Iceberg's manifest scanner automatically excludes files where the maximum date is earlier. In production environments, this approach has been shown to significantly reduce query planning time for large tables.

To take advantage of Iceberg's rich metadata and statistics, you first create a table as usual; Spark and other engines will automatically populate file- and manifest-level statistics during writes:

```
CREATE TABLE iceberg_sales (
  transaction_id STRING,
  sale_time TIMESTAMP,
  product_sku STRING,
  amount DECIMAL(9,2))
USING ICEBERG
PARTITIONED BY (days(sale_time));
```

## Apache Hudi

Hudi implements a multi-modal metadata table that precomputes column ranges and stores them in a distributed metadata index, backed by an internal MoR table optimized for fast lookups. In real-world deployments, this has enabled sub-second metadata queries on petabyte-scale tables with billions of records. For instance, at Uber, Hudi's indexing strategy reduced query latency significantly for their real-time analytics workloads. Here is how you can create indexes:

```
CREATE INDEX idx_product_stats ON hudi_inventory USING column_
stats(product_id);


SELECT warehouse_id, SUM(stock)
FROM hudi_inventory
WHERE product_id BETWEEN 1000 AND 2000
GROUP BY warehouse_id;
```

## Delta Lake

Delta Lake implements optimizations through transaction log annotations and enhances partition pruning with dynamic techniques. At Databricks, customers have reported noticeable performance improvements for selective queries using Z-order clustering. Here is how you can create clustering:

```
OPTIMIZE retail.products ZORDER BY (category_id, price);


SELECT product_name
FROM retail.products
WHERE category_id = 215 AND price BETWEEN 50 AND 100;
```

# Bloom filters and advanced indexing strategies

High-cardinality column filtering has become increasingly important in modern data architectures. For example, in e-commerce platforms handling millions of SKUs, efficient filtering can reduce query times from minutes to seconds.

## Apache Iceberg

Iceberg exposes Bloom filter support through table properties that configure Parquet or ORC writers. To enable a Bloom filter on a specific column, you set the corresponding `write.parquet.bloom-filter-enabled.column.<col>` property (or `write.orc.bloom.filter.columns` for ORC). For example, to enable a Bloom filter on the `error_code` column in a Parquet-backed Iceberg table and set a false positive rate of 1%:

```
ALTER TABLE iceberg_logs SET TBLPROPERTIES (
   'write.parquet.bloom-filter-enabled.column.error_code' = 'true',
   'write.parquet.bloom-filter-fpp.column.error_code'     = '0.01'
);
```

These properties instruct Iceberg's Parquet writer to embed a Bloom filter for error_code in each data file, which allows engines to quickly discard files that definitely do not contain a given error code, reducing I/O for highly selective filters

## Apache Hudi

Hudi's asynchronous Bloom filter indexing has demonstrated low false positives in production environments. The following example shows how Hudi's bloom_filters index can be configured and queried for selective lookups on user_id:

```
CREATE INDEX idx_bloom_users ON hudi_social USING bloom_filters(user_id);


SELECT *
FROM hudi_social
WHERE user_id = 'U-9XQ9T3P';
```

## Delta Lake

On Databricks, Delta Lake supports Bloom filter *indexes* as an optional data skipping feature. Bloom filters are created and managed using the CREATE BLOOM FILTER INDEX command and are **Databricks-specific**, not part of open-source Delta Lake.

As discussed in the *Clustering* section earlier, Z-ordering and liquid clustering in Delta Lake organize data to improve multi-dimensional data skipping. Here, they work in conjunction with Bloom filters and statistics to reduce the number of files scanned. For example, to create a Bloom filter index on product_id in a Delta table:

```
CREATE BLOOM FILTER INDEX idx_products_pid
  ON TABLE retail.products
  FOR COLUMNS (product_id)
  OPTIONS ('fpp' = '0.01', 'numItems' = '1000000');
```

At query time, the engine consults the Bloom filter index to skip files that cannot contain the requested product_id, improving performance for highly selective equality filters.

For non-Databricks environments using open-source Delta Lake, Bloom filter indexes are not available; other techniques such as Z-ordering or clustering (discussed earlier) are preferred for multi-dimensional pruning.

# Vectorized execution and hardware-accelerated processing

The shift from row-wise to vectorized execution has revolutionized big data analytics, with many organizations reporting 2-10x performance improvements for analytical workloads. Modern CPU architectures with SIMD instructions can process up to eight double-precision values simultaneously, significantly accelerating data processing.

## Apache Iceberg

Iceberg's vectorized readers for Parquet and ORC files have shown exceptional performance in production environments. At Netflix, the combination of Iceberg's vectorized reading with Spark's Tungsten engine resulted in faster scan performance for their content analytics platform. Here is an example on how to enable vectorized reads:

```
-- Example of Iceberg configuration for vectorized reads
ALTER TABLE iceberg_analytics SET TBLPROPERTIES (
  'read.parquet.vectorization.enabled' = 'true',
  'read.parquet.vectorization.batch-size' = '4096');
```

## Apache Hudi

Hudi's hybrid approach combines vectorized readers with row-oriented Avro log merging. At Uber, this architecture has reported noticeable improvements in reduced query latency for real-time analytics while maintaining update latencies. Here is an example to create a table with optimized read/write settings:

```
CREATE TABLE hudi_metrics (
  metric_id STRING, timestamp TIMESTAMP, value DOUBLE) USING hudi
TBLPROPERTIES (
  'hoodie.parquet.max.file.size' = '128000000',
  'hoodie.parquet.compression.codec' = 'snappy',
  'hoodie.clustering.inline' = 'true');
```

## Delta Lake

Delta Lake's integration with Spark's Tungsten engine has demonstrated significant performance gains. Microsoft reported faster processing for their large-scale log analytics after implementing vectorized execution. Here is an example on how to enable vectorized reads in Delta Lake:

```
SET spark.sql.parquet.enableVectorizedReader = true;
SET spark.sql.inMemoryColumnarStorage.batchSize = 10000;
```

# CBO and query planning

Modern cost-based optimizers have evolved to leverage detailed table statistics, resulting in up to 10x performance improvements for complex analytical queries. In production environments, intelligent query planning can reduce resource utilization by 40-60%.

## Apache Iceberg

In Iceberg setups that use Spark as the query engine, cost-based optimization (CBO) relies on table and column statistics stored in the catalog. Spark's Catalyst optimizer uses these statistics to choose better join orders, join strategies, and filter pushdown plans. To enable CBO, you first compute statistics on your Iceberg tables using ANALYZE TABLE:

```
-- Enable CBO in Spark
SET spark.sql.cbo.enabled = true;

-- Collect table and column statistics for an Iceberg table
ANALYZE TABLE iceberg_users
  COMPUTE STATISTICS FOR ALL COLUMNS;
```

Once these statistics are collected, Spark can generate more efficient execution plans for queries that join iceberg_users with other tables, often reducing shuffle volume and overall runtime.

## Apache Hudi

Hudi's global index has enabled efficient query planning across distributed datasets. At ByteDance, this reduced shuffle operations significantly during MERGE operations:

```
-- Configure global index for MERGE optimization
SET hoodie.index.type = GLOBAL_SIMPLE;
SET hoodie.bloom.index.update.partition.path = true;

-- MERGE operation with shuffle optimization
MERGE INTO hudi_transactions AS target
USING updates_stream AS source
ON target.account_id = source.account_id
WHEN MATCHED THEN UPDATE SET *
WHEN NOT MATCHED THEN INSERT *;
```

# Delta Lake

Delta Lake's low shuffle merge optimization has proven particularly effective for large-scale data updates. Databricks customers have reported faster MERGE operations. The following low-shuffle merge optimization is available on managed runtimes that extend Delta Lake (such as Microsoft Fabric or Databricks), and is not part of the core open-source Delta Lake feature set:

```
SET spark.databricks.delta.merge.lowShuffle.enabled = true;


MERGE INTO delta_customers AS target
USING updates AS source
ON target.customer_id = source.customer_id
WHEN MATCHED THEN UPDATE SET *;
```

# Intelligent caching architectures

Effective caching strategies have become crucial for modern data platforms, with some organizations reporting noticeable reductions in cold query latencies through intelligent cache management.

# Apache Iceberg

Iceberg can cache the contents of manifest files in memory to avoid repeatedly reading small metadata files from remote storage during planning. This can reduce metadata I/O and improve planning latency for append-heavy tables, especially in cloud object stores. Manifest caching is configured as catalog properties (engine/session configuration), not as Iceberg table properties.

```
-- Configure Iceberg manifest caching (catalog-
level; set before running queries)
SET spark.sql.catalog.iceberg_prod.io.manifest.cache-enabled = true;
SET spark.sql.catalog.iceberg_prod.io.manifest.cache.expiration-interval-
ms = 600000;


-- Required sizing knobs when enabling manifest caching
SET spark.sql.catalog.iceberg_prod.io.manifest.cache.max-total-
bytes = 104857600;     -- 100 MB default
SET spark.sql.catalog.iceberg_prod.io.manifest.cache.max-content-
length = 8388608;    -- 8 MB default
```

Those property names and defaults come from Iceberg's CatalogProperties constants.

## Apache Hudi

Hudi's hybrid caching model has demonstrated exceptional performance for mixed workloads. At Uber, this approach reduced average query latency significantly while maintaining real-time data freshness:

```
-- Configure Hudi's record-level indexing with caching
CREATE TABLE hudi_realtime (
 id STRING, data STRING) USING hudi
TBLPROPERTIES (
 'type' = 'mor',
 'hoodie.compact.inline' = 'false',
 'hoodie.index.type' = 'GLOBAL_BLOOM',
 'hoodie.bloom.index.use.caching' = 'true');
```

## Delta Lake

Delta Lake's distributed caching has shown impressive results in cloud environments. Microsoft Azure customers reported faster query performance for frequently accessed data:

```
-- Enable and configure Delta caching
SET spark.databricks.delta.caching.enabled = true;
SET spark.databricks.delta.caching.maxAge = '7d';
```

> `spark.databricks.delta.caching.enabled` is specific to Databricks Runtime. On other platforms, similar benefits can be achieved using Spark's built-in caching (`df.cache()` / `CACHE TABLE`) or vendor-specific file caching mechanisms.

# Precomputed aggregates and secondary indexing

Precomputed aggregate tables and secondary indexes are common techniques for reducing query latency in analytical workloads. By materializing frequently used groupings or filter paths, engines can avoid scanning full detail tables and instead operate on smaller derived tables or leverage index structures tailored to typical access patterns.

## Apache Iceberg

Many query engines that support Iceberg allow you to create precomputed aggregate tables (sometimes called materialized views) on top of base Iceberg tables. Even if the engine does not support CREATE MATERIALIZED VIEW natively, you can achieve a similar effect using CREATE TABLE AS SELECT (CTAS) and refreshing the table on a schedule:

```
CREATE TABLE iceberg_daily_metrics USING ICEBERG AS
SELECT
    date_trunc('day', event_time) AS day,
    event_type,
    COUNT(*) AS event_count
FROM iceberg_events
GROUP BY date_trunc('day', event_time), event_type;
```

This pattern precomputes daily aggregates, significantly reducing the cost of repeated dashboard queries over the raw iceberg_events table.

## Apache Hudi

Hudi's global secondary indexes are not materialized views but can serve a similar purpose for accelerating filtered or pre-aggregated access patterns. For example, creating a global secondary index on order_status enables efficient queries that group or filter by status:

```
CREATE INDEX gsi_order_status ON hudi_orders (order_status);

SELECT customer_id, SUM(total) AS total_spent
FROM hudi_orders
WHERE order_status = 'shipped'
GROUP BY customer_id;
```

Here, the index helps Hudi locate matching records more quickly across partitions, reducing scan cost for common reporting queries.

## Delta Lake

Delta Lake's liquid clustering has demonstrated significant benefits for materialized view performance. Databricks has reported substantially faster queries for customer analytics workloads when using liquid clustering:

```
ALTER TABLE delta_events SET TBLPROPERTIES (
  'clusteringColumns' = 'event_category,user_tier');

OPTIMIZE delta_events;
```

# Summary

In this chapter, we explored the critical performance optimization techniques required for efficient data processing in modern lakehouse architectures. We began by examining storage optimization strategies, including partitioning, compaction, clustering, and cleaning, which minimize data scanning and I/O costs. Apache Iceberg, Hudi, and Delta Lake leverage these techniques differently, providing flexibility and scalability for varied analytical workloads.

We then delved into advanced query optimization methods, highlighting the role of column statistics, Bloom filters, and vectorized execution in enhancing query performance. These approaches effectively prune data and utilize intelligent indexing strategies to minimize query latency and maximize resource efficiency. Additionally, we discussed CBO, intelligent caching architectures, and materialized view optimization, demonstrating their impact on high-performance analytics in distributed data ecosystems.

Through practical examples and real-world scenarios, this chapter illustrated how to apply these techniques using compute engines such as Apache Spark and Flink. By mastering these strategies, data engineers can build scalable, high-performance lakehouse systems that effectively handle large-scale data processing demands.

Building on these optimization strategies, the next chapter delves into data governance and security, focusing on data quality, life cycle management, and robust access controls to ensure compliance with regulatory requirements in scalable lakehouse environments.

# Questions

1. What is the primary purpose of partitioning in lakehouse architectures?
2. How does Apache Iceberg handle partition evolution without rewriting data?
3. What is the small file problem, and how does compaction solve it?
4. What is the difference between Z-ordering and Hilbert curves for clustering?
5. How does Apache Hudi leverage its metadata table for partition pruning?
6. What role do Bloom filters play in query optimization?
7. How does vectorized execution improve query performance compared to row-wise processing?
8. What is cost-based optimization, and how does it enhance query planning?
9. How does intelligent caching architecture improve query latency in modern data systems?
10. What is the purpose of materialized views in query optimization?

# Answers

1. Partitioning logically segments data based on specific columns, allowing query engines to target only relevant partitions, thereby minimizing I/O operations and improving query performance.

2. Apache Iceberg supports partition evolution as a metadata-only change by committing a new partition spec in table metadata. New data can be written with the new spec while existing data remains readable under older specs, no eager rewrite of existing files is required.

3. The small file problem occurs when numerous small files accumulate over time, increasing metadata overhead and slowing query execution. Compaction merges small files into larger ones, reducing file count and enhancing query efficiency.

4. Z-ordering (Morton/Z-order curve) clusters data by mapping multi-dimensional values to a 1-D ordering that preserves locality reasonably well. Hilbert curves are another space-filling curve that often provides better locality/clustering than Z-order in practice (especially in low dimensions), which can improve multi-column pruning effectiveness.

5. Apache Hudi's metadata table can maintain auxiliary indexes such as column statistics (min/max, null counts, etc.) and partition statistics. Query engines can use these to skip files and even entire partitions more efficiently (data skipping / faster pruning), reducing planning and scan overhead.

6. Bloom filters are probabilistic data structures that efficiently filter out non-matching records, reducing point lookup latency for high-cardinality fields.

7. Vectorized execution processes data in batches using modern CPU architectures, minimizing function call overhead and enabling parallel processing, significantly speeding up query execution.

8. Cost-based optimization uses table statistics to generate optimal execution plans, reducing resource utilization and improving query performance by minimizing unnecessary data scans.

9. Intelligent caching architectures store frequently accessed metadata or data in-memory or on local SSDs, reducing redundant I/O operations and enhancing query performance.

10. Materialized views store pre-aggregated or pre-joined query results, enabling faster query responses by reducing computation overhead during query execution.

## Get This Book's PDF Version and Exclusive Extras

UNLOCK NOW

Scan the QR code (or go to packtpub.com/unlock). Search for this book by name, confirm the edition, and then follow the steps on the page.

**Note:** *Keep your invoice handy. Purchases made directly from Packt don't require an invoice.*

# 9

# Data Governance and Security in Lakehouses

Data governance and security represent critical pillars in modern lakehouse architecture, especially those built on open table formats such as Apache Iceberg, Apache Hudi, and Delta Lake. This chapter provides a comprehensive examination of governance practices, quality frameworks, lifecycle management, and security protocols essential for enterprise-grade lakehouse implementations.

Organizations implementing data lakehouses face unique challenges as they attempt to maintain the flexibility of data lakes while ensuring the governance capabilities traditionally associated with data warehouses. The following sections will guide you through establishing robust governance mechanisms, implementing comprehensive data quality measures, managing complete data lifecycles, securing access to sensitive information, and navigating the complex landscape of regulatory compliance.

By implementing these practices, organizations can ensure that their lakehouse implementations deliver trusted, high-quality data that supports critical business decisions while maintaining appropriate safeguards.

In this chapter, we will cover these main topics:

- Understanding data quality and lineage
- Data lifecycle management
- Security and access control
- Compliance and regulations

# Understanding data quality and lineage

Data quality serves as the foundation of effective data governance in lakehouse architectures. Without reliable, accurate data, even the most sophisticated analytics and machine learning models will produce questionable results, undermining trust in the entire data ecosystem.

## Data quality fundamentals in lakehouses

Data quality in lakehouses involves establishing clear definitions, metrics, and processes to ensure that data remains reliable throughout its lifecycle. Quality begins with understanding the unique characteristics of the lakehouse architecture, where data may exist in various forms, from raw files to refined tables. The challenge lies in maintaining consistency across these different representations while leveraging the strengths of open table formats.

A robust data quality framework starts by defining organization-specific quality requirements that align with business objectives. These requirements should be specific, measurable, and actionable, providing clear guidelines for data stewards and engineers. Organizations must identify the critical data assets within their lakehouse and prioritize quality efforts accordingly, focusing resources on data elements that drive key business decisions. This targeted approach ensures that quality initiatives deliver maximum business value rather than treating all data with equal importance.

When implementing data quality in lakehouses, organizations should leverage the metadata capabilities of open table formats. Apache Iceberg, Delta Lake, and Apache Hudi all provide rich metadata layers that can be utilized to enforce quality rules, track changes, and facilitate remediation when issues arise. This metadata-driven approach to quality management provides visibility into data assets and their quality characteristics without requiring data movement or duplication.

## Role of open table formats in governance

Open table formats such as Apache Iceberg, Delta Lake, and Apache Hudi play a critical role in data governance by embedding governance capabilities directly into the storage layer. Iceberg's centralized REST catalog enables fine-grained authorization and consistent metadata management, while Delta Lake's transaction logs provide lineage and auditability at the file level. Hudi's DeltaStreamer automates ingestion validations for data completeness and schema consistency, ensuring high data quality as data flows into the lakehouse.

## Key data quality dimensions

Effective data governance requires organizations to focus on multiple quality dimensions that collectively determine fitness for use.

The following diagram highlights the four key dimensions of data quality in lakehouses—completeness, freshness, accuracy, and consistency—each of which must be monitored to ensure reliable analytics.

# Key Dimensions of Data Quality

## Consistency
Maintains ciherence and prevents contradictions in data.

## Completeness
Ensures all required data is present and accounted for.

## Accuracy
Validates data representation against real-world entities.

## Freshness
Measures how current the data is relative to real-world events.

*Figure 9.1 – The four core dimensions of data quality in lakehouses: completeness, freshness, accuracy, and consistency*

**Consistency** ensures that data remains coherent and free from contradictions across the lakehouse. This dimension becomes particularly challenging in open table format environments where multiple writers may update the same datasets. The transaction support provided by formats such as Delta Lake, Iceberg, and Hudi helps maintain consistency by preventing concurrent modifications from creating inconsistent states.

**Completeness** represents one of the most fundamental quality attributes, measuring whether all required data is present and accounted for. In lakehouse environments, completeness checks must occur at multiple levels, from verifying that all expected data files have been ingested to ensuring that individual records contain all mandatory fields.

**Accuracy** measures how well data represents the real-world entities or events it describes. Ensuring accuracy in lakehouses requires validating data against known reference sources, business rules, and statistical expectations. Implementing accuracy checks often involves comparing data against trusted sources of truth or applying domain-specific validation rules. These checks should be implemented as close to the ingestion point as possible, flagging or rejecting inaccurate data before it propagates through the system.

**Freshness** indicates how current the data is relative to real-world events or source systems. This dimension becomes particularly important in lakehouses that combine batch and streaming data, where timeliness expectations may vary across use cases. Organizations must establish clear freshness requirements for different data assets and implement monitoring to verify that data arrives and becomes available within expected timeframes. Open table formats provide transaction logs and time travel capabilities that can be leveraged to measure and monitor data freshness effectively.

## Data lineage implementation

Data lineage provides visibility into the origin, movement, and transformation of data throughout its lifecycle. In lakehouse architectures, lineage becomes particularly important as data may undergo multiple transformations while moving between raw, refined, and consumption zones. Effective lineage tracking enables root cause analysis when quality issues arise, supports impact assessments when changes are proposed, and facilitates compliance with regulatory requirements.

Implementing technical lineage with open table formats involves capturing metadata about data sources, transformation operations, and the relationships between datasets. This metadata should include information about when transformations occurred, who performed them, and what business logic was applied. Delta Lake, Iceberg, and Hudi all provide transaction logs that can be leveraged as building blocks for lineage implementation, capturing the history of changes to each dataset.

Organizations should consider implementing both backward and forward lineage capabilities. Backward lineage allows users to trace data back to its origins, understanding how it was created and modified along the way. Forward lineage shows the downstream impact of specific datasets, identifying which reports, models, or decisions might be affected by quality issues or changes. The combination of these perspectives provides a comprehensive understanding of data flows throughout the lakehouse.

Visualization plays a crucial role in making lineage information accessible to different stakeholders. Technical users may require detailed transformation logic and code references, while business users need higher-level views of data flows between systems and business processes. Modern lineage tools provide interactive visualizations that allow users to navigate complex data landscapes, drilling down into specific areas of interest while maintaining context.

Open source tools such as **OpenLineage** and **Marquez** can integrate with lakehouse pipelines to automatically capture lineage metadata. Combined with Iceberg's metadata and Delta's transaction logs, these tools visualize end-to-end data flows, enabling both technical and business users to understand dependencies, transformations, and data ownership across the lakehouse ecosystem.

# Monitoring and remediation

Continuous monitoring forms the backbone of sustainable data quality management in lakehouse environments. Organizations should implement automated quality checks that are executed at different stages of the data lifecycle, from ingestion to consumption. These checks should verify compliance with the quality dimensions described earlier, generating metrics that can be tracked over time to identify trends and patterns.

When quality issues are detected, timely notification allows for rapid intervention before downstream processes or decisions are affected. Alerting mechanisms should be configured to notify appropriate stakeholders based on the severity and scope of identified problems. Critical issues affecting key business processes may require immediate attention, while less severe problems might be addressed through regular maintenance cycles.

Remediation workflows define the steps taken when quality issues are identified. These workflows should specify responsibilities, timeframes, and escalation paths for different types of problems. The time travel capabilities provided by open table formats can be valuable during remediation, allowing organizations to revert to previous consistent states while issues are being addressed.

Together, these practices establish a strong foundation for maintaining trusted, high-quality data in a lakehouse. By continuously monitoring, remediating, and leveraging features such as time travel, organizations can ensure that data remains reliable even as it evolves. With quality and lineage in place, the next step is to manage how data moves through its entire lifecycle, from ingestion to eventual archiving or deletion, which we will explore in the following section.

# Practical tools for monitoring data quality

In practice, organizations can leverage open source tools to measure and monitor data quality in their lakehouses. Tools such as Great Expectations provide a framework for defining and validating expectations about datasets, allowing automated checks for completeness, accuracy, and consistency. These can be integrated with open table formats by reading Iceberg, Hudi, or Delta tables directly through Spark or Python APIs.

Additionally, **dbt** (which stands for **data build tool**) can complement governance practices by tracking data transformations and lineage as part of model development. When integrated with Delta Live Tables or Iceberg pipelines, dbt's documentation and lineage graph offer visibility into dependencies across datasets, making governance more transparent and traceable.

# Data lifecycle management

Effective **data lifecycle management (DLM)** ensures that data assets are properly handled from creation to eventual archival or deletion, maximizing their value while minimizing storage costs and compliance risks.

## Lifecycle fundamentals for lakehouses

DLM provides a structured approach to handling data throughout its useful life, ensuring that it remains accessible, secure, and compliant with relevant policies. In lakehouse architectures, DLM must address the diverse nature of data assets, from structured tables to semi-structured documents and unstructured files. The decoupled storage and compute model common in lakehouses presents both opportunities and challenges for lifecycle management.

Designing an effective lifecycle strategy requires organizations to categorize data assets based on business importance, usage patterns, and regulatory requirements. These categories then determine appropriate policies for retention, access controls, and quality management. Open table formats provide mechanisms to implement these policies through metadata, partitioning, and versioning capabilities, allowing organizations to manage data at a granular level without extensive data movement.

The lakehouse lifecycle typically begins with data generation from various sources, including operational systems, applications, and external providers. From there, data moves through ingestion, storage, processing, and consumption phases before eventually reaching retention, archiving, and deletion stages. Each phase requires specific governance controls to ensure proper handling according to organizational policies and external regulations.

## Data ingestion and processing strategies

Data ingestion represents the entry point for the lakehouse, where data from diverse sources is brought into the ecosystem. Effective ingestion processes must validate incoming data, ensuring that it meets basic quality requirements before being accepted. This validation may include schema verification, completeness checks, and business rule application, rejecting or quarantining data that fails to meet defined standards.

Processing and transformation convert raw data into forms suitable for analysis and consumption. In lakehouse architectures, these operations often follow the medallion architecture pattern, with data progressing through bronze (raw), silver (cleansed), and gold (business-ready) stages. Open table formats facilitate this progression by maintaining metadata about data quality and processing status, enabling downstream consumers to understand data readiness.

When designing processing workflows, organizations should prioritize reproducibility and auditability. Each transformation step should be documented, versioned, and traceable, allowing for recreation of results and validation of processing logic. The transaction logs maintained by Delta Lake, Iceberg, and Hudi provide a foundation for this auditability, recording each operation performed on datasets throughout their lifecycle.

## Storage optimization and organization

Storage optimization balances performance, cost, and accessibility considerations in the lakehouse. Data organizations must determine appropriate retention periods for different data categories, considering both business requirements and regulatory constraints. Frequently accessed data may warrant premium storage with higher performance characteristics, while rarely accessed historical data might be moved to lower-cost alternatives.

File format selection significantly impacts storage efficiency and query performance in lakehouses. Columnar formats such as Parquet are commonly used with open table formats due to their compression efficiency and query performance benefits. Organizations should establish standards for file sizes, compression techniques, and encoding methods based on expected access patterns and processing requirements.

Partitioning and clustering strategies organize data to optimize query performance and facilitate lifecycle management. Effective partitioning schemes align with common query patterns while supporting efficient data retirement and archiving. Time-based partitioning is particularly valuable for lifecycle management, allowing organizations to easily identify and process data based on age or relevance.

## Retention, archiving, and purging

Data retention policies establish how long different types of data should be kept within the lakehouse. These policies must balance analytical needs, historical reference requirements, and storage costs while ensuring compliance with relevant regulations. Open table formats provide time travel capabilities that can simplify retention management by allowing access to historical versions without maintaining separate archives.

Archiving moves less frequently accessed data to lower-cost storage tiers while maintaining its availability for occasional use. In lakehouse architectures, archiving can be implemented through storage tiering, where data remains logically part of the lakehouse but physically resides on different storage media. This approach preserves the unified access model while optimizing storage costs.

Data purging permanently removes data that has exceeded its retention period and no longer provides business value. Purging processes must be carefully controlled, documented, and auditable to demonstrate compliance with retention policies and regulations. Organizations implementing open table formats can leverage features such as Iceberg's partition evolution or Delta Lake's VACUUM command to efficiently remove expired data while maintaining system integrity.

Version management represents another critical aspect of lifecycle management in lakehouses. Open table formats provide built-in versioning capabilities that allow organizations to track changes over time, roll back to previous states when needed, and understand how data has evolved. These capabilities support both operational needs, such as recovery from processing errors, and governance requirements, such as maintaining audit trails of data modifications.

While lifecycle management ensures that data is properly organized, retained, and eventually retired, these measures alone do not protect sensitive information from misuse or exposure. To safeguard data throughout its lifecycle, lakehouses must incorporate robust security and access controls. The next section examines the security architecture, identity models, and protection mechanisms that underpin secure data operations.

# Security and access control

Comprehensive security measures are essential to protect sensitive data assets and ensure that access is limited to authorized users for legitimate business purposes.

## Security architecture for lakehouses

A robust security architecture for lakehouses must address multiple layers, from the underlying infrastructure to application-level controls. Organizations should implement defense-in-depth strategies that provide redundant protections, ensuring that a failure at one layer does not compromise the entire system. This multi-layered approach is particularly important in lakehouse environments where data may be accessed through diverse tools and services.

When designing security frameworks, organizations must consider the distributed nature of lakehouse architecture. Storage, compute, and metadata services may be provided by different components, each with its own security model. Ensuring consistent protection across these components requires careful integration and centralized policy management. The security capabilities provided by open table formats can help bridge these gaps by embedding access controls within the data layer itself.

Threat modeling helps organizations identify and prioritize potential security risks to their lake-house implementations. This process involves systematically analyzing the architecture to identify vulnerabilities, assess potential impacts, and determine appropriate mitigations. Effective threat models consider both external threats, such as unauthorized access attempts, and internal risks such as privilege misuse or accidental data exposure.

## Authentication and authorization mechanisms

Identity management forms the foundation of lakehouse security, establishing who users are and what credentials they present. Organizations should integrate lakehouse authentication with enterprise identity providers, ensuring consistent user management and enabling single sign-on experiences. This integration simplifies administration while strengthening security through centralized control of account lifecycles.

**Role-based access control** (**RBAC**) assigns permissions based on job functions or responsibilities, simplifying administration by grouping users with similar access needs. In lakehouse environments, RBAC can be implemented at multiple levels, from coarse-grained table access to fine-grained column-level security. Open table formats support various RBAC implementations, allowing organizations to enforce consistent controls regardless of the access method.

**Attribute-based access control** (**ABAC**) extends RBAC by incorporating additional factors such as user location, time of access, or data sensitivity into access decisions. This dynamic approach allows for more nuanced security policies that adapt to changing conditions. ABAC becomes particularly valuable in lakehouses handling sensitive data, where access might depend on multiple contextual factors beyond simple role assignments.

For example, the **Iceberg REST catalog** supports **scoped tokens** that allow fine-grained authorization for data operations. This enables secure, role-specific access without exposing full credentials. Similarly, **Apache Hudi's DeltaStreamer** can perform data validation checks during ingestion to verify schema compatibility, completeness, and accuracy before committing data. These built-in governance features reduce the need for external tools and provide a unified, metadata-driven approach to data integrity and access control.

Service accounts and applications represent non-human entities that require access to lakehouse resources. Managing these identities requires special attention, as they often need persistent credentials rather than interactive authentication. Organizations should implement strict controls for service account creation, permission assignment, and credential rotation, ensuring that these accounts operate with minimal necessary privileges.

# Data protection mechanisms

Encryption provides a fundamental layer of protection for lakehouse data, rendering it unreadable without appropriate decryption keys. Organizations should implement encryption for data at rest, protecting stored files from unauthorized access, and encryption in transit, securing data as it moves between components. Both types of encryption are essential in distributed lakehouse architectures where data traverses multiple systems and networks.

Tokenization and masking protect sensitive data elements while preserving analytical utility. These techniques replace original values with surrogates that maintain format and distribution characteristics without exposing actual sensitive data. In lakehouse environments, these protections can be applied dynamically based on user context, allowing different levels of access for different roles or use cases.

Key management systems centralize the storage, protection, and lifecycle management of encryption keys. Organizations should implement robust key management practices, including regular rotation, secure backup, and strict access controls. Integration between key management systems and lakehouse components ensures that encryption remains effective while minimizing operational complexity. The implementation should support the unique requirements of open table formats, where data may be accessed through multiple paths and tools.

# Auditing and monitoring

Access auditing captures detailed records of who accessed what data, when, and how. These audit trails provide visibility into system usage, support compliance verification, and enable investigation of potential security incidents. In lakehouse environments, comprehensive auditing requires capturing access events across all entry points, from SQL queries to API calls and filesystem operations.

Pattern analysis examines audit data to identify unusual or suspicious activities that might indicate security problems. This analysis can detect potential threats like privilege escalation attempts, unusual access volumes, or off-hours activity. Modern security approaches use machine learning to establish baselines of normal behavior and flag anomalies for investigation, providing an additional layer of protection for lakehouse environments.

Security incident detection combines audit data, pattern analysis, and threat intelligence to identify potential breaches or policy violations. When suspicious activities are detected, response processes should trigger appropriate actions, from additional monitoring to active intervention. These detection capabilities should be integrated with enterprise security operations to ensure coordinated responses to potential threats.

Security measures protect data from unauthorized access and misuse, but organizations must also demonstrate that their practices align with external legal and industry requirements. Compliance frameworks add this layer of accountability, mapping governance and security controls to regulations such as GDPR, CCPA, and HIPAA. The following section explores how lakehouses support compliance through classification, consent management, and automated reporting.

# Compliance and regulations

Regulatory compliance ensures that lakehouse implementations meet legal and industry requirements for data handling, protection, and governance.

## Regulatory landscape for data lakehouses

The regulatory environment for data management continues to evolve rapidly, with new requirements emerging across different jurisdictions and industries. Key regulations such as the **General Data Protection Regulation (GDPR)**, **California Consumer Privacy Act (CCPA)**, and industry-specific rules such as **Health Insurance Portability and Accountability Act (HIPAA)** impose specific obligations on organizations handling personal or sensitive data. Lakehouse implementations must incorporate controls to meet these requirements while maintaining analytical flexibility.

Understanding the implications of these regulations for lakehouse architecture requires mapping regulatory requirements to specific technical and procedural controls. For example, GDPR's right to be forgotten necessitates mechanisms to identify and remove personal data upon request, while CCPA's disclosure requirements demand accurate data inventories and lineage tracking. The transaction logging and time travel capabilities of open table formats can be leveraged to implement many of these controls efficiently.

Organizations operating globally face additional challenges in navigating potentially conflicting requirements across jurisdictions. Data residency restrictions may limit where certain data can be stored, while differing consent standards might require maintaining multiple versions of consent records. Lakehouse architecture must be designed with sufficient flexibility to accommodate these variations while maintaining consistent governance practices.

## Implementing compliance controls

Data classification and tagging provide the foundation for effective compliance by identifying regulated data elements within the lakehouse. This process involves analyzing datasets to detect personal information, sensitive attributes, and other regulated elements, then applying appropriate metadata tags. These tags enable automated enforcement of compliance policies and simplify reporting for regulatory purposes.

Consent management tracks user permissions for data collection, storage, and processing. In lakehouse environments, consent records should be maintained alongside the data they govern, ensuring that usage restrictions can be easily verified. The versioning capabilities of open table formats support this approach by maintaining historical consent states and allowing traceability of changes over time.

The following diagram illustrates a maturity model for compliance control strategies in lakehouses, ranging from basic implementations such as classification and consent tracking to advanced practices such as data minimization and automated compliance reporting:

## Compliance Control Strategies in Lakehouses

*Figure 9.2 – Compliance control strategies in lakehouses, organized along two axes: basic to advanced implementation, and data management to compliance enforcement*

Implementing the right to be forgotten requires mechanisms to identify and remove personal data upon request. This capability becomes particularly challenging in lakehouse environments where data may exist in multiple forms across raw, refined, and consumption layers. Solutions must balance complete removal with maintaining referential integrity and audit trails, often leveraging techniques such as pseudonymization rather than outright deletion.

Data minimization limits collection and retention to what is strictly necessary for stated purposes. In lakehouse implementations, this principle translates to thoughtful data modeling that avoids unnecessary duplication, careful retention policies that remove data when no longer needed, and processing controls that limit exposure of sensitive elements. These practices not only support compliance but also improve system efficiency and reduce storage costs.

## Compliance monitoring and reporting

Automated compliance checks verify adherence to regulatory requirements and internal policies on an ongoing basis. These checks should examine multiple aspects of the lakehouse, from data presence and quality to access patterns and retention practices. Results should be captured in compliance dashboards that provide visibility to appropriate stakeholders and highlight areas requiring attention.

Regulatory audits require organizations to demonstrate compliance with specific requirements, often with limited preparation time. Lakehouse implementations should maintain comprehensive documentation of governance practices, including policies, procedures, and evidence of control effectiveness. The audit trails provided by open table formats can be valuable during these assessments, offering detailed records of data handling throughout its lifecycle.

Compliance dashboards consolidate metrics and findings into accessible views for different stakeholders. These dashboards should track key compliance indicators, highlight exceptions or violations, and provide trending data to identify emerging issues. Effective dashboards go beyond simple reporting to enable action, connecting directly to remediation workflows when problems are identified.

## Evolving compliance requirements

The regulatory landscape continues to evolve as new privacy laws emerge and existing regulations are refined. Organizations must establish mechanisms to monitor these changes and assess their impact on lakehouse implementations. This ongoing vigilance requires collaboration between legal, compliance, and technical teams to translate regulatory language into specific control requirements.

Building adaptable compliance frameworks allows organizations to respond efficiently to changing requirements without redesigning their entire governance approach. These frameworks separate fundamental principles from specific implementation details, providing a stable foundation that can accommodate evolving regulations. Open table formats support this adaptability through their flexible metadata capabilities, versioning support, and extensible security models.

**Governance in action: Iceberg, Hudi, and Delta Lake in the enterprise**

In enterprise environments, data governance is enforced through various capabilities offered by modern table formats. Apache Iceberg provides robust auditability and security through features like time travel, version tracking, and catalog-level access policies exposed via REST APIs. Apache Hudi strengthens governance with its DeltaStreamer and incremental pull mechanisms, which enable automated validation and ensure data completeness. Meanwhile, Delta Lake supports schema evolution with constraint enforcement and native ACID transactions, delivering reliable and consistent governance at scale.

# Summary

In this chapter, we explored how robust data governance and security practices form the cornerstone of modern lakehouse architectures. We examined how open table formats empower organizations to ensure data quality through precise metadata management, enabling effective data lineage, lifecycle management, and regulatory compliance. By establishing clear policies and leveraging fine-grained access controls, encryption, and comprehensive audit trails, organizations transform governance from a compliance burden into a strategic enabler of trusted, data-driven decision-making.

Effective governance not only safeguards sensitive information but also optimizes DLM—from ingestion and processing to retention, archiving, and purging—thus reducing storage costs and enhancing operational efficiency. As lakehouse architectures continue to evolve, adapting governance practices while incorporating new capabilities is essential. The flexibility provided by open table formats positions organizations to make incremental improvements without disruptive changes, ensuring that their governance frameworks remain resilient in the face of emerging technologies, evolving business needs, and shifting regulatory landscapes.

Taken together, governance, lifecycle management, security, and compliance ensure that data in a lakehouse is both trustworthy and protected. These capabilities not only reduce operational and regulatory risk but also create the foundation for making informed technology choices. In the next chapter, we shift from governance practices to the practical question of selecting the right open table formats and query engines for different workloads.

Building on this foundation, the next chapter, *Decisions on Open Table Formats*, will guide you through selecting optimal query engines and table formats for specific use cases. By leveraging real-world insights from industry leaders, you will learn how to evaluate production scenarios, cluster sizes, and technology choices to further optimize your lakehouse architecture.

# Questions

1. What are the key dimensions of data quality discussed in the chapter?

2. How does metadata management facilitate effective data lineage?

3. What benefits does DLM provide in lakehouse architectures?

4. How do open table formats help in maintaining regulatory compliance?

5. In what way do fine-grained access controls enhance lakehouse security?

6. Why is encryption important for protecting data in distributed systems?

7. How do comprehensive audit trails contribute to data governance?

8. What role do transaction logs play in ensuring data consistency and supporting rollback operations?

9. Why is it important to adapt governance practices as lakehouse architectures evolve?

10. How does a robust governance framework transform data governance from a burden into a strategic enabler?

# Answers

1. **Key dimensions of data quality**: The chapter highlights completeness, freshness, accuracy, and consistency as critical dimensions for ensuring data quality.

2. **Metadata management and lineage**: Effective metadata management captures detailed information about data origins, transformations, and history, which helps trace data flow and supports data lineage.

3. **Benefits of DLM**: It organizes data from ingestion to purging, optimizing storage usage, ensuring efficient retrieval, and supporting regulatory requirements.

4. **Regulatory compliance**: Open table formats incorporate features such as versioning, time travel, and detailed audit trails that enable organizations to meet compliance requirements such as GDPR and CCPA.

5. **Fine-grained access controls**: These controls restrict data access to authorized users based on roles or attributes, ensuring that sensitive data is protected throughout the system.

6. **Importance of encryption**: Encryption secures data both at rest and in transit, preventing unauthorized access and ensuring the confidentiality and integrity of sensitive information.

7. **Role of audit trails**: Comprehensive audit trails log every data access and modification, providing visibility into system operations and supporting compliance audits and incident investigations.

8. **Transaction logs**: Transaction logs maintain a detailed history of data operations, which is crucial for ensuring consistency, enabling rollbacks, and supporting effective data lineage.

9. **Adapting governance practices**: As data ecosystems evolve, governance practices must adapt to incorporate new technologies and regulatory changes, ensuring sustainable and effective oversight.

10. **Transforming governance**: A robust governance framework, underpinned by open table formats, enables organizations to optimize data management processes and drive strategic, trusted data use across the enterprise.

# 10

# Evaluating and Selecting Open Table Formats

While Apache Iceberg, Apache Hudi, and Delta Lake share foundational capabilities such as ACID transactions, schema evolution, and time travel, their architectural designs and optimization strategies cater to distinct use cases. Selecting the right table format is a foundational decision in building a scalable and efficient lakehouse architecture. This choice extends far beyond storage; it dictates how data is ingested, updated, and queried, while also shaping the broader ecosystem of compute engines, metadata catalogs, and downstream applications such as BI tools and ML platforms.

This chapter should provide a systematic approach to evaluating and selecting the most appropriate table format depending on workload type and size. It will bring together some of the core strengths of Iceberg, Hudi, and Delta Lake (discussed in *Chapters 3*, *4*, and *5*), how they integrate with different ecosystems, and real-world adoption patterns that illustrate their practical applications. By the end, you should have a structured framework for making an informed choice based on specific workload requirements.

> A key takeaway from this chapter is that no single table format will be a definitive "winner." In many cases, multiple formats can effectively serve the same use case. The choice ultimately depends on a combination of critical factors, which we will explore in this chapter. We also discussed before how projects such as Apache XTable (incubating) can provide interoperability between the formats regardless of the initial choice.

A well-informed decision on table formats helps you bring in the right tools for specific workloads and keeps your data architecture future-proof, allowing new compute engines and tools to be added as needed. On the other hand, a poorly considered selections can introduce the following:

- **Performance bottlenecks**: Suboptimal data skipping techniques, partitioning, or metadata management leading to slow query execution
- **Ingestion constraints**: Lack of efficient upserts/deletes, resulting in data duplication, low write concurrency (leading to contention), high ingestion latency, or write amplification
- **Ecosystem limitations**: Poor interoperability with compute engines and other tools in the stack, leading to vendor lock-in or limited tool compatibility
- **Operational complexity**: Excessive metadata overhead, lack of automatic table maintenance, or inefficient optimization strategies (such as compaction, clustering, or async indexing), causing high operational costs

The topics covered in this chapter include:

- Key decision factors in evaluating table formats
- Table evolution and versioning
- Platform tools and operational capabilities
- Strengths at the feature level and practical selection guidelines
- Support available across the open ecosystem
- Real-world case studies

# Key decision factors in table format evaluation

To avoid the pitfalls discussed in the previous bullet list, a structured evaluation is required. In this section, we will go over some of the key factors to consider when selecting a table format. These practical considerations are some of the critical questions to ask when evaluating a format.

## Read versus write optimization: understanding workload patterns

One of the most fundamental considerations when selecting a table format is the nature of the workload – whether it is predominantly query-intensive (read-heavy), ingestion-intensive (write-heavy), or requires some balance between the two.

A table format optimized for fast and scalable queries may not handle high-frequency updates, inserts, or deletes efficiently, while a format designed for efficient data ingestion and mutation may introduce performance overhead for analytical queries. While every format offers some level of support for both reads and writes, their design decisions and optimizations make them better suited for specific scenarios.

## Read-heavy workloads

These workloads prioritize efficient data retrieval, optimized query performance, and analytical scalability. When assessing them, the key considerations include the following:

- Are large datasets being scanned for batch analytics, reporting, and BI workloads?
- Is reducing query latency a priority through data skipping and storage optimization techniques?
- Are ad hoc and interactive queries common, where minimizing full-table scans is essential?
- Does the system need to manage small files effectively through compaction to reduce I/O overhead and improve query performance?

For query-heavy workloads, the key requirement is minimizing read amplification (i.e., ensuring that queries scan only the necessary data without reading irrelevant records).

## Write-heavy workloads

These workloads focus on high-throughput data ingestion, efficient record-level modifications, and transactional consistency. When evaluating them, keep the following factors in mind:

- Is continuous ingestion needed from event streams, **Change Data Capture** (CDC) pipelines, or batch sources?
- Does the system need to handle upserts and deletes efficiently, enabling faster and frequent updates?
- Is bulk data loading necessary to efficiently ingest large volumes of data for initial table population, periodic batch ingestion, or large-scale **extract, transform, load** (ETL) pipelines while minimizing write amplification?
- Does the workload require support for high concurrent writes, ensuring that multiple writers (engines) and background table services can operate simultaneously without conflicts or data corruption?
- Is there a need to write new records while preventing duplicates, particularly in CDC processing or streaming ingestion, where retries, late-arriving data, or reprocessing failures can introduce duplicate records?

These considerations help ensure the ingestion layer remains reliable, scalable, and resilient under real-world conditions. Choosing the right approach here lays the groundwork for consistent downstream performance.

## Ecosystem compatibility

The table format is not an isolated decision; it directly affects how well the data integrates with the existing architecture and long-term ecosystem strategy. Unlike traditional data warehouses, which are often tied to a single vendor's ecosystem, open table formats provide the flexibility to interact with multiple compute engines, catalogs, and storage backends. However, this flexibility varies between formats depending on the type of support and maturity, making compatibility evaluation a critical step in the selection process. Key aspects to assess include how well the format integrates with compute engines, metadata catalogs, cloud and storage backends, and application-layer tools:

- **Compute engine support:** Does the table format integrate well with the primary compute engines in use, such as Spark, Flink, Trino, or Presto? Do they support read, write, and table maintenance capabilities?

- **Metadata catalogs:** Can the format work seamlessly with the organization's catalog of choice, whether it's Hive Metastore, AWS Glue, Apache Polaris, or Unity Catalog?

- **Cloud and storage backends:** Does the format provide native support for cloud storage solutions such as Amazon S3, Google Cloud Storage, or Azure Data Lake?

- **Application layer integrations:** Can the format interact effectively with business intelligence tools, machine learning platforms, or orchestration frameworks such as dbt and Airflow?

Since every organization has an existing data stack, evaluating how seamlessly a table format integrates with that stack is the first important step. The choice of format also influences future architecture decisions and may introduce limitations if a format lacks native support for required components. Hence, it is critical to have that understanding when evaluating the formats.

For example, organizations that rely heavily on Apache Flink for multiple low-latency writes must ensure that the chosen table format fully supports Flink's stateful streaming and effective concurrency control mechanisms. Some formats may provide these integrations natively, while others may just offer basic streaming reads. Alternatively, if a company uses Trino or Presto for interactive ad hoc queries, the table format must optimize metadata pruning and data skipping to avoid expensive full-table scans, but not every format may have that level of support with the compute engine.

# Table maintenance and optimization services

A table format, along with its storage engine, provides a set of table maintenance and optimization services that are essential for ensuring query performance, ingestion efficiency, and storage scalability. We learned about these services in *Chapter 8*. These services determine how well a table format manages data layout over time, impacting both read and write performance as the dataset grows. This is one of the important factors to consider for evaluation as organizations productionize lakehouse architecture.

A well-designed optimization system should do the following:

- **Balance ingestion and optimization** (e.g., ensuring that compaction and clustering do not disrupt ongoing writes)
- **Provide automation** (e.g., automatic scheduling of table services rather than requiring manual intervention)
- **Be workload-aware** (e.g., tuning the frequency of maintenance tasks based on ingestion rates and query workloads)

The maturity of these table services varies across formats and plays a critical role in format selection. If a workload has high-frequency streaming writes (small batches can lead to small files), it requires a format that can compact small files efficiently without impacting ingestion. Similarly, if a workload relies on fast lookups, a format that supports better metadata pruning will be more effective.

Here are some of the key table maintenance services and why they matter when selecting a format:

- **Data skipping and pruning**: Data skipping ensures that queries read only the relevant data files, improving performance by avoiding unnecessary disk scans. Metadata-driven optimizations allow formats to filter out irrelevant data before execution, thereby reducing query latency and compute costs significantly for analytical workloads. Considerations include the following:

    - Does the format store column statistics (min/max values) at the file or row-group level for fine-grained pruning?
    - Does the format support predicate pushdown, allowing query filters to be applied before reading data?
    - Are bloom filters or other indexing techniques used to accelerate point lookups and range scans?

- **Partitioning**: Partitioning is one of the most fundamental techniques for improving query performance. However, how partitioning is managed varies across formats. Considerations include the following:

    - Does the format require explicit partitioning, or does it support hidden partitioning?
    - Can partition schemes evolve over time without rewriting existing data?
    - Does the format allow dynamic partition pruning for query optimization?

- **Clustering**: Clustering groups similar records together within data files, improving query locality and data skipping efficiency. Considerations include the following:

    - Does the format support different clustering techniques (linear sorting, multi-dimensional clustering, etc.) to cater to different data sizes and workloads?
    - Can clustering be performed asynchronously, without blocking writes?

- **Indexing**: Indexes help in finding out where a particular record exists within immutable data files (such as Parquet) in the data lake storage, so the compute engine can write to (update) or read from quickly, thereby improving latency. Considerations include the following:

    - Does the format provide index support? What kind of index is it?
    - How well does indexing scale as the dataset grows?
    - Does the format offer secondary indexing options for faster record lookups?

- **Compaction**: Compaction is essential for managing small files, which are common in streaming and high-frequency batch ingestion workloads. A table format should support automatic compaction to merge small files and optimize read performance. Considerations include the following:

    - Can compaction run asynchronously without disrupting ingestion?
    - Does the format support automatic triggering of compaction based on file size thresholds?

- **Cleaning and retention policies**: Cleaning ensures that old, unreferenced, or deleted data is efficiently removed, preventing unnecessary storage consumption and metadata bloat. Considerations include the following:

    - Does the format support automatic retention policies?
    - Can users configure retention based on data lifecycle policies?

Effective table maintenance and optimization are key to sustaining high performance, efficient ingestion, and scalable storage as datasets grow. Selecting a format with mature, automated, and workload-aware services ensures the lakehouse can handle evolving data demands reliably and efficiently.

# Table evolution and versioning

Table evolution and versioning are critical aspects of lakehouse architecture, influencing how data evolves and how historical versions are retained. A table format's ability to support flexible schema and partition evolution, and efficient versioning directly impacts data consistency and long-term maintainability. When selecting a table format, organizations must evaluate the following:

- How seamlessly schema changes can be applied without requiring costly table rewrites
- How efficiently past table versions can be accessed for rollback, auditing, or time travel
- Ways to evolve partitions without a full data rewrite

Effectively managing table evolution and versioning ensures that data remains consistent, auditable, and easy to maintain over time. Choosing a format that handles these aspects efficiently lays the foundation for a resilient and future-proof lakehouse architecture.

## Schema and partition evolution

Schema evolution determines how well a table format supports schema modifications such as adding, renaming, or dropping columns over time. Without proper schema evolution support, updates to table structures can lead to compatibility issues, data loss, or require full-table rewrites. Additionally, there could be a need to change partitions for large tables, hence it's important to evaluate factors such as:

- Does the format allow schema changes without rewriting existing data?
- Are backward and forward compatibility supported? Can new readers handle old schema versions and vice versa?
- Does the format enforce schema constraints, or does it allow schema-on-read flexibility?
- Is there a way to change partitions in storage without costly rewrites?

Robust schema evolution ensures tables can adapt to changing data requirements without risking data loss or operational disruptions. Choosing a format that supports flexible, compatible, and efficient schema changes is essential for long-term maintainability.

# Data versioning and rollback

Versioning and rollback capabilities ensure that historical table states can be retained and accessed efficiently, which is crucial for the following:

- **Auditing and compliance**: Querying previous table versions for regulatory reporting
- **Time travel queries**: Accessing historical snapshots to debug or analyze past data states
- **Error recovery**: Rolling back to a consistent snapshot after accidental data modifications

When evaluating a table format, it is important to consider questions such as:

- Does the format support snapshot-based time travel?
- Can rollback operations be performed at the snapshot level or based on a timestamp?
- How does versioning impact storage and metadata size over time? Does that have performance implications?
- Are there ways to implement blue-green deployments?

Data versioning and rollback allow access to historical states for auditing, analysis, and error recovery. Choosing a format with snapshot-based support ensures data integrity and consistent performance.

# Platform tools and operational features

While the factors discussed before are critical to format selection, many table formats also provide additional platform tools and operational features that enhance usability, automation, and manageability.

These features can significantly reduce operational overhead depending on the organization's requirements. For example, built-in open ingestion tools may be beneficial for teams that are building ingestion frameworks from scratch or require a native way (with integrated features) to work with the format.

When evaluating table formats, organizations should consider these features not as deal-breakers, but as value-added services that can simplify table management and improve operational efficiency:

- **Ingestion frameworks and built-in connectors**: Some table formats provide pre-integrated ingestion frameworks that simplify data onboarding from both batch and streaming sources. The ease of ingesting data at scale is a key factor, especially for organizations dealing with CDC pipelines, event streams, or scheduled batch jobs. Considerations include the following:
  - Are there pre-built ingestion tools available, or is ingestion fully external?
  - Does the format offer connectors for streaming sources (e.g., Kafka, Kinesis, Pulsar)?
  - How much additional setup is required for transactional ingestion?

- **CLI and management APIs**: Some table formats offer CLI tools and APIs for managing table lifecycle operations, making it easier to handle schema evolution, snapshot retention, and optimization tasks programmatically. Considerations include the following:

  - Does the format provide a CLI for table management, or are all operations API-driven?

  - How easily can key operations (e.g., compaction and rollback) be triggered?

  - Are there built-in monitoring or logging capabilities?

- **Failure handling and transaction safeguards**: Handling job failures, partial writes, and transaction conflicts is a key concern in large-scale data pipelines. Some table formats offer built-in mechanisms to detect and handle failures, reducing the need for manual intervention. Considerations include the following:

  - How does the format handle partial or failed writes?

  - Are there built-in rollback mechanisms, or must failures be handled externally?

  - How is transactional integrity maintained under high concurrent workloads?

These additional platform tools and operational features provide value by simplifying table management and reducing manual effort. Evaluating them helps organizations improve efficiency and ensure smoother operations without compromising core functionality.

## Based on use cases

The choice of a table format should align with the specific execution patterns and data processing needs of an organization. This section focuses on how different formats must support the three key processing models.

## Batch processing

Batch processing is the backbone of large-scale analytics, ETL pipelines, and data transformations. Batch workloads involve processing large datasets at scheduled intervals, often in high-throughput, compute-intensive operations. Many of the architectural and operational considerations for batch workloads have already been discussed in previous sections:

- **Read versus write optimization**: Since batch workloads involve high-volume writes, the format must efficiently handle bulk ingestion without excessive write amplification

- **Table maintenance and optimization**: Since batch processing produces large output datasets, effective compaction, clustering, and partitioning strategies are essential to keep query performance high over time

- **Schema evolution and versioning**: Long-lived batch tables often require non-disruptive schema evolution to accommodate changes without rewriting historical data
- **Snapshot consistency**: Bulk ingestion jobs should write transactionally, allowing queries to read from a consistent snapshot while new data is being ingested.

Key considerations for batch workloads include the following:

- Can the format efficiently ingest large datasets in a single batch commit without excessive metadata overhead?
- Does it support bulk insert modes to optimize ingestion performance for large ETL workloads?
- Can batch jobs read from a consistent snapshot while new data is being ingested?
- Does the format enable efficient table scans (predicate pushdown and data skipping)?

Batch processing requires table formats that handle large-scale ingestion, maintain performance, and support consistent snapshots. Choosing a format that meets these needs ensures reliable and efficient batch operations.

## Stream processing

Streaming workloads require low-latency ingestion, continuous updates, and transactional consistency to process real-time or near-real-time event streams. Unlike batch processing, where data is written at scheduled intervals, streaming workloads handle small, high-frequency writes, requiring the format to efficiently merge updates, prevent inconsistencies, and optimize storage layout dynamically. When evaluating table formats for streaming workloads, keep in mind the following:

- Can the format handle continuous low-latency ingestion without excessive write amplification?
- How does the format efficiently merge new events?
- What mechanisms exist to prevent small file accumulation from continuous writes, and does the format provide asynchronous background compaction and dynamic file layout optimization without disrupting active ingestion?
- Does the format ensure correct event-time ordering and late data handling, preventing inconsistencies from out-of-order events while supporting ordered merges (e.g., database **Log Sequence Number** (**LSN**) order) and latest-writer-wins semantics?
- How does the format manage concurrent writes and transactional integrity?

Streaming workloads demand formats that handle continuous ingestion, dynamic updates, and maintain transactional integrity. Selecting a format that meets these requirements ensures real-time data consistency and efficient storage management.

## Incremental processing

Incremental processing enables efficient data pipeline optimizations by allowing downstream queries or transformations to process only the newly changed records since the last run, rather than scanning the full dataset.

This is especially beneficial in the following:

- CDC ingestion, where only updated records need to be processed
- Event-driven architectures, where downstream consumers need to react to new data without reprocessing everything
- Real-time analytics, where only recent data updates are relevant

Key questions to evaluate for incremental processing include:

- Does the format natively offer streaming primitives to enable near-real-time data ingestion and processing on a data lake without requiring external real-time systems?
- How does the format track change history across writes and background table services? Can change tracking persist across operations such as clustering and compaction without relying solely on snapshot retention?
- Does it support partial updates?
- Can it handle frequent updates (e.g., ingesting 1 GB into a 1 TB table every 5–10 minutes) without bottlenecks?
- Does the format provide native support for event-time ordering and late data handling in streaming and incremental workloads?

Now that we have outlined the key decision factors in selecting a table format, it's time to map these considerations to the architectural strengths of Apache Iceberg, Apache Hudi, and Delta Lake.

# Feature-level strengths and practical selection criteria

This section highlights how each format aligns with specific requirements and provides a comparative feature-level analysis for structured decision-making.

# Apache Iceberg

Apache Iceberg is recognized for its strong alignment with read-optimized **analytical** workloads. Its architectural design emphasizes efficient data and metadata management, flexible partition handling, and support across multiple engines, making it a natural choice for organizations focused on large-scale batch analytics and query performance. Let's look at some of its key strengths.

## Key architectural strengths in practice

Iceberg is designed for high-performance analytical queries, large-scale batch processing, and multi-engine interoperability. It introduces a modern approach to table management, allowing flexible schema evolution, partition handling, and metadata pruning while maintaining compatibility with multiple query engines. Here are some of the key design strengths of Iceberg.

- **Hidden partitioning and partition evolution**: Iceberg automatically manages partitions without the need to explicitly define partition columns and allows partitions to be modified dynamically without rewriting data.

- **Advanced data skipping and metadata optimization**:

  - Manifest file-based pruning ensures that queries only scan relevant data files, avoiding full-table scans

  - Puffin file-based statistics allows using advanced statistics, such as sketches (estimating **number of distinct values (NDVs)**)

- **Branching and tagging**: It supports multi-versioned data environments for the following:

  - **Experimentation and rollback**: Create separate table versions without duplicating data

  - **Data reproducibility**: Enables consistent dataset snapshots (versions) for ML training

- **Ecosystem compatibility**:

  - Iceberg is a lightweight table format, making it easy to integrate with various analytics stacks and compute engines such as Spark SQL, Trino, Flink, and StarRocks

  - It also provides a REST API standard (Apache Iceberg REST catalog protocol), allowing the format and engine to easily integrate with catalogs that implement the specification, such as Unity, Apache Polaris, and Nessie

It is best suited for the following:

- **Enterprise-scale BI and batch analytics**: Iceberg's advanced data skipping, manifest-based metadata pruning, and Puffin statistics optimize query performance for read-heavy workloads, making it ideal for large-scale batch analytics and BI use cases.

- **Easy adoption for analytics-driven lakehouse architectures**: Iceberg's lightweight design makes it easy to plug into analytics (read-side) use cases. For example, an organization using a data lake (such as S3) for machine learning workloads can adopt Iceberg to expose tables efficiently to query engines such as Trino for ad hoc analysis. The REST catalog standard further simplifies integration with catalogs such as Trino, Snowflake, Polaris, and Nessie.

- **Workloads requiring flexible schema, partition changes**: Iceberg's schema evolution and partition evolution make it well-suited for dynamically changing schemas without costly data rewrites.

- **Use cases that require multi-versioned data environments**: Branching and tagging capabilities provide isolated data environments that allow for safe experimentation and reproducibility, ideal for machine learning workloads and data quality checks.

Iceberg's design delivers high-performance queries, flexible schema and partition management, and multi-engine compatibility. These strengths make it well-suited for large-scale analytics, evolving schemas, and multi-versioned data environments.

# Apache Hudi

Apache Hudi stands out for its strong alignment with write-optimized ingestion and CDC workloads. Hudi's architecture is purpose-built for handling continuous data streams, frequent updates, and incremental processing. This makes it particularly attractive for real-time pipelines, mutable datasets, and use cases where automated table services are critical to sustaining performance. Let's look at its key strengths.

## Key architectural strengths in practice

Hudi is optimized for write-heavy ingestion workloads, CDC, and incremental processing. Its architecture is deeply optimized for handling mutable change streams, ensuring efficient writes, fast record lookups, and automated table maintenance. Listed here are some of the key architectural strengths of Hudi:

- **First-class support for indexes**:
  - Hudi treats indexing as an integral part of its design, ensuring that both ingestion performance and query efficiency are optimized
  - Multiple indexing strategies (Bloom, record-level, bucket, and HBase) enable fast record lookups, avoiding costly full-table scans during updates

- **Built-in automated table services for optimized write performance:**

  - Hudi provides automated table services such as compaction, clustering, indexing, archiving, TTL enforcement, and cleaning, all executed without external orchestration or manual SQL commands

  - Hudi's marker mechanism efficiently cleans up uncommitted or orphaned files during writes, avoiding the need for expensive cloud storage scans that can take hours or even time out

- **Out-of-the-box platform tools:**

  - Hudi offers fully production-ready ingestion tools for Spark, Flink, and Kafka, allowing users to build lakehouse pipelines

  - Native support for popular CDC formats (Debezium, AWS DMS, and MongoDB) and sources such as S3, GCS, Kafka, and Pulsar makes it easy to ingest change data efficiently

  - It enables syncing tables to multiple catalogs via its native tool

- **Streaming-first design:**

  - Hudi is natively optimized for streaming ingestion, offering event-time ordering and late data handling within storage, particularly for merge-on-read tables

  - Hudi's RecordPayload/RecordMerger APIs ensure that updates follow the correct database LSN order for accurate event sequencing (dealing with out-of-order data)

- **Efficient incremental processing and change data queries:**

  - Hudi supports incremental queries and CDC-based queries, enabling downstream consumers to process only changed records between two time intervals instead of reprocessing entire tables

  - By using scalable metadata, an LSM-tree-backed timeline history, and record-level change tracking, Hudi supports long-term retention for incremental streams, critical for transactional datasets and log processing

It is best suited for the following:

- **Write-heavy ingestion pipelines**: Hudi's built-in indexing and upsert optimizations ensure fast ingestion with minimal table scans, making it ideal for workloads with frequent updates and deletes.

- **Streaming and real-time analytics**: Hudi's **Merge-on-Read (MoR)** storage format and event-time handling enable continuous, low-latency ingestion, making it ideal for event-driven architectures and real-time data processing.

- **Workloads requiring built-in optimization and self-managed table services**: Automated compaction, clustering, and cleaning services reduce manual table maintenance, balancing write performance with read efficiency. Hudi fits well with workloads that demand this balance.

- **Incremental data processing**: Change data queries and incremental processing allow downstream systems to consume only modified records, making Hudi a great fit for efficient ETL pipelines and analytics workloads.

Hudi's architecture delivers efficient writes, fast record lookups, and automated table maintenance for streaming and incremental workloads. These strengths make it ideal for write-heavy pipelines, real-time analytics, and change-data-driven processing.

# Delta Lake

Delta Lake is relevant for teams building on top of the Apache Spark (Databricks for managed services) ecosystem. Its deep integration with Spark makes it a straightforward choice for organizations that want strong transactional guarantees, schema flexibility, and native support for data science and machine learning pipelines.

## Key architectural strengths in practice

Delta Lake is optimized for read-heavy analytics workloads while maintaining transactional consistency and schema flexibility. It is deeply integrated into the Python/Rust ecosystem, making it a strong choice for data science, ML workloads, and ad hoc analytics use cases. Here are some of its key design strengths:

- **Tight integration with Apache Spark**: Delta Lake sits on top of Apache Spark, simplifying the process of building lakehouse pipelines. The close coupling between the format and compute layer allows for seamless ingestion, transformation, and querying within Spark-based environments.

- **Change data feed (CDF) for tracking data modifications**: Delta Lake enables efficient downstream consumption of changed records (row-level changes) via CDF, making it easier to build incremental ETL pipelines.

- **Liquid clustering for automatic query optimization:**

  - Unlike traditional clustering methods, liquid clustering dynamically organizes data based on query patterns without requiring costly rewrites.

  - It reduces query latency and optimizes file layout for faster access without manual intervention.

- **Multi-language API Support (Python, Rust, and beyond):** Delta Lake provides native APIs for Python and Rust, making it a strong fit for compute engines such as pandas, Polars, DuckDB, and DataFusion.

- **Data sharing and governance via Delta Sharing:**

  - It supports secure, cross-platform data sharing with Delta Sharing, enabling organizations to share Delta tables externally without requiring full table copies.

  - It ensures governance and controlled access while maintaining interoperability across different environments.

It is best suited for the following:

- **Python/Rust-based ML and data science workloads:** Delta Lake's native table format capabilities, especially in the Python/Rust ecosystem, make it a strong fit for data science and ML model training and experimentation. It integrates seamlessly with MLflow, pandas, Polars, Ray, and so on, needed for these tasks.

- **Read-heavy analytics:** Features such as Z-ordering, liquid clustering, and auto compaction in Delta Lake optimize query execution, ensuring efficient data retrieval in batch analytics use cases. This is where Delta could work best.

- **Apache Spark-based data pipelines:** Delta Lake's native integration with Spark makes it a strong choice for Spark-driven ETL, batch processing, and streaming analytics, ensuring simpler implementation and optimized performance in Spark-centric architectures.

Now that we have explored the key decision factors and feature-level strengths of Apache Iceberg, Apache Hudi, and Delta Lake, it's time to visualize these insights in a structured way.

The following selection matrix maps each format's strengths against critical considerations, providing a practical guide for choosing the right table format based on specific workload needs. Instead of ranking formats as "better" or "worse," this table highlights their relative strengths in different areas, helping engineers make informed decisions based on their data architecture and use cases.

| Consideration | Apache Iceberg | Apache Hudi | Delta Lake |
|---|---|---|---|
| Read vs. write optimization | Shines with read-heavy workloads; best for batch analytics, BI, and ad hoc analysis. | Shines with write-heavy workloads; excels in incremental ingestion and CDC | Shines with read-heavy workloads; supports batch analytics and ML pipelines |
| Ecosystem compatibility | Stands out with analytical stack (Trino, Snowflake, Dremio, and Superset) | Stands out with streaming engines and tools (Flink, Kafka, and Spark Streaming) | Stands out with Python/Rust-based stack (analytics and ML ecosystems) |
| Table maintenance and optimization services | No built-in services; requires external compute trigger (compaction, clustering, and cleaning) | Fully automated table maintenance services (compaction, clustering, cleaning, and indexing) | Limited automation (compaction and liquid clustering); offers Spark APIs for maintenance |
| Table evolution and versioning | Flexible schema evolution and partition evolution; supports multi-version environments (branches) | Supports schema evolution; offers expression-based indexing but lacks multi-version environments | Supports schema evolution but lacks multi-version environments |
| Platform tools and operational features | No native platform tools; relies on external compute (for ingestion, data quality checks, and recovery) | Provides built-in ingestion tools, catalog sync, and operational services for data quality and recovery | Includes Delta Sharing for cross-platform data access |
| Use cases | Best suited for large-scale batch processing and analytical workloads; replacing Hive in cloud object stores | Best suited for faster ingestion, incremental processing, and low-latency writes | Best suited for Spark-based pipelines, batch analytics, and ML/AI workloads |

*Table 10.1: Comparison of Iceberg, Hudi, and Delta Lake*

Up to this point, we have focused on the feature-level strengths and use cases of individual table formats. However, evaluating a format in isolation is not enough – its practical success often depends on the surrounding tooling, compute engines, and metadata catalogs that enable these formats to be operational.

# Support within the open ecosystem

As with any architecture, a data lakehouse offers two primary approaches:

- Using open source technologies to build an open lakehouse
- Adopting a managed lakehouse solution from a vendor

Each approach has its trade-offs in flexibility, performance, maintenance, and cost.

The open ecosystem consists of various compute engines and metadata catalogs that provide different levels of read/write support, feature compatibility, and integration capabilities with Apache Iceberg, Apache Hudi, and Delta Lake. While open source solutions offer greater flexibility and control, they often require operational expertise and specialized engineering resources to build, maintain, and optimize.

On the other hand, managed lakehouse platforms provide turnkey solutions with automated optimizations, built-in table services, and native security features. However, these platforms may introduce vendor lock-in, pricing constraints, or limited interoperability with other open source components.

In this chapter, our scope is limited to evaluating some of the commonly used open compute engines and catalogs. This section explores their capabilities to help organizations determine the best fit for their needs.

> Since lakehouse formats are a constantly evolving technology, support of these open compute engines and catalogs is subject to change.

# Compute engine

Let's now examine how major compute engines interact with Apache Iceberg, Apache Hudi, and Delta Lake, focusing on read/write support, table optimization, and key feature compatibility. The following table highlights the strengths and limitations of each engine for different table formats.

| Compute engine | Read/write support | Table optimization support | Key feature support |
|---|---|---|---|
| Apache Spark | Full support for Iceberg, Hudi, and Delta | Supports all major methods: compaction, clustering, and cleaning | Supports all major features |
| Apache Flink | Full support for Iceberg and Hudi; limited support for Delta | Good support for Hudi, limited support for Iceberg; no support for Delta | Supports most major features for Hudi and Iceberg; restricted support for Delta |
| Trino | Excellent read/write support for Iceberg, limited write support for Delta, read-only for Hudi | Limited support for Iceberg and Delta; no support for Hudi | Strong support for Iceberg, partial support for Delta, and restricted support for Hudi |
| Presto | Excellent read/write support for Iceberg; read-only for Hudi and Delta | Great support for Iceberg; no support for Delta and Hudi | Supports major features for Iceberg; lacks feature support for Hudi and Delta |
| Clickhouse | Read-only for Iceberg, Hudi, and Delta | No support | Restricted support for all three |
| StarRocks | Read-only for Iceberg, Hudi, and Delta | No support | Limited support for Iceberg; no major support for Hudi and Delta |
| Apache Doris | Read-only for Iceberg and Hudi; no support for Delta | No support | Basic Iceberg and Hudi support; no Delta support |

*Table 10.2: Compute engine support across Iceberg, Hudi, and Delta Lake*

Spark provides the broadest support across all formats, while engines such as ClickHouse, Star-Rocks, and Apache Doris offer limited or read-only functionality. Understanding these differences is essential for aligning compute engines with workload requirements.

## Catalogs

Key metadata catalogs vary in their support for open table formats, file types, and unstructured data, with some offering broader compatibility than others. The following table highlights the strengths and limitations of each catalog and connector gaps to consider.

| Metadata catalog | Open table format support | File type and unstructured data support | Notable connector gaps |
|---|---|---|---|
| Unity Catalog | Delta, Hudi, and Iceberg | Parquet, ORC, Avro, CSV, JSON, TSV, and XML | Limited to data lakes; no Flink or Trino |
| Apache Polaris | Iceberg only | Structured only | Nothing besides Iceberg support |
| Hive Metastore | Iceberg, Hudi, and Delta | Structured only | Thrift server scaling issues, legacy |
| Apache Gravitino | Hudi and Iceberg | Parquet, ORC, TXT, Avro, and JSON (supports FileSets for unstructured objects) | No Delta Lake support |

*Table 10.3: Metadata catalog compatibility with Iceberg, Hudi, and Delta Lake*

Unity Catalog provides the widest format and file support, while Apache Polaris and Apache Gravitino have more limited compatibility. Choosing the right catalog ensures alignment with table formats and workload requirements.

# Real-world case studies

So far, we have explored the key decision factors in choosing a table format and examined their architectural strengths in practice. However, technical comparisons alone don't always provide a complete picture; real-world implementations reveal practical challenges, trade-offs, and lessons learned when deploying these formats at scale.

In this section, we analyze three production deployments, each showcasing a different open table format (Iceberg, Hudi, and Delta), not just to highlight their strengths, but to emphasize the idea of "format fit": choosing a table format based on the dominant workload patterns and platform needs.

We go beyond generic comparisons and look closely at why a particular format was chosen, what architectural decisions were made, and how challenges were addressed.

## Case study 1: Scaling analytics with Apache Iceberg at Orca Security

Orca Security needed a table format that could support a petabyte-scale security analytics platform with streaming ingestion, multi-engine query access (Spark and Athena), and constant schema evolution. Apache Iceberg was selected because it fulfilled several critical requirements:

- ACID guarantees and snapshot isolation enabled concurrent streaming writes and batch reads without conflicts

- Engine interoperability allowed querying from both Apache Spark and Amazon Athena (Trino)

- Metadata pruning and hidden partitioning delivered scalable query performance and simplified SQL access patterns

- Partition evolution made it possible to shift from daily to hourly partitions without re-writing data

- Schema evolution support enabled teams to iterate on data models without downtime

These capabilities made Iceberg a strategic foundation for Orca's goal of unified, transactional data access across both analytical and machine learning pipelines.

Here is the architectural overview:

- **Storage layer**: Apache Parquet files stored in Amazon S3, with table layout managed by Iceberg

- **Catalog and metadata**: AWS Glue Data Catalog

- **Streaming ingestion**:

  - Data from security and access logs sent to Amazon MSK (Kafka)

  - Apache Spark Structured Streaming on EMR writes to Iceberg tables

- **Query engines**: Amazon Athena (Trino-based) and Apache Spark SQL

- **ML and feature engineering**: Amazon SageMaker and AWS SDK for pandas for model training, normalization, and pipeline integration

- **Security and governance**: IAM-based fine-grained access control over S3 and Glue

The architectural choices and design outcomes at Orca Security reflect a deliberate alignment with the decision criteria we introduced earlier in this chapter. Let's walk through how this real-world case reinforces the rationale for choosing Apache Iceberg in specific scenarios.

| Evaluation category | Why Iceberg? |
| --- | --- |
| Read vs. write optimization | Orca processes petabyte-scale, read-heavy workloads using Athena and Spark. Iceberg's snapshot isolation and manifest-based pruning ensure low-latency reads without blocking concurrent writes. |
| Ecosystem compatibility | It uses an AWS-native stack: MSK to Iceberg on S3, queried via Athena and Spark, with ML via SageMaker. Iceberg integrates natively across these tools. |
| Schema and partition evolution | Iceberg enables schema evolution without rewrite, and supports Orca's shift from daily to hourly partitions, critical for timely security event processing. |

*Table 10.4: Evaluation of Apache Iceberg for Orca Security's analytics platform*

These results demonstrate how Iceberg's features, such as scalable reads and writes, seamless engine interoperability, and flexible schema and partition evolution, directly enabled Orca Security to build a robust, high-performance analytics platform at petabyte scale.

## Case study 2: Building an update-heavy terabyte-scale data lakehouse at Notion

Notion needed a table format capable of handling continuous updates, CDC, and efficient incremental processing. Their existing architecture with Postgres shards feeding into Snowflake couldn't sustain frequent updates or rapidly growing datasets.

Apache Hudi was selected as the core table format because it is purpose-built for high-frequency, write-heavy ingestion workloads while maintaining analytical query performance:

- Hudi supports native upserts and incremental processing out of the box for update-dominated workloads
- It integrates with Debezium CDC and Kafka, enabling low-latency ingestion from Postgres into S3

In their evaluation, Iceberg and Delta Lake were considered but rejected for this workload: Iceberg lacked an out-of-the-box Debezium consumer, while Delta Lake's certain capabilities were not open source.

Here is the architectural overview:

- **Storage layer**: Apache Parquet files on Amazon S3, managed as Hudi tables (the COPY_ON_WRITE type) **Ingestion layer**:

    - Debezium connectors capture CDC events from sharded Postgres
    - Events streamed via Apache Kafka
    - Spark-based Hudi DeltaStreamer jobs consume the Kafka topics and upsert into Hudi tables on S3.

- **Processing and query engines**: Apache Spark (PySpark for lighter jobs, Scala Spark for heavy transformations) is used for complex processing such as block tree traversal and denormalization

- **Table services/maintenance**: Notion employed partitioning by source shard (480 logical shards) to align with Postgres sharding, used event_lsn ordering to sort updates, and leveraged Bloom-filter indexing to optimize upsert performance

Now, let's relate this to our decision matrix and understand the rationale behind selecting Apache Hudi.

| Evaluation category | Why Hudi? |
|---|---|
| Read vs. write optimization | Notion's workloads are write-heavy – over 90% of writes are updates. Hudi's record-level upsert and incremental ingestion via Debezium + Kafka + Spark allowed continuous low-latency writes. |
| Ecosystem compatibility | Hudi integrated seamlessly with Postgres, Debezium, and Kafka, forming a fully open source ingestion pipeline. |
| Table maintenance and optimization services | Hudi's built-in services for compaction, cleaning, and indexing automated maintenance, reducing manual overhead. Partitioning by 480 Postgres shards and Bloom-filter indexing further optimized both ingestion and query performance. |
| Platform tools and operational features | Hudi's DeltaStreamer served as a turnkey ingestion framework, continuously streaming data from Kafka into S3. Running on EKS alongside Kafka, it scaled seamlessly with minimal operational overhead or upgrades. |
| Use cases | Ideal for update-heavy, CDC-driven pipelines requiring near-real-time freshness. Enabled Notion to cut ingestion time from > 1 day to minutes/hours and achieve >$1 million net savings in 2022. |

*Table 10.5: Evaluation of Apache Hudi for Notion's update-heavy data lakehouse*

Apache Hudi's native support for upserts, incremental processing, and built-in table services enabled Notion to efficiently manage update-heavy, CDC-driven workloads. This choice delivered low-latency ingestion, simplified maintenance, and significant operational cost savings.

## Case study 3: Using a Delta Lake-based lakehouse for T-Mobile's data science and analytics

T-Mobile's **data science and analytics (DSNA)** team faced growing complexity as data was scattered across disconnected systems supporting network planning, procurement, and supply chain operations. Their first **massively parallel processing (MPP)**-based data lake (TMUS) improved reporting speed but suffered workload contention, unreliable refreshes, and a lack of governance as user queries competed for shared resources.

To resolve these issues, the team adopted a data lakehouse architecture built on Delta Lake, unifying data warehousing principles with open data lake storage. Delta Lake's ACID transactions, compute/storage separation, and workload isolation addressed the scalability and governance challenges of TMUS:

- ACID compliance and versioned tables ensured reliable updates and reproducible analytics
- Separation of compute and storage eliminated resource contention between analytical and operational workloads
- Serverless SQL and Spark endpoints provided consistent performance and clear SLAs for all users

Here is the architectural overview:

- **Storage layer:** Azure **Data Lake Storage (DLS)** and Delta Lake tables
- **Ingestion layer:** Source systems continue writing to ADLS; audit DB added for governance and lineage
- **Processing and query engines:** Apache Spark notebooks; Serverless SQL endpoints
- **Governance and access:** Schema-based data segregation; SLA-based access model

Now, let's understand how their decision relates to our decision matrix.

| Evaluation category | Why Delta Lake? |
|---|---|
| Read vs. write optimization | Balanced performance for analytical and operational workloads; transactional updates supported via Delta's ACID engine |
| Ecosystem compatibility | Seamless integration with Azure DLS, Apache Spark, and Serverless SQL; supports both batch and ad-hoc analysis |

| Table maintenance and optimization services | Delta's compaction, vacuuming, and Z-ordering maintain query efficiency and predictable performance |
| Table evolution and versioning | Built-in versioned history and time-travel simplify debugging and reproducibility across bronze-silver-gold tables |

*Table 10.6: Evaluation of Delta Lake for T-Mobile's data science and analytics lakehouse*

Delta Lake's ACID transactions, workload isolation, and built-in optimization services enabled T-Mobile to unify their data landscape while maintaining reliable performance and governance. This architecture delivered reproducible analytics, reduced contention, and simplified maintenance across diverse data workloads.

# Summary

In this chapter, we explored the critical considerations for evaluating and selecting open table formats in a modern lakehouse architecture. By analyzing core design trade-offs such as read versus write optimization, ecosystem compatibility, and operational tooling, we've seen how Apache Iceberg, Apache Hudi, and Delta Lake each cater to distinct workload patterns and organizational needs. These choices have downstream implications across the data stack, influencing ingestion pipelines, query performance, governance, and long-term maintainability.

While format selection remains a foundational architectural decision, it's important to note the emergence of technologies such as Apache XTable (discussed in *Chapter 7*), which enable cross-format interoperability. Projects such as XTable allow organizations to embrace the unique strengths of each format while minimizing fragmentation and improving flexibility in multi-engine, multi-tool environments. However, you should consider the practical integration aspects for such interoperability layers in the lakehouse stack.

In the next chapter, we will delve into the practical aspects of a lakehouse implementation by walking through real-world examples and applying our overall learnings through hands-on code.

# References

- https://aws.amazon.com/blogs/big-data/orca-securitys-journey-to-a-petabyte-scale-data-lake-with-apache-iceberg-and-aws-analytics/
- https://www.notion.com/blog/building-and-scaling-notions-data-lake
- https://delta.io/blog/2022-09-14-why-migrate-lakehouse-delta-lake-tmo-dsna/

## Get This Book's PDF Version and Exclusive Extras

UNLOCK NOW

Scan the QR code (or go to packtpub.com/unlock). Search for this book by name, confirm the edition, and then follow the steps on the page.

*Note: Keep your invoice handy. Purchases made directly from Packt don't require an invoice.*

# 11

# Real-World Applications and Learnings

The promise of the lakehouse architecture lies not just in its conceptual elegance but in its ability to solve real-world data challenges at scale. In this final chapter, we move from theory to practice by walking through three hands-on implementations of commonly seen use cases, each powered by an open table format best suited for the job.

These use cases will reflect common workflows in the analytics realm, ranging from analytical workloads (BI) and real-time ingestion to machine learning pipelines, and show how open source lakehouse-native tools and patterns such as **write-audit-publish (WAP)**, incremental processing, and **change data capture (CDC)** can be put into action.

Each use case will demonstrate the following:

- A real-world-inspired scenario
- A curated set of open source tools tightly integrated with an open table format
- Step-by-step implementation with architecture details
- A "build once, scale anywhere" mindset, enabling you to translate these learnings into production pipelines

We will cover the following three scenarios in this chapter:

- Acme Manufacturing's journey to an Iceberg-based lakehouse
- GlobalMart's real-time analytics with Apache Hudi CDC
- Visionary Telecom's machine learning workflow modernization with Delta Lake

# Scenario overview: Acme Manufacturing's journey to an Iceberg-based lakehouse

Acme Manufacturing is a growing industrial equipment manufacturer producing custom precision parts across multiple factory locations. Over the past few years, Acme has invested heavily in digitization, equipping production lines with IoT sensors, automating quality checks, and capturing detailed records of maintenance, productivity, and energy usage.

To extract insights from this data, Acme built a traditional two-tier analytics architecture: an enterprise data warehouse for structured analytics and reporting and a separate data lake that served as the central repository for all raw data, used for ad hoc exploration and transformations via batch query engines. While functional, this setup introduced new challenges:

- High infrastructure costs (for cloud warehouses) due to repeated ETL jobs and materialized views
- Delayed analytics caused by data staleness between lake and warehouse syncs
- Scattered, inconsistent copies of data across tools and teams
- Limited flexibility for running ad hoc queries or building unified dashboards

Despite having rich operational data, Acme's analytics teams in production, supply chain, and quality control struggled to make timely, cross-functional decisions.

The company's leadership decides to overhaul its analytics infrastructure by building an in-house lakehouse architecture that can enable near real-time monitoring, root-cause analysis, and predictive insights across business units.

Their first goal is to consolidate key operational metrics into a central Apache Iceberg table, enabling the following:

- Unified data access via SQL

- Interactive dashboards for cross-team analysis

- Cost-effective and open storage using formats such as Parquet

# Solution: A lakehouse for unified manufacturing analytics

To address the pain points, Acme embarks on a journey to build a lakehouse architecture using Apache Iceberg as the open table format on top of their current cloud data lake storage (S3-compatible object storage, MinIO).

## Why Apache Iceberg?

Acme's decision to adopt Apache Iceberg as the table format is driven by a combination of architectural evolution, analytical workload characteristics, and usability requirements:

- **From Hive to Iceberg**: Acme historically relied on Hive tables over HDFS for batch analytics. As they migrate to the cloud and adopt S3-compatible object storage (MinIO), they need a modern table format that could seamlessly plug into their new environment while overcoming the limitations of Hive (such as lack of atomicity and inefficient schema evolution). Iceberg provides a drop-in, cloud-native alternative with strong backward compatibility.

- **Read-heavy analytical workloads**: Most teams at Acme are consumers of data; they run dashboards, slice reports, and perform trend analysis. Tables are written infrequently but read often. Iceberg is optimized for such read-heavy workloads, with metadata and partition pruning features.

- **Schema and partition evolution**: Over time, Acme's data models are expected to change. New attributes will be added, and partition strategies may need to adapt. Iceberg offers flexible schema and partition evolution without forcing full rewrites of historical data, making it ideal for long-lived, evolving datasets.

- **SQL accessibility across engines**: Acme's data analysts and operations teams are fluent in SQL and want to continue using familiar tools and dialects. Iceberg's support for multiple SQL-native engines, such as Dremio, Trino, Flink SQL, and Spark SQL, makes it easy to plug into their ecosystem without retraining teams or introducing custom code.

- **Data quality before publication**: Acme also wants the ability to test and audit data before making it available to production applications such as BI dashboards. Iceberg natively supports Git-like branching with compute engines such as Apache Spark, but also, with catalogs such as Nessie, Acme's data team can achieve catalog-level branching, which would allow them to implement data quality checks for all of their tables. Their goal is to achieve a WAP workflow:

  - Write new data to a staging branch
  - Run validation or exploratory queries
  - Merge to the main branch only after quality checks are passed

## Architecture details

To implement their analytics-driven lakehouse, the Acme data platform team designs a modular architecture centered around open standards and interoperable tools. This allows them to power analytical workloads (BI reports and ad hoc queries) directly on their data lake, without duplicating data into a warehouse or managing complex ETL jobs.

Raw data lands from various sources in the data lake (MinIO) and is ingested as Apache Iceberg tables using Dremio as the compute engine. These tables progress through the Bronze → Silver → Gold layers as the data is cleaned, enriched, and transformed. Project Nessie ensures these tables are cataloged and versioned in a Git-like model, allowing structured governance and isolated data environments. Finally, Apache Superset connects to Dremio to query Gold-layer Iceberg tables, enabling the analytics team to build interactive dashboards using familiar SQL.

## Tooling stack breakdown

Here are the various open source tools that Acme uses to make their lakehouse operational:

- **Apache Iceberg**: Serves as the open table format enabling schema evolution, partitioning, and time travel across all data layers.
- **Project Nessie**: Acts as the open catalog and versioning system that stores all the Iceberg tables and offers Git-like branching for managing table states, which is especially useful for isolating transformations or audits.
- **MinIO**: A self-hosted, S3-compatible object store used as the backing data lake storage. All data is stored in Apache Parquet format, allowing efficient columnar reads.

- **Dremio OSS**: The SQL-based compute engine responsible for reading/writing Iceberg tables, applying transformations between Bronze → Silver → Gold, and serving queries to downstream tools.

- **Apache Superset**: A lightweight, open source visualization tool connected to Dremio to create real-time visualizations and interactive dashboards.

This is the high-level architecture for Acme's new lakehouse. You can run this architecture locally using the Docker assets provided in the book's companion code repository at https://github. com/PacktPublishing/Engineering-Lakehouses-with-Open-Table-Formats/tree/main/ch11.

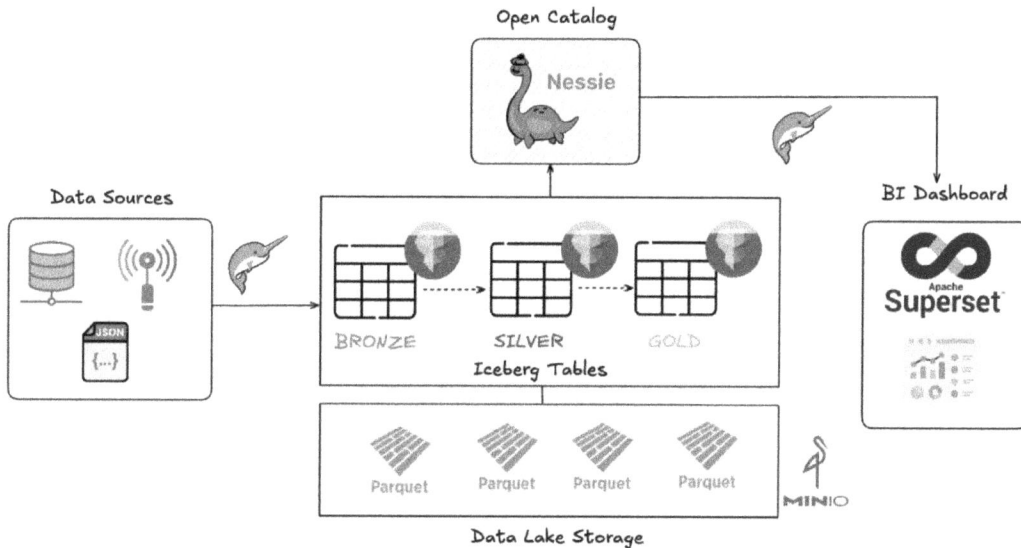

Figure 11.1 – High-level architecture for Acme's open lakehouse

## Catalog configuration

As we discussed in *Chapter 3, Apache Iceberg Deep Dive* configuring a catalog is the first step in the journey to an Iceberg-based lakehouse. A catalog is what brings ACID guarantees in Iceberg. Since the team relies on Dremio as the SQL compute engine, they start by configuring a catalog source in Dremio.

Acme uses Nessie as their open catalog to store all of their Iceberg tables:

**Add Data Source**                                                    ✕

Q  Search data source

**Nessie Catalogs**

Nessie (Preview)

**Metastores**

AWS Glue Data Catalog

Hive 2.x

Hive 3.x

**Object Storage**

Amazon S3

Azure Data Lake Storage Gen1

Azure Storage

Google Cloud Storage

HDFS

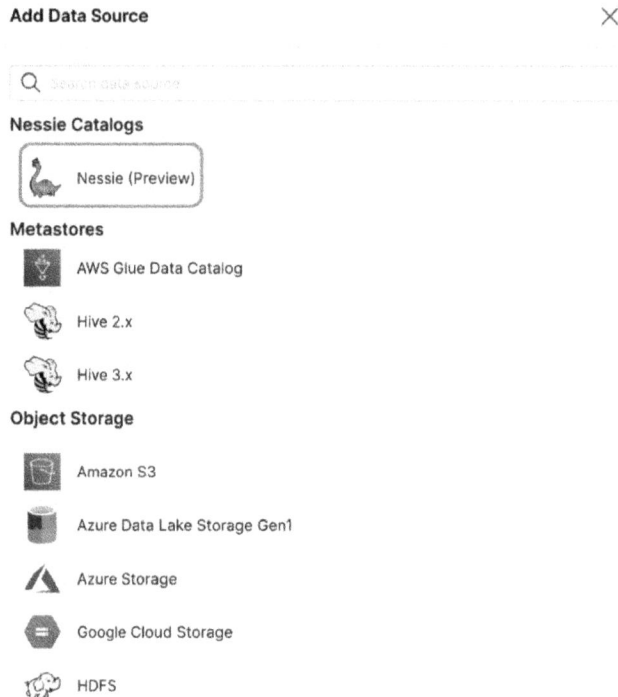

*Figure 11.2 – Different catalog options within Dremio's platform*

In order to configure Nessie, the team needs to first provide the Nessie endpoint URL (this is where Nessie is running) and select the right authentication type, as shown here:

**Source Settings**

General                          Nessie Source

Storage
                                 Name
Advanced Options
                                 nessie
Reflection Refresh

                                 Nessie endpoint URL

                                 http://nessie:19120/api/v2

                                 Nessie authentication type

                                 ◉ None    ○ Bearer

                                 No authentication is enforced on Nessie server.

*Figure 11.3 – Configuring the Nessie endpoint and authentication types*

Now, for Dremio to read and write data files related to the Iceberg table (via the catalog), the storage settings for the catalog need to be configured with the right authentication method, along with some of the additional properties:

General

**Storage**

Advanced Options

Reflection Refresh

**S3 Storage**

AWS root path (i)

s3://  /warehouse

**S3 Authentication**

Authentication method

◉ AWS Access Key    ○ EC2 Metadata    ○ AWS Profile    ○ No Authentication

AWS access key

admin

AWS access secret

••••••••••••••••••••••

IAM role to assume

**Other**

Connection properties

| Name | Value |
| --- | --- |
| fs.s3a.path.style.access | true |
| Name | Value |
| fs.s3a.endpoint | minio-storage:9000 |
| Name | Value |
| dremio.s3.compat | true |

*Figure 11.4 – Configuring storage settings for the catalog*

Dremio provides various other catalogs and storage systems options to choose from.

## Implementing Write-Audit-Publish (WAP) with Project Nessie:

Before the Acme team begins ingesting or transforming data, they enable a Write-Audit-Publish workflow using Project Nessie. Nessie allows catalog-level branching and merging, like Git, which gives Acme:

- Isolated data pipelines (no risk of corrupting production tables)
- A staging area for data quality validation
- Fully version-controlled data workflows

The team begins by creating a dedicated staging branch for the ETL job and switches context using USE  BRANCH so all new writes go to the etl_staging branch.

```
CREATE BRANCH etl_staging AT BRANCH main IN nessie;
USE BRANCH etl_staging IN nessie;
```

> In Dremio, USE  BRANCH applies within the current multi-statement script/session. If you run statements separately, specify the branch explicitly using AT  BRANCH in each statement.

We can see the output:

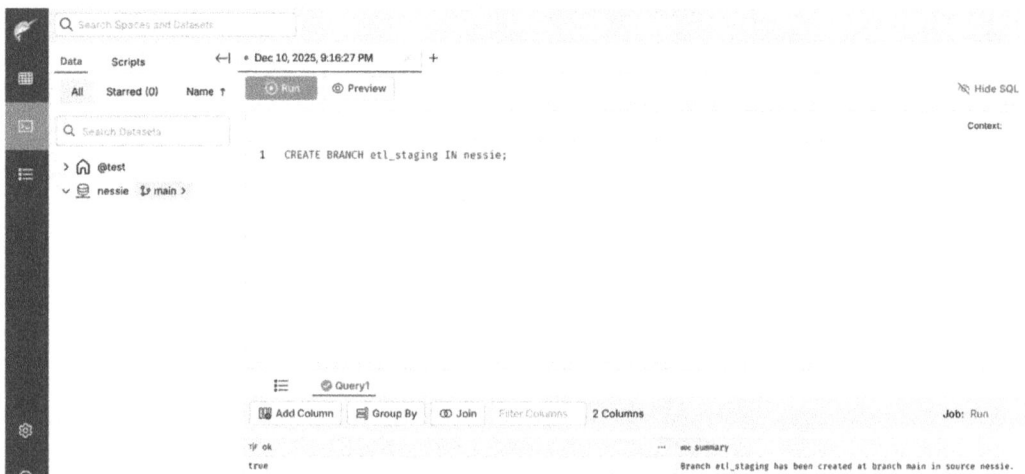

*Figure 11.5 – Creating a new Nessie branch using SQL*

# Initial load/ingestion (raw data to Bronze)

Once the catalog is configured and the staging branch created, the team is now ready to start with their first ingestion workload. Note that whatever operations the team executes from now on, will only apply to the etl_staging branch.

Acme accumulates all of their production data from internal systems (manufacturing logs, sensor outputs, and operational reports) and stores it as raw files in their data lake (MinIO).

The data engineers' first task is to ingest this raw data as an Iceberg table without modifying or transforming it. This creates a durable, immutable snapshot of raw data that can be queried and versioned if needed.

The team uses Dremio's SQL interface to quickly create Iceberg tables by using a CTAS statement:

```
CREATE TABLE nessie.acme_manu AT BRANCH etl_staging
AS (SELECT * FROM "@test"."Acme_manufacturing");
```

This creates a Bronze Iceberg table that mirrors the raw schema but adds the benefits of an open table format:

**nessie**   ⅙ etl_staging >

**Name**

acme_manu

*Figure 11.6 – Newly created Iceberg table in the Bronze layer*

## Data cleaning and normalization (Bronze to Silver)

With the raw data now safely ingested and versioned in the Bronze Iceberg table, Acme's data engineering team moves to the next stage: standardizing and preparing the data for analytics.

Their objective in this layer is to ensure the data is clean, consistent, and structured enough to be trusted by downstream consumers. This means enforcing correct data types, filtering out incomplete or malformed records, and aligning column names to a standard convention.

The engineers materialize the Silver layer as a new Iceberg table on the etl_staging branch. This keeps the cleaned dataset versioned in Nessie, so it can be audited and promoted together with the rest of the pipeline.

```
SELECT
  -- Normalized column naming (snake_case)
  CAST(ProductionVolume AS INTEGER)     AS production_volume,
  CAST(ProductionCost AS FLOAT)         AS production_cost,
  CAST(SupplierQuality AS FLOAT)        AS supplier_quality,
  CAST(DeliveryDelay AS INTEGER)        AS delivery_delay,
  CAST(DefectRate AS FLOAT)             AS defect_rate,
  CAST(QualityScore AS FLOAT)           AS quality_score,
  CAST(MaintenanceHours AS INTEGER)     AS maintenance_hours,
  CAST(DowntimePercentage AS FLOAT)     AS downtime_pct,
  CAST(InventoryTurnover AS FLOAT)      AS inventory_turnover,
  CAST(StockoutRate AS FLOAT)           AS stockout_rate,
  CAST(WorkerProductivity AS FLOAT)     AS worker_productivity,
```

```
    CAST(SafetyIncidents AS INTEGER)        AS safety_incidents,
    CAST(EnergyConsumption AS FLOAT)        AS energy_consumption,
    CAST(EnergyEfficiency AS FLOAT)         AS energy_efficiency,
    CAST(AdditiveProcessTime AS FLOAT)      AS additive_process_time,
    CAST(AdditiveMaterialCost AS FLOAT)     AS additive_material_cost,
    CAST(DefectStatus AS INTEGER)           AS defect_status
  FROM nessie.acme_manu AT BRANCH etl_staging
  -- Filter out incomplete records
  WHERE ProductionVolume IS NOT NULL
    AND ProductionCost IS NOT NULL
    AND DefectRate IS NOT NULL
    AND QualityScore IS NOT NULL
```

During this step, note the following:

- All numeric columns are explicitly cast to appropriate types (e.g., `FLOAT` or `INTEGER`) to avoid type ambiguity later
- All column names are renamed to `snake_case` for consistency across engineering and analytics workflows
- Records with missing or null values in critical columns such as `ProductionVolume`, `ProductionCost`, and `DefectRate` are filtered out to preserve data quality

By the end of this step, Acme has a clean, standardized Iceberg table (Iceberg view: `https://iceberg.apache.org/view-spec/`) in their Silver layer that acts as a trusted foundation for building business logic, aggregations, and dashboards in the Gold layer:

**nessie**  ⑂ etl_staging  >

**Name**

🗄 acme_manu

🗄 silver_acme_manu

*Figure 11.7 – Newly created Iceberg table in the Silver layer*

## Business logic and aggregation (Silver to Gold)

With the data now cleaned and normalized in the Silver layer, Acme's data engineering team turns their attention to creating the Gold layer - the final application layer powering production applications such as BI dashboards in Superset.

The goal of this step is to transform operational data into business-ready metrics that support real-time visibility, trend analysis, and decision-making across departments such as production, quality, energy, and workforce operations.

Working alongside analysts and factory leads, the engineers define a set of **key performance indicators (KPIs)** and categorical insights. These include the following:

- Overall production volume and cost metrics
- Quality indicators such as defect rate and defect level classification
- Operational efficiency via cost-per-unit and a custom efficiency score
- Safety incident totals and maintenance trends
- Supplier performance and inventory health

To support time-series dashboards, the team also generates a `production_date` column by synthetically assigning a day to each record, simulating a realistic daily ingestion pattern.

Here is the code to do so:

```
WITH numbered_data AS (
 SELECT
   *,
 ROW_NUMBER() OVER (ORDER BY production_volume) - 1 AS row_num
 FROM nessie."silver_acme_manu" AT BRANCH etl_staging
)
SELECT
 DATE_ADD(DATE '2024-01-01', row_num) AS production_date,
 -- Core output & cost metrics
 SUM(production_volume) AS total_production_volume,
 SUM(production_cost) AS total_production_cost,

 CASE
   WHEN SUM(production_volume) > 0 THEN SUM(production_cost) /
SUM(production_volume)
   ELSE NULL
 END AS cost_per_unit,
 -- Operational & energy efficiency
 AVG(worker_productivity) AS avg_worker_productivity,
 AVG(energy_efficiency) AS avg_energy_efficiency,
 (0.6 * AVG(worker_productivity) + 0.4 * AVG(energy_efficiency) * 100) AS
```

```
efficiency_score,
  -- Quality metrics
 AVG(defect_rate) AS avg_defect_rate,
 AVG(quality_score) AS avg_quality_score,
 CASE
    WHEN AVG(defect_rate) >= 5 THEN 'High'
    WHEN AVG(defect_rate) >= 2 THEN 'Moderate'
    ELSE 'Low'
 END AS defect_level,
 -- Workforce and reliability metrics
 SUM(safety_incidents) AS total_safety_incidents,
 AVG(maintenance_hours) AS avg_maintenance_hours,

 -- Inventory and supply chain metrics
 AVG(inventory_turnover) AS avg_inventory_turnover,
 AVG(stockout_rate) AS avg_stockout_rate,
 AVG(supplier_quality) AS avg_supplier_quality,
 AVG(delivery_delay) AS avg_delivery_delay
FROM numbered_data
GROUP BY DATE_ADD(DATE '2024-01-01', row_num)
```

All of this is done using Dremio SQL and materialized as a Gold Iceberg table in the Nessie catalog on the etl_staging branch.

With this, Acme now has a Gold-layer virtual dataset containing fully refined, business-ready metrics where all aggregations, categorizations, and business logic have been applied:

*Figure 11.8 – Newly created Iceberg table in the Gold layer*

This curated dataset is optimized for direct use by analytical tools, enabling fast, reliable access to actionable insights across teams.

## Auditing Metrics Before Promotion to Production

Once Acme's data engineering team has completed the first few steps of their ETL pipeline, i.e. loading raw files into the bronze table and enriching them into a Gold-level dataset, they are not ready to publish it to production just yet.

Instead, they want to audit key metrics on the etl_staging branch and verify if the transformed data looks trustworthy and consistent. Once satisfied, they can then publish them to the main branch (production) using Git-like operations. This is the advantage of using catalogs like Nessie with table format like Apache Iceberg.

In Acme's case, two important quality signals are:

- The average defect rate of manufactured units
- The average quality score across plants

They use a simple SQL query to assess these:

```
SELECT
  AVG(avg_defect_rate) AS avg_defect_rate,
  AVG(avg_quality_score) AS avg_quality_score
FROM nessie.gold_acme_manu AT BRANCH etl_staging;
```

This query returns aggregated metrics, allowing the team to answer questions like:

- Is the average defect rate below their threshold (e.g., 3%)?
- Are quality scores consistent across time or spiking abnormally?

If the metrics are within acceptable bounds, the team decides that the data is good enough to promote to production.

## Merging into Production

Once the audit checks are completed successfully, Acme uses Nessie's Git-like branching model to promote the trusted data to the main branch. This makes the changes visible to downstream consumers such as BI dashboards, external APIs, or ML pipelines that rely on the production data.

Here's the SQL syntax to merge the changes from the staging branch to the main branch:

```
MERGE BRANCH etl_staging INTO main IN nessie;
```

This operation is transactional, ensuring that either all the changes are made visible or none at all. Under the hood, this updates the metadata pointer in Nessie's catalog to now reference the latest snapshot created by the `etl_staging` branch.

From this point onward, all readers of `nessie.gold_acme_manu` (defaulting to the `main` branch) will see the updated, audited data.

Acme's team is also able to have complete version control for all their data workflows running on top of Iceberg (backed by Nessie).

This allows every table mutation, schema evolution, and transformation to be fully tracked, reproducible, and auditable, giving engineers the ability to inspect historical states, understand how a dataset changed over time, and reconstruct previous versions for debugging or compliance.

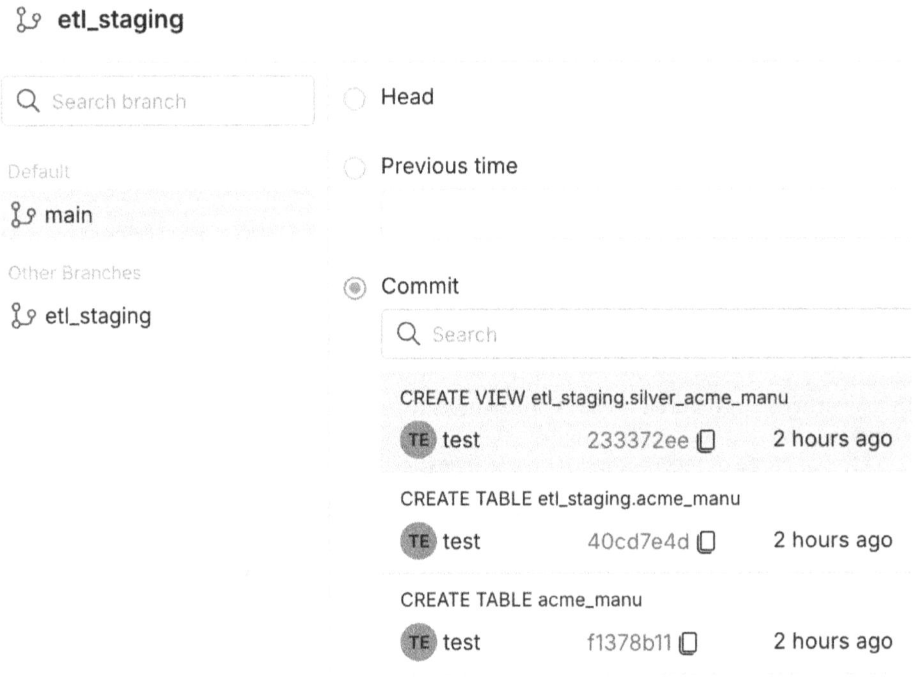

*Figure 11.9 – Commit history for the etl_staging branch*

## Analytics layer: Building BI dashboards directly on the lakehouse

Now that Acme's data engineering team has curated clean, high-quality Gold-layer Iceberg tables, the analytics team can connect directly to these Iceberg datasets using Dremio as the compute engine, without moving or copying data out of the data lake. This enables them to build rich, interactive dashboards in Apache Superset, powered entirely by open standards.

Using the Gold-layer tables, the analytics team built operational dashboards that track production output, efficiency scores, quality indicators such as defect levels, safety incidents, and supply chain metrics:

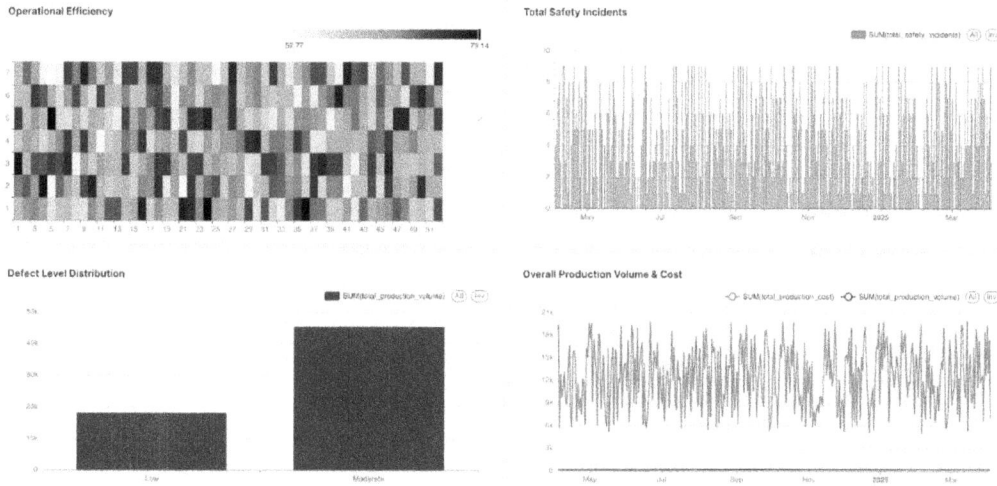

*Figure 11.10 – Operational dashboards built using Iceberg tables*

This lakehouse-native analytics approach brings powerful benefits compared to traditional two-tier architectures. Here's a comparison that highlights how Acme's shift to a lakehouse architecture directly addresses the core pain points of their previous setup:

| Challenge area | Before (two-tier architecture) | After (lakehouse architecture with Iceberg) |
|---|---|---|
| Data freshness | Delayed insights due to sync lag between data lake and warehouse | Near-real-time analytics using Gold-layer Iceberg tables queried directly from the data lake |
| Infrastructure costs | High costs from ETL pipelines, staging zones, and warehouse compute/storage | Lower costs by eliminating warehouse dependencies; compute pushed down via Dremio on MinIO |
| Data consistency | Multiple, conflicting data copies across BI tools and departments | Single source of truth with versioned Iceberg tables and Nessie catalog |
| Analytics flexibility | Analysts blocked by pipeline delays and schema rigidity in data marts | Self-service exploration and ad hoc querying with a SQL engine on Iceberg tables |
| BI and reporting workflow | Extract-based dashboards with performance trade-offs and vendor lock-in | Open, interactive dashboards built in Superset, powered by open formats and near-real-time access |

*Table 11.1 – Comparison showing how Acme's shift to a lakehouse architecture directly addresses the core pain points of their previous setup*

# Scenario overview: GlobalMart's real-time analytics with Apache Hudi CDC

GlobalMart is a multinational retail corporation with hundreds of stores and a robust e-commerce platform. The company collects vast amounts of operational data from multiple systems, including point-of-sale transactions, inventory management, customer profiles, and online shopping behavior.

Previously, GlobalMart relied on a batch-oriented data architecture where transactional systems were synchronized with their data warehouse through nightly ETL jobs. This approach created several challenges:

- Data staleness, affecting decision-making and operational efficiency
- Complex, brittle ETL pipelines that were difficult to maintain
- Inability to track historical changes and data lineage
- Limited capability to detect and respond to real-time business events
- High infrastructure costs for duplicate storage and compute resources

To address these limitations, GlobalMart's data engineering team decided to implement a modern CDC pipeline using Apache Hudi as their open table format. Their goal was to create a near-real-time data pipeline that could do the following:

- Capture changes from source databases immediately as they occur
- Maintain a complete history of data changes for audit and compliance
- Support both batch and streaming analytics from the same dataset
- Enable time travel queries for point-in-time analysis
- Reduce data duplication and infrastructure costs

## Solution: Real-time CDC pipeline with Apache Hudi

The team chose to implement a CDC solution using Apache Hudi as the foundation for their lakehouse architecture. This allowed them to build a unified platform that supports both streaming and batch workloads while maintaining the complete history of data changes.

# Why Apache Hudi?

GlobalMart's decision to adopt Apache Hudi was driven by several technical requirements:

- **CDC support**: Hudi's unique capability to efficiently track record-level changes made it ideal for CDC use cases, where only incremental changes need to be processed.

- **Upsert capability**: Hudi's support for upsert operations (via **copy-on-write (COW)** or **merge-on-read (MOR)** tables) enables efficient processing of database change events without full table scans or rebuilds.

- **Time travel and historical data**: Compliance requirements mandate that GlobalMart maintain a complete audit trail of data changes. Hudi's time travel and incremental querying capabilities provide this without complex versioning schemes.

- **Streaming and batch unification**: GlobalMart needed to support both real-time dashboards and traditional batch analytical workloads. Hudi's architecture allows querying the same dataset efficiently through both paradigms.

- **Schema evolution**: As business requirements evolve, Hudi's flexible schema evolution allows GlobalMart to adapt without disrupting existing pipelines or requiring data migrations.

# Architecture details

To implement their real-time CDC solution, GlobalMart designed a modular architecture centered around Apache Hudi, leveraging open source tools for each stage of the pipeline:

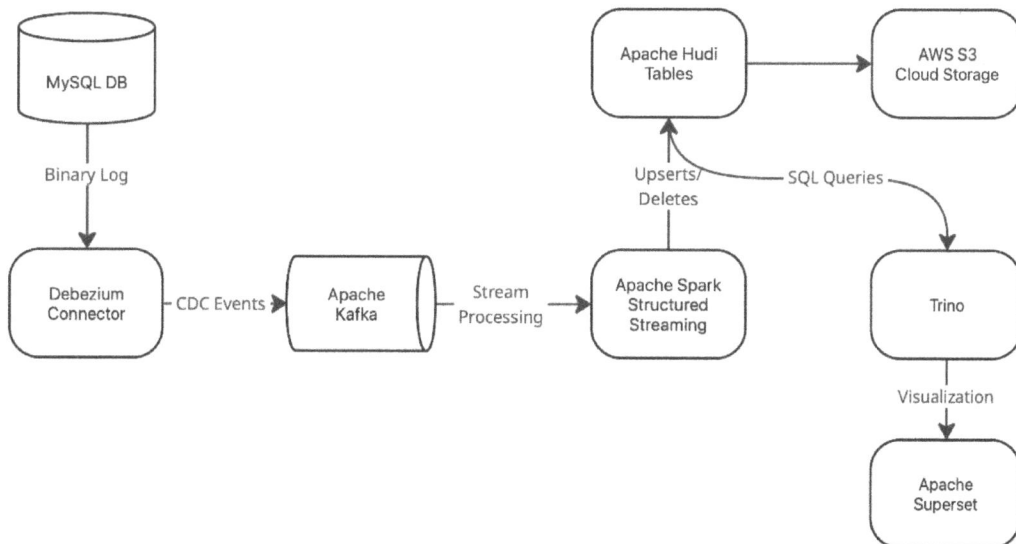

*Figure 11.11 – Real-time CDC pipeline with Apache Hudi*

## Tooling stack breakdown

GlobalMart's CDC pipeline uses the following open source components, each responsible for a clear stage of ingestion, transport, processing, storage, and serving:

- **Apache Hudi**: Serves as the open table format, providing upsert capabilities, time travel, and incremental processing for all CDC events
- **MySQL:** The RDBMS data store that has all the transactional data.
- **Debezium**: A CDC connector that captures changes from MySQL databases by reading the binary log and converting changes to Kafka messages
- **Apache Kafka**: A message broker that receives CDC events from Debezium and buffers them for processing
- **Apache Spark Structured Streaming**: A processing engine that consumes CDC events from Kafka and applies them to Hudi tables
- **Trino**: A SQL query engine enabling analysts to run interactive queries against Hudi tables
- **Apache Superset**: A visualization layer providing dashboards and reports on top of the near-real-time data

## Implementation steps

Let's walk through how GlobalMart implemented their CDC pipeline with Apache Hudi.

### Step 1: Configuring the Debezium MySQL connector

First, the team configured Debezium to capture changes from their MySQL transactional database containing product, inventory, and sales data. This required setting up a connector configuration to monitor the binary log:

```
{
    "name": "globalmart-mysql-connector",
    "config": {
      "connector.class": "io.debezium.connector.mysql.MySqlConnector",
      "database.hostname": "mysql-primary",
      "database.port": "3306",
      "database.user": "debezium",
      "database.password": "dbz_password",
      "database.server.id": "1",
      "database.server.name": "globalmart",
      "database.include.list": "retail",
      "table.include.list": "retail.products,retail.inventory,retail.sales",
```

```
        "database.history.kafka.bootstrap.servers": "kafka:29092",
        "database.history.kafka.topic": "schema-changes.retail",
        "include.schema.changes": "true"
    }
}
```

This configuration captures all changes (inserts, updates, and deletes) from the specified tables and pushes them to Kafka topics following this naming pattern:

```
globalmart.retail.[table_name]
```

Debezium change events are typically emitted as an "envelope" that contains metadata fields (for example, an operation code) and row images in `before` and `after`. In this chapter's Spark job, we assume the Kafka message value is a JSON document that preserves this envelope structure so it can be parsed into fields such as `before`, `after`, and `op`. In production, many teams add a lightweight unwrapping/flattening step (either in-stream or as a small parsing layer) to consistently extract these envelope fields and normalize the payload into a stable schema for downstream processing. This unwrapping step does not change the connector configuration; it simply standardizes how consumers interpret and project the Debezium event into the fields needed for upserts and deletes.

## Step 2: Defining a Hudi table schema and configuration

For each source table being tracked, the team created a corresponding Hudi table with appropriate schema and configurations. Here's an example for the `products` table:

```python
from pyspark.sql.types import StructType, StructField, IntegerType,
StringType, DoubleType, TimestampType

# Define schema based on source table
product_schema = StructType([
    StructField("product_id", IntegerType(), False),
    StructField("name", StringType(), True),
    StructField("category", StringType(), True),
    StructField("price", DoubleType(), True),
    StructField("description", StringType(), True),
    StructField("updated_at", TimestampType(), True)
])
# Hudi table options
```

```
hudi_options = {
    "hoodie.table.name": "products_hudi",
    # Some Hudi/Spark configurations also expect this explicit table-name
key:
    "hoodie.datasource.write.table.name": "products_hudi",

    "hoodie.datasource.write.recordkey.field": "product_id",
    "hoodie.datasource.write.precombine.field": "updated_at",
    "hoodie.datasource.write.partitionpath.field": "category",
    "hoodie.datasource.write.table.type": "MERGE_ON_READ",

    "hoodie.bulkinsert.shuffle.parallelism": "4",
    "hoodie.upsert.shuffle.parallelism": "4",
    "hoodie.datasource.write.operation": "upsert",
    "hoodie.datasource.write.payload.class": "org.apache.hudi.common.
model.DefaultHoodieRecordPayload",

    "hoodie.compact.async.enable": "true",
    "hoodie.clustering.async.enabled": "true"
}
```

The team chose the MOR table type for tables with frequent updates to optimize write performance, while using COW for tables with less frequent changes but more read operations.

## Step 3: Creating a Spark Structured Streaming job for CDC processing

With the Hudi table configuration defined, the team implemented a Spark Structured Streaming job to consume CDC events from Kafka and apply them to the Hudi tables:

> Spark requires the Structured Streaming Kafka integration (`spark-sql-kafka-0-10`) on the classpath to use `.format("kafka")`. If you are running this example via the chapter's Docker environment, this dependency is included. Otherwise, add it when starting Spark (for example, via `--packages`).

```
from pyspark.sql.functions import col, from_json, current_timestamp, lit,
when, coalesce
from pyspark.sql.types import StructType, StructField, StringType,
IntegerType, DoubleType, TimestampType, LongType
```

```python
# Debezium emits an envelope with before/after/op/ts_ms.
# For deletes: after is null and before contains the deleted row.

row_schema = StructType([
  StructField("product_id", IntegerType(), True),
  StructField("name", StringType(), True),
  StructField("category", StringType(), True),
  StructField("price", DoubleType(), True),
  StructField("description", StringType(), True),
  StructField("updated_at", TimestampType(), True)
])

cdc_schema = StructType([
  StructField("before", row_schema, True),
  StructField("after", row_schema, True),
  StructField("op", StringType(), True),
  StructField("ts_ms", LongType(), True)
])

# Read CDC events from Kafka
cdc_stream = (
  spark.readStream
    .format("kafka")
    .option("kafka.bootstrap.servers", "kafka:29092")
    .option("subscribe", "globalmart.retail.products")
    .option("startingOffsets", "latest")
    .load()
)

# Parse the CDC event payload
parsed_stream = (
  cdc_stream
    .select(from_json(col("value").cast("string"), cdc_schema).
alias("data"))
    .select("data.*")
)
```

```python
# Transform to a Hudi-ready shape.
# IMPORTANT: Hudi interprets deletes via the _hoodie_is_deleted flag (true
# for deletes, false/null otherwise).

transformed_stream = (
  parsed_stream
    .select(
        # record key must be present even for deletes
        # (where after is null)
        coalesce(col("after.product_id"), col("before.product_id"))
        .alias("product_id"),
        # keep latest state for upserts; for deletes, these may be null
        # (acceptable) or can fall back to "before"

        coalesce(col("after.name"), col("before.name")).alias("name"),
        coalesce(col("after.category"), col("before.category")).
alias("category"),
        coalesce(col("after.price"), col("before.price")).alias("price"),
        coalesce(col("after.description"), col("before.description")).
alias("description"),

        current_timestamp().alias("updated_at"),
        when(col("op") == "d", lit(True)).otherwise(lit(False)).alias("_
hoodie_is_deleted")
    )

)

# Write to Hudi table with upsert semantics; deletes are applied via
# _hoodie_is_deleted = true

query = (
  transformed_stream
    .writeStream
    .format("hudi")
    .options(**hudi_options)
    .outputMode("append")
    .option("path", "/path/to/products_hudi")
```

```
        .option("checkpointLocation", "/tmp/checkpoint/products")
        .trigger(processingTime="30 seconds")
        .start()
)
query.awaitTermination()
```

> For deletes, Hudi's Spark DataSource does not automatically "physically delete" rows just because the CDC event has an operation type. The writer must be able to interpret a delete marker in the dataframe. In this example, delete events are represented by setting the Hudi-supported `_hoodie_is_deleted` column to `true` (and `false` for inserts/updates). When `_hoodie_is_deleted = true`, Hudi treats the record as a delete during the upsert write.

This streaming job does the following:

1.  Consumes CDC events from Kafka

2.  Parses the Debezium change-event envelope (before/after/op)

3.  Derives the record key for all operations (including deletes where `after` is null)

4.  Applies upserts and deletes to the Hudi table by setting `_hoodie_is_deleted = true` for delete events

## Step 4: Enabling time travel queries for audit and analysis

One of the key advantages of using Hudi for CDC is the ability to query the data at different points in time. GlobalMart's data scientists leveraged this capability to perform point-in-time analysis:

```
spark.read.format("hudi").load("/path/to/products_hudi").
createOrReplaceTempView("products_hudi")

-- Query the current state of products
SELECT * FROM products_hudi;
-- Query products as they were yesterday at 9 AM
SELECT * FROM products_hudi TIMESTAMP AS OF '2024-04-13 09:00:00';
-- Track how a specific product changed over time
SELECT _hoodie_commit_time, product_id, name, price
FROM products_hudi
WHERE product_id = 1234
ORDER BY _hoodie_commit_time;
```

This time travel capability proved invaluable for the following:

- Regulatory compliance and audit requirements
- Tracking pricing changes over time
- Analyzing inventory fluctuations
- Recreating reports as they would have appeared at a specific point in time

## Step 5: Implementing incremental processing for downstream applications

For downstream applications that needed to process only the latest changes, the team leveraged Hudi's incremental processing capabilities:

```python
# Get the last processed commit time
# Application-specific method. This must be a Hudi commit instant time
# (for example, a previous _hoodie_commit_time).
last_processed_commit = get_last_processed_commit()


# Application-specific method
# Read only incremental changes since last processed commit
incremental_changes = spark.read \
.format("hudi") \
.option("hoodie.datasource.query.type", "incremental") \
.option("hoodie.datasource.read.begin.instanttime", last_processed_commit) \
.load("/path/to/products_hudi")
# Process only the changed records
incremental_changes.createOrReplaceTempView("recent_changes")
# Aggregate the latest changes for real-time dashboard
spark.sql("""
SELECT
category,
COUNT(*) as product_count,
AVG(price) as avg_price
    FROM recent_changes
GROUP BY category
""").write \
.format("parquet") \
```

```
  .mode("overwrite") \
  .save("/path/to/category_metrics")
```

This pattern allowed GlobalMart to build efficient downstream pipelines that processed only the deltas, rather than reprocessing the entire dataset each time.

## Benefits and results

After implementing their Hudi-based CDC pipeline, GlobalMart experienced significant improvements across their data platform:

| Area | Before (Batch ETL) | After (Hudi CDC) |
|------|--------------------|------------------|
| Data freshness | 24-hour lag | Near-real time (minutes) |
| Infrastructure costs | High (duplicate storage) | Reduced by 40% (single source) |
| Data quality | Manual reconciliation | Automated lineage tracking |
| Query performance | Slow (full table scans) | Fast (incremental processing) |
| Compliance and audit | Manual exports | Built-in time travel queries |
| Development time | Weeks per new pipeline | Days with reusable patterns |

Table 11.2 – Before-and-after comparison of GlobalMart's batch ETL architecture versus the Hudi-based CDC pipeline

The solution also provided business value by enabling the following:

- Near-real-time inventory visibility across stores
- Rapid detection of price discrepancies
- Immediate alerts for low-stock situations
- Historical analysis of product performance over time
- Reduced development time for new data initiatives

## Key learnings and best practices

Through this implementation, GlobalMart's data team identified several best practices for Hudi-based CDC pipelines:

1. **Tune Hudi table types carefully**: Use MOR tables for write-heavy workloads and COW tables for read-heavy workloads.

2. **Plan partitioning strategy**: Choose partition fields that balance query performance with partition size.

3. **Set appropriate compaction intervals**: Configure automatic compaction based on data volumes and latency requirements.

4.  **Enable clustering for large tables**: Use Hudi's clustering feature to optimize file sizes and improve query performance.

5.  **Implement error handling**: Build robust error handling for CDC events that fail processing.

6.  **Monitor commit metrics**: Track Hudi commit sizes and timing to optimize performance.

7.  **Test time travel queries**: Verify that historical queries work correctly before relying on them for compliance reporting.

In summary, Apache Hudi provided GlobalMart with a robust foundation for building real-time CDC pipelines, unifying their batch and streaming workloads, and enabling powerful time travel capabilities—all while reducing infrastructure costs and complexity.

## Scenario overview: Visionary Telecom's machine learning workflow modernization with Delta Lake

Visionary Telecom is a direct-to-consumer telecom provider offering internet, mobile, and subscription bundles. Over the last few years, the company has invested heavily in digital transformation, launching a self-service customer portal, introducing real-time usage monitoring, and collecting customer interaction signals across channels.

Despite this digital footprint, Visionary Telecom's machine learning workflows remained largely siloed and brittle:

- Feature data lived in disconnected files or was regenerated from scratch per model run

- Models were trained ad hoc, without a clear delineation between datasets, parameters, and versions

- No reproducibility existed for past runs, and deploying models to production environments required significant manual overhead

As the business grew more reliant on predictive analytics for churn management, upsell campaigns, and customer segmentation, the limitations of their fragmented approach became a bottleneck.

To address these issues, the platform engineering team set out to re-architect their machine learning life cycle with data versioning, model governance, and reproducibility at its core— choosing Delta Lake, Apache Spark, and MLflow as foundational components of a modern lakehouse-driven MLOps stack.

# Solution

Visionary Telecom reimagined its machine learning life cycle as a first-class citizen of the lakehouse, unifying model development, feature pipelines, and experiment tracking using Delta Lake and MLflow. The goal was not just to train an ad hoc model but to build an end-to-end workflow that is versioned, reproducible, and production-ready.

The team's reference use case? A churn prediction model trained on customer behavior and service attributes—tracked, versioned, and registered seamlessly via MLflow.

## Why Delta Lake?

Delta Lake is chosen as the backbone of this pipeline for several reasons:

- **Dataset versioning for reproducible ML:** Delta Lake's time travel makes it easy to record the exact dataset version used for training (for example, by logging the Delta table version as an MLflow tag), enabling repeatable experiments and audits.

- **ACID guarantees and schema enforcement:** As data science pipelines evolve, Delta's schema validation and transactional writes ensure consistency and reliability in long-running jobs

- **Time travel and reproducibility:** With versioned tables and snapshots, data scientists can retrain or debug a model using the exact data state from any historical point

- **Streaming and batch flexibility:** Delta supports both modes of processing, making it a strong candidate for extending to near-real-time inference in the future

- **SQL and PySpark compatibility:** Feature pipelines could be authored using familiar Spark SQL and PySpark, allowing data engineers and scientists to collaborate without tooling friction

## Architecture details

The re-architected machine learning stack followed a modular design:

- **Feature engineering:** Raw CSV data is ingested into Delta tables with enforced schemas and persisted for reuse.

- **Model training:** A classification model (Random Forest) is trained using Spark MLlib or scikit-learn (via PySpark integration).

- **Tracking and versioning:** MLflow is used to log parameters, metrics, and model artifacts. The Delta table version used for training is also recorded for full lineage.

- **Model registry and inference:** After registration, models can be promoted and served with guarantees around dataset compatibility and versioned reproducibility.

## Tooling stack breakdown

Visionary Telecom's lakehouse-driven MLOps stack combines the following tools to cover storage, compute, experiment tracking, and model governance:

- **Delta Lake:** Open table format for storing training datasets, feature stores, and model outputs
- **MLflow:** Experiment tracking, model registry, and lineage management
- **Apache Spark (PySpark):** Compute layer for feature transformations and model training
- **Python/scikit-learn/Spark MLlib:** Machine learning libraries used for model experimentation
- **Notebook environment:** Used by data scientists for interactive experimentation

## Ingesting raw churn records as a Delta table

After evaluating their machine learning platform gaps, the Visionary Telecom team kicks off their modernization initiative by consolidating all machine learning datasets inside a unified Delta Lake environment. Their first goal is to ingest customer churn records from the CSV files scattered across analyst-owned folders, notebooks, and siloed pipelines into a governed, versioned, and queryable Delta table.

These churn records represent customer-level behavioral data, including usage patterns, support call interactions, voicemail activity, international plan details, and whether or not the customer eventually churned.

The data engineering team's objective in this step is clear:

- Persist the raw records in Delta Lake table format, enforcing schema consistency
- Enable downstream reproducibility by capturing data snapshots through Delta versioning
- Lay the foundation for feature engineering, with ACID guarantees and time travel support

Because all of their experimentation and model training happens within a notebook environment powered by Spark, they use Delta Lake's native Python API (delta-spark) to run their pipelines:

```
from pyspark.sql import SparkSession
from delta import configure_spark_with_delta_pip
builder = SparkSession.builder \
    .appName("ChurnDeltaMLPipeline") \
    .config("spark.sql.extensions", "io.delta.sql.
DeltaSparkSessionExtension") \
```

```
      .config("spark.sql.catalog.spark_catalog", "org.apache.spark.sql.
  delta.catalog.DeltaCatalog")
  spark = configure_spark_with_delta_pip(builder).getOrCreate()
  csv_path = "Downloads/telecom_churn_8000.csv"
  df = spark.read.option("header", "true").option("inferSchema", "true").
  csv(csv_path)
  delta_path = "Downloads/telco_delta"
  df.write.format("delta").mode("overwrite").save(delta_path)
```

This Delta table can now be seen in the storage system along with the Delta transaction log file:

*Figure 11.12 – Delta Lake metadata and data files in the storage system*

This foundational table now acts as the single source of truth for all churn-related experimentation at Visionary Telecom. The team no longer needs to manually track which CSV version was used or worry about schema drift between runs—every ingestion is recorded as a Delta version that can be referenced or rolled back if needed.

## Feature engineering and label preparation

With the raw churn data now versioned in Delta Lake, Visionary Telecom's data science team moves into the feature engineering phase. The raw dataset includes a mix of categorical attributes (such as whether a customer is on an international plan), numeric metrics (such as total minutes used across time periods), and a churn flag.

Before any model training can happen, the following must be done to this data:

- It must be cleaned and encoded into machine-readable formats
- It should be transformed into a numeric feature vector
- It should be labeled correctly for classification (binary: e.g., churned versus not churned)

To ensure this step is modular and reproducible, the team builds a Spark machine learning pipeline, chaining together feature transformers that index categorical variables, convert the label column, and assemble all features into a single vector:

```python
from pyspark.ml.feature import StringIndexer, VectorAssembler
from pyspark.ml import Pipeline
from pyspark.sql.functions import col
df_raw = spark.read.format("delta").load(delta_path)
df_raw = df_raw.withColumn("Churn", col("Churn").cast("string"))
categorical_cols = ['International_plan', 'Voicemail_plan']
numeric_cols = [
    'Account_length', 'Number_vmail_messages', 'Total_day_minutes',
    'Total_eve_minutes', 'Total_night_minutes', 'Total_intl_minutes',
    'Customer_service_calls'
]
label_col = 'Churn'
indexers = [StringIndexer(inputCol=col, outputCol=f"{col}_index") for col
in categorical_cols]
indexers += [StringIndexer(inputCol=label_col, outputCol="label")]
feature_cols = numeric_cols + [f"{col}_index" for col in categorical_cols]
assembler = VectorAssembler(inputCols=feature_cols, outputCol="features")

# Create transformation pipeline
pipeline = Pipeline(stages=indexers + [assembler])
model = pipeline.fit(df_raw)
df_processed = model.transform(df_raw).select("features", "label")
```

This results in a transformed Spark DataFrame with two columns: features (a dense vector of all input variables) and label (a binary flag for churn).

By persisting this pipeline and reusing the transformers, Visionary Telecom ensures that every feature is preprocessed consistently, whether for training, testing, or inference.

## Training a Random Forest classifier with Spark MLlib

With a labeled, vectorized dataset ready, the data scientists proceed to train a binary classification model using Random Forest, a commonly used model for churn prediction.

They split the dataset into training and testing subsets, fit the model on the training data, and evaluate its performance using the **area under the ROC curve (AUC)**—a widely accepted metric for classification quality. Here is the code to do so:

```
from pyspark.ml.classification import RandomForestClassifier
from pyspark.ml.evaluation import BinaryClassificationEvaluator
train_df, test_df = df_processed.randomSplit([0.8, 0.2], seed=42)
rf = RandomForestClassifier(labelCol="label", featuresCol="features",
numTrees=50, maxDepth=5)
rf_model = rf.fit(train_df)
predictions = rf_model.transform(test_df)
evaluator = BinaryClassificationEvaluator(labelCol="label",
metricName="areaUnderROC")
auc = evaluator.evaluate(predictions)
print(f"Test AUC: {auc:.4f}")
```

The model gives an AUC score of 0.9738, which is great for using it as the benchmark to build future models.

## Logging the model and metrics with MLflow

After training the model, the team logs the full experiment run to MLflow, including model parameters, the performance metrics, and the trained model itself.

They also take advantage of Delta's versioning by recording the exact Delta table version that was used to generate the training dataset. This allows complete reproducibility, and they can always retrain a model using the same data version.

Let's see this in action:

```
import mlflow
import mlflow.spark
from delta.tables import DeltaTable
# Set the MLflow experiment
mlflow.set_experiment("/VisionaryRetail/ChurnPrediction")
# Path where your Delta table is stored
delta_path = "/Users/dipankarmazumdar/Downloads/telco_delta"
# Start an MLflow run and log metadata
with mlflow.start_run(run_name="RandomForest_v1"):
    # Log model hyperparameters and metrics
    mlflow.log_param("num_trees", 50)
```

```
mlflow.log_param("max_depth", 5)
mlflow.log_metric("test_auc", auc)
# Log the trained Spark MLlib model
mlflow.spark.log_model(
    rf_model,
    artifact_path="model",
    registered_model_name="ChurnPredictorV1"
)
dt = DeltaTable.forPath(spark, delta_path)
history_df = dt.history()
latest_version = history_df.select("version").first()["version"]
# Log the version used to train this model
mlflow.set_tag("delta_version", latest_version)
```

Now, the experiment is fully tracked in MLflow with lineage to the Delta training data. Future iterations or rollbacks are now fully auditable. This tight integration is one of the key reasons Visionary Telecom selected Delta and MLflow as their Lakehouse machine learning stack: everything is tracked and reproducible by default, and it works seamlessly within their existing Spark-based environment.

## Training a new model on new data (v2)

The data platform team then receives some new data as part of regular ETL jobs, which they ingest into the existing Delta Lake table. This enables the data scientists to train a different classification model on this new dataset.

Because the existing Delta table is already materialized with features and label, training becomes straightforward. MLflow is again used to track artifacts for this new model. This provides full lineage and reproducibility for each model run.

```
import mlflow
import mlflow.spark
from pyspark.ml.feature import StringIndexer, VectorAssembler
from pyspark.ml.classification import RandomForestClassifier
from pyspark.ml import Pipeline

# Set experiment
mlflow.set_experiment("/VisionaryRetail/ChurnPrediction")

# Load latest version of Delta table (v2 includes appended data)
df = spark.read.format("delta").load(delta_path)

df = df.withColumn("Churn", col("Churn").cast("string"))

# Prepare label and features
indexer = StringIndexer(inputCol="Churn", outputCol="label")
assembler = VectorAssembler(
    inputCols=[
        "Account_length", "Number_vmail_messages", "Total_day_minutes",
        "Total_eve_minutes", "Total_night_minutes", "Total_intl_minutes",
        "Customer_service_calls"
    ],
    outputCol="features"
)

# Model
rf = RandomForestClassifier(featuresCol="features", labelCol="label")

# Pipeline
pipeline_new = Pipeline(stages=[indexer, assembler, rf])

# Train with MLflow tracking
with mlflow.start_run():
    model_new = pipeline_new.fit(df)

    # Log model
    mlflow.spark.log_model(model_new, artifact_path="model", registered_model_name="ChurnPredictorV2")

    # Add a tag with Delta version (latest)
    dt = DeltaTable.forPath(spark, delta_path)
    version = dt.history().select("version").first()["version"]
    mlflow.set_tag("delta_version", version)

    print(f"✅ Model trained on Delta version {version} and registered as 'ChurnPredictorV2'")
```

```
2025/04/09 16:17:22 WARNING mlflow.models.model: Model logged without a signature and input example.
n logging the model to auto infer the model signature.
✅ Model trained on Delta version 1 and registered as 'ChurnPredictorV2'
Successfully registered model 'ChurnPredictorV2'.
Created version '1' of model 'ChurnPredictorV2'.
```

*Figure 11.13 – Training model with full lineage and reproducibility for each run*

## Loading a past Delta version for reproducible scoring

Once the model is trained on the most recent data (Delta version 1), the Visionary Telecom team wants to validate how well it performs on older snapshots of customer behavior. This is a common enterprise requirement, especially in environments where data drifts over time, and historical reproducibility is key for audits or governance.

Thanks to Delta Lake's time travel capabilities, this becomes effortless. By specifying `.option("versionAsOf", 0)` in the Spark read operation, the team can load exactly how the dataset looked during version 0, prior to the new records being appended.

The model is then applied to this past snapshot to evaluate generalization. This also allows the team to simulate backtesting, compare across time periods, and maintain MLflow experiment lineage tied to a specific Delta version.

> No data copies or pipelines need to be rebuilt for this, just version-controlled reads and deterministic scoring.

Here's how to load a specific Delta version for reproducible scoring:

```
# Load Delta version 0 for reproducible scoring
df_v1 = spark.read.format("delta").option("versionAsOf", 0).load(delta_
path)
df_v1 = df_v1.withColumn("Churn", col("Churn").cast("string"))
df_v1_transformed = model_new.transform(df_v1)
# Show predictions
df_v1_transformed.select("label", "prediction", "probability").show(5)
```

*Figure 11.14* shows the predictions and probabilities produced by the model for this dataset.

```
+-----+----------+--------------------+
|label|prediction|         probability|
+-----+----------+--------------------+
|  0.0|       0.0|[0.94810782061112...|
|  0.0|       0.0|[0.93990984170554...|
|  0.0|       0.0|[0.90156352813804...|
|  0.0|       0.0|[0.88055437221243...|
|  0.0|       0.0|[0.94316936979824...|
+-----+----------+--------------------+
only showing top 5 rows
```

*Figure 11.14 – Prediction and probabilities from the new model in earlier versions of the dataset*

## Comparing MLflow runs for governance and auditability

With multiple model versions trained on different Delta table versions, the Visionary Telecom team uses MLflow's programmatic inspection for model performance, metadata, and lineage. They use MLflow's Python API to list and compare recent runs from their experiment:

```
import mlflow
client = mlflow.tracking.MlflowClient()
```

```
experiment = client.get_experiment_by_name("/VisionaryRetail/
ChurnPrediction")
# List latest runs
runs = client.search_runs(experiment_ids=[experiment.experiment_id],
order_by=["attributes.start_time DESC"])
for run in runs[:5]:
    run_id = run.info.run_id
    tags = run.data.tags
    metrics = run.data.metrics
    print(f"\n Run ID: {run_id}")
    print(f"Model Name: {tags.get('mlflow.log-model.history', 'N/A')}")
    print(f"AUC: {metrics.get('areaUnderROC', 'N/A')}")
    print(f"Delta Table Version: {tags.get('delta_version', 'N/A')}")
```

*Figure 11.15* shows a snippet of the logged model performance, metadata, and dataset lineage captured through MLflow.

Run ID: df95860682a64c6684f50214d8bf33da
Model Name: [{"run_id": "df95860682a64c6684f50214d8bf33da", "artifact_path": "model", "utc_time_created": "2025-04-09 20:17:07.762518", "mode
l_uuid": "f53fc72793d545a293d1efe24b0d6f13", "flavors": {"spark": {"pyspark_version": "3.4.4", "model_data": "sparkml", "code": null, "model_
class": "pyspark.ml.pipeline.PipelineModel"}, "python_function": {"loader_module": "mlflow.spark", "python_version": "3.11.5", "data": "spark
ml", "env": {"conda": "conda.yaml", "virtualenv": "python_env.yaml"}}}}]
AUC: N/A
Delta Table Version: 1

Run ID: bec0fde51e574d669c243fd499664679
Model Name: [{"run_id": "bec0fde51e574d669c243fd499664679", "artifact_path": "model", "utc_time_created": "2025-04-09 16:47:52.644252", "mode
l_uuid": "8032c17befa343a2b21bb0a5169f3756", "flavors": {"spark": {"pyspark_version": "3.4.4", "model_data": "sparkml", "code": null, "model_
class": "pyspark.ml.pipeline.PipelineModel"}, "python_function": {"loader_module": "mlflow.spark", "python_version": "3.11.5", "data": "spark
ml", "env": {"conda": "conda.yaml", "virtualenv": "python_env.yaml"}}}}]
AUC: N/A
Delta Table Version: 0

*Figure 11.15 – Inspection model performance, metadata, and lineage using MLflow*

Each model training run automatically logs the following:

- The associated Delta table version (via a custom tag)
- The run ID, making it easy to trace back

This allows the team to answer critical questions such as the following:

- "Which model was trained on which dataset version?"
- "How did its performance vary across time or data drift?"
- "Which run should be promoted to staging or production?"

## Batch inference on a critical new dataset using a registered MLflow model

Weeks after deploying their churn prediction model, the Visionary team receives a new batch of customer data, representing customers acquired through a new marketing campaign. This dataset is outside the training window and contains customer behavior patterns not seen before.

Given the importance of understanding churn risk early for these new customers, the data science team decides to use the most recently approved version of the model (version 2) of ChurnPredictorV2, already tracked in MLflow, to score this dataset:

```
# Load the newly ingested Delta table
df_score = spark.read.format("delta").load(scoring_path)
# Load production model from MLflow
model_uri = "models:/ChurnPredictorV2@prod_model"
prod_model = mlflow.spark.load_model(model_uri)
predictions = prod_model.transform(df_score)
predictions.select("State", "prediction", "probability").show(10)
```

*Figure 11.16* shows the predictions and probabilities produced by the most recently approved model.

```
+-----+----------+--------------------+
|State|prediction|         probability|
+-----+----------+--------------------+
|   CA|       0.0|[0.62756559690772...|
|   NY|       0.0|[0.72214544068916...|
|   TX|       0.0|[0.94727331144314...|
|   NY|       1.0|[0.46004931559784...|
|   NY|       0.0|[0.91393269601472...|
|   NJ|       0.0|[0.73059610848167...|
|   TX|       0.0|[0.65893628737161...|
|   TX|       0.0|[0.79352147748035...|
|   TX|       1.0|[0.35852197695168...|
|   NY|       0.0|[0.88889699173589...|
+-----+----------+--------------------+
only showing top 10 rows
```

*Figure 11.16 – Prediction and probabilities from the recently approved model*

This completes the end-to-end life cycle: from ingestion to model training to version tracking (in MLflow) to reproducible scoring, and, finally, production inference. The team at Visionary Retail now has the following:

- Complete lineage of model versions with associated data versions
- One-click reproducibility for past experiments
- Production-grade inference capability without extra engineering overhead

# Summary

This chapter showcased the practical application of open table formats—Apache Iceberg, Apache Hudi, and Delta Lake—through real-world use cases that span manufacturing analytics, real-time CDC, and machine learning workflows.

We began with Acme Manufacturing's journey to unify operational data using an Iceberg-based lakehouse. Their architecture, built with MinIO, Dremio, Nessie, and Superset, demonstrated how to implement a Bronze-Silver-Gold table model with Git-like data branching for WAP workflows. Iceberg's support for schema evolution and SQL accessibility enabled seamless team adoption and real-time insights.

Next, we explored how GlobalMart leveraged Apache Hudi to implement a real-time CDC pipeline. By integrating Debezium, Kafka, Spark Structured Streaming, and Hudi, the team achieved near-real-time data freshness, time travel, and incremental query support. This architecture streamlined compliance reporting, reduced infrastructure costs, and empowered timely decision-making across the enterprise.

Finally, we examined Visionary Telecom's re-architecture of its machine learning workflows using Delta Lake and MLflow. With Delta's versioned storage, ACID guarantees, and MLflow's experiment tracking, the team established reproducibility, model lineage, and production-grade scoring with ease. Delta's integration with PySpark and machine learning libraries enabled collaboration across teams and seamless deployment.

These scenarios demonstrate how a "build once, scale anywhere" mindset can unlock powerful analytics and operational capabilities through lakehouse-native patterns—transforming complex data operations into simplified, governed, and real-time pipelines.

This book set out to offer a practical, engineering-first perspective on building modern lakehouse systems. We started with the foundational principles, understanding why open table formats emerged, and walked through the architectural foundations, transactional capabilities, and performance techniques that make them production-ready. Through detailed chapters on Apache Iceberg, Apache Hudi, and Delta Lake, as well as hands-on examples, we explored the decisions practitioners face when adopting and operating these formats.

As this final chapter showed, real-world lakehouse implementations are never one-size-fits-all. They're shaped by use cases, constraints, and ecosystem choices. Our goal was not to prescribe a silver bullet but to equip you with the vocabulary, mental models, and technical depth needed to make informed decisions.

## Questions

1. What challenges led Acme Manufacturing to adopt a lakehouse architecture?

2. Why did Acme choose Apache Iceberg as their open table format?

3. How does the Write-Audit-Publish workflow help maintain data quality in Iceberg?

4. What role does Project Nessie play in Acme's architecture?

5. What are the main advantages of using Apache Hudi for CDC at GlobalMart?

6. How does GlobalMart ensure time travel and auditability in their data pipeline?

7. What tools are used in GlobalMart's real-time CDC architecture?

8. Why did Visionary Telecom choose Delta Lake for its machine learning workflows?

9. How does Delta Lake support experiment reproducibility in machine learning pipelines?

10. What advantages does MLflow provide when integrated with Delta Lake?

## Answers

1. Acme faced issues with data staleness, high warehouse costs, and inconsistent analytics across teams, which prompted their shift to a lakehouse model for unified and timely insights.

2. Apache Iceberg met Acme's needs for schema/partition evolution, broad SQL-engine compatibility, and optimized analytical reads. WAP can be enabled in Iceberg (for example via write.wap.enabled in supported engines), and when paired with Project Nessie, Acme also gains Git-like catalog branching/merging to implement audited promotion workflows.

3. The WAP workflow allows data to be validated and tested in staging branches before being merged to production, ensuring high data integrity.

4. Project Nessie acts as a catalog and version control layer, enabling Git-like branching, data isolation, and structured governance in Iceberg-based pipelines.

5. Hudi's upsert support, efficient handling of record-level changes, time travel queries, and incremental reads make it ideal for CDC and real-time analytics.

6. GlobalMart leverages Hudi's commit timeline and built-in time travel to run point-in-time queries (for example, Spark SQL TIMESTAMP AS OF ...), enabling auditability and compliance reporting.

7. Their CDC pipeline includes Debezium for MySQL change capture, Kafka for streaming, Spark for processing, and Hudi as the target storage format, queried via Trino and visualized with Superset.

8. Delta Lake was chosen for its ACID guarantees, schema enforcement, and built-in time travel, which make dataset versions reproducible. MLflow complements this by tracking experiments and logging the Delta table version used for training, enabling end-to-end lineage.

9. Delta Lake captures the exact version of the dataset used for training, allowing models to be retrained or evaluated consistently on historical data.

10. MLflow tracks model runs, parameters, and metrics and links them to the dataset versions in Delta Lake, enabling governance, auditability, and repeatability.

## Get This Book's PDF Version and Exclusive Extras

UNLOCK NOW

Scan the QR code (or go to packtpub.com/unlock). Search for this book by name, confirm the edition, and then follow the steps on the page.

*Note: Keep your invoice handy. Purchases made directly from Packt don't require an invoice.*

# 12

# Unlock Your Exclusive Benefits

Your copy of this book includes the following exclusive benefits:

- ☁ Next-gen Packt Reader
- 📄 DRM-free PDF/ePub downloads

Follow the guide below to unlock them. The process takes only a few minutes and needs to be completed once.

## Unlock this Book's Free Benefits in 3 Easy Steps

### Step 1

Keep your purchase invoice ready for *Step 3*. If you have a physical copy, scan it using your phone and save it as a PDF, JPG, or PNG.

For more help on finding your invoice, visit https://www.packtpub.com/unlock-benefits/help.

> **Note**: If you bought this book directly from Packt, no invoice is required. After *Step 2*, you can access your exclusive content right away.

## Step 2

Scan the QR code or go to packtpub.com/unlock.

On the page that opens (similar to *Figure 12.1* on desktop), search for this book by name and select the correct edition.

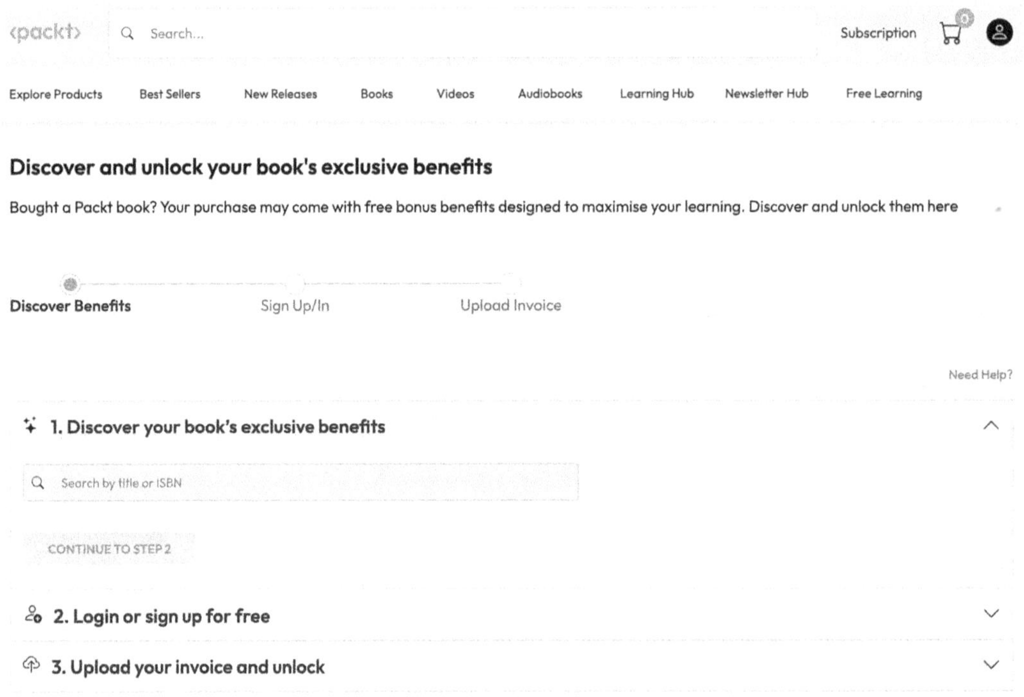

<packt>    Q  Search...                                                          Subscription  🛒  👤

Explore Products    Best Sellers    New Releases    Books    Videos    Audiobooks    Learning Hub    Newsletter Hub    Free Learning

### Discover and unlock your book's exclusive benefits

Bought a Packt book? Your purchase may come with free bonus benefits designed to maximise your learning. Discover and unlock them here

**Discover Benefits**              Sign Up/In              Upload Invoice

Need Help?

**✦  1. Discover your book's exclusive benefits**                                           ⌃

Q   Search by title or ISBN

CONTINUE TO STEP 2

**⚟  2. Login or sign up for free**                                                          ⌄

**☁  3. Upload your invoice and unlock**                                                     ⌄

*Figure 12.1: Packt unlock landing page on desktop*

## Step 3

After selecting your book, sign in to your Packt account or create one for free. Then upload your invoice (PDF, PNG, or JPG, up to 10 MB). Follow the on-screen instructions to finish the process.

## Need help?

If you get stuck and need help, visit `https://www.packtpub.com/unlock-benefits/help` for a detailed FAQ on how to find your invoices and more. This QR code will take you to the help page.

**Note:** If you are still facing issues, reach out to `customercare@packt.com`.

# ‹packt›

packtpub.com

Subscribe to our online digital library for full access to over 7,000 books and videos, as well as industry leading tools to help you plan your personal development and advance your career. For more information, please visit our website.

## Why subscribe?

- Spend less time learning and more time coding with practical eBooks and Videos from over 4,000 industry professionals
- Improve your learning with Skill Plans built especially for you
- Get a free eBook or video every month
- Fully searchable for easy access to vital information
- Copy and paste, print, and bookmark content

At www.packtpub.com, you can also read a collection of free technical articles, sign up for a range of free newsletters, and receive exclusive discounts and offers on Packt books and eBooks.

# Other Books You May Enjoy

If you enjoyed this book, you may be interested in these other books by Packt:

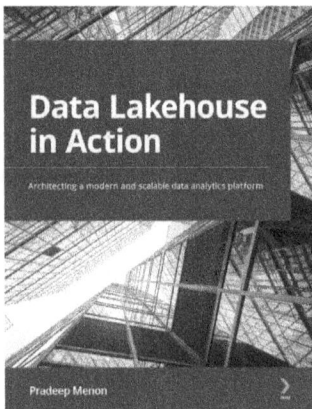

**Data Lakehouse in Action**

Pradeep Menon

ISBN: 978-1-80181-593-2

- Understand the evolution of the Data Architecture patterns for analytics
- Become well versed in the Data Lakehouse pattern and how it enables data analytics
- Focus on methods to ingest, process, store, and govern data in a Data Lakehouse architecture
- Learn techniques to serve data and perform analytics in a Data Lakehouse architecture
- Cover methods to secure the data in a Data Lakehouse architecture
- Implement Data Lakehouse in a cloud computing platform such as Azure
- Combine Data Lakehouse in a macro-architecture pattern such as Data Mesh

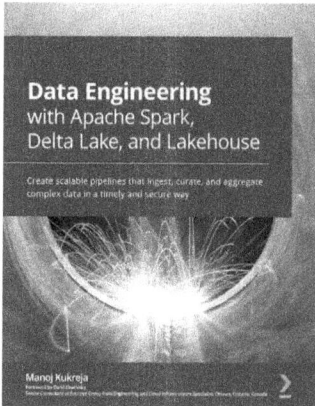

**Data Engineering with Apache Spark, Delta Lake, and Lakehouse**

Manoj Kukreja

ISBN: 978-1-80107-774-3

- Discover the challenges you may face in the data engineering world
- Add ACID transactions to Apache Spark using Delta Lake
- Understand effective design strategies to build enterprise-grade data lakes
- Explore architectural and design patterns for building efficient data ingestion pipelines
- Orchestrate a data pipeline for preprocessing data using Apache Spark and Delta Lake APIs
- Automate deployment and monitoring of data pipelines in production
- Get to grips with securing, monitoring, and managing data pipelines models efficiently

# Packt is searching for authors like you

If you're interested in becoming an author for Packt, please visit authors.packt.com and apply today. We have worked with thousands of developers and tech professionals, just like you, to help them share their insight with the global tech community. You can make a general application, apply for a specific hot topic that we are recruiting an author for, or submit your own idea.

# Share your thoughts

Now you've finished *Engineering Lakehouses with Open Table Formats*, we'd love to hear your thoughts! Scan the QR code below to go straight to the Amazon review page for this book and share your feedback or leave a review on the site that you purchased it from.

https://packt.link/r/1836207239

Your review is important to us and the tech community and will help us make sure we're delivering excellent quality content.

# Index